SECOND EDITION

Handbook of
Training
Evaluation and
Measurement
Methods

Building Blocks of Human Potential/Leonard Nadler,
Series Editor

*An *Instructor's Guide* to the *Handbook of Training Evaluation and
Measurement Methods* is also available to qualified users of the text.
For details write Gulf Publishing Company, Book Division, P.O. Box
2608, Houston, Texas 77252-2608.

SECOND EDITION

Handbook of
Training
Evaluation and
Measurement
Methods

Jack J. Phillips

Gulf Publishing Company
Houston, London, Paris, Zurich, Tokyo

Handbook of
Training Evaluation
and
Measurement Methods
Second Edition

Library of Congress Cataloging-in-Publication Data

Phillips, Jack J., 1945-
    Handbook of training evaluation and measurement methods / Jack J. Phillips.—2nd ed.
      p. cm.
    Includes bibliographical references and index.
    ISBN 0-87201-174-7
    1. Employees, Training of—Evaluation. I. Title.
HF5549.5.T7P43 1991
658.3′12404—dc20   91-12239
                                          CIP

Gulf Publishing Company
Book Division
P.O. Box 2608 Houston, Texas 77252-2608

10 9 8 7 6 5 4 3 2 1

Contents

Part III: Evaluation Methods and Mechanics

About the author

Jack J. Phillips, Ph.D., received his B.S. in physics and mathematics from Oglethorpe University, his M.A. in decision sciences from Georgia State University, and his Ph.D. in human resources development from the University of Alabama. Dr. Phillips has 25 years of human resources management experience and is executive vice-president, human resources and support services, of Secor Bank in Birmingham, Alabama.

Preface

The Importance of Evaluation

The Human Resource Development (HRD) field has grown at a phenomenal rate in recent years. The exact amount of growth and the size of the industry are difficult to pinpoint. One report has placed the total dollars budgeted for formal training by U.S. organizations at $45.5 billion.* Perhaps the informal training would account for an equal amount. The total number of individuals who receive formal, employer-sponsored training annually is about 39.5 million. The total dollars budgeted by HRD departments for outside expenditures, such as seminars, computers and packaged training programs, stands at $9.2 billion. Consistent with other trends involving computers, 41% of organizations are now providing computer-based training. This brief profile shows how dramatic the HRD field has increased and the tremendous potential impact it can have on U.S. organizations.

Among the hottest issues in the HRD field are evaluation, results-oriented training, and bottomline contribution. When any of these topics are discussed, they attract attention. Why? Because there is more pressure today than ever before to produce results with HRD programs. Training and development departments are struggling to meet demands from management for profit contributions and from participants who want a program that produces results.

---

* C. Lee, "Industry Report: 1990," Training, *October 1990, p. 29–32.*

This trend toward accountability is probably the most significant development in the HRD field in recent years. Yet, many HRD professionals are reluctant to change, contending that evaluation and measurement are too difficult or too costly. Some evaluation models make it appear that way, but evaluation can be simple and inexpensive. Practical ideas can work for any training and development department. With all the tremendous growth and expenditures in this field, today's HRD professionals can no longer ignore the basic responsibility to evaluate programs and measure the results of their department's efforts.

This handbook equips HRD professionals with the tools necessary to evaluate their programs. Presented in a systematic format from a practical viewpoint with many examples and illustrations, it is based on actual experiences, and each technique or idea has been tested and proven.

I have been fortunate to experience evaluation from four important perspectives. First, and most important, I have been directly involved in the evaluation process for many years as a full-time trainer and HRD manager. As part of this experience, I served as a training director for two Fortune 500 firms. In these direct roles, I applied many of the concepts reported in this book and refined them in a search to improve evaluation techniques.

Second, while serving as a key staff executive, the HRD department reported directly to me. In this role, I required the HRD staff to emphasize evaluation in a results-oriented approach.

Third, as a line executive, I was a major user of HRD services. In this role, I insisted that the HRD staff show contributions for their programs, which could only be derived from a comprehensive approach to evaluation. I often required that specific evaluation techniques be implemented.

Last, but not least, I have had the opportunity to provide consulting assistance in organizations that sought to revamp their overall evaluation process. In this outside observer role, I have helped these organizations improve evaluation techniques and strategies.

Why this Handbook?

A basic question faces every author: "Is there a need for this book?" The answer is based on my experience with evaluation. For years I searched for information on program evaluation and, when I found a useful technique or approach that was feasible for my organization, I applied it. I often achieved excellent results and began to tell others through articles and professional presentations. I soon realized that others had a keen interest in the subject, too.

There appeared to be a void unfilled by the current literature, although there have been many publications on the subject of evaluation and measurement. Most articles are theoretically based or cover only small bits or pieces of the evaluation process. The books on evaluation have been even more disappointing. Many are laced with too much theory and not enough practical substance to make a valuable contribution to the field. Others represent a collection of articles. To my knowledge, until now no book has been developed which provides a systematic process to evaluate HRD from a practical viewpoint.

General Considerations

This book is designed to be a valuable reference to individuals new to the field as well as seasoned professionals. The simplistic presentation with examples will provide the novice with the foundation to develop a sound program of evaluation. For the seasoned professional, the book contains numerous ideas that can add to the evaluation effort in a fully functioning HRD department. The information presented will apply equally to small or large HRD staffs. Even a one-person department can pick up many ideas to evaluate the HRD effort in the organization.

An important strength of this book is the many examples taken from a variety of settings. Since so much of HRD occurs in business and industry, most of the examples come from the private sector. However, there are examples from government, health care, and education. The examples cover a broad range of different types of training, although the emphasis is on management and supervision, an area of HRD that is difficult to evaluate.

Some additional explanation is necessary for the terminology used throughout the book. The term "human resource development (HRD)" is used instead of training, training and development, manpower development, or management development. "Participant" is used instead of trainee or conferee. "Program" is used instead of course, and in most cases the term "HRD professional" is used in place of trainer, training specialist, or instructor. Finally, "he" and "his" are used consistently to reduce the awkwardness of "he/she" and "his or her." This label does not refer to the gender of the person referenced but makes for smoother reading.

The Structure of the Book

The book is divided into four major parts. In the two chapters that consitute Part I, The Measurement Imperative, the importance of measurement is outlined, along with the need for evaluating HRD programs. Recent trends toward measurement are documented to set the proper perspective for evaluation.

Part II is Preparation for Evaluation. The five chapters of this part include all the necessary steps to prepare for evaluation. Useful techniques for developing a results-oriented approach in the organization are presented, along with an 18-step results-oriented HRD model. Evaluation design is covered in two chapters—one dealing with evaluation instruments, and the other discussing the overall evaluation strategy. Finally, uncomplicated methods for determining program costs are provided in a separate chapter.

Part III is Evaluation Methods and Mechanics. Five chapters are included in this section, with a key chapter on methods of data collection. The most effective techniques for collecting both soft and hard data are presented with a variety of illustrations and examples. One chapter is devoted to techniques for analyzing the data after collection. Another chapter presents approaches to measuring the return on HRD, an ultimate goal for many professionals. This chapter discusses ideas for assigning dollar values to data and subsequently calculating the return on investment (ROI). Numerous examples and a case study are presented. A chapter on computer-based training has been added in this second edition. The final chapter in this section covers evaluation of outside resources, including outside seminars, packaged programs, and the use of external consultants.

Part IV is Factors Affecting Program Results. Two chapters are presented: one on management influence on program results, and another on communicating results. Management influence includes methods to increase management commitment, support and reinforcement, and ways to secure additional management involvement in the HRD process. The final chapter examines effective methods to communicate the results obtained in an evaluation. These communication strategies are almost as important as achieving results.

Seven appendices give additional information and examples related to the chapters.

Generally, each chapter is self-contained, although some build on the information of another. It is not required that the chapters be read in the sequence presented. Experienced professionals may want to refer to selected chapters, depending on their individual evaluation needs.

What this Handbook Will Do for You

This book explores the key issues of HRD program evaluation and measurement. It will show you how to:

☐ Assess the attitude toward results in your organization.
☐ Define the purposes of evaluation.
☐ Develop programs with an emphasis on achieving results.
☐ Design instruments to use in program evaluation and measurement.
☐ Select the optimum evaluation strategy.
☐ Determine the costs of HRD programs.
☐ Compare and select the most effective and efficient data-collection methods.
☐ Analyze evaluation data collected from HRD programs.
☐ Assign dollar values to HRD program data.
☐ Calculate the ROI for HRD programs.
☐ Explore the use of computers in the HRD process and as a part of evaluation strategy
☐ Evaluate the use of outside resources such as seminars, consultants, and packaged programs.
☐ Improve management commitment and support for the HRD function.
☐ Secure management involvement in the HRD process.
☐ Communicate the results of HRD programs.

In summary, this is the first book presenting concise, practical methods to evaluate any type of HRD program. With its systematic process, ranging from determining the purposes of evaluation to communicating the results of an evaluation, it is designed to be a standard reference on evaluation and measurement for every HRD professional. In addition, it will serve as an excellent text for a course on evaluation. I welcome comments and criticisms and particularly any suggestions for improvement.

Acknowledgments

No book represents the work of the author alone. Many people contribute to the final product, and this book is no exception. Many colleagues have shared their thoughts which have been refined, developed, and ultimately presented here. The many organizations that supplied material for this book are given credit throughout the publication.

The number of individuals who have influenced, supported, or encouraged me in this effort are almost too numerous to mention, but some deserve special attention. Robert H. Hudson, retired manager of education and training at Lockheed-Georgia, inspired me to pursue evaluation projects when I challenged the effectiveness of the programs at Lockheed. In addition, he stimulated my interest in HRD and challenged me with high standards of performance. To him and my former colleagues at Lockheed, I owe a large debt of gratitude.

Through the years I have worked with several colleagues who share an equal interest in evaluation. Jac Fitz-Enz is one of those individuals. Through his work at the Saratoga Institute and his publications, he has heightened the interest in evaluation. His encouragement and support is appreciated.

Much gratitude goes to Leonard and Zeace Nadler, for their meticulous review of the manuscript and very thoughtful suggestions for improvement, the vast majority of which were implemented. Len has been rightfully labeled "Mr. HRD" based on his contribution to the profession. He has an extraordinary insight into the HRD field and makes an excellent series editor.

And finally I owe much appreciation to my wife, Johnnie, who provided encouragement, support, and assistance throughout the effort. She made many sacrifices to make this book a reality.

Jack J. Phillips, Ph.D.
Birmingham, Alabama

CHAPTER 1

The Need for
Results-Oriented HRD

Evaluation Myths

There are many faulty assumptions about the "mysterious" process of evaluation which have kept HRD professionals from measuring the contribution of their efforts. Eleven myths are presented here, and each deserves a few comments.

Myth #1: I can't measure the results of my training effort. A persistent myth about training is that the value of a training program cannot be quantitatively measured. Some myth makers will concede that the effects of training might be measurable, but they continue to perpetuate the myth that the value of professional and management development programs cannot be identified and calculated. This is simply not true.[1] The technology and methods are readily available to measure the impact of almost any program. The primary decision is whether or not to measure results instead of selecting the most appropriate method. A change in attitude toward evaluation is needed.

Myth #2: 1 don't know what information to collect. If a program is designed properly and the objectives are precise and measurable, then

1

there should be some idea about what type of information to collect to determine whether or not the program worked. When training focuses on performance, much of the confusion about data collection evaporates. Today there is more information available to HRD professionals for performance measurement than ever before. An analysis of the jobs of those being trained will usually reveal some quantifiable measures of performance—even for the most difficult jobs.

Myth #3: If I can't calculate the return on investment, then it is useless to evaluate the program. The ultimate evaluation is determining the return on investment (ROI), and it should be a concern of every HRD professional. It shows the efficiency of using the organization's financial resources. However, the ROI of a training effort is usually based on a few subjective premises; consequently, the calculation may not be as specific as the ROI of a capital expenditure.[2] Also, there may be reasons other than economics for conducting a program.

For some programs, the cost of an objective and precise evaluation may outweigh the cost of the program. For these situations, it does not make sense, economically, to undertake an evaluation. Instead, a brief and somewhat subjective evaluation might suffice.

This approach can be illustrated with an example:

> A listening course was conducted for 10 supervisors. The 15-hour course concentrated on building skills to be an effective listener. The total cost of the course—including participants' time, cost of materials, instructor salaries, and other administrative expense—was $2000. The impact of the program can be measured. A very detailed and sophisticated evaluation can be undertaken involving direct observation of all participants over a period of time, extensive interviews with each participant, follow-up testing, and interviews and surveys of the subordinates of those supervisors. All of this evaluation can be combined in a detailed study that gives a fairly reliable estimate as to what change, if any, the program brings about in those 10 supervisors. The approximate economic impact of that change can be calculated. An evaluation of this type can easily cost $50,000. No sane person is going to pay $50,000 to determine the impact of a $2000 course.

While this is an extreme example, a very important and relevant question should always be asked before approaching the subject of evaluation: "Is it worth it?" or, "How much evaluation is warranted?"

It may be worthwhile to spend $50,000 on evaluation for a course that costs $500,000 annually to conduct.

Myth #4: Measurement is only effective in the production and financial areas. Every functional area of business is being subjected to the cries of accountability. Today, measures exist in all functional areas. Functional specialists who prospered during good economic times and were severely reduced in numbers during economic difficulties are now scurrying to find ways to show their contribution. HRD is one of those areas. Because of this need, creative minds in the field have produced measurements that are meaningful and realistic.

Myth #5: My chief executive officer (CEO) does not require evaluation, so why should I do it? This is an easy trap. If top management does not demand measurable results, and no evaluation takes place, the HRD department is possibly heading for trouble. The CEO may change and suddenly demand justifications for the department's existence, or a new CEO can assume command and require measurement.

More important, although measurement may not be required, key decisions affecting the HRD department are made routinely. The chief executive will evaluate the efforts either explicitly or implicitly. The CEO will use any information available to assign a value to the department's efforts. In the absence of realistic evaluation data, the chief executive will draw a conclusion about the department based on this information. It is dangerous to wait until someone forces evaluation.

Myth #6: There are too many variables affecting the behavior change for me to evaluate the impact of training. Many research studies have been conducted which show the impact of training when the other variables remained fairly constant. It is possible to isolate the variables for which the HRD staff has primary control, namely those involved in the learning process.

On the job, many variables can affect a participant's performance after a program is completed. Common among these are the self-motivation of the participant, the environment in which a participant is working, and the supportive reinforcement from the participant's boss. While these are significant factors not directly under the control of most HRD departments, they should not be the basis for discarding evaluation.

Waiting for simpler work situations is like waiting for taxes to go away. It will never happen. Jobs are becoming more complicated and require the analysis of many interrelated variables. Although measurements may not be precise, they are better than no measurement of change at all.

Myth #7: Evaluation will lead to criticism. Evaluation results can reflect unfavorably on those who designed the program and those who conducted it . . . and possibly even on the participants' supervisors who have failed to support it. Unless an organization is ready for criticism, evaluation should not be undertaken. Comments and feedback will not always be positive, particularly when reactions and observations are solicited. For a light-hearted look at criticism and evaluation, see Appendix 1.

Myth #8: I don't need to justify my existence, I have a proven track record. Many HRD professionals have established an excellent reputation for their individual efforts and do not have to justify their existence. But, the HRD function needs consideration. The impact of the HRD department is at stake, not the efforts of any individual. Reputations are usually short-lived and forgotten during an economic crunch. Management needs clear-cut data to show the worth of a department or section and the contribution being made.

Myth #9: The emphasis on evaluation should be the same in all organizations. The interest in evaluation depends on the size of the organization and the scope of the HRD activities. Small organizations with no formal training programs will have little interest in evaluation, although some might argue otherwise. Large organizations must be concerned about evaluation.
Consider these two extremes:

McKee Advertising Specialties has about 12 salespersons selling advertising specialties. Johnnie McKee, president, trains each of the salespersons individually and has developed a training manual outlining the effective procedures and tips to be a successful salesperson. She considers training to be a major part of her job but has little or no interest in formal evaluation. To her, the evaluation is whether or not a salesperson is effective and is ultimately a producer for the company.

At IBM, on any given day, 18,000 of its 390,000 employees take part in some kind of formal education event—in a classroom, through self study or via computer-based training. IBM employees around the world complete a staggering five million student days per year, giving each one an average of about 12 days. The yearly education budget of $900 million includes the costs for people, equipment, and facilities needed to deliver training, but does not include the salaries of the people being trained. With the magnitude of its investment, IBM must be concerned about evaluation. According to Jack Bowsher, former director of education for IBM, measurements are the key to justifying education.[3]

Myth #10: Measuring progress toward objectives is an adequate evaluation strategy. Training program objectives are typically narrowly focused on course content, learning activities, and immediate end-of-program improvements. In today's competitive environment, measuring progress toward these objectives is inadequate. Evaluation strategies must include the long-term impact of programs, measured in terms of organizational change, ultimate outcomes, or business results. Measurements that assess the long-term impact of training and education are an important part of the evaluation process.

Myth #11: Evaluation would probably cost too much. Evaluation represents only a small part of the total cost of a program. If integrated into program conception, design, development, and delivery, the evaluation process can be inexpensive and not very time consuming. The key issue is this: If evaluation is necessary to determine a payoff from training, then how can an HRD department afford *not* to allocate expenses for evaluation?

These myths need not hinder the evaluation efforts of any HRD department. The chapters ahead will expose these faulty assumptions and pave the way for a successful evaluation program. The next section examines why a change in approach is needed.

Needed: A Change in Approach

More Talk than Action

When it comes to measurement and evaluation, there still appears to be more talk than action. HRD executives are reluctant to disclose their approaches to evaluation and admit that there are few bottom-line ties to their training efforts. In a meeting with several training directors, the following comment was offered by a human resource director who refused to be quoted by name:

". . . I can't win," he said. "If I tell you we don't measure bottom-line benefits, you run a headline that says 'XYZ Corporation Doesn't Evaluate Its Training.' If I say we do, you ask me how, and I can't answer because I don't believe you can hang dollar signs on the value of professional or management training."[4]

Some of the most prestigious companies with extensive training budgets do not always have a comprehensive approach to tying their training investment to bottom-line results. Consider IBM, mentioned earlier. At the time when the company was spending $900 million a year on education, which represented 4% of its total operating budget, IBM was hitting a plateau in its growth. During a period of heavy expense control, a management committee asked the education division to give back $200 million. Jack Bowsher, director of education, told them it would be difficult to know what to cut without damaging the company. No one knew what was good and what needed work in education at IBM. According to Bowsher, "All we knew was that we were doing a lot of it. My message to the directors of education was that either we were going to show that education had value or it would be taken down $200 million."[5]

It is increasingly common to see descriptions of successful programs in publications or have them discussed at professional meetings. However, when some of these programs are examined in detail in regard to securing evidence of success, there appears to be more talk than action. For example, consider the General Motors Fellowship Plan, a program in place for more than forty years with a tremendous payoff.[6] The program selects outstanding employees to send to graduate school. The employee is guaranteed a position upon returning to General Motors and receives the following:

- ☐ All tuition and fee payments.
- ☐ Compensation based on 50% of base salary.
- ☐ Continued participation in all benefit plans.
- ☐ Eligibility for merit salary consideration and accrual of vacation time.
- ☐ A one-time personal computer allowance and annual book and software allowances.
- ☐ Relocation expenses for the fellow and spouse.
- ☐ Reimbursements for one trip per year to the sponsoring unit of GM and any trips necessary for a final research project.

Clearly, this is a considerable investment, easily exceeding $100,000 per participant, depending on school and location. Currently, GM selects

125 candidates per year for this program, representing a tremendous total investment.

Unfortunately, there are no measures of the program's success. According to the program's administrator, "although there are no formal measures of participants' lengths of tenure or degrees of success at the corporation, the general consensus is that returning participants make a significant, long-term contribution to their sponsoring units."[7]

In today's world this falls short of an appropriate program evaluation. Expenditures of this magnitude should have objective measures of success. It is disappointing for this type of program not to be evaluated, because it probably does produce some important long-term contributions to the organization. These contributions can and should be tabulated, analyzed, and reported to management. Without measurement and evaluation, the program may be placed in jeopardy as was evident in 1987 when GM suspended the program for one year in the midst of plant closings and layoffs. This example further underscores the need for evaluating all types of programs, not just the typical classroom variety.

Other examples of more talk than action occur when impressive results are attributed to a program with no explanation of how the results are calculated. For example, Frito Lay attributed a substantial savings to the implementation of three creative problem solving courses. According to Frito Lay's group manager, Dave Morrison, ". . . we saved major dollars—more than $500 million during the first six years."[8] Morrison attests that there is a direct connection between employees learning and using creative problem solving techniques and profit. He goes no further to indicate how the savings were generated and provides no additional details about the connection between the training programs and profitability. While there may be some connection, there is no hint of how the $500 million was tabulated. Admittedly, creativity training and problem solving programs are very difficult to evaluate. When claims are made that are difficult to believe and are not substantiated, it places the entire evaluation process in jeopardy.

Since the first edition of this book, additional surveys have revealed the status of evaluation in use by practitioners. One study involved the Fortune 500 and analyzed their approach to evaluation of management training. Responses to a variety of questions still showed disappointing news for evaluation efforts. Only 15% of the respondents measured change in performance on the job, and only 8% measured change in company operating results that were traceable to training. Equally disturbing was that in response to a question of how management training fund expenditures are justified, only 6% responded "by showing a favorable return on investments."[9] The study shed some light on the problems of evaluation. Twenty-two percent of the respondents said that a lack of adequate evaluation methodology was a constraint to management training program evaluation efforts. Also, a lack of standards and yardsticks was indicated as the most significant shortcoming to evaluation as was reported by 42% of the respondents. The most troubling part of the study revealed that 53% of the respondents planned no changes, either short-range or long-range, in their evaluation program.

Another study, reported in the *Harvard Business Review,* indicated that 30% of corporations conduct no formal evaluation of their training and development programs. According to the study's authors, "Surely no other area of business endeavor is managed so casually."[10]

A final study, conducted by *Human Resource Executive* magazine and Pittsburgh, Pennsylvania-based Development Dimensions International, focused on the status of management training. Table 1-1 shows the responses to questions concerning evaluation of training. While there is some comfort that 52% have some type of evaluation, it is disappointing to see that 13% in the study have no systemic evaluation and that only an equal number evaluate changes in organizational performance. This study was mailed to 2,000 human resource executives where 486 responded.[11]

In the mid 1980s, the HRD Futures Task Force of the American Society for Training and Development made some predictions for the HR profession for the 1990s.[12] One prediction focused on evaluation and measurement. The trend was that HRD will be expected to contribute

Table 1-1
Status of Program Evaluation: Ways Respondents Evaluated the Effectiveness of Their Training

Method	Percent Responding
Assess participants' satisfaction with training	52%
Assess applications of skills to job	17%
Evaluate changes in organizational performance	13%
Test for skill acquisition immediately after training	5%
Do no systematic evaluation	13%

Based on a study by Human Resource Executive magazine and Development Dimensions International, 1990.

directly toward organizational goals. In the short-term, training will become more effective and transfer and maintenance of training will increase. HRD professionals will have to evaluate and demonstrate its effectiveness to management. In the long-term, the task force predicted more sophisticated cost benefit analysis techniques would be developed to demonstrate HRD's economic impact. Now, in the 1990s, we have to ask ourselves, do we have more sophisticated cost benefit analysis techniques? Is evaluation mandated? Unfortunately, the answer to both of these questions is no. Although the trend is in this direction, it is painfully slow and widespread adoption is still yet to come.

Painful Lessons

Unfortunately, the following scene has been repeated many times:

A phone call is received from an acquaintance employed in the HRD field. Asking if there are any vacancies, the caller explains: "Business is down with my company, and they're cutting back on the training department. I'm looking for a job." A few questions revealed the cause. A general feeling among top management of the organization was that the training and development department could be cut without seriously affecting the operation. In other words, there was little or no bottomline contribution.

Management training and development has taken on much criticism in recent years. In most organizations, teaching managers how to manage has been a difficult, haphazard and often unsuccessful exercise. After years of observing corporations, business and industry struggle with a variety of approaches to management training, some researchers suggest that management training has failed because it has no connection to real life in the company.[13] Ask a manager six months after completing a program how it changed his or her behavior and you will probably get a vague answer. Each year, companies spend millions of dollars on programs to help supervisors, managers, and executives become more competent. How many such programs really affect the organization's ability to compete? Not very many according to one leader, who claims that management development programs fail to add value to corporate strategy.[14] Five common reasons for failure are offered:

1. Programs are not linked specifically to strategies, challenges, or problems in the organization.

2. Programs designed to create awareness and understanding, but not competence.
3. Programs focus on individuals rather than operating units.
4. Participants attend programs for reasons other than personal or organizational need.
5. Programs fail to help participants confront reality.

These problems can be partially overcome with a comprehensive, results-oriented approach, using measurement and evaluation.

For years many HRD observers have suspected a direct correlation between training departments that suffer cutbacks during recessions and a lack of evaluation and measurement. In the early 1970s one large defense contractor had a training staff of almost 300. There were instructors, specialists, coordinators, artists, supervisors, and managers at all levels performing a variety of training activities. When defense spending was reduced, the organization began to cut back on employment. This organization had not learned the difference between training, education, and development.

No other department suffered reductions of the magnitude and frequency of that of the training department. The staff went from almost 300 down to just under 30 in about two years, with the majority of the reductions coming in the first few months. Only the essential required training was retained. The primary reason: In all of its courses and programs, among hundreds, not one could be tied to a direct bottomline contribution. There were few attempts to evaluate any of the programs. The programs may have been effective, but there was no way to prove to anyone that they were. The department could not show top management what would happen if a program was no longer conducted.

It is understandable that management, when faced with severe reductions, will chop away those functions which can be eliminated with the least amount of disruption in the operation. Had the training department shown a strong contribution with most of the programs, it would have been more difficult to cancel them. The timing of the reductions and the numbers probably would have been different.

It is a painful lesson to learn. Unfortunately, the previous situation has occurred in many organizations—not only defense-related but those facing recession. Training departments were put in the same category as public relations and government affairs. These departments were nice to have, but when times got tough, they were trimmed. It is a lesson that need not be repeated.

These painful lessons not only occur during tough times, but sometimes they surface during good times. For example, a training manager was terminated from a large motel chain. He offered little explanation as to why he left, saying "things just didn't work out." Later, in a conversation with his former boss, some of the specifics on the termination were uncovered. More than any other reason, he was terminated because he could not justify the existence of his department. To quote his former boss,

> He had some good ideas, some popular programs, and he seemed to enjoy what he was doing. But, he could not show us how effective his programs were and what they were doing for the company. We need someone who can make a contribution and let us know about it.

That is indeed a painful lesson for anyone to learn.

Why Change?

Why should HRD departments change their approach? Based on the previous examples, some reasons are rather obvious, but here is a comprehensive listing.

Good economic sense. Evaluation should be required of any activity which represents a significant expenditure of funds from the organization. The pressures of cost cutting, scarce resources, and highly competitive industries have led to an increased pressure on HRD departments to make a bottomline contribution.

Measurement trend in our society. In almost every function people are attempting to quantify the impact of their activities. Most executives want to know what impact their departments, programs, and services have with clients, consumers, and customers. This trend toward measurement certainly applies to the HRD profession.

Approval for HRD budgets. A difficult task facing HRD managers is securing budget approval. Specific measurements of a past program's success can help secure additional funds in the future. With zero-based budgeting, which is becoming more popular, departments must justify their existence to obtain funds for next year's operation. Without evaluation, this task is almost impossible.

Pressure from the top to make a contribution. It is becoming increasingly common for a chief executive to express the need for HRD departments to achieve results from their efforts. Many executives say it is now time for the HRD department to show what it can do in hard, undisputable facts. Some require it now. More will require it in the future.

Peer pressure from HRD professionals. Peer pressure causes some departments to strengthen their efforts in evaluation and measurement. When the HRD department in one organization sees another HRD department making progress in this fertile field, others feel obligated to try to do the same. This pressure is healthy and a part of any professional organization.

Self-satisfaction. There is a certain sense of self-satisfaction when a person sees the results of his efforts. Also, learning new techniques can lead to high levels of job satisfaction. This result is best described from an experience of a training and development manager who wishes to remain anonymous:

> I once accepted a training manager's job which had been occupied previously by a line manager. That line manager wrestled with the job unsuccessfully for about three years. Finally, in a fit of frustration, he gave it up and went back to the line organization as a plant manager. His biggest frustration, as he shared with me later, was the fact that he never had a feeling of accomplishment in the job of training manager. While in line management, he could go home each day and see how much work had been accomplished, by counting the tons of production. But in the training job, it was different. He would go home frustrated not knowing whether his programs worked, not knowing if what he did was the right thing. He never knew the extent of the contribution of these programs because no effort was made to evaluate them or measure their results. He did not know the difference between evaluating learning and job performance.

More information available. The field of evaluation and measurement is embryonic, but it is mushrooming, as described in Chapter 2. Information is being shared in professional journals, meetings, and books, although much of this information is still theory. (There still seems to be a shortage of practical ideas.) Although each situation is different, techniques which work for one situation may work for another. Techniques can be borrowed, results cannot.

Professionalism. The extent to which evaluation and measurement is conducted differentiates an amateur from a professional. Part of the process of professionalism in any field is to show the worth of a function. It has become an integral part of the HRD profession. Evaluation is becoming part of the career development for beginning professionals.

Many professional development courses for HRD personnel cover evaluation strategies and techniques.

Survival. One final reason for changing is survival. Those who do not evaluate their efforts may be left out in the future. Organizations may reach a point where they will not hire or promote HRD personnel who do not attempt to evaluate what they are doing to show their contributions.

How Results-Oriented Are Your HRD Programs?
A Quick Test for the HRD Manager

Before pursuing the topic of results-oriented training, a review of the attitude toward evaluation in HRD departments is in order. This section presents a test that should be taken by each staff member involved in HRD. It is brief and can be taken in just a few minutes. When taking the test, try to be candid in selecting the appropriate response. The test should be taken now, before reading the analysis which follows. Select the most correct response.

1. HRD programs are:
   A. Activity-oriented (All supervisors attend the "Performance Appraisal Workshop.")
   B. Individual results-oriented (The participant will reduce his or her error rate by at least 20%.)
   C. Organizational results-oriented (The cost of claims processing will decrease by 25%.)

2. The investment in HRD is measured primarily by:
   A. Accident; there is no consistent measurement.
   B. Observations by management, reactions from participants.
   C. Dollar return through improved productivity, cost savings, or better quality.

3. The concern for the method of evaluation in the design and implementation of HRD programs occurs:
   A. When a program is completed.
   B. When a program is developed; before it is conducted.
   C. Before a person is developed.

4. HRD efforts consist of:
   A. Usually one-shot, seminar-type approaches.
   B. A full array of courses to meet individual needs.

C. A variety of education and training programs implemented to bring about change in the organization

5. Cost/benefits comparisons of HRD programs are:
   A. Never developed.
   B. Occasionally developed.
   C. Frequently developed.

6. HRD programs, without some formal method of evaluation, are implemented:
   A. Regularly
   B. Seldom
   C. Never

7. The results of HRD programs are communicated:
   A. When requested, to those who have a need to know.
   B. Occasionally, to members of management only.
   C. Routinely, to a variety of selected target audiences.

8. The HRD staff involvement in evaluation consists of:
   A. No specific responsibilities in evaluation, with no formal training in evaluation methods.
   B. Part of the staff has responsibilities for evaluation, with some format training.
   C. All members of the staff have some responsibilities in evaluation, even if some are devoted full time to the effort; all staff members have been trained in evaluation.

9. In an economic downturn the HRD function will
   A. Be the first to have its staff reduced.
   B. Be retained at the same staffing level.
   C. Go untouched in staff reductions and possibly beefed up.

10. Budgeting for HRD is based on:
    A. Whatever is left over.
    B. Whatever the department head can "sell."
    C. A zero-based system.

11. HRD is funded through:
    A. The training department budget.
    B. The administrative budget.
    C. Line operating budgets.

12. The principal group that must justify HRD expenditures is:
    A. The training department.
    B. Various staff areas, including personnel and industrial relations.
    C. Line management.

13. Over the last two years, the HRD budget as a percent of operating expenses has:

A. Decreased
B. Remained stable
C. Increased

14. The CEO interfaces with the manager responsible for HRD:
    A. Never; it is a delegated responsibility.
    B. Occasionally, when someone recommends it.
    C. Frequently, to know what is going on.

15. The CEO's involvement in the implementation of HRD programs is:
    A. Limited to sending invitations, extending congratulations, passing out certificates, etc.
    B. Monitoring progress, opening/closing speeches, presentation on the outlook of the organization, etc.
    C. Program participation to see what's covered, conducting major segments of the program, requiring key executives to be involved, etc.

16. On the organization chart, the HRD manager:
    A. Is more than two levels removed from the CEO.
    B. Is two levels below the CEO.
    C. Reports directly to the CEO.

17. Line management involvement in implementing HRD programs is:
    A. Nil; only HRD specialists conduct programs.
    B. Limited to a few specialists conducting programs in their area of expertise.
    C. Significant; on the average, over half of the programs are conducted by key line managers.

18. When an employee completes an HRD program and returns to the job, his or her supervisor usually:
    A. Makes no reference to the program.
    B. Asks questions about the program and encourages the use of the material.
    C. Requires use of the program material and gives positive rewards when the material is used successfully.

19. When an employee attends an outside seminar, upon return, he or she is required to:
    A. Do nothing.
    B. Submit a report summarizing the program.
    C. Evaluate the seminar, outline plans for implementing the material covered, and estimate the dollar savings as a result of attendance.

20. With the present HRD organization and attitude toward results, the HRD function's impact on profit:
    A. Can never be assessed accurately.

B. Can be estimated but probably at a significant cost.
C. Can be estimated (or is being estimated) with little cost.

Analysis of Test Scores

Score the test as follows. Allow:

> 1 point for each (A) response.
> 3 points for each (B) response.
> 5 points for each (C) response.

The total should be somewhere between 20 and 100 points.

The score can reveal much about HRD in an organization and in particular the attitude toward evaluation and measurement. A perfect score of 100 is probably unachievable. It represents utopia and is an ultimate goal of many HRD departments. Conversely, a score of 20 reveals an ineffective organization with inappropriate methods and probably one that will not exist for very long. The test has been administered to several hundred HRD managers, who were primarily responsible for the HRD function. The average score has been 55 with a standard deviation of 10. An analysis of a score can be best described by examining four ranges:

Score Range	Analysis of Score
81-100	This organization represents results-oriented education and training in action. There is little room for improvement and little need to take any additional concentrated efforts to improve evaluation of the HRD function. Departments with this rating are leaders in this important field of evaluation and setting examples for others. Chances are the organization will be extremely effective with this attitude toward HRD and evaluation.
61-80	This organization is probably better than average in HRD and evaluation. There is room for improvement, but the efforts appear to be headed in the right direction. There is some attention to obtaining results and evaluation of programs. Some methods appear to be appropriate, but additional emphasis is needed to make the department contribute more in the future.

| 41-60 | Improvement is needed in this organization. The attitude and approach to HRD and evaluation are less than desirable. Most methods are ineffective. Emphasis needs to be placed on securing the appropriate management involvement in changing the philosophy of the organization. |
| 20-40 | In this organization there is little or no concern for measuring results of the HRD function. The department is very ineffective and needs improvement if it is to survive. Urgent attention is needed from top management to change the approach of the HRD function. |

The analysis of the scores is simplistic and may not be exact, but the point is obvious. Achieving results from HRD is more than just evaluating a single program. It is an entire philosophy that involves active participation of many and an attention to evaluation at several stages in the process. The remainder of this book is devoted to practically every area covered on this test. The rationale for selecting what is considered the best response will become obvious in the chapters ahead.

Discussion Questions

1. How realistic are the 11 myths presented in this chapter? Please elaborate.
2. Cite specific examples of the myths in action, (i.e. situations when the myths inhibited a comprehensive evaluation process.)
3. Review these myths with the HRD staff within your organization (or one with which you are familiar). Discuss the level of attachment to these myths.
4. Which myths cause the most problem in the evaluation process? Why?
5. Why are HRD practitioners reluctant to change their approaches to evaluation?
6. Why is there "more talk than action" when examining the effectiveness of the evaluation process?
7. Consider the case of IBM where the evaluation process was not as comprehensive as top management required, yet their budget was one of the largest in the United States. What has IBM done about this? What success has been achieved?

8. Is there really a *need* to have dollar value results from the evaluation processes? Please explain.
9. What is considered an adequate score on the results-oriented status test?
10. Compare the test scores in your organization (or one with which you are familiar) to other organizations. Explain the differences.
11. In what ways can the results-oriented status test be used in an organization?
12. What is the greatest obstacle that keeps organizations from evaluating HRD programs?

References

1. Fitz-enz, J., "Proving the Value of Training," *Personnel,* March 1988, p. 20.
2. Asgar, J., "Give Me Relevance or Give Me Nothing," *Training,* July 1990, p. 50.
3. Galagan, P. A., "IBM Gets Its Arms Around Education," *Training and Development Journal,* January 1989, p. 35.
4. Gordon, J., "Romancing the Bottom Line," *Training,* June 1989, p. 33.
5. Galagan, P., p. 37
6. Varholy, C. M., "GM Boosts Employees' Drive for Excellence Through Education," *The Human Resources Professional,* Summer 1990, pp. 27–34.
7. Ibid, p. 34.
8. Solomon, C. M., "What an Idea: Creativity Training," *Personnel Journal,* May 1990, p. 68.
9. Clegg, W. H., "Management Training Evaluation: An Update," *Training and Development Journal,* February 1987, pp. 66–68.
10. Bernhard, H. B. and Ingols, C. A., "Six Lessons for the Corporate Classroom," *Harvard Business Review,* September–October 1988, p. 46.
11. Scovel, K., "What's Topping the Charts in Management Training?" *Human Resource Executive,* April 1990, p. 39.
12. American Society for Training and Development, "HRD Tomorrow," *Training and Development Journal,* November 1984, p. 58.
13. Mironoff, A., "Teaching Johnny to Manage," *Training,* March 1988, p. 49.
14. Berry, J. K., "Linking Management Development to Business Strategies," *Training and Development,* August 1990, pp. 20–21.

CHAPTER 2

The Trend Toward Measurement

Now, for the good news. There is an important and steady trend in the HRD field: a move toward more relevant programs whose impact and results are monitored, evaluated, and reported.

The entire human resources management function is responding to the demands to measure its impact, and training and development appears to be taking the lead. This is probably one of the most difficult changes occurring in this profession, and there is growing evidence of this trend in every direction. The HRD professional, already aware of this trend, may find this chapter elementary and may wish to proceed to Chapter 3.

View from the Top

A new and persistent trend toward measurement is the requirement from chief executives that HRD programs show evidence of their impact. Perhaps this trend is one of the most significant because a few years ago it was difficult to find comments from chief executives regarding what results should be achieved from the HRD function. This view from the top is important because it determines to what extent the HRD department will evaluate their efforts. When a CEO expects results and communicates that expectation, chances are the department will produce those results. It can have a tremendous impact on the organization.

Many comments from chief executives have been solicited by two significant publications in the HRD field. First, the *Training and Development Journal* regularly features interviews with chief executives. There is usually a standard set of questions, and several focus on measurement and evaluation of the HRD function. These comments were important and probably had an impact on other chief executives. Although many of the interviews were probably prepared in part by HRD professionals in that organization, it served the purpose of getting chief executives and the HRD staff together to define and clarify what the CEO wants from that department.

In another effort *Training, The Magazine of Human Resources Development* features many articles of interest to top management as well as interviews with chief executives who have demonstrated strong support and involvement in the HRD function. Many of these interviews and articles feature comments about the expectations of chief executives and how HRD is evaluated in their organizations. These independent efforts by the two leading publications in the HRD field provide a major impetus in getting chief executives more attuned to evaluation of HRD and more involved in the process.

Just what did these chief executives say about evaluation of training? In analyzing issues of the two publications, the responses vary from vague and noncommittal comments to strong and specific statements about results. For instance, one CEO had this comment, ''While we can't measure the absolute results of training programs, our record as an organization indicates we're doing something right.'' The message is unclear—except that training seems to be difficult to measure at this company. This comment also gives the HRD department little incentive to attempt evaluation. Fortunately, it was not representative of all the comments. Most were more specific.

An excellent example of the results-oriented training occurs at the Digital Equipment Corporation of Maynard, Massachusetts. On any given Monday morning, more than 6,000 trainees enter DEC's worldwide training network. They may be learning how to tap into a powerful software system, how to trouble shoot hardware, or how to sell a computer system that will satisfy a customer's needs.[1] With more than 300,000 students taking 13,000,000 hours of instruction each year, DEC is truly an industrial university.

The commitment to training is very strong at the top of the organization. According to Ken Olsen, DEC's chairman and CEO, the commitment to training shows up in results-oriented programs. Because the educational services department is in business to provide training support for customers and employees, it is both a cost and a profit center. DEC's arrangement is geared to ensure that the training organization focuses on delivering high quality, responsive, and flexible training in the most cost effective ways. The bottom line is to ensure that the time and money invested in training pay off.

Another example is from Xerox Corporation, which has a strong commitment to training. In 1989, Xerox won the Malcolm Baldridge National Quality Award, which is given annually to American companies that exemplify excellence in quality. Xerox's quest for quality included a commitment of $125 million to training. According to David T. Kearns, Xerox's CEO, the training produced significant payoffs. Although it is difficult to estimate, Xerox related the savings to the cost of quality, which was placed at $2 billion.[2]

Another organization with an impressive commitment is Cummins Engine where training is designed to help lower costs and improve quality. As part of Cummins' commitment, full-time trainers report directly to managers in the line organizations, but are accountable for production related outcomes relevant to their training areas. Quantitative measures of training success—not just smile sheets or testimonials—are used for evaluation.[3]

These examples are only a few of the representative statements about measurement and evaluation of HRD from the nation's largest organizations. Public comments illustrate a definite trend of encouraging—and even demanding—measurable results from HRD programs.

View from One Level Above

The HRD function may fit into an organization in several different ways. The most common approach, at least for a medium-to-large organization, is illustrated in Figure 2-1. The HRD manager reports to a vice-president of human resources who in turn reports to the chief executive. The level between the HRD manager and the chief executive is critical to the results-oriented approach.

It is increasingly common to find the vice-president of human resources with a background in training and development. In years past, in a traditional unionized setting, the vice-president of industrial relations or personnel, as it was called, historically had come through the labor relations field. Labor relations was a function regarded as extremely critical to the organization. It was assumed that any manager heading

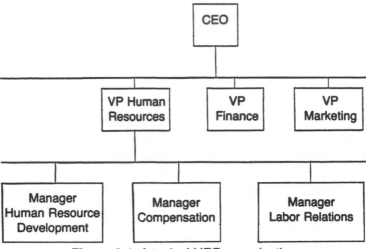

Figure 2-1. A typical HRD organization.

up the entire function must have a strong background in that area. In a non-union setting, the person filling the job would typically be a generalist, with exposure to all functions in a smaller environment or a specialist in employment or employee relations. Rarely did you see a training director fill this top personnel job.

The role is changing. As the top positions become filled with training and development people, their emphasis will differ significantly from those in the past. Former training managers will require evaluation and measurement from their current HRD managers if they believe evaluation to be an integral part of their function. One human resources manager, who was formerly a training manager, characterized it this way:

> I now require the training and development department to submit plans for evaluation along with their plans for conducting a program. I pass the proposal along to our chief executive. This procedure is followed without exception. It continues to place the training and development department in a good posture to grow and develop and make a contribution to the organization.

Also, the HRD department is one of the most dispensable functions of the personnel and industrial relations field, at least in the past. Without good measurement of the results, there never was a strong justification for keeping the training department. Compensation and benefits administration are necessary if employees are paid and have benefits. Labor relations activities are necessary if there is a union, and recruitment is necessary if new employees are needed. But, training was unnecessary. Training could occur directly on the job under management's direction. Without clear-cut evaluation, training departments grew and diminished along with good and bad economic times. Now, human resources vice-presidents are demanding evaluation of the HRD effort to keep the current staff and recruit additional staff as needed.

Reporting Relationship

The most common arrangement for the HRD reporting relationship was depicted in the previous section. However, an increasingly common arrangement has the individual responsible for HRD on the same level as the director of human resources. For example, at SouthTrust Bank, a $9 billion regional financial institution, the senior vice-president, human resources development is at the same level in the organization as the senior vice-president, human resources, both reporting to the president. Some experts argue that HRD should be separated from the traditional personnel or human resources function. Because HRD focuses on change and improvement, maybe it should not be grouped with compensation and benefits, labor relations, employee relations, and recruiting.

This reporting arrangement enhances the overall influence of the HRD department and increases the prospects for accountability. As a general rule, the higher the reporting level of a function in an organization, the greater the expectations from the function. As a result, top executives will have clearly defined accountability measures for HRD, along with similar expectations from the human resources function.

Professional Exposure

In the past it was difficult to find an article, or even references, on the evaluation process. Quite often, when found, the material was general, vague, or somewhat theoretically based. Success stories (i.e., companies that evaluated their efforts successfully) were rare. Now it is different. Articles on evaluation appear in almost every issue of the *Training and Development Journal* and *Training, The Magazine for Human Resources Development*. They regularly feature evaluation as one of their key areas of coverage, and the programs described in these magazines contain information on how the program was evaluated; and in many cases, the actual results are presented.

HR Magazine, the magazine of the Society for Human Resource Management, occasionally has articles devoted to evaluation. One issue each year is devoted to training and development. Also, *Personnel Journal, Personnel, The Human Resource Professional,* and *Human Resource Management* frequently contain HRD evaluation articles. Even the *Harvard Business Review* has featured articles that focus on evaluation.[4]

There is strong evidence of a trend toward evaluation in the meetings of the professional societies involved in the training and development field. As with publications a few years ago, meetings had few sessions and discussions devoted to evaluation. Now evaluation has become a key subject in the meetings of the American Society for Training and Development and those sponsored by *Training.* Annual training conferences have a results-oriented theme such as *Training* magazine's annual Cost Effective Training Conference. In addition, meetings sponsored by professional organizations, such as the National Society for Performance and Instruction, The American Society for Healthcare Education and Training, the Society for Human Resource Management, and the American Management Association, have more sessions devoted to evaluations of training and development. Video conferences have been developed that focus on evaluation such as the recent Value-Added Assessment Conference at Oklahoma State University. Additional seminars and courses on evaluation are available, including college courses required for HRD degrees. (This text has been adopted for use in several college courses on evaluation.)

Job Requirements for HRD Personnel

Successful experience in evaluation is becoming more important in the list of credentials needed for an effective HRD professional seeking employment. One human resource vice president who had the responsibility for hiring an HRD manager in his organization put it this way,

> I would virtually disregard any resume for our HRD manager position that did not address the issue of evaluation. I would like to know what the candidate has accomplished and what was done to evaluate the most significant programs.

It is not unusual to see an ad for a training manager that refers to evaluation. Consider the ad shown in Figure 2-2. It is from *The Wall Street Journal* and requires significant evaluation experience. The trend appears to be spreading. An informal analysis of want ads for training/HRD positions revealed that approximately one-half of the ads mentioned the word "evaluation" either in the skills and experience required or in the duties and responsibilities of the position.

HRD professionals must be prepared to discuss experiences in evaluation. Then too, the job requirements for future HRD positions will require experience in evaluation. This view may appear to be extreme, but the signs are in that direction. Sound advice for any individual seeking opportunities in this field would be to include references to either knowledge, skill, or experience in the evaluation process. Even if it is not required for the job, this experience will impress executives recruiting HRD professionals.

Also, the job descriptions of many HRD specialists, coordinators, instructors, and other positions now include evaluation duties as part of their key responsibilities. The following section is a job description for a training and education specialist who designs, develops, conducts, and evaluates the HRD process. As can be seen, several key responsibilities are in the area of evaluation.

Figure 2-2. An ad from The Wall Street Journal.

Job Description

Job Title: Training and Education Specialist.

Summary: Plan, develop, conduct, and evaluate training and education programs for all departments in the company.

Work Performed:

1. Plan and develop training and education programs such as new employee orientation, apprenticeship training, supervisory development, on-the-job training, and special seminars as required for company personnel.
2. Prepare training materials, visual aids, and other support materials needed to implement training and education programs.
3. Develop program objectives, course content, determine methodology, develop schedules, and select media for the effective implementation of training and education programs.
4. Develop methods, techniques, and criteria for evaluating the effectiveness of training and education programs.
5. Corroborate with program participants, their supervisors, and other appropriate personnel to evaluate the impact of training and education programs.
6. Prepare summary reports on program evaluations and present them to appropriate management personnel.
7. Determine training needs in various functional areas of the company.
8. Identify and select additional sources of support for training and education such as outside instructors, internal instructors, and consultants.
9. Counsel individual employees on vocational guidance and career development plans.

The American Society of Training and Development (ASTD) has analyzed the roles of HRD practitioners including the competencies needed for success on the job. After two years of research, ASTD published the models for practice that focus on these important issues.[5] As part of this study, ASTD identified eleven key roles of HRD personnel. One of these roles is the evaluator. In this role, the evaluator identifies the impact of an intervention on individual or organizational effectiveness. The outputs from this role are evaluation designs and plans, evaluation instruments, evaluation findings, conclusions and recommendations, evaluation processes, and evaluation feedback.

The study identified HRD competencies in four areas: technical, business, interpersonal, and intellectual. Some of the competencies are closely related to measurement and evaluation. Among the technical competencies are:

☐ Objective preparation skills: preparing clear statements that describe desired outputs.
☐ Performance-observation skills: tracking and describing behaviors and their effects.
☐ Research skills: selecting, developing, and using methodologies such as statistical and data collection techniques for formal inquiry.

Among the business competencies are:

☐ Cost benefit analysis skills: assessing alternatives in terms of their financial, psychological, and strategic advantages and disadvantages.
☐ Record management skills: storing data in an easily retrievable form.

Among the interpersonal competencies are:

☐ Feedback skills: communicating information, opinions, observations and conclusions so that they are understood and can be acted upon.
☐ Questioning skills: gathering information from and stimulating insight in individuals and groups through the use of interviews, questionnaires, and other probing methods.

Among the intellectual competencies are:

☐ Data reduction skills: scanning, synthesizing and drawing conclusions from data.
☐ Model building skills: conceptualizing and developing theoretical or practical frameworks that describe complex ideas in understandable, usable ways.
☐ Observing skills: recognizing objectively what is happening in or across situations.

These competencies and role of an evaluator clearly place measurement and evaluation as a key part of an HRD specialist's job.

HRD Structure and Practice Within the Organization

Additional evidence of the trend toward measurement is the way the HRD function is structured in many organizations, particularly in the larger ones, where a department or unit is devoted to evaluation. Sometimes, evaluation and research are performed by the same group, as shown in the HRD department organization in Figure 2-3.

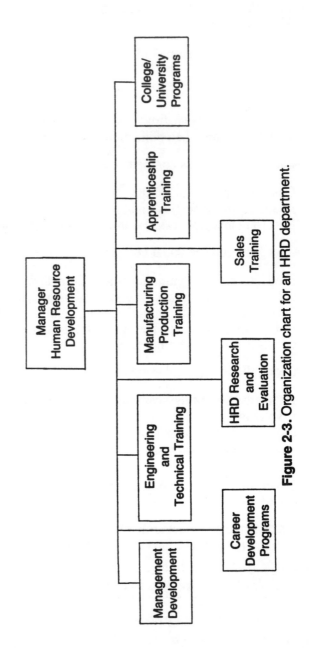

Figure 2-3. Organization chart for an HRD department.

The functions and responsibilities of the research and evaluation section may be presented as follows:

Functions and Responsibilities

Human Resource Development Research and Evaluation

Reports To: Manager, Human Resource Development.

Summary: In concert with all sections within the HRD department, provide basic research and evaluation assistance for all current and proposed HRD programs. In an advisory capacity make recommendations as to specific methods, techniques, and strategies for program evaluation. Provide necessary assistance to initiate and complete evaluation projects.

Specific Responsibilities:

1. Explore, investigate, and keep abreast of new HRD innovations and techniques.
2. Establish HRD standards, policy, and evaluation guidelines.
3. Provide research and analysis to develop and implement HRD programs.
4. Conduct needs analyses to determine overall direction of new HRD programs.
5. Develop and implement systems for collecting data to use in measuring the results of programs.
6. Design and develop evaluation instruments used to measure results of HRD efforts.
7. Assist HRD personnel in selecting evaluation methods and determining the overall evaluation strategy for each proposed and current program.
8. Assist HRD personnel in preparing and presenting proposals for new projects.
9. Develop systems for estimating, monitoring, and reporting HRD program costs.
10. Assist HRD personnel in testing programs on a pilot basis to make adjustments and evaluate their results.
11. Analyze and interpret evaluation data and report conclusions to appropriate management personnel.
12. Recommend program adjustments to HRD personnel based on evaluation data.
13. As requested, calculate cost/benefit ratios, returns on investments, and other measures of economic justification for HRD programs.

(continued on next page)

(continued)

14. Develop guidelines for communicating HRD program results to appropriate personnel.
15. Keep abreast of the latest computer software designed for research and analysis applications.

More company policy statements on HRD contain references to training evaluation. One example is contained in a statement by Aetna Life and Casualty:

> Training evaluation and monitoring go beyond simple evaluation of a course or instructor. From the beginning, both the trainer and the client must ask "How will we know if we made a difference?" There is no shortage of methods and techniques for evaluating training, but what is missing too often is the evaluation mindset. Evaluation is not merely a last step to the training process but a continual concern of the trainer.[6]

Finally, some organizations have developed standard procedures for conducting evaluations. Appendix 2 presents the detailed procedures and requirements in effect at a large utility company.

Surveys and Studies

Surveys are routinely conducted among HRD professionals to determine the state of the art in the profession. Although the surveys vary with the purpose and type of questions, many of them gather information on the status of evaluation because of the popularity of the subject. As discussed in the previous chapter, a survey a few years ago would reveal almost no efforts at evaluation and would contain almost no references to evaluation success stories. Lip service was the order of the day. Recent surveys have shown significant activity in the area of evaluation.

One important survey focused on the extent of human resource development in the Fortune 500, America's most prestigious companies.[7] Questionnaires were completed by 280 of the senior HRD managers in the organizations surveyed. Responses to several questions revealed the level of commitment to evaluation. When asked, "What do you believe is the most important issue within the next five years for you as an HRD professional?" 23% gave the highest rating to "Effectively measuring and evaluating HRD results.'' A total of 88% rated that issue ranging from important to extremely important. This response was third only to "Keeping in touch with client needs" (#1), and "Having an excellent knowledge of the business and strategic plans of the company" (#2). This shows a significant trend in the importance of evaluation.

One interesting survey comes from the Readership Survey of *Training* Magazine and focuses on the extent to which HRD practitioners apply the systems approach to training.[8] The use of specific evaluation techniques are an important part of this approach. Participants were provided 23 statements and were asked whether they did or did not employ the practices in their organizations. Among the important conclusions related to evaluation are as follows:

- ☐ 57% indicated that "Once a program is developed we pilot test it before it goes on line."
- ☐ 68% agreed with the statement, "Our evaluation measures are tied to our written instructional objectives."
- ☐ 87% agreed with the statement, "Trainee feedback and test performance is used to modify our programs."
- ☐ An impressive 48% agreed with the statement, "We use specific follow-up procedures to ensure training transfers to the job."
- ☐ 24% agreed with the statement, "We do formal results studies to determine the actual on-the-job performance as a result of training."

While these percentages would ideally be higher, they represent an encouraging trend in the use of evaluation practices.

There has been a consensus among HRD professionals that when times get tough in an organization, the training staff is the first to be cut. It has been assumed that cuts are taken because there is no clear cut connection between training efforts and bottom line results. Perhaps this changed in the 1980s. There is evidence to suggest that the trend has been inhibited or does not exist to the extent that was otherwise thought. A survey of readers of *Training* Magazine suggests that budget cutbacks of the HRD department when economic times get tough, were no worse than other departments.[9] The survey involved readers who had experienced layoffs and those who were asked to predict what would happen to their department should bad times prevail. This is an encouraging trend for trainers who have been haunted with the fear that during tough times, their department would be the first to feel the chop of the ax.

Government Research

Another very significant piece of evidence about trends in evaluation involves recent government research on evaluation of training and development. Under the auspices of the Office of Personnel Management several research and development efforts were undertaken to assist various government agencies to develop procedures and models for evaluating their training programs. This provided a systematic approach for formulating and implementing an overall evaluation plan.

The federal government has been creative and diligent in its evaluation efforts despite facing budget reductions. Not only is its work very helpful in understanding evaluation, but it is willing to share it with others. Table 2-1 summarizes some of the evaluation projects in the federal government. The evaluation practices covered different types of courses, audiences, data-gathering techniques, and levels of sophistication. Many are tied to previous needs analysis or tasks analysis.[10]

Table 2-1
Typical Government Evaluation Projects*

Title of Evaluation Project	Government Agency
1. Evaluation of New Officer Training	Department of Agriculture, APHIS, Plant Protection and Quarantine
2. Evaluation of Supervisory Skills Training Program	Department of Agriculture, Forest Service Region 5
3. Evaluation of the Basic Supervisory Training Program	Department of Education
4. Evaluation of the Skills for Performance and Career Development Course	U.S. General Accounting Office
5. Evaluation of Desk Audit Training	Department of Labor, Employment Standards Administration
6. Evaluation of District Office Managers Workshop on Federal Employees' Compensation	Department of Labor, Employment Standards Administration
7. Evaluation of Career Action Planning Seminar	National Aeronautics and Space Administration
8. Evaluation of Interaction Management Course	Department of Navy, Finance Center
9. Evaluation of Portuguese Language for Technical and Scientific Staff	Department of Navy, Naval Research Laboratory

10. Participant Action Plan Approach: A Generic Follow-up Evaluation Method	U.S. Office of Personnel Management

*Salinger, R. D. "Judging from the Feds," Training and Development Journal, August 1985, pp. 63–65.
For additional information contact the Office of Training and Development, U.S. Office of Personnel Management, Box 7230, Washington, D.C. 20044.

Another important key indicator of increasing government interest in training evaluation is the recent award of $750,000, two-year grant by the U. S. Department of Labor to the ASTD. The award was granted to examine workplace training practices and their transferability throughout public and private employment systems. The project, labeled "Best Practices: What Works in Training and Development," began in 1986 and was completed at the end of 1988.

Although the entire project had a results orientation, two important parts focused directly on measurement and evaluation. The first of these two parts involved accounting systems where the best practices in accounting for training was explored. The absence of standardized accounting practices for training and development currently makes it difficult to integrate training and development into strategic thinking of employment situations.

Until an accounting structure that integrates training and development is established, employers cannot effectively use training as a tool to adapt to change or implement cost effective training. The second part on evaluating training effectiveness is closely linked with the accounting study area. Standard evaluation methods are not currently in use or at any rate progressively promoted. Identifying model best practices and promoting their transferability was the focus of this part of the study.

The evaluation and cost accounting portions of the study were featured in the July 1990 issue of *Training and Development Journal.* This move by the Department of Labor and the continuing efforts of other federal agencies have helped to move evaluation into the forefront in federal government HRD systems.

Outcome Measurement And Management Education

A major education innovation important to business is on the horizon. If fully implemented, the innovation would have a significant impact on collegiate business and management education in the 1990s and beyond.

This innovation, referred to as the Outcome Measurement Project (OMP), was developed by the American Association of Collegiate Schools of Business (AACSB). The project requires the evaluation of the quality of education students receive from collegiate business and management programs. The outcome measures include various tests and exercises designed to evaluate the results of the educational process.

The project is designed to address the need for accountability from business schools. Currently, the marketplace is a primary vehicle to judge the success of business schools, but markets are not always perfect. Academicians, politicians, and business leaders are all interested in exploring accountability issues. The measures would be applied at the end of the educational process, before the student enters the marketplace. In addition, it would be useful for assessing the knowledge and skills of the business school graduates during the educational process.

Knowledge and Skills

An important part of this project was to identify the content areas in which to test students. The seven content areas are accounting, business environment and strategy, finance, human resources and organization theory, marketing, management information systems, and quantitative analysis/operations research/production and operations management. In addition to the content areas, nine skill and personal characteristics areas have been identified. These are believed to be valuable attributes to business success. These are leadership, oral communication/presentation skills, written communication, planning and organizing, information gathering and problem analysis, decision making, delegation and control, self-objectivity, and disposition to lead.

Progress

To date, instruments have been developed for measuring the content areas and skills and personal characteristics. For the seven content areas, the American College Testing Program has developed written tests. For the nine skills and personal characteristics, Development Dimensions International, a leading training producer has developed a battery of behavioral simulations including in-basket exercises, role plays, and group discussion exercises. The Edwards Personal Preference Schedule rates the disposition to lead characteristic.

Both types of measures have been applied on an experimental basis with fourteen schools cooperating in the initial testing for content areas.

Four schools have participated in the use of the simulations for assessing skills and characteristics. Experimentation with the Outcome Measurement Project is continuing. This may be one of the most significant measurement and evaluation projects undertaken in the United States.[11]

Packaged Programs/Training Suppliers

Finally, additional evidence in the trend toward measurement appears in the packaged training programs available for sale. The marketing strategy, for at least the more progressive firms selling packaged programs, is to show tangible results achieved from those programs. Many ads now show how the program was evaluated and what results were achieved by others. Figure 2-4 shows an example of such an ad.

Organizations such as Xerox Learning Systems go to extremes to test a program before introducing it to the general public. In test marketing emphasis is placed on evaluating the impact of the program and this, in turn, is a major factor in the decision to go public with the program. If inadequate results are achieved, the program is not introduced.

This trend toward more responsible evaluation by program developers is in response to questions HRD professionals have been asking in recent years. Potential purchasers want to know what results have been achieved and how they were developed. Effective sales representatives must give specific answers and not vague, general responses to evaluation questions. There was a time when an impressive client list was convincing enough that the program worked. This is no longer the case. Programs have failed in the most prestigious companies. And too, just because a program works in one organization does not mean that it will work in another.

Supplier brochures contain convincing information about the results achieved from programs. In the brochure describing the interaction management program from Development Dimensions, International, Bill Byham, CEO responded to the question, "What about results?" Bill's comments, printed on the brochure, are:

> "Improved job performance, increased productivity. Better communications among departments and organizational levels. Results are real, immediate, and noticeable. Independent studies and organizational evaluations prove year in and year out that IM works."

This effort on the part of suppliers even goes beyond displaying results. Some have adopted names that reflect evaluation and measurement, such as Measurable Performance Systems or the Effectiveness Institute, Inc.

FACT: Supervisors dramatically improve skills

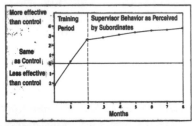

SST supervisors were perceived by subordinates to be using SST skills at levels significantly above those of the controls.

FACT: Production per person achieves 17% increase

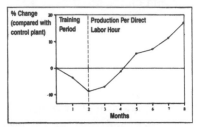

The six month running average of total monthly production *per direct* worker-hour improved 17% when compared to control plant.

FACT: Average daily production achieves 25% increase

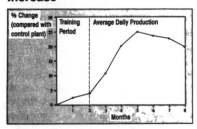

Average daily production relative to controls increased 25% in month 5 and remained substantially above the rate prior to the beginning of the intervention.

FACT: $250,000 saved in six months through waste reduction

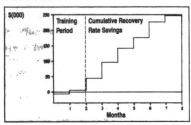

Relative to controls, raw material converted to end product improved at a rate equivalent to a decrease in cost from $40,000-$50,000 per month during the six month research period.

FACT: These results clearly indicate that MOHR'S custom designed behavior modeling based intervention substantially changed the behavior of the supervisors and managers in the SST plant.

Figure 2-4. An ad for behavior modeling. (Reprinted with permission from MOHR Development, Inc.; Stamford, CT.)

Others have developed philosophy statements concerning evaluation such as this statement from the Training House credo:

We believe that professional trainers owe their management a report on the impact of the training effort, with success documented in terms of measurably improved performance. Our survey instruments, tests, and assessment exercises are designed to measure impact and not simply satisfaction.

Training House is a Princeton, New Jersey-based supplier of training programs.

Summary

This chapter presented the good news. There is growing evidence of more evaluation in every aspect of the HRD field, from those directly involved in the process to those working on the sidelines. It is a trend which should continue in the future. Chapter 3 explores ways that an organization can develop and put into practice a results-oriented HRD philosophy.

Discussion Questions

1. Have you noticed a trend toward measurement and evaluation in the HRD field? If so, please cite specific examples. What developments have occurred in your organization (or one with which you are familiar)?
2. Why is it important for a CEO to communicate expectations for the HRD function—both privately and publicly?
3. How does the reporting relationship affect the accountability of the HRD function?
4. Do the requirements for training and education jobs in your organization (or one with which you are familiar) contain specific statements about measurement and evaluation? Please explain.
5. Discuss the relationship between the models for HRD practice and evaluation.
6. How will the outcome measurement project affect business education?
7. Although more want ads for training positions require evaluation experience, the majority still do not. Why?
8. Discuss the federal government's role in evaluation. Why is it important?
9. Most organizations measure participant reaction to training programs yet few measure the actual results. Why?
10. Why are training suppliers more responsive to requests for measurable results from their programs?

References

1. Lee, C., "All Hands on DEC," *Training*, December 1989, p. 35.
2. Galagan, P., "David T. Kearns: A CEO's View of Training,"*Training and Development Journal*, May 1990, p. 44.
3. Baldwin, T. T., Wagner, R. J., and Chasteen, C., "A Real Commitment to Training," *Training and Development Journal*, September 1989, p. 64.
4. Bernhard, H. B. and Ingols, C. A., "Six Lessons for the Corporate Classroom," *Harvard Business Review*, September–October 1988, p. 46.
5. McLagan, P. A., "Models for HRD Practice," *Training and Development Journal*, September 1989, pp. 54–57.
6. American Society for Training and Development, "How Can HRD Be More Relevant?" *Training and Development Journal*, January 1985, p. 18.
7. Ralphs, L. T. and Stephan, E., "HRD In the Fortune 500,"*Training and Development Journal*, October 1986, p. 70.
8. Zemke, R., "The Systems Approach: A Nice Theory But . . . ," *Training*, October 1985, p. 103.
9. Gordon, J., "The First Thing Cut?" *Training*, November 1987, pp. 43–51.
10. Salinger, R. D., "Judging From the Feds,"*Training and Development Journal*, August 1985, p. 63–65.
11. For additional information on this project contact the Academy of Management. Several articles have appeared on this subject in the Academy of Management *Newsletter* in 1989 and 1990. Portions of the material in this chapter were taken from a *Newsletter* article by Robert Albanese, Texas A&M University.

C H A P T E R 3

Developing a Results-Oriented Approach

What Is Results-Oriented HRD?

Results-oriented HRD is a term used occasionally in HRD literature, and it will be used throughout this book. What does it mean? It represents an HRD philosophy which emphasizes results and is characterized in the following ways:

☐ *HRD programs are not usually undertaken unless tangible results can be obtained.* If the impact of the program cannot be measured, then perhaps the program should not be implemented. If a program represents a significant effort or cost, then should it be conducted if its effectiveness cannot be determined? Maybe there are other reasons for proceeding with a program. However, if this philosophy toward getting results is adopted, it may cause a review of the process and possibly the creation of additional evaluation approaches.

☐ *At least one method to measure the results of an HRD program is included in the program design.* The evaluation strategy is usually determined when program objectives are established. With this philosophy, evaluation strategy is placed on a level of equal importance with the content of the program, the objectives, the delivery system, and the instructor or program director. It should be an equal consideration if the results are to be measured.

☐ *Each member of the HRD staff should be required to measure the results of their efforts.* Each member of the HRD staff must see the importance of evaluation and the necessity for including it as an integral part of the HRD process. If possible, each staff member should participate directly in the measurement of results of his or her programs.

☐ *Management is involved in the HRD process at all phases.* From inception through evaluation and follow-up, management's active involvement is critical to the success of any program. It will enhance the process and facilitate the communication of results to the management group.

☐ *There is an active effort to increase management commitment and support of the HRD effort.* Management support is critical to the allocation of resources to the HRD department. Securing results and properly communicating those results will increase support. This increased support will allow for additional efforts to evaluate programs. It is a continuous cycle, and a very important part of a results-oriented HRD philosophy.

Purposes and Uses of Evaluation

Evaluation is undertaken for several purposes, which usually fall into one of two categories: (1) to improve the HRD process, or (2) to decide whether or not to continue it. The following list presents in more detail each specific reason:

☐ *To determine whether a program is accomplishing its objectives.* Every properly designed program should have objectives. These objectives should be stated in generally accepted terms (i.e., measurable, specific, challenging, etc.). A very important purpose of the evaluation process is to determine whether or not objectives are being (or have been) met.

☐ *To identify the strengths and weaknesses in the HRD process.* An evaluation can help to determine the effectiveness of the various components of an HRD program. This is probably the most common purpose of evaluation. These include, but are not limited to, methods of presentation, learning environment, program content, training aids, facility, schedule, and the instructor. These variables do make a difference in the HRD effort and need to be evaluated to make improvements in the program.

☐ *To determine the cost/benefit ratio of an HRD program.* An increasingly common reason for evaluation is to determine whether or not the program justifies the cost. This aspect of evaluation compares the cost of a program to its usefulness or value. For example, an HRD program is conducted for salespersons to increase sales output. The sales volume is compared before and after the training program. The resulting benefit or value of the program can be approximated. This value, in turn, is compared with the cost of the program to calculate a cost/benefit ratio over a predetermined time period. Overall, this evaluation provides management with data to eliminate an unproductive program, to increase support for programs which yield a high payoff, or to make adjustments in a program to increase the benefits.

☐ *To decide who should participate in future programs.* Sometimes a follow-up evaluation simply determines the benefits of the program. Communicating these benefits to prospective participants can help them decide whether or not they need to be involved in the program. For example, an advanced management seminar was offered to all members of a management group. Part of the program involved the implementation of specific projects after the program was completed. Information collected on the follow-up evaluation revealed the type of projects undertaken and what results were achieved. The communication of this information to other members of the management group enabled potential participants to help decide if they should attend the program.

☐ *To test the clarity and validity of tests, questions, and exercises.* It is extremely important for exercises, questions, and tests used in the training process to be valid. They must measure the skills, knowledge, and abilities the program is designed to teach. Evaluation often provides a mechanism for instruments to be validated.

☐ *To identify which participants benefitted the most or the least from the program.* An evaluation can determine which participants excelled and which failed in implementing the skills or knowledge taught. For example, an HRD program on decision making was offered to a large segment of professional and managerial employees. The selection of participants was left up to the user organization. After the program was completed, follow-up evaluations were conducted with all participants. The follow-up served to identify which participants were most successful in their efforts. This type of evaluation yields more information on the assessment of the individual rather than the effectiveness of the HRD program.

☐ *To reinforce major points made to the participant.* A follow-up evaluation can reinforce the information covered in a program by attempting to measure the results accomplished by participants. It reminds the participants of what they should have accomplished or should be accomplishing. For example, a communications training program was conducted for first-line supervisors. As part of the program, participants were asked to conduct group meetings with employees on a regular basis to solve problems and enhance two-way communication between the employees and the supervisor. In the follow-up evaluation, supervisors were reminded of what they were asked to do. Several questions focused on the number of meetings, the success of the meetings, and the problems encountered. This follow-up evaluation served to reinforce to participants that they should be conducting group meetings.

☐ *To gather data to assist in marketing future programs.* In many situations HRD departments or organizations delivering seminars are interested in why participants attend a specific program. This is particularly true for larger organizations where many programs are offered and the sponsoring organization does not always know why someone is selected to attend. An evaluation can yield information to assist the marketing strategy for future programs. Questions which become relevant are:

- Why did you attend this program?
- Who made the decision for you to attend?
- How did you find out about the program?
- Would you recommend it to others?

This information can easily be obtained as part of the evaluation at the end of the program. For example, the Society for Human Resource Management (SHRM) presents a number of professional seminars as part of their continuing education program for its members. As part of SHRM's seminar evaluation form, information is secured on the previous questions, providing program developers and administrators some insight into how participants are selected to attend their programs and how they found out about a particular seminar. This information, in turn, is useful for planning future promotional efforts.

☐ *To determine if the program was appropriate.* Sometimes evaluation can determine whether or not the original problem was indeed a training problem. Too often a training program is conducted to correct problems that cannot be corrected by training. There may be other reasons for the performance deficiencies, such as procedures, work flow, or supervision. An evaluation may yield some insight into whether or not training was actually required.

Consider this example:

A training program was conducted to reduce the number of errors on time cards. Most of these errors appeared as written changes on the time card. Management thought that supervisors did not know the proper procedures and did not understand the importance of proper time card records. The training and development department was asked to present a short program to all supervisors. The training and development manager wanted to determine if indeed it was a training problem. Top management would not listen, and insisted that the department conduct a training program "to see what happens." A program was developed and conducted. The evaluation data were time card errors. They were calculated each week as part of the routine information developed for, and reported to, supervision. After the program was conducted, the percentage of errors actually went up, much to the displeasure of top management. Additional evaluation showed that the training program, as presented, was effective when considering the program content and the instructional technology. However, the results were not achieved. When asked why, the supervisors gave many reasons, none of which indicated that there was a knowledge or skill deficiency in the first place. Other reasons, including poor time clock maintenance, lack of accountability, and employee discipline were strong factors leading to the original problem. This information appeared on the follow-up evaluation form.

In this case evaluation revealed that training was not required in the first place. Although this result is unusual, it can be another reason for the evaluation process.

☐ *To establish a data base which can assist management in making decisions.* The central theme in most evaluations is to make a decision about the future of an HRD program. This information can be used by a variety of people concerned with the program: the instructors, the management of the HRD department, and top executives who must allocate resources for future programs. A comprehensive evaluation system can build a data base to help make these decisions.

Levels of Evaluation: Basic Models

According to most experts, evaluation is a systematic process to determine the worth, value, or meaning of something. In regard to HRD, evaluation usually provides information for a decision about the fate of the HRD program.

The question of what to evaluate is crucial to the evaluation strategy. This depends on the type of HRD program, the organization, and the purposes of evaluation. The information collected and used for evaluation can usually be grouped into different categories. For a given category, some methods of evaluation are more appropriate than others. The types of groupings vary slightly with the different experts in the HRD field. The following section presents seven models. The specific evaluation techniques mentioned here will be discussed later.

The Kirkpatrick Approach

Probably the most well-known framework for classifying areas of evaluation comes from Kirkpatrick.[1] In his model he developed a conceptual framework to assist in determining what data are to be collected. His concept calls for four levels of evaluation, and answers four very important questions:

Level	Questions
1. Reaction	Were the participants pleased with the program?
2. Learning	What did the participants learn in the program?
3. Behavior	Did the participants change their behavior based on what was learned?
4. Results	Did the change in behavior positively affect the organization?

Reaction. Reaction is defined as what the participants thought of the program, including materials, instructors, facilities, methodology, content, etc. It does *not* include a measure of the learning that takes place.

The reaction of the participants is often a critical factor in the continuance of HRD programs. Responses on reaction questionnaires help to ensure against decisions based on the comments of a few very satisfied or disgruntled participants. Most trainers believe that initial receptivity provides a good atmosphere for learning the material in the program but does not necessarily lead to high levels of learning.

Learning. This level of evaluation is concerned with measuring the learning of principles, facts, techniques, and skills presented in a program. It is more difficult to measure than reaction. The measures must be objective and quantifiable indicators of how the participants understood and absorbed the material. There are many different measures of learning, including paper-and-pencil tests, learning curves, skill practices, and job simulations.

Behavior. The term "behavior" is used in reference to the measurement of job performance. Just as favorable reaction does not necessarily mean that learning will occur, superior achievement in a program does not always result in improved behavior on the job. Evaluations in this category may include:

☐ Before-and-after comparisons
☐ Observations from the participant's superiors, subordinates, and peers
☐ Statistical comparisons
☐ Long-range follow-ups

Results. Evaluations at this level relate the results of the program to organizational improvement. Some of the results that can be examined include costs savings, work output improvement, and quality changes. This involves collecting data before and after the program and analyzing the improvement. In this evaluation every effort should be made to isolate the variables which could have caused the improvement.

The Bell System Approach

A slightly different approach was developed as a result of a study at AT&T and the Bell System units. Prior to the divestiture of AT&T, Jackson and Kulp presented their classification of results in an ASTD conference on "Determining the Payoff of Management Training."[2] The following levels of program results, or outcomes, were presented:

☐ Reaction outcomes
☐ Capability outcomes
☐ Application outcomes
☐ Worth outcomes

Reaction outcomes. This presents the participants' opinions of the program as a whole or as specific components such as content, materials, methods, or activities. In a word, did they *accept* the program?

Capability outcomes. This covers what participants are expected to know, think, do, or produce by the end of the program.

Application outcomes. This involves what participants know, think, do, or produce in the real-world setting(s) for which the HRD program has prepared them.

Worth outcomes. This is a most significant result because it shows the value of training in relation to its cost. This outcome represents the extent to which an organization benefits from training in terms of the money, time, effort, or resources invested.

The first two levels represent the immediate goals of training; the second two levels represent the long-term results.

The CIRO Approach

A third general approach to classifying types of evaluation comes from Warr, Bird, and Rackham.[3] This rather unique approach to classifying evaluation has been used in their work in Europe, and it has a much broader scope than the traditional use of the term "evaluation" in the United States.

As with the three previous approaches, there are four general categories of evaluation studies. They form the letters C I R O:

☐ *C*ontext evaluation
☐ *I*nput evaluation
☐ *R*eaction evaluation
☐ *O*utcome evaluation

Context evaluation. This involves obtaining and using information about the current operational situation (or context) to determine training needs and objectives. This evaluation determines if training is needed. During this process, three types of objectives may be evaluated:

☐ *Ultimate objectives* (the particular deficiency in the organization that the program will eliminate or overcome).
☐ *Intermediate objectives* (the changes in employees' work behavior that will be necessary for the ultimate objectives to be attained).
☐ *Immediate objectives* (the new knowledge, skills, or attitudes that the employees must acquire to change their behavior as required to reach the intermediate objective).

Context evaluation consists of collecting information about a performance deficiency, assessing that information to establish HRD needs and, on the basis of those findings, setting objectives at three levels.

Input evaluation. Input evaluation consists of obtaining and using information about possible training resources to choose between alternative inputs to HRD. This type of evaluation involves analyzing the resources available and determining how they can be deployed so that there is a maximum chance of achieving the desired objectives. Factors such as budget and management requirements may limit the options available. Questions which become relevant during this evaluation are:

☐ What are the relative merits of the different HRD methods?
☐ Is it feasible for an outside organization to be more efficient at conducting the program?
☐ Should it be developed with internal resources?
☐ Should the line organization be involved?
☐ How much time is available for HRD?
☐ What results were achieved when a similar program was conducted in the past?

Thus, input evaluation refers to the process of collecting evidence and using it to decide on the HRD methods.

Reaction evaluation. This involves obtaining and using information about participant's reactions to improve the HRD process. The distinguishing feature of this type of evaluation is that it relies on the subjective reports of the participants, and their views can prove extremely helpful if they are collected in a systematic manner.

Outcome evaluation. This involves obtaining and using information about the results (or outcomes) of HRD to improve future programs. This is the most important part of evaluation. If outcome evaluation is to be successful, it requires careful preparation before the training program begins. There are four stages which form outcome evaluation:

☐ Defining trend objectives.
☐ Selecting or constructing some measures of those objectives.
☐ Making the measurements at the appropriate time.
☐ Assessing the results and using them to improve later programs.

In determining the results of training it is helpful to think in terms of a hierarchy of HRD outcomes. These correspond to the three levels of objectives discussed earlier and are the immediate outcomes, intermediate outcomes, and ultimate outcomes.

Successful HRD will produce some change in a participant. This is an immediate outcome. Initially, this training is reflected in the changes of knowledge, skills, or attitude. Although these three characteristics are interrelated, it is often useful for the purposes of analysis to consider them separately. Changes in knowledge, skill, or attitude can be measured as soon as the course has been completed and before the participant leaves the HRD program.

HRD is not conducted primarily for the sake of learning something. Its main concern is to bring about positive change in the participant, or intermediate outcomes. This involves on-the-job behavior change without which there will be no change in job performance. The change in knowledge, skills, or attitude does not necessarily guarantee a change in job performance.

If changes occur in the performance of the participants on the job, then the organization will be affected in some way. The impact on the organization is the ultimate outcome of any HRD program. For example, there may be improvements in the department's output, cost, scrap rates, accident frequencies, etc. This type of change is measured in terms of a department or section as a whole, and not necessarily on the part of individuals. This measurement represents one of the most difficult areas of evaluation.

Saratoga Institute Approach

As an outgrowth of a measurement task force created by the Society for Human Resource Management, the Saratoga Institute has developed four levels of training evaluation.[4] Similar to the Kirkpatrick model, this approach evaluates the following levels:

Training satisfaction. The degree to which participants are satisfied with the training they have received.

Learning change. The actual learning that has occurred, with pre- and post-course instruments.

Behavior change. The on-the-job change in behavior as a result of the training program.

Organizational change. The improvements in the organization as a result of the training program, measured in quantitative terms.

HRD programs, evaluated on each of these four levels are reported annually by the Saratoga Institute in the SHRM/Saratoga Institute Human Resource Effectiveness Survey. The ultimate evaluation is a return on investment, which is related to the fourth level, organizational change.

The IBM Approach

IBM, whose training budget totals almost $1 billion, also evaluates its training on four levels.[5] Another variation of the Kirkpatrick model, these levels are defined as follows:

Reaction. A satisfaction rating that asks trainees how valuable they found the program.

Testing. Pre- and post-program measurements that assess knowledge and skills improvement as a result of the training program.

Application. The extent to which participants applied new skills on the job and the results achieved from the application.

Business results. What IBM expected from the program in the form of a return that can be converted to a dollar value.

IBM admits that their ultimate level is business results, showing the dollar impact. They take some measurements to this level, although only in certain cases, and most of those cases involve technical or hard skills training.

Xerox Approach

Another model for evaluation is the category used by Xerox Corporation in their evaluation efforts.[6] As with the other models, evaluation focuses on four levels:

Entry capability. An evaluation of trainees at the time they enter a program to determine if the prerequisites for the program are satisfied.

End-of-course performance. Addresses the issue of whether or not trainees achieve the desired training outcomes. This is linked to training objectives.

Mastery job performance. Focuses on the question of whether or not graduates of the program exhibit mastery performance under normal job conditions after a practical period of on-the-job experience.

Organizational performance. Focuses on which program participants meet or exceed organizational targets after a practical period of on-the-job experience.

This approach is very similar to other models but has a different twist with the entry measurements.

CIPP Model

Another model that is receiving widespread use in several organizations is the CIPP Model, which is an acronym of the four basic types of evaluation in the model—context, input, process, and product. Developed by leading educators on the National Study Committee on Evaluation of Phi Delta Kappa, an international society of professional educators, the CIPP model is valuable for evaluation of management training and development.[7] Its developers claim it is practical, effective, efficient, comprehensive, balanced and useful. The four levels are:

Context evaluation. Useful for providing a rationale for determined executives, context evaluation defines a relevant environment, identifies needs and opportunities and diagnoses specific problems. A needs analysis is a common example of context evaluation.

Input evaluation. Provides information to determine how to use resources to best meet program goals. It is used to decide if outside assistance is necessary and to help determine general strategy for planning and designing the program. The results of input evaluation are often seen as policies, budgets, schedules, proposals, and procedures.

Process evaluation. Provides feedback to individuals responsible for implementation. It is accomplished through monitoring potential sources for failure, providing information for preplanned decisions during implementation and describing what actually occurs. Both informal approaches are used in data collection. These include reaction sheets, rating scales, and analysis of existing records.

Product evaluation. Measures and interprets the attainment of objectives. It should measure intended as well as unintended outcomes. Evaluation at this level can take place both during and after program. The traditional review of evaluation has meant product evaluations. Any traditional evaluation procedure may be used at this level, providing it is a good fit for the situation.

In summary, context evaluation assists in forming goals; input evaluation aids in program planning; process evaluation guides implementation; and product evaluation helps in recycling decisions. The CIPP model has received favorable attention and may be a model of preference over the Kirkpatrick Model. A study of 300 members of the ASTD revealed the extent of use of the CIPP Model. With an 80% response rate and high validity and reliability in the research project, it appears that the CIPP Model wins out. According to the respondents, 126 out of 225 preferred the CIPP Model, whereas 82 of the 225 preferred the Kirkpatrick Model. Seventeen had no preference.[8]

Which Model Is Best?

Describing seven models for levels of evaluation invites confusion. Unfortunately, the literature is not limited to seven. There are many others, most of which are variations of those presented here. Now comes the important question, "Which one is best?" There is no right answer. What is best for one organization, may be inappropriate for another. The most important course of action is to select a model around which the organization will focus its evaluation. The models represented by Kirkpatrick, AT&T, Saratoga Institute, and IBM are very similar. Although the words differ, they focus on reaction or satisfaction at the first level, learning or achievement at the second level, behavior or measurable job performance at the third level, and business results or ultimate outcomes at the fourth level. Because of these similarities and the popularity of this four-level distinction, reference will be made to these four levels throughout the remainder of this book.

Evaluation should occur at each of the four levels and a comprehensive evaluation process will focus on all four levels in the same program. The common thread among most evaluation experts is that emphasis should be placed on the ultimate outcome, which results in improved group or organization performance. It is the most difficult to obtain, document, and measure. The other three levels will not suffice in an ultimate evaluation. There is evidence in studies to indicate that the fourth level, a results orientation, is a method most desired and receives the most support.[9]

What is needed from many training programs is business results—bottom-line achievements as depicted in Table 3-1. This table shows the results attained from participants attending a basic management skills course conducted by the corporate management and training department at the Cigna Corporation.[10] Each of the plan results can be converted to a dollar value savings. It is this type of data that is convincing to management in terms of continuing training efforts and justifying future programs, which are two of the most important purposes for undertaking evaluation.

The focus on business results should be integrated into the overall program, as is discussed in the next chapter. As programs are developed, the business results focus should be highlighted. For example, a review of the course catalog for training programs offered by Motorola reveals the name of the program, the target audience, the overall goal of the program, the method of delivery and probably most importantly, the business issue addressed.[11] Among the business issues addressed in a sampling of courses are the following:

1. Total quality improvement
2. Planning product marketing strategy
3. Improving organizational productivity
4. Ten-fold quality improvement
5. Return on net assets
6. Business planning

This up-front communication leaves little room for confusion over what ultimate outcome is expected from a program.

It is for these reasons, or assumptions, that much of the material in this book has been developed and presented. Emphasis will be placed on examining ways to measure results. The term "evaluation" will be used as an all-inclusive term and, occasionally, measuring results will be used to be more specific for that important part of the evaluation.

Table 3-1
BMS Case Studies on Bottom-Line Results

Case No.	Manager Function	Plan Results
1	Reinsurance coding unit	$18 K in savings, 730% ROI
2	Premium collections	$80 K increased investment income, 3,100% ROI
3	Premium collections	$150 K increased investment income, 5,900% ROI
4	Exchange department	$95 K increased revenue, 4,475% ROI
5	Benefits administration	60% improvement on timing standard
6	Benefits administration	80% improvement on accuracy standard
7	Benefits administration	80% improvement on accuracy standard
8	Systems processing unit	20% productivity increase, $110 K in budget savings, 4,500% ROI, plus increased tape mounts, improved turn-around on service requests
9	Financial analysis unit	35% improvement on on-time service, plus 25% productivity increase on job set-ups
10	Systems testing unit	165% efficiency increase against production standard
11	Actuarial unit	15% improvement on timing standard, 70% improvement in accuracy while production volume increased by 20%, no staff increases
12	Actuarial unit	15% improvement in on-time reporting, 30% increase in quality review standard
13	Actuarial unit	30% increase on service timing and 10% improvement in accuracy standard
14	Actuarial unit	5% increase on service timing and 10% improvement in accuracy standard

Source: Paquet, B., Kasl, E., Weinstein, I., and Waite, W. "The Bottom Line," Training and Development Journal, May, 1987, p. 30.

Developing a Results-Oriented Attitude

Developing a results-oriented HRD effort depends, to a large extent, on a proper philosophy and attitude among the HRD staff and the employees. Evaluation goes beyond reaction forms, measuring output data, and presenting statistical analysis of improved performance. There are so many factors which can affect the outcome of HRD programs that evaluation must be an overall philosophy.

For example, participants can attend a training program, not put it to use for six months after the last evaluation, and then be inspired to apply some of the techniques presented in the program. Unless the evaluation considers the long-term effect, it will fall short of its optimum effectiveness.

The HRD staff's attitude toward evaluation is something more. It involves:

☐ How they think about evaluation.
☐ How they plan for it, implement it, and use it.
☐ How much time they are willing to spend on it.
☐ How they feel about its relative priority.

The HRD staff member who asks the question, "Do we really have to develop evaluation procedures before the program is conducted?" does not have the proper orientation for an effective evaluation. HRD staff members who are not committed to the process will not make the most of an evaluation.

A key to this proper philosophy of evaluation is involvement on the part of HRD personnel. The simplest, most straightforward, uncomplicated option for improving anything is to get involved and take responsibility for oneself. Only a few steps can be taken at a time. No one is born a veteran.

Attitude and Performance

The link between attitude and performance is an important issue with HRD professionals. Is there a definite correlation? (i.e., Can the attitude of a person affect performance?) Much research has indicated that there is a definite tie. A positive attitude can produce more results than a negative attitude. Sometimes referred to as the Pygmalion effect or the self-fulfilling prophecy, this phenomenon has been demonstrated in many research efforts. It is illustrated in Figure 3-1 and probably is best described as the powerful influence of one person's expectations on another's behavior. If a manager's expectations are high, productivity is likely to be excellent. If expectations are low, productivity is likely to be poor. The self-fulfilling prophecy phenomenon, documented in a number of case studies prepared during the past decade for major industrial concerns, has revealed the following:[12]

☐ What a manager expects of his subordinates and the way he or she treats them largely determines their work performance and career progress.
☐ A unique characteristic of superior managers is their ability to create high performance expectations that subordinates fulfill.
☐ Less-effective managers fail to develop similar expectations and, as a consequence, the productivity of their subordinates suffers.
☐ Subordinates, more often than not, do what they believe they are expected to do.

A recent example of the Pygmalion Effect in action comes from the fast-food industry in an experimental program in Philadelphia.[13] In an area where there is a shortage of entry-level workers, an extremely high turnover rate has plagued the industry. A program called Project Transition developed entry-level training using Pygmalion. Welfare recipients seemed to be the natural source of employees

Figure 3-1. The self-fulfilling prophecy in action. (Reprinted with permission from *Training Today,* CRM McGraw-Hill.)

for the program. Using Pygmalion techniques, none of the 57 participants in the first year of Program Transition went back on welfare. The program designers credit Pygmalion factors such as gut reaction, work ethic, initiative, work quality, reliability and availability, as being the key to the program's success.

The comparison of attitude and performance to attitude and HRD program results should be apparent. If participants are expected to obtain results from the application of knowledge and skills gained in the training program, then that expectation will enhance the results achieved. An active effort undertaken to develop a results-oriented attitude among participants should improve results.

This assumption can be checked by conducting an experiment using a control group and an experimental group. In the control group the HRD program is presented in its usual manner with little emphasis on what is expected of the participants. There is no pressure for them to put into practice what they are being taught. They are told that a follow-up will be conducted to help measure the effectiveness of the program. In the experimental group, at periodic intervals in the program, discussions are held with the participants regarding what is expected of them and what others have achieved in previous programs. The follow-up is mentioned in the same way except that the participants are expected to improve on the performance of others before them. This positive attitude toward expectation is interjected throughout the program. If the two groups are approximately the same in terms of their ability and motivation and the HRD program content is the same except for the expectations of results, the experimental group should obtain greater results.

Communicating Expectations

Several discussions about results should be held with HRD program participants. They must understand the expectations, and there should be no doubt that they should put into practice what they are being taught. Typical discussions are held at the beginning, at the end, and at appropriate times during the program, depending on the type and duration. Some specific evaluation methods require an explanation of the procedures required of the participants. This explanation, when coupled with a reminder about results, enhances the evaluation effort and helps to ensure that the material taught is actually put into practice.

Most important, participants should be aware of what has been accomplished by others if the course has been conducted previously. Knowing about tangible results from others can trigger thought processes in participants to meet or exceed those results. If no previous results are available, discussing what can be accomplished through applications of the program material can be effective. As will be presented later, an integral part of evaluation is a follow-up to see what results were achieved. These follow-up evaluations should be thoroughly discussed with participants.

This discussion is illustrated by the remarks of a chief executive at the beginning of an HRD program:

> The participants who have preceded you have achieved excellent results by putting into practice the material covered in this program. In follow-up surveys those supervisors who have used the safety practices, rules, and tips presented here have reduced, on a combined basis, the accident frequency rate from 2.2 to 1.5 over a period of 6 months after attending the training program. This represents a 32% reduction, a significant result when you consider the average cost of an accident and the human suffering involved. Those statistics dealt with the number of supervisors who used the material in the program. Not all did, and that's disappointing. In the follow-up survey 20% did not use it. With improvements in our training program and with the ability of this group, I am sure that you can beat both records. It can be done, and we expect you to do it.

That introduction leaves no doubt what is expected as a result of attending this HRD program. It would be difficult for anyone to ignore the material in the program.

Responsibility for Results

Achieving results from HRD programs is a multiple responsibility. The primary responsibility must lie with the participants. They must understand the material, put it into practice, and get the desired results.

Others play a very important part in making this process work effectively and smoothly. The reinforcement (or lack of reinforcement) from the participant's supervisor can have a significant effect on the results. The supervisor must show support for the HRD effort and make a commitment to help get the expected results. Positive reinforcement is a key part of results-oriented HRD and will be discussed in detail in a later chapter.

Discussion leaders have a significant role in achieving results. They must conduct programs in an effective manner so that the content is understood. Program designers and subject-matter experts share in the responsibility, since they must develop a program relevant to the needs of the participants.

Last, but not least, top management shares in the responsibility for results. When top management demands results-oriented programs, requires evaluation of all the programs, and communicates their expectations to all parties involved, then the subsequent results will be enhanced. It is only through a shared responsibility for results, with each party accepting their respective roles, that maximum results will be obtained.

Policy Statements

Another key to developing a results-oriented attitude is to have the organization's intentions clearly defined and communicated to all. Functions and responsibilities, policies and procedures, and statement(s) of philosophy of an organization can have an impact on the attitude toward measuring the results of an HRD effort. A results-oriented philosophy must be communicated to all members of management and in some cases to all employees. For example, the role of training and development at Chevron U.S.A. Inc.[14] is detailed in the following box. Characteristic 3 sets the tone for evaluation at Chevron: "If no measurement can be developed, training is not undertaken. Measurement can be either objective or subjective, but is based on observable data, preferably, in dollars of cost reduction or productivity increase." There can be little doubt in the minds of the HRD staff and other members of management about the importance of evaluation at Chevron.

In defining the responsibilities for training and development it might be appropriate to state who is responsible for evaluation and the various roles in the evaluation process. The HRD staff, the line organization, and the support functions all have evaluation responsibilities. This communication puts a proper emphasis on evaluation and defines the responsibilities. The impact on program results may be surprising.

Summary

This chapter presented the information necessary to understand and develop a results-oriented approach to HRD in an organization. It began with a thorough definition of results-oriented HRD. Next, the purposes

THE ROLE OF TRAINING AND DEVELOPMENT
AT CHEVRON U.S.A. INC.

Philosophy

The purpose of training and development is to maintain and improve effectiveness and efficiency of individuals within the organization. This can only have sustained effect if it influences the actions and practices of line managers so as to serve better both the self-interest of employees (personal return, both tangible and intangible) and the needs of the corporation (profit return, both short and long range).

All training and development within the company is based on the firm belief that:
1. Employees have a need for growth and self-fulfillment which can be compatible with the goals of the organization for the benefit of both.
2. Learning is a self-activity; all employee development is self-development.
3. The primary job of a trainer is not to train; it is to manage the learning process for those individuals with whom the trainer interfaces.
4. Training, to be effective, must be a function of line management.

Characteristics

A training and development system should have the following characteristics:
1. It requires management commitment and follow-up. This only comes about when training helps individuals accomplish:
   • Their established objectives;
   • The changes they desire; and
   • The mission of their organization.
2. It recognizes that most performance problems are not caused by lack of skill but are execution problems—caused by lack of feedback, either positive or negative.
3. If no measurement can be developed, training is not undertaken. Measurement can be either objective or subjective but is based on observable data, preferably in dollars of cost reduction or productivity increase.
4. Programs are tested both on the job and in the classroom before publication—and they are revised until they meet standards.
5. It is based on the fact that new employees learn how to do most jobs very quickly. Therefore, training concentrates only on major payoff areas of what they are not performing after some time on the job, (This is in sharp contrast to the organization that believes new employees must be formally taught everything.)
6. As company goals change, the training system adjusts to meet the new goals of the company.
7. It recognizes the difference between:
   • Training (improve performance in current job);
   • Education (improve competency in a specified career direction); and
   • Development (prepares employee to move with the job as it changes and grows).
8. It has qualified individuals who:
   • Maintain both knowledge and skill, in depth, to identity and formulate concepts and implementation techniques which will strengthen management at all levels;
   • Stay abreast of and evaluate changes in managerial practices;
   • Stay abreast of training and development techniques and procedures; and
   • Recommend and/or adopt changes as appropriate.

THREE CATEGORIES OF TRAINING

The total context of training can be subdivided into three categories:

Training can be defined as those activities designed to improve performance on the job the employee is presently doing, is being hired to do, or is being promoted into (provided the promotion is to a position having the same basic area of activity—merely greater responsibility, more authority, a larger scope, etc.).

Education includes those activities which are designed to improve the overall competence of an employee in a specified direction beyond the job now held. The employee is being prepared for a different place in the organization from that he now holds. Education includes

(Continued on page 60)

(Continued from page 59)

preparation for promotion into a position with new areas of activity: it also includes learning inputs for long-range career advancement.

Development activities are those which increase the competence and ability of an employee to move with the organization as it changes and grows. Development is concerned with the future of the organization and the individual and usually has goals which cannot be stated in specific behavioral terminology. The current job is evolving and changing and what it will be in the future probably has not been identified: the future conditions and standards of proficiency are not today's reality. Employee development is designed to produce a viable and flexible work force as the organization moves into the future

Reprinted with permission from Training, The Magazine of Human Resources Development.

and uses of evaluation were presented in detail. Seven popular approaches for placing evaluation into categories or levels were outlined. This categorization helps develop a better understanding of the full scope of the evaluation process. Finally, the factors necessary to develop a positive attitude toward getting results were presented. This results-oriented attitude, instilled in all who have a responsibility for results, can be an important part of the evaluation strategy. The next chapter presents a results-oriented HRD model.

Discussion Questions

1. Why is the "results-oriented approach" advocated as a necessary philosophy in an organization?
2. How much of a "results orientation" does your organization (or one with which you are familiar) have?
3. Which purposes of evaluation are the most commonly used? Which are most important? Least important?
4. Discuss a recent evaluation project. What were the purposes of evaluation?
5. Contrast the basic models for the levels of evaluation? Which one is best suited for your organization (or one with which you are familiar)?
6. Why is the Kirkpatrick Model (or variations of it) so popular?
7. How can HRD staff members be motivated to pursue evaluation?
8. Cite examples or personal experiences of the self-fulfilling prophecy.
9. Why is it important to communicate performance expectations to trainees?
10. Secure a training policy statement from an organization. What does it reveal about obtaining results? Why?
11. Why are long-term results from a program difficult to achieve?

References

1. Kirkpatrick, D. L., "Four Steps to Measuring Training Effectiveness," *Personnel Administrator*, November 1983, pp. 19–25.
2. Jackson, S. and Kulp, M. J., "Designing Guidelines for Evaluating the Outcomes of Management Training," *Determining the Payoff of Management Training*, ASTD, Washington, D.C., 1979, pp. 7–8.
3. Warr, P., Bird, M., and Rackham, N., *Evaluation of Management Training*, Gower Press, London, 1970.
4. Fitz-enz, J., *ASPA/Saratoga Institute Human Resource Effectiveness Survey: 1990 Annual Report*, Saratoga Institute: Saratoga, CA, 1991.
5. Gordon, J., "Romancing the Bottom Line," *Training*, June 1987, pp. 31–42.
6. Alden, J., Manager Training Systems, Xerox Corporation, reported at a senior HRD managers forum on "Measuring HRD," February 24, 1983.
7. Galvin, J. G., "What Can Trainers Learn from Educators about Evaluating Management Training?" *Training and Development Journal*, August 1983, p. 52.
8. *Ibid*, p. 55.
9. Kusy, M. E., Jr., "The Effects of Types of Training Evaluation on Support of Training Among Corporation Managers," *Training and Development Journal*, April 1987, p. 82.
10. Paquet, B., Kasl, E., Weinstein, L., and Waite, W., "The Bottom Line," *Training and Development Journal*, May 1987, p. 30.
11. Galagan, P., "Focus on Results at Motorola," *Training and Development Journal*, May 1986, p. 45.
12. Eden, D., *Pygmalion in Management: Productivity as a Self-Fulfilling Prophecy*, Lexington Books: Lexington, MA 1990.
13. Shimko, B. W., "The McPygmalion Effect," *Training and Development Journal*, June 1990, pp. 64–70.
14. Zemke, R., "In Search of a Training Philosophy," *Training*, October 1985, pp. 93–98.

CHAPTER 4

A Results-Oriented HRD Model

There are a variety of models for the design and implementation of HRD programs. Most are sound and logical and produce an effective program. Some focus on impact instead of activity[1]; others focus on efficiency and effectiveness.[2] However, many of them do lack steps in the design process which emphasize the evaluation of a program, and more specifically, the desired results. A model can be very useful to observe the total HRD process and examine the relationship of one step to another. The model presented in this chapter is appropriate for almost any HRD activity. It involves 18 logical steps, with at least 11 of the steps directly involving evaluation. The reaction to this model in the first edition of this book was very favorable.[3]

As presented earlier, evaluation is a systematic process with several important parts. Most successful evaluations are planned at the beginning of the needs assessment process, when the questions that will shape the training program are asked.[4] Evaluation efforts must be undertaken before, during, and after a program. Before a program is developed, basic questions related to evaluation which must be answered, such as:

☐ Who?
☐ What?
☐ Where?
☐ When?
☐ How?

During the program, activities are geared toward achieving results, and in some cases data are actually collected. After the program, additional data are collected, analyzed, and reported.

Table 4-1 shows the complete HRD model that emphasizes evaluation. The model is designed to allow a termination of the process whenever appropriate. The complete model may be too detailed for some organi-

Table 4-1
A Complete Results-Oriented HRD Model

1. Conduct a Needs Analysis and Develop Tentative Objectives

2. Identify Purposes of Evaluation

3. Establish Baseline Data

4. Select Evaluation Method/Design

5. Determine Evaluation Strategy

6. Finalize Program Objectives

7. Estimate Program Costs/Benefits

8. Prepare and Present Proposal

9. Design Evaluation Instruments

10. Determine and Develop Program Content

11. Design or Select Training and Development Methods

12. Test Program and Make Revisions

13. Implement or Conduct Program

14. Collect Data at Proper Stages

15. Analyze and Interpret Data

16. Make Program Adjustments

17. Calculate Return on Investment

18. Communicate Program Results

zations. It can be shortened, if necessary. However, for a results-oriented approach, the steps in this model related directly to evaluation are considered necessary. They must be included to improve the evaluation and subsequent results. In this chapter each step will be discussed. The comments on the steps not related to evaluation will be very brief, with more explanation devoted to the steps related directly to evaluation.

1. Conduct a Needs Analysis and Develop Tentative Objectives

This is an obvious first step for any HRD program design. There must be a determination of the need for the program. This step could be triggered by the discovery of a performance deficiency, a request for training from top management, a general observation of a problem, a need to improve productivity, a requirement to meet a government regulation, or an effort to improve employee morale. Whatever triggered the need for the program, a needs analysis should be conducted to determine specific deficiencies in performance or lack of information necessary for a job. Needs analyses are typically conducted by interviews with potential candidates to be trained, or in interviews with their superiors, or by administering attitude surveys and questionnaires. To the extent that it is feasible, the environment surrounding the performance deficiency should be examined to see what other factors are affecting performance. This could involve procedures, systems, leadership climate, compensation, or many other factors.

Typical questions that might be appropriate for a detailed needs analysis are:

☐ Is there a performance problem?
☐ What is the gap between desired and actual performance?
☐ How important is the problem?
☐ What happens if we do nothing?
☐ Is there a lack of skill contributing to the problem?
☐ Do employee attitudes need to be improved?
☐ Is this program designed to meet some outside requirement or to satisfy an external influence? If so, what is it/are they?
☐ Which employees will need the training?
☐ Are there alternative ways to satisfy the need?
☐ To what extent will other departments be involved?
☐ Are there natural barriers to accomplishing the program?
☐ Who supports this new program?

These and other questions will help HRD professionals focus more specifically on the need for the new program. In reality, this step becomes a performance audit and several models have been developed to focus exclusively on this process.[5]

The result of the needs analysis is a description of the performance deficiencies of the target employees (i.e., skills, knowledge, or abilities). At this point, the effort could be terminated if it is determined that not enough deficiencies exist to justify the design and implementation of the HRD program.

The second part of this step involves developing tentative program objectives. The needs analysis should reveal information to develop objectives—what must be accomplished with the new program. The objectives are only tentative and will be finalized in Step 6, after determining if data are available and can be collected. See Step 6 for more information about objectives.

2. Identify the Purposes of Evaluation

As presented in Chapter 3, there may be more than one purpose of evaluation. Before pursuing any development work, the purposes of evaluation must be determined. More than likely, evaluation will be undertaken to help make a decision about the future status of the program (i.e., whether or not it should be continued). But there could be additional reasons for evaluation, and these reasons will affect the baseline data collected and the evaluation method(s) chosen. For example, if an evaluation is undertaken to improve the instructional methods of the course, a reaction questionnaire at the end of the program will probably be appropriate.

3. Establish Baseline Data

Before any comparisons can be made, data must be collected prior to the program and after its completion. Data may exist in a variety of forms and generally reflect the conditions which have necessitated the training. Ideally, data should be collected for a period of time necessary for a realistic comparison. Data collection answers the basic question of *what* to evaluate. Examples include the number of grievances in the last six months, the number of errors in processing claims in the past year, the accident frequency rate for the last quarter, or the average monthly sales cost for the previous year. Baseline data reflects the information which is most important and represents the performance deficiency.

Establishing baseline data after the needs analysis enables the HRD professional to focus more clearly on what change the program should bring about. This process is not very difficult when specific baseline data exist.The difficulty arises when a program is being designed to improve something when there is no clear evidence of the current state of affairs. If this is the case, then it might be appropriate to begin this step of the model by asking the question again, "Is this training really necessary?" If the current performance level cannot be clearly defined, then is there any need to improve on that? And, more important, how can we tell if there has been improvement?

Most of the difficulty in establishing baseline data occurs in the supervisory and management area. These programs are aimed at improving the effectiveness of supervisors, and very little baseline data may be available on their current level of effectiveness. While evaluation is difficult, many organizations have made significant improvements in developing individualized performance data such as absenteeism, turnover, grievances, etc. In addition, work unit output, quality, costs, and time delays are group outputs directly tied to those supervisors.

If supervisors do not have clear-cut measures of their effectiveness, perhaps such measures should be developed to determine which ones need improvement. For this situation, there are two suggested alternatives:

1. *Ask the question, "What necessitated the training program?"* If a needs analysis was done and performance deficiencies were identified, the analysis may contain measurements of the current situation. It may involve soft data such as making improper decisions, or a lack of open communication between the employee and the supervisor. Somehow, there must be deficiencies tied to some measurable item, although the estimate of that baseline might be subjective.
2. *Develop some baseline data.* If a deficiency exists, but no data are present to measure the present level of deficiency, then possibly some data should be developed for a short period. For instance, suppose that there is an indication that employee complaints are increasing, yet there is no mechanism in the organization to know how many complaints are being made. If this is a serious problem, it might be appropriate to ask the supervisors to note the frequency and types of complaints received from employees over a period of time. With this collection of baseline data, the HRD program could focus on reducing those complaints.

4. Select Evaluation Method/Design

The next step is to select the evaluation method(s) and design. It may seem unusual that this step precedes the step of finalizing program objectives, but the selection of the evaluation method may influence the objectives established for the program. It is useless to set an objective in an area for which there is no way of gathering information. Therefore, if the methods of gathering information are finalized first, then the objectives are tailored to those methods. Some might disagree with this approach, feeling that the objective should be set first and the methods selected afterward to evaluate those objectives. While that approach may seem logical, there are only a finite number of evaluation methods, and these methods have to be tailored to the organization and to the proposed program. Selecting the method before finalizing the objectives can make a difference in thought processes when compared to the reverse sequence. Realistically, the two steps may be performed concurrently.

This step answers the question of *how* to evaluate. The method or methods are selected which are appropriate for the type of data, the learning environment, the participants, and the content of the program. The following methods will be discussed in more detail in a later chapter:

- ☐ Precourse and post-course examinations
- ☐ Participant feedback
- ☐ Feedback from others
- ☐ Participant follow-up
- ☐ Action plan audit
- ☐ Performance contracts
- ☐ Ex post facto evaluation
- ☐ Job simulations

Also, in this step the evaluation design must be selected—a decision as important as the evaluation method. There are a number of possible designs, all of which will be discussed later.

5. Determine Evaluation Strategy

This step in the process answers the questions of *who, where,* and *when* as it relates to the evaluation. These are key questions whose answers are important in planning the evaluation. The HRD department has a significant role in evaluation, as do the program participants. Some questions about responsibility assignments need to be asked:

☐ Will the instructors conduct the evaluation? If not, who will?
☐ Will information be collected from the supervisors of the partici-
pants?
☐ Will information be collected from the peer group or subordinates
of participants?
☐ Who will analyze the data?
☐ Who will interpret the data?
☐ Who will conduct the follow-up evaluation?
☐ Who will make the decision to stop or alter the evaluation process?

These questions regarding *who* should be answered before any further action is taken. In most cases, one individual will be responsible for collecting all of the data, analyzing the results, and communicating them to the appropriate people.

The *where* relates to the location for the evaluation. Some relevant questions are:

☐ Will all the evaluations occur in a classroom, on the job, or a
combination of the two?
☐ Will the participants need to be taken off the job to conduct a
follow-up a few months after the program?
☐ Will observations of employees at the work station be necessary?

The question of *when* involves timing and requires careful planning. Generally, an evaluation can occur at these times:

☐ During the course (to gather reaction and measure learning).
☐ At the end of the course (to gather reaction and measure learning).
☐ On the job (to observe behavior change).
☐ At a specified follow-up date (to measure the results achieved by the
individual or the group).

A very thorough and complete evaluation and measurement system will gather data at all of these times, but most important, the results are gathered at a follow-up date.

This step completes the evaluation strategy by answering the questions of *who* will evaluate, *where* will it be done, and *when* will it be done. When combined with previous steps, all the questions are answered that form the initial approach to evaluation.

6. Finalize Program Objectives

The next step is to finalize the objectives for the program. This step purposely comes after all the questions regarding the evaluation approach have been answered, since they may influence the final selection of objectives. Ideally, each objective should be related to baseline data that has been collected. For example, suppose an HRD program is conducted to improve the relationship between supervisors and employees. The baseline data might include the number of grievances in the last six months. One objective might be to reduce the grievances by 20% in the next six-month period. A more complete training objective then becomes:

> To enable supervisors to hold effective disciplinary discussions and administer the labor contract so that the number of grievances are reduced by 20% in the next six-month period.

Training objectives provide direction to course developers, participants in the program, as well as management who must determine whether or not the program should be conducted. HRD program objectives should follow the normal criteria for any sound objective. They should be:

☐ Challenging
☐ Precise
☐ Dated
☐ Achievable
☐ Understood by all those involved

To meet these criteria and to have objectives that are understood and accepted by all parties, it is important to use a participative objective setting process. This helps to ensure that the problem objectives are precisely what management wants and are related to the jobs performed in the organization. This process, according to some experts, is essential to produce a high-quality training system.[6]

It is sometimes useful to consider training objectives at different levels or hierarchies. For example, there may be lesson objectives that relate to a particular session in the training program. There may be end-of-course objectives that define what learning will occur as a result of the program. There may be on-the-job performance objectives that define what will change on the job as a result of the program. Finally, there may be ultimate or outcome objectives that focus on the end results of the program.[7] This approach ties objectives to the framework of different levels of evaluation discussed in the previous chapter.

---

7. Estimate Program Cost/Benefits

The next step is to calculate the approximate cost for developing and conducting the program. This step is undertaken before any course development work is initiated to see if a go/no-go decision might be in order. Up to this point, a needs analysis could reveal a definite performance deficiency. Base-line data are established, the evaluation strategy is determined, and the objectives of the program are finalized. The cost for developing and conducting the program is then estimated and compared to the potential benefits derived from the program. The anticipated return on investment can then be calculated.

These are only estimates of the cost, but they will satisfy the need at this point. Costs can be tabulated in several basic areas such as:

☐ Analysis costs
☐ Development costs
☐ Delivery costs
☐ Evaluation costs

Once these costs are tabulated, the potential cost savings are estimated. For example, if $2000 can be saved for each person who completed the training program, and there are 100 people to be trained, then there is a potential cost savings of $200,000. More information on cost calculations will be presented in a later chapter.

This step may be unnecessary in some situations. If, in the opinion of the program designers, the program will be conducted regardless of the cost, then there is little need to get an estimate. This may not mean that costs are not a consideration, but there is a definite need for the program other than for an economic reason. It will need to be conducted as long as the costs are reasonable. Efforts are then concentrated on being efficient in the program development and delivery.

This is a worthwhile step to complete if there is any question about the cost, since it tends to keep HRD personnel aware of the magnitude of their efforts and the expense of their function to the entire organization.

8. Prepare and Present Proposal

At this stage, a formal proposal for management is recommended prior to the implementation of the program. The proposal should focus on the information collected and should be presented in a formal and professional manner.

There are many ways to prepare a proposal. The time invested in preparing and presenting a professional proposal will ensure that the proposal receives the proper attention.

The following action checklist is useful when preparing a proposal for a significant training project:

☐ Develop an audience profile, determining who will receive and approve the proposal.

☐ Determine the best timing to present proposal, after all appropriate individuals have concurred with the contents of the proposal.

☐ Select the best location for presenting the proposal. Is an HRD conference room best or would an executive conference room be more appropriate?

☐ Arrange the audience carefully, placing key decision makers in the best location to understand the presentation and ask questions as necessary.

☐ Consider rehearsing the presentation for effective delivery.

☐ Make notes to stay on track and deliver a smooth presentation.

☐ Consider appropriate visual aids. Charts, graphs and slides are very helpful to develop audience understanding.

☐ Anticipate the types of questions from each member of the audience and be prepared with appropriate responses. Expect difficult questions and be prepared to inhibit individuals who may be biased against your proposal.

☐ Understand the numbers in the financial justification part of the proposal. Be prepared to explain the rationale for any assumptions made when developing the proposal.

☐ Discuss the advantages and disadvantages of the recommended program.

☐ Explain what can happen if the program is not conducted, particularly in terms of dollars lost.

☐ Present the proposed implementation schedule for the program with estimated completion dates.

☐ Discuss follow-up sessions when updated data will be presented.

☐ Ask for approval to proceed with the program.
☐ Leave a copy of the report.

These simple steps can make the difference in an effective, successful presentation.

9. Design Evaluation Instruments

This step involves the design, or possibly the selection, of specific instruments to be used in the evaluation process. In the context of evaluation an instrument is a data-gathering tool. It collects data on attitudes, learning, behavior change, or the results achieved from the program. Instruments may include record-keeping systems, questionnaires, examinations, attitude surveys, interviews, focus groups, observations, or job simulations. The instrument should be statistically reliable and easy to use. The various features of, and the basis for choosing, a specific instrument will be discussed later. It is important that the instrument be designed before the program is developed, since some additional information might be uncovered that will alter course development and course content.

10. Determine and Develop Program Content

Probably the most time-consuming step of this model is to determine the content and develop the program. The content may be determined by subject-matter experts who decide what participants need to know (principles, facts, and skills) to meet the program objectives. It is very time consuming and requires careful review by the appropriate members of management. Reviewing and revising are continuous actions for all parts of the HRD design process.

Program developers may rely on previous programs or similar programs conducted with other groups. For example, action taken to improve safety in one organization may be useful to improve the safety record in another.

Completing the previous steps in this model will focus attention only on those areas that will produce the desired results. Material that is nice to know but not related to program objectives will probably be omitted because of the emphasis on getting results. Program development is beyond the scope of this book. Other works provide detail on this topic.[8]

11. Design or Select Training and Development Methods

Selecting the development methods appropriate for the program is the next step. Instructional systems and audio-visual makeup are primary issues here. The designer must choose between a variety of methods.

Mayo and Dubois[9] have identified fourteen methods of training delivery:

☐ Presentation-discussion (including lectures and listening and questioning)
☐ Conference (including seminars)
☐ Case study
☐ Role play
☐ Workshop
☐ Computer-based instruction (including computer-assisted instruction and computer-managed instruction)
☐ Simulations, simulation games and games
☐ On-the-job training
☐ Peer training
☐ Programmed instruction
☐ Team teaching/training
☐ Demonstration
☐ Field trips
☐ Preparatory (short-course) format

The selection of a method (or methods) depends on such factors as:

☐ Budget
☐ Resources available
☐ Program objectives
☐ Time frame
☐ Ability of participants
☐ Ability of program developers
☐ Ability of instructors
☐ Location of training

The effectiveness of these methods vary depending on the previous factors. Lectures are considered to be among the least effective, while those methods that require significant trainee involvement are the most effective. For example, one study revealed that participants in behavior modeling training significantly outperformed those in a lecture method on measures of performance.[10] Although lectures have been very popular, there is some evidence to suggest that their use is declining.[11] A presentation on training methods is beyond the scope of this book. Others provide excellent coverage on the topic.[12]

Methods of presentation can exert considerable influence on the outcome of the program. It is just as important as the content and needs careful attention.

12. Test Program and Make Revisions

After the program is developed, a tryout may be needed. Pilot testing is often overlooked in the HRD process. It is particularly useful when the program will be repeated with many participants; whereas, with a one-time program, there is little reason to test on an experimental basis unless there are unusual circumstances. This step also gives the program developers a chance to test, at least to a certain extent, some of the evaluation methods. Pre-program and post-program evaluations, participants' reactions, and behavior simulations can be observed on a test basis and adjusted if necessary.

A well planned pilot program can help make the months of analysis, interviews, and program development pay off. Taking the appropriate steps before, during, and after the pilot can turn the odds in favor of a flawless, fail-safe pilot program, while at the same time, finding an opportunity to analyze the strengths and weaknesses of the program.[13] This fail-safe approach involves choosing the audience carefully for the pilot, establishing ground rules during the pilot test, developing group cohesiveness during the program, and watching for warning signals as the program is delivered.

13. Implement or Conduct Program

The integral part of the HRD process is to implement or conduct the program. This step needs little comment except that participants should be made aware of what results are expected. As discussed in the previous chapter, communicating expectations can influence the results achieved.

Note that this step does not specifically deal with classroom training programs. The HRD model may involve programs that are not of the traditional classroom variety. For instance, an on-the-job management development program should be subjected to the same development process and evaluation model.

14. Collect Data at Proper Stages

Another logical step of evaluation is the collection of data. A system of collections at the appropriate times must be devised and implemented. The predetermined schedule for data collection must be followed closely in the actual execution of the evaluation. It is easy to establish elaborate plans for an evaluation and have them fall short of their expectations because of failure to collect the data at proper intervals. This situation is common in follow-up evaluations after a program is conducted. Consider this situation: an HRD program generated favorable initial reaction, learning was statistically improved, and the initial on-the-job application appears to be good. With this positive information, there may be a tendency not to execute the follow-up evaluations as planned. Without follow-up, the overall evaluation will be incomplete.

15. Analyze and Interpret Data

A very difficult step involves analyzing data and making interpretations from data analysis. All data are collected for a predetermined purpose. As Mark Twain once said, "Collecting data is like collecting garbage, you must know in advance what you are going to do with the stuff before you collect it."

This step involves the analysis of the data and the interpretation of that analysis. Responses to questionnaires should be tabulated and prepared for presentation. Variances need to be analyzed.

When analyzing data, statistics are usually needed. There are three general groups of the statistical analysis that are useful for analyzing evaluation data: (1) measures of central tendency, (2) measures of dispersion, and (3) measures of association.

Measures of central tendency include the mean, median, and mode. They convey the general idea of the impact on participants as a group. For example, the average error rate is now 5.2 compared to 9.5 before the HRD program.

Measures of dispersion, which use standard deviations and analysis of variance, calculate how widely the performance of the participants varied when compared with each other and over time. Individuals who have different levels of performance can be compared to determine whether or not there was actual improvement of the group.

Measures of association use correlation to show a quantitative relationship of different elements of the HRD program to performance. For instance, the comparison of a participant's performance on the job with the examination score at the end of the program can show correlation between the two. Also, a comparison can be useful in drawing conclusions about other participants in the future based on their examination scores.

Statistical methods and data interpretation will be covered in more detail in a later chapter. The dollar value of the results achieved is calculated at this step if appropriate for the analysis. Judgmental factors may be involved in arriving at dollar values. These factors will have to be explained in the overall evaluation report.

The analysis and interpretation of results may be done in different stages. For example, data collected during the course will most likely be evaluated at that time to provide information for possible program adjustments. Other on-the-job performance data or follow-up information can be collected later and combined with other data for a complete program evaluation. The overall results need to be packaged and made ready for presentation in a format that can easily be understood by the various audiences.

---

16. Make Program Adjustments

Based on the analysis of the information collected, changes in the program may be necessary. If the program produced no results, then something went wrong. Adjustments or a possible cancellation of the program may be necessary. If parts of the program are not effective according to the evaluation, then those parts need to be redesigned.

Unacceptable results should be examined to determine the cause of failure. Some common reasons for failure are improper content, poor presentation, inadequate reinforcement on the job, or lack of motivation of the participants. Every part of the program should be examined.

---

17. Calculate Return on Investment (ROI)

The next logical step in the sequence is to calculate the ROI if an economic justification is planned. Although the ROI should be calculated whenever possible, it may not be necessary in some instances, or it might be too unreliable to be useful. If the economic justification is planned, a basic formula is

$$\text{Rate of return} = \frac{\text{dollar value of results}}{\text{program costs}}$$

When ROIs are calculated, they should be compared to a target for such programs. Sometimes these targets are determined based on company standards for capital expenditures. Others are based on what top management expects from an HRD program, or what level they would require to approve the implementation.

The calculation of the ROI will be covered in a later chapter. It is an area that deserves much attention, since it represents the ultimate approach to evaluation and should be an important part of the future of this profession. It provides a sound basis for calculating the efficient utilization of the financial resources allocated to HRD activities.

---

18. Communicate Program Results

The final step in the process involves communicating the results of the program. While there are many audiences which should receive evaluation information, three very important groups are discussed here.

One of the most important groups is the HRD staff, which needs this information to make improvements in the program. Only through refinement, based on good feedback, will programs be improved with even greater results in the future.

Another important group is management, i.e., those who must make a decision regarding the future of the program. A fundamental purpose of evaluation is to make decisions. These decisions can be cold and rational. Should the funds be expended to continue this effort? Was the program worthwhile? Answers to these questions should be communicated to the management group.

The third major group is the participants who need to know how well they have done in the program and see their performance compared to others. This feedback can enhance their future efforts as well as the efforts of others who will be involved in the program.

Communicating results is an often overlooked final step in HRD. Although evaluation data which has been analyzed and interpreted will usually be given to someone, problems occur when others who need this information do not receive it. Care must be taken to present information in an unbiased, effective manner. Because of its importance, an entire chapter is devoted to ways to communicate HRD program results successfully.

Summary

The HRD model presented in this chapter represents an effective results-oriented approach to designing, developing, and implementing an HRD program. Evaluation is emphasized at different stages in the process. These steps are necessary to produce HRD programs which focus on results.

In implementing this process, Murphy's laws, or variations thereof, should be considered:

☐ If things can go wrong, they will.
☐ Nothing is as easy as it looks.
☐ Everything takes longer than you expect.
☐ Projects take longer than they do.

Armed with this wisdom and knowledge, an HRD professional can develop a results-oriented program.

Discussion Questions

---

1. Why is it important to focus on evaluation at virtually all stages of the training and development process?
2. Is there a need for another model for developing a new training program? Please explain.
3. Contrast the results-oriented model with other models with which you are familiar.
4. In this model, program objectives are not established in final form until step 6. Why does this occur so late in the process?
5. Examine the objectives of a training program. At what level of evaluation are these objectives aimed?
6. A training needs analysis is sometimes regarded as a performance audit. Please explain.
7. In what type of programs would a cost benefit analysis be appropriate in the proposal stage, prior to development of the program?
8. One HRD Executive stated "few proposals for new training programs contain the right types of information." What do you think is the problem?

9. How can the design and selection of the methods of delivery have an impact on program results? Please explain.
10. When is pilot testing appropriate for a new program?
11. Examine a data collection scheme for a training evaluation project. At what point is data collected? Why?
12. Why is the return on investment important in this model?
13. Examine an evaluation project. How were the results communicated? To what audiences and why?

References

1. Robinson, D. G. and Robinson, J. C., *Training for Impact: How to Link Training to Business Needs and Measure the Results,* Jossey-Bass: San Francisco, CA, 1989.
2. Brinkerhoff, R. O., *Achieving Results from Training,* Jossey-Bass: San Francisco, CA, 1987.
3. Phillips, J. J., "Training Programs: A Results-Oriented Model for Managing the Development of Human Resources," *Personnel,* May–June 1983, pp. 11–18.
4. Schwartz, A. E. and Mahoney, M., "What to Measure, and When: Tailoring Evaluation to Organizational Objectives," *Training News,* October 1987, p. 12.
5. Hobbs, D. L., "A Training-Appropriations Process," *Training and Development Journal,* May 1990, pp. 109–115.
6. Garen, M. E. and Daniel, J., "Construct a Training Quality Control System," *Personnel Administrator,* November 1983, pp. 33–38.
7. Hoffman, F. O., "The Hierarchy of Training Objectives," *Personnel,* August 1985, pp. 12–16.
8. For example, see Buckley, R. and Caple, J., *The Theory and Practice of Training,* University Associates, Inc.: San Diego, CA, 1990.
9. Mayo, G. and Dubois, P. H., *The Complete Book of Training: Theory, Principles and Techniques,* University Associates, Inc.: San Diego, CA, 1989.
10. Gist, M. "The Influence of Training Method on Self-Efficacy and Idea Generation Among Managers," *Personnel Psychology,* Vol. 42, 1989, pp. 787–789.
11. Harris, O. J. and Bethke, A. L., "HR Professional Two Decades Later," *Personnel Administrator,* February 1989, p. 69.
12. Silberman, M., *Active Training: A Handbook of Techniques, Designs, Case Examples and Tips,* Lexington Books: Lexington, MA, 1990.
13. Derven, M. G., "Fail-Safe Pilot Programs," *Training and Development Journal,* March 1989, pp. 63–64.

CHAPTER 5

Evaluation Instrument Design

Preliminary Design Considerations

Parts of the HRD model presented in Chapter 4 focused on the design aspects of evaluation. Chapters 5 and 6 cover these topics thoroughly. Although evaluation instrument design occurs after the decision has been made to develop the program, it is more appropriate to present the topic in conjunction with the design strategy. Therefore, this chapter covers the design of evaluation instruments, while the next chapter focuses on the overall evaluation design.

Types of Instruments

An evaluation instrument is a data-gathering device administered at the appropriate stages in the HRD process. Instruments may come in a variety of forms and are usually divided into the following categories:

☐ Questionnaires
☐ Attitude surveys
☐ Tests
☐ Interviews
☐ Focus groups
☐ Observations
☐ Performance records

After reviewing a few general design considerations, each of these types of instruments will be briefly discussed. The advantages and disadvantages will be presented, along with a few specific design considerations.

Preliminary Questions

Before designing an instrument, several issues must be addressed. These questions provide data to focus on the optimum design for the intended purpose.

How will the data be used? Before selecting or designing an instrument, the basic purpose(s) of evaluation must be reviewed. Will the data be used to calculate ROI? Will it be used to strengthen the HRD process? Will it be used to bring in new participants? The answers can have an impact on the type of instrument needed.

How will the data be analyzed? Data are usually collected to be tabulated, summarized, and reported to others. The types of analyses, including the statistical comparisons, should be considered at design time.

Who will use the information? Another important consideration is the target audience. Who will be reviewing the information in its raw state or in a summarized manner? This determination can lead to specific questions for the instrument.

What facts are needed? Facts are needed for an effective evaluation. Which ones are best for the evaluation? Specific costs, output, time, quality, attitudes, reactions, or observations may be collected by the instrument.

Should the instrument be tested? It may be appropriate to test an instrument before using it to evaluate a program. This is appropriate for a program which represents a significant investment or one that will be repeated many times. Testing gives an opportunity to analyze the data to see if there are any problems with the instrument.

Is there a standard instrument? In some cases standard instruments can be effective with less cost than custom-designed instruments. Broad-based areas such as communications, human relations, or leadership may be suitable for standard instruments. Of course, the program content and objectives must be appropriate for the areas covered in the instrument. For example, in a general communications course for supervisors, an inventory on communications may be an appropriate standard instrument to use in evaluating the program.

What are the consequences of wrong answers or biased information? An often overlooked part of this process is the consequence of participants supplying biased information on the instrument. Sometimes, evaluation data are supplied on a voluntary basis—even anonymously. The participant's biases can enter into the information. Unless opinions and attitudes are sought, the information will not be reliable. Purposeful wrong answers can possibly have a significant influence on an individual, a budget, or a group of employees. If so, steps should be taken to prevent it. One technique involves asking similar questions at different times and cross-checking the answers. Similar answers to similar questions can show whether or not the information is consistent.

Characteristics of Effective Evaluation Instruments

Regardless of the type of instrument, there are basic design principles which can lead to a more effective instrument. The most common are presented here.

Validity

Probably the most important characteristic of an evaluation instrument is validity. A valid instrument measures what the person using the instrument wishes to measure. The degree to which it performs this function satisfactorily is usually called the relative validity.

Primarily, the HRD professional should be concerned with validity when there are skeptics who would question the appropriateness of a particular instrument. The economic consideration of design may dictate that little time is spent with the subject, whereas the evaluation of elaborate programs will demand more attention to validity.

Basically, there are four approaches to determining if an instrument is valid. These approaches, adopted by the American Psychological Association, are: (1) content validity, (2) construct validity, (3) concurrent validity, and (4) predictive validity. The actions taken to make the instrument valid are usually referred to as "defending" the validity of the instrument.[1]

Before discussing validity, the term "correlation" should be defined. Correlation refers to the strength of the relationship between two measures. It is expressed in terms of a correlation coefficient and can be positive or negative, ranging from -1 to $+1$. Methods for calculating the coefficient are presented in a later chapter.

Content validity. Content validity refers to the extent to which the instrument represents the content of the program. Content validity is probably the most important approach. Is it a representative sample of the skill, knowledge, or ability presented in the HRD program? Low-content validity means that the instrument does not represent a true sample of what was covered. High-content validity means that the instrument represents a good balance of all the information presented. To ensure content validity, no important items, behaviors, or information covered in the program should be omitted from the instrument. Also, there should not be any imbalance of the material. The number of items or questions in the instrument should correspond roughly with the amount of time, exposure, or importance of the material presented. A seven-step procedure for ensuring content validity is contained in Smith and Merchant.[2]

Construct validity. Construct validity refers to the extent to which an instrument represents the construct it purports to measure. A construct is an abstract variable such as the skill, attitude, or ability that the instrument is intended to measure. Examples of constructs are:

☐ Attitude toward supervisor
☐ Ability to read a scale
☐ Skill in conducting an effective performance discussion

As a first step in defending the construct validity, define all parts of the construct, and make a case to show that the instrument is an adequate measure of that construct. The definition of the construct should be as detailed as possible to make it easy to understand. Then construct validity can be defended by one or more ways:

☐ Expert opinion
☐ Correlations
☐ Logical deductions
☐ Criterion group studies

Expert opinion is a relatively easy approach. A group of experts state that the instrument, in their opinion, is an accurate measurement of the construct. Correlations are more complex. In this case another instrument is used to measure the same or a similar construct, and the results are correlated with the first instrument. Positive correlations could show construct validity. Logical deduction is more subjective. The instrument designer must logically conclude, through a series of deductions, that the instrument does represent a measure of the construct. The criterion group studies can be more useful. A group of people possessing an abundance or deficiency of the construct in question has the instrument administered to them. If, indeed, the results agree with the existing knowledge about the group, then it helps make the case for construct validity.

Construct validity is a complex matter. Perhaps an example can help illustrate the process. An HRD program is conducted to improve the company loyalty of a group of employees. An instrument must be designed to measure the extent of loyalty before and after the program. During the program analysis, the following conclusions are made. Employees with high levels of company loyalty:

☐ Have a desire to work hard for the organization (high productivity).
☐ Become part of the organization's goals and values (high job satisfaction, job involvement).
☐ Have a strong desire to remain with the organization (low turnover, low absenteeism).

The construct in this example is company loyalty. The instrument is designed to measure job satisfaction, job involvement, and productivity. Data are also collected on absenteeism and turnover. Employees who are perceived to have a high degree of company loyalty have the instrument administered to them. Data collected from the instruments show a positive relationship between company loyalty and job satisfaction, involvement, and productivity. There is a negative correlation between company loyalty and absenteeism and turnover. This provides necessary support for the validity of the company loyalty construct.

Concurrent validity. Concurrent validity refers to the extent to which an instrument agrees with the results of other instruments administered at approximately the same time to measure the same characteristics. For example, an attitude survey is conducted to measure the attitudes of employees toward their benefit programs. Another attitude survey, designed for the same purpose, is administered to the same group. If both instruments show the same results, then it can be argued that the instrument is valid based on concurrent validity. Concurrent validity is determined by calculating the correlation coefficient between the results of the instrument in question and the results of a similar instrument.

Predictive validity. Predictive validity refers to the extent to which an instrument can predict future behaviors or results. Although this approach has less application in program evaluation, it may be useful in some situations. For example, the results obtained from an end-of-the-program evaluation may be used to predict future behavior on the job.

The predictive validity must be defended over a period of time. If an instrument predicts a behavior, and a significant number of participants do exhibit that behavior, then the instrument possesses predictive validity. Predictive validity can be calculated and expressed as a correlation coefficient relating the instrument in question to the measure of the predicted results or behavior.

Methods to Improve Validity

There are no magic formulas to ensure that an instrument is valid when it is designed. However, here are a few simple guidelines that may help improve validity.

Include an ample number of appropriate items. Too few items on an instrument can hamper the validity, while too many can be cumbersome and time-consuming. Strive for the right balance to improve the validity.

Reduce response bias. Participants responding to questions on an instrument may tend to say what they think the administrators want them to say. This desire to please can make an instrument invalid. Participants should be encouraged to give candid responses.

Be objective in administering the instrument. In some cases the staff administering the instrument may be biased in how they expect the outcomes to be. For instance, if it is revealed that one group is expected to outperform another, it can sometimes influence the results. The participants may give responses that show improvement when actually those improvements do not exist.

Recognize the weak link between attitude and behavior. Attitudes do not always predict behavior. A person may indicate certain attitudes but behave in a different manner. Even the most carefully designed instrument can miss in a prediction of behavior or performance.

Reliability

Reliability is another important characteristic of an evaluation instrument. A reliable instrument is one which is consistent enough that subsequent measurements of an item give approximately the same results. For example, an attitude survey is administered to an employee. The same survey is administered to the same employee two days later. The results should be the same, assuming that nothing happens in the interim period to change the attitude of the employee. A reliable instrument will get the same results. If there is a significant difference, then the instrument is unreliable, since the results fluctuated without additional effort to change the employee's attitude.

The causes of these potential fluctuations are called errors. There are a number of sources of errors which affect the reliability of instruments.[3] They include:

☐ Fluctuations in the mental alertness of the participants.
☐ Variations in the conditions under which the instrument is administered.
☐ Differences in interpreting the results from the instrument.
☐ Random effects caused by the personal motivation of the participants.
☐ The length of the instrument. With a longer instrument, more data are collected, but reliability may be increased at the expense of other factors.

In precourse and post-course examinations where data are collected from participants before and after a program, it is essential to have reliable instruments; otherwise, the changes in scores cannot be attributed to the HRD program.

Four procedures, which can help ensure that an instrument is reliable, are: (1) test/retest, (2) alternate form, (3) split half and (4) inter-item correlations. For more information on reliability, see Ghiselli, Campbell and Zedeck.[4]

Test/retest. This procedure involves administering the same test or survey to the same group of employees at two different time periods and calculating the correlation of the scores. If there is a high degree of positive correlation, then the test is reliable.

Alternate-form method. This procedure involves constructing two similar instruments and administering those to employees at the same time and analyzing the correlation between the two scores. If there is a high positive correlation, then the instrument is considered to be reliable. Constructing a similar instrument is time consuming, which may make this approach impractical.

Split-half procedure. This method involves splitting the instrument into two equal parts and comparing the results. For example, it might be appropriate to compare the even-numbered questions with the odd-numbered questions. The scores of the two halves are compared, and their correlations are checked. Once again, a high correlation indicates a reliable instrument.

Inter-item Correlations. A fourth procedure to measure reliability is to calculate correlations between each of the items on the instrument. For example, a test with 25 items is divided into 25 parts. A correlation is developed comparing each item with all of the others.

Ease of Administration

An instrument should be easy to administer. It should not be burdensome or difficult for the participant or the HRD staff member. Directions and instructions should be simple and straightforward, increasing the likelihood that it will be administered consistently among different individuals. Written instructions to participants (as well as verbal explanations) will help to ensure consistent application.

Simple and Brief

Another characteristic of a good instrument is simplicity and brevity. The level of readability should be appropriate for the participant's knowledge, ability, and background. Short objective responses, whenever practical, should be sought. Long responses and essay answers detract from the simplistic approach. The least number of questions necessary to cover a particular topic is recommended. There seems to be a natural tendency to over-survey (ask more questions than necessary), and this adds to the length and possible frustration of the participants.

Economical

As with every other stage of the HRD development process, economics must be considered in the design and/or selection of an instrument. A good instrument will be one that is economical for its planned use. Economics must be considered in the cost of designing, developing, or purchasing an instrument. The length of time to administer an instrument is another cost consideration. The time necessary to analyze the data collected and present it in a meaningful format also adds to the costs.

Questionnaires

Probably the most common form of program evaluation instrument is the questionnaire. Ranging from short reaction forms to detailed follow-up instruments, questionnaires come in all sizes. They can be used to obtain subjective information about participants' feelings as well as document measurable results for use in an economic analysis. With this versatility and popularity, it is important that questionnaires be designed properly to satisfy their intended purposes. Improperly worded questionnaires are often the cause of problems in research methods.[5]

Types of Questions

Basically, there are five types of questions. A questionnaire may contain any or all of these types of questions:

☐ *Open-ended question*—has an unlimited answer. The question is followed by an ample blank space for the response.
☐ *Checklist*—a list of items where a participant is asked to check those that apply to the situation.
☐ *Two-way question*—has alternate responses, a yes/no or other possibilities.
☐ *Multiple-choice question*—has several choices, and the participant is asked to select the most correct one.
☐ *Ranking scales*—requires the participant to rank a list of items.

The following box shows examples of each of these types of questions.

---

1. *Open-Ended Question:*
   What problems have you encountered in using the customer contact skills presented in the program?

   _____
   _____
   _____

2. *Checklist:*
   In the following list check the items classified as job motivators in the Herzberg model.
   ☐ Responsibility
   ☐ Company policy and administration
   ☐ Achievement
   ☐ Interpersonal skills
   ☐ Job security
   ☐ Technical supervision
   ☐ Advancement
   ☐ The work itself
   ☐ Salary
   ☐ Status

□ Recognition
□ Possibility of growth
□ Working conditions

3. *Two-Way Question:*
As a result of this program, I have a better understanding of my job as an air traffic controller.
YES □   NO □

4. *Multiple-Choice Question:*
The absenteeism rate for our company last year was:
a. 2.0%
b. 2.8%
c. 3.2%
d. 4.1%

5. *Ranking Scales:*
The following list contains five important aspects of a supervisor's job. Place a one (1) by the item that is most important to you, a two (2) by the item that is second most important, and so on. The five (5) will be the least important item on the list.

Salary   _____
Nature of the job   _____
Authority   _____
Responsibility   _____
Working environment   _____

Questionnaire Design

Questionnaire design can be a simple and logical process. There is nothing more confusing, frustrating, and potentially embarrassing than a poorly designed or an improperly worded questionnaire. The following steps can ensure that a valid, reliable, and effective instrument is developed.

Determine the information needed. This is the first step of any instrument design. Itemize the subjects, skills, or abilities covered in the program or that were in some way related to the program. Questions can be developed later. It might be appropriate to develop this information in outline form so that related questions can be grouped together.

Select the type(s) of questions. Using the previous five types, select the type(s) that will be best for the intended purpose, taking into consideration the planned data analysis and variety of data to be collected.

Develop the questions. The next step is to develop the questions based on the type of question(s) planned and the information needed. The questions should be simple and straightforward to avoid confusion or lead the participant to a desired response. Terms or expressions unfamiliar to the participant should be avoided. Develop the appropriate number and variety of questions consistent with the validity and reliability discussions presented earlier.

Test the questions. Once the questions are developed, they should be tested for understanding. Ideally, the questions should be tested on a group of participants in a pilot program. If this is not feasible, they should be tested on a group of employees at approximately the same job level as the potential participants. Collect as much input and criticism as possible, and revise the questions to improve them.

Develop the completed questionnaire and prepare a data summary. The questions should be integrated to develop a clean, crisp questionnaire, one with proper instructions so that it can be administered effectively. In addition, a summary sheet should be developed so that the data can be tabulated quickly for summary and interpretation.

After completing these steps, the questionnaire is ready to be administered. Because questionnaire administration is a critical element in the data-collecting process, several ideas will be presented on this topic later in this chapter. For additional information on questionnaire design see Sudman and Bradburn.[6]

Attitude Surveys

Attitude surveys represent a specific type of questionnaire with several applications for measuring the results of HRD programs. A program may be designed to change employee attitudes toward work, policies, procedures, the organization, and even the immediate supervisor. Before-and-after program measurements are required to show changes in attitude. Sometimes an organization will conduct an attitude survey to assess employee attitude toward one of the areas listed previously. Then, based on these results, HRD programs are undertaken to change attitudes in areas where improvement is needed. In addition, attitude surveys can help evaluate HRD when they are used to:

☐ Provide feedback to managers on how well they are balancing their various managerial and supervisory responsibilities.

☐ Build a data base that can inform the organization of the content and processes of selecting, developing, and training managers.

☐ Assist in the design and modification of personnel policies, management systems, and decision-making processes, thereby improving overall organizational effectiveness.

☐ Provide a way to assess progress during periods of change.

☐ Assess the organization's internal employee relations climate and monitor the trends.[7]

Measuring attitudes is a complex task. It is impossible to measure an attitude precisely, since information gathered may not represent the participant's true feelings. Also, the behavior, beliefs, and feelings of an individual will not always correlate. Attitudes tend to change with time, and there are a number of factors that form an individual's attitude. Recognizing these short-comings, it is possible to get a reasonable fix on the attitude of an individual.

Surveys alone are not the only way to measure attitudes. Interviews and observations, two other ways to check attitudes, are discussed later.

Guidelines for Developing Attitude Surveys

The principles of attitude survey construction are similar to question-naire design which were discussed earlier. However, there are a few guidelines unique to the design or purchase of an attitude survey.[8]

Involve appropriate management. The executives involved in this process must be committed to take action based on survey results. Involve them early in the process, before the survey is constructed. Address management concerns, issues, and suggestions, and try to win commitment.

Determine precisely the attitudes that must be measured. While this is obvious, it is easy to stray into areas unrelated to the subject. "Let's check their attitude on this" is a familiar trap. While it may be interesting information, if it is not related, it should be omitted.

Keep survey statements as simple as possible. Participants need to understand the meaning of a statement or question. There should be little room for different interpretations. Also, the participants should be capable of expressing an attitude or opinion on the subject. For example, suppose employees are asked about their attitude toward a job posting system in the company. If the system has just been installed and little information was given about it beforehand, it is difficult for the employees to respond with accurate information.

Ensure that participant responses are anonymous. If feasible, participants must feel free to respond openly to statements or questions. The confidentiality of their responses is of the utmost importance. Research has indicated a link between survey anonymity and accuracy.[9] If data are collected which can identify a respondent, then a neutral third party should collect and process the data.

Communicate the purpose of the survey. The participants will cooperate in an activity when they understand its purpose. When a survey is administered, participants should be given an explanation of its purpose and be told what would be done with the information. Also, they should be encouraged to give correct and proper statements or answers.

Identify survey comparisons. Attitudes by themselves are virtually meaningless. They need to be compared to other attitudes before or after the HRD program or compared to another group. A group of employees may be compared to all employees or a division or a department. For purchased surveys, information may be available on a national scale in similar industries. Specific comparisons should be planned before administering the survey.

Design for easy tabulation. In an attitude survey, yes/no remarks or varying degrees of agreement and disagreement are the usual responses. These two kinds of responses are illustrated in the following box.

Typical Attitude Survey Questions

Yes/No Responses				*Yes*	*No*
My supervisor gives us credit for work well done				☐	☐
My supervisor secures our ideas about our job				☐	☐

Agreement/Disagreement Responses

	Strongly Agree	Agree	Neutral	Disagree	Strongly Disagree
Our organization has too many policies that interfere with doing a good job.	☐	☐	☐	☐	☐
Management gives me support on my personal problems.	☐	☐	☐	☐	☐

These uniform types of responses make it easier for tabulation and comparisons. On a scale of strongly agree to strongly disagree, numbers are usually assigned to reflect their response. For instance, a one (1) may represent strongly disagree and a five (5) strongly agree. An average response of 2.2 on a preprogram survey followed by a post-program average response of 4.3 shows a significant change in attitude. Some argue that a five-point scale merely permits the respondent to select the midpoint and not be forced to make a choice. If this is a concern, an even-numbered scale should be used.

Purchasing an Existing Survey

Many organizations purchase existing surveys to use in program evaluation. There can be several advantages. They can save time in development and pilot testing. Most of the reputable companies producing and marketing surveys have designed them to be reliable and valid for their intended purposes. Also, outside surveys make it easy to compare your results with others. For instance, suppose a survey is conducted to determine what employees think about the employee benefit program. As a result, a communications program is planned to inform the employees about the benefits and improve their attitude about them. The survey should be conducted before and after the training program. The results can also be compared with other organizations within the same industry or in similar industries. Outside organizations that market surveys sometimes can easily tabulate the results, thereby saving additional time and expense. There are several organizations that produce and market attitude surveys. A definitive listing of survey publishers and other information on purchased surveys is contained in Henerson, Morris, and Fitz-Gibbon.[10]

Tests

Testing is important in program evaluations for measuring learning. Precourse and post-course comparisons using tests are very common. An improvement in test scores shows the change in skill, knowledge, or ability of the participant which should be attributed to the program. By any measure, there was a dramatic increase in the use of tests in the 1980s. And predictions for the 1990s call for more testing. One source has identified more than 3,000 commercially available tests.[11] The principles of test development are similar to the design and development of questionnaires and attitude surveys. Additional information is presented in this section on the types of tests and test construction.

Types of Tests

There are several types of tests used in the HRD field and there are three different ways in which tests can be classified. The first way is based upon the medium used for administering the test. The most common media for training tests are paper and pencil performance tests, using simulated tools or the actual equipment; and computer-based tests, using computers and video displays. Written tests are by far the most common type of knowledge and skills tests used in the training process. Performance tests are usually more costly to develop and administer than written examinations. Computer-based tests and those using interactive video are relatively new developments in testing. A computer monitor or video screen presents the test questions or situations. Trainees respond by typing on a keyboard or touching the screen.[12] Interactive videos have a strong element of realism because the person being tested can react to images, often moving pictures and video vignettes, that reproduce the real job situation. Additional information on computer-based tests is included in Chapter 11, "Computers and HRD Evaluation."

The second way to classify tests is by purpose and content. In this context, tests can be divided into aptitude tests or achievement tests. Aptitude tests measure basic skills or innate or acquired capacity to learn an occupation. An achievement test assesses a person's knowledge or competence in a particular subject. It measures the end result of education and training.

A third way in which to classify tests is by test design. The most common are oral examinations, essay tests, objective tests, norm-referenced tests, criterion-referenced tests, and performance tests. Oral examinations and essay tests have limited use in HRD program evaluation. They are probably more useful in academic settings. Objective tests have answers which are specific and precise, based on the objectives of a program. Attitudes, feelings, creativity, problem-solving processes, and other intangible skills and abilities cannot be measured accurately with objective tests. A more useful form of objective test is the criterion-referenced test discussed later. The last three types of tests listed above are more common in HRD evaluation efforts and are described here in more detail.

Norm-referenced test. Norm-referenced tests compare participants with each other or to other groups rather than to specific instructional objectives. They are characterized by using data to compare the participants to the "norm" or average. Although norm-referenced tests have limited use in some HRD evaluations, they may be useful in programs involving large numbers of participants where average scores and relative rankings are important. In some situations participants scoring highest on the exams are given special recognition or awards or made eligible for other special activities.

In an example, suppose the top 50% of the graduates from an HRD program are selected for promotion. The measurement would be norm-referenced so that participants are ranked rather than held to a specific cut-off score. If a minimum passing score is established and participants are selected on that basis, then the measurement device is a criterion-referenced measurement, discussed next.

Criterion-referenced test. The criterion-referenced test (CRT) is an objective test with a predetermined cut-off score. The CRT is a measure against carefully written objectives for the HRD program. In a CRT the interest lies in whether or not participants meet the desired minimum standards—not how that participant ranks with others. The primary concern is to measure, report, and analyze participant performance as it relates to the instructional objectives.

Table 5-1 examines a reporting format based on criterion-referenced testing. This format helps explain how a CRT is applied to an evaluation effort. Four participants have completed a program with three measurable objectives. Actual test scores are reported, and the minimum standard is shown. For example, on the first objective, Participant 4 received a pass rating for a test which has no numerical value and which is simply rated pass or fail. The same participant passed objective 2 with a score of 14 (10 was listed as the minimum passing score). Participant 4 also scored 88 on objective 3 but failed it because the standard was 90. Overall, Participant 4 satisfactorily completed the program of study. The grid on the far right shows that the minimum passing standard for the program is at least two of the three objectives. Participant 4 achieved two objectives, the required minimum.

Criterion-referenced testing is a popular measurement instrument in HRD. Its use is becoming widespread and is frequently computer-based. It has the advantage of being objective-based, precise, and relatively easy to administer. It does require programs with clearly defined objectives which can be measured by tests.

Table 5-1
Reporting Format for CRT Test Data

	Objective 1	Objective 2			Objective 3			Total Obj's Passed	Minimum Program Standard	Overall Program Score
	P/F	Raw Score	Std	P/F	Raw Score	Std	P/F			
Participant 1	P	4	10	F	87	90	F	1	2 of 3	Fail
Participant 2	F	12	10	P	110	90	P	2	2 of 3	Pass
Participant 3	P	10	19	P	100	90	P	3	2 of 3	Pass
Participant 4	P	14	10	P	88	90	F	2	2 of 3	Pass
Totals 4	3 Pass 1 Fail			3 Pass 1 Fail			2 Pass 2 Fail	8 Pass 4 Fail		3 Pass 1 Fail

Performance testing. Performance testing allows the participant to exhibit a skill (and occasionally knowledge or attitudes) which has been learned in an HRD program. The skill can be manual, verbal, or analytical, or a combination of the three. Performance testing is used frequently in job-related training where the participants are allowed to demonstrate what they have learned. In supervisory and management training, performance testing comes in the form of skill practices or role plays. Participants are asked to demonstrate discussion or problem-solving skills they have acquired. To illustrate the possibilities of performance testing, three examples are presented:

Example 1: Aspiring industrial engineers are required to attend a course on motion and time study. As a final test of the program, participants are given the assignment to conduct a motion and time study on an actual job in a plant. Participants make the study and are observed by the instructor. The instructor performs the same study and compares his results with participants. These comparisons provide an evaluation of the program and represent an adequate reflection of the skills learned in the course.

Example 2: As part of a management training program, managers are trained to motivate an average performer. Part of the course evaluation requires managers to write a skill practice session in an actual situation involving an average performer in their organization. Participants are then asked to conduct the skill practice on another member of the group using the real situation and applying the principles and steps taught in the program. The skill practice is observed by the instructor, and a written critique is provided at the end of the practice. These critiques provide part of the evaluation of the program.

Example 3: Potential aircraft assemblers attend a course on the basics of aircraft production assembly techniques. At the end of the course, students are required to complete a special project. They are provided a blueprint and a list of materials and are asked to build the item according to the specifications outlined on the blueprint. The time of completion, quality, and accuracy of the construction of the project make up the evaluation. A successful combination is necessary for the potential employee to advance to the permanent job of an aircraft assembler.

Design and administration of a performance test. For a performance test to be effective, the following steps are necessary in the design and administration of the test.

☐ *The test should be a representative sample of the HRD program.* The test should allow the participant to demonstrate as many skills as possible that are taught in the program. This increases the validity of the test and makes it more meaningful to the participant.

☐ *The test should be thoroughly planned.* Every phase of the test should be planned—the timing, the preparation of the participant, the collection of necessary materials and tools, and the evaluation of the results.

☐ *Thorough and consistent instructions are necessary.* As with other tests, the quality of the instructions can influence the outcome of a performance test. All participants should be given the same instructions. They should be clear, concise, and to the point. Charts, diagrams, blueprints, and other supporting information should be provided if they are normally provided in the work setting. If appropriate and feasible, the test should be demonstrated by the instructor so that participants observe how the skill is practiced.

☐ *Develop procedures for objective evaluation.* Acceptable standards must be developed for a performance test. Standards are sometimes difficult to develop because there can be varying degrees of speed, skill, and quality associated with test outcomes. Predetermined standards must be developed so that employees know in advance what has to be accomplished to be considered satisfactory and acceptable for test completion.

☐ *Do not include information that will lead participants astray.* The program is conducted to train participants in a particular skill. They should not be led astray or tricked into obvious wrong answers, unless they face the same obstacles in the real-world environment.

Following these general guidelines, performance tests can be developed into effective tools for program evaluation. Although more costly than written tests, performance tests are essential in situations where a high degree of fidelity is required between work and test conditions.

Interviews

Another useful evaluation instrument is the interview, although it is not used as frequently as the other methods. Interviews can be conducted by the HRD staff, the participant's supervisor, or an outside third party. Interviews can secure data not available in performance records, or data difficult to obtain through written responses or observations. Also, interviews can uncover success stories that can be useful in the overall evaluation. Participants may be reluctant to describe their results in a questionnaire but will volunteer the information to a skillful interviewer who probes for it. The interview process will uncover changes in behavior, reaction, and results. In some programs, the interview process comprises the total evaluation, although it's not recommended.[13]

A major disadvantage of the interview is that it is time consuming. It can also require the training or preparation of interviewers to ensure that the process is conducted in an effective manner. The same principles involved in designing questions for a questionnaire can also apply to the interview.

Types of Interviews

Interviews usually fall into two basic types: (1) structured, and (2) unstructured. A structured interview is much like a questionnaire. Specific questions are asked with little room to deviate from the desired responses. The primary advantages of the structured interview over the questionnaire are that the interview process can ensure that the questionnaire is completed and the interviewer understands the responses supplied by the participant.

The unstructured interview allows for probing for more information. This type of interview employs a few general questions which can lead into more detailed information as data are uncovered. The interviewer who conducts an unstructured interview should be skilled in the probing process. Typical probing questions are:

☐ Can you explain that in more detail?
☐ Can you give me an example of what you are saying?
☐ Can you explain the difficulty that you say you encountered?

These questions probe more deeply into the information needed from the participant. Probes used in an unstructured interview follow no definite format. In addition to the previous types of probes, they may also be acknowledgments of what has been said with a follow-up question for more information, or a restatement of the previous comment that leaves the interviewee obligated to respond with more information.

Interview Design

As with the other instruments, there are specific steps in the development of an interview which can lead to a more effective instrument. These are outlined here.

List basic questions to be asked. Once a decision has been made about the type of interview, specific questions need to be itemized. They need to be brief, precise, and designed for easy response.

Try out the interview. The instrument should be tested on a number of participants and their responses analyzed. If possible, the interviews should be conducted as part of the trial run of the HRD program.

Train the interviewers. The interviewer should be trained in the interview process, including conducting probes, collecting information, and summarizing it in a meaningful form. If the interviewer is already skilled in this process, this training can be shortened or eliminated.

Give clear instructions to the interviewee. The person being interviewed should understand the purpose of the interview and know what will be done with the information. Expectations, conditions, and rules of the interview should be thoroughly discussed. If the participant's statements are to be kept confidential, they should understand that. Often the participants will be nervous during an interview and may develop signs of anxiety. The participant should be made to feel at ease, and the information should be collected in a non-threatening manner.

Administer the interviews according to a scheduled plan. As with the other evaluation instruments, interviews need to be conducted according to a predetermined plan. The timing of the interview, the person to conduct the interview, and the place of the interview are all issues which become relevant in developing an interview plan. In some cases, if there is a large number of participants, a sampling plan may be necessary to save time and reduce the cost of the evaluation.

The following box shows an interview form to help evaluate a program to train supervisors in handling emotional situations.

Interview Form

Handling Emotional Situations

Name _____   Department _____

Instructions to Interviewer: Complete all parts of this form where applicable. Use probing questions to obtain specific information.

1. Have you had a chance to use the skill "handling emotional situations"? _____ (If not, terminate the interview.)
2. If Yes, How many discussions have you held?

   _____

---

3. How many would you classify as successful? _____
Somewhat Successful? _____ Unsuccessful? _____ Don't
Know? _____ Describe your most successful experience.
_____
_____

4. Did you finally resolve the situation causing the emotional
outburst? Please explain.
_____
_____

5. Critique the way you handled the discussion.
_____
_____

6. Were you able to use all the steps? Yes _____ No _____ Explain
_____

7. Which steps were most difficult? Explain.
_____
_____

8. Which steps were most helpful? Explain.
_____
_____

9. Did you encounter any problem? Explain.
_____
_____

10. Describe your least successful experience in "handling emotional
situations."
_____
_____

11. Critique the way you handled the discussion.
_____
_____

12. What could have made it successful? Explain.
_____
_____

13. Are you comfortable using the steps? Explain.
_____
_____

14. Do you consider the steps appropriate for your situations? Explain.
_____
_____

15. Do you consider this an important skill for supervisors? Why?

   _____

   _____

16. Please give any other comments related to using this skill and how it has improved your skills as a supervisor.

   _____

   _____

Interviewer _____ Date _____

Interviewer's Comments:

   _____

   _____

Focus Groups

Focus groups are particularly helpful when in-depth feedback is needed for training program evaluation. For many cost conscious trainers, the focus group process is becoming the evaluation instrument of choice.[14] The focus group is a small group discussion conducted by an experienced facilitator. It is designed to solicit qualitative judgments on a particular topic or issue. Group members are all required to provide their input and individual input builds on group input.

For years, the HRD profession has largely ignored the focus group potential for evaluating training. In other types of research—particularly marketing research—the focus group has long been used to generate quality information on which to make decisions. Marketing researchers have used the focus group to test new products, marketing campaigns, and questionnaire wording. It is also used to collect information for training needs analyses, secure input for changes in company policies, and provide feedback on problems and concerns within an organization.

Applications for HRD

The focus group is particularly helpful when information is needed about the quality of a training program or an assessment of behavior change resulting from a training program. For example, the focus group can be used in the following situations:

☐ To evaluate training design and the training process in a pilot test program.
☐ To evaluate the reactions to specific exercises, cases, simulations, or other components of a training program.
☐ To assess the overall effectiveness of the program as perceived by the participants immediately following a program.
☐ Assess the impact of the program in a follow-up evaluation after the program is completed.

Essentially it is helpful when evaluation information is needed which cannot be collected adequately with simple, quantitative methods.

Advantages

When compared with questionnaires, surveys, tests, or interviews, the focus group strategy has several advantages. The basic premise of using focus groups is that when quality judgments are subjective, several individual judgments are better than one. It is a standardized evaluation situation with explicit review criteria, a review procedure, and a method for synthesizing individual judgments. Frequently cited advantages for focus groups include the following[15]:

☐ It is inexpensive and can be quickly planned and conducted.
☐ The group process, where participants often motivate one another, is an effective method for generating new ideas and hypotheses.
☐ The interview format is flexible to allow for in-depth probing and confirmation.
☐ Its flexibility makes it possible to explore a training program's unexpected possible outcomes or applications.

Guidelines

While there are no set rules on how to use focus groups for evaluation, the following guidelines should be helpful:

Plan topics, questions, and strategy carefully. As with any evaluation instrument, planning is the key. The specific topics, questions, and issues to be discussed must be carefully planned and sequenced. This enhances the comparison of results from one group to another and ensures that the group process is effective and stays on track.

Ensure that management buys into the process. Because this is a relatively new process, it might be foreign to some management groups. Managers may need to be educated about focus groups and their advantages. This should raise their level of confidence in the information obtained from focus group sessions.

Select an appropriate number of groups. While there is no magic number of total groups, it is important that enough focus groups are assembled to provide the quality information that can be used to reach conclusions. While it is dangerous to suggest a percentage, a range of 5 to 20% of the target population may be appropriate for most focus group applications. This depends on many factors such as the importance of having complete group representation of the target population and the cost involved in conducting additional focus groups.

Keep the group size small. If the group is too small, there will not be much opportunity for one person to build on another's comments. While, there is no magic group size, a range of 6 to 12 seems to be appropriate for most focus group applications. A group has to be large enough to ensure different points of view, but small enough to give every participant a chance to talk freely and exchange comments.

Ensure that there is a representative sample of the target population. It is important for groups to be stratified appropriately so that participants represent the target population. The group should be homogeneous in experience, rank, and influence in the organization.

Insist on facilitators having appropriate expertise. The success of a focus group rests with the facilitator. The facilitator must be trained adequately in the focus group process and have an opportunity to practice before using evaluation data. Facilitators must be experienced in group dynamics and know how to listen to opinions from strong members of the group as well as knowing how to diffuse the comments from those who want to dominate the group. Also, facilitators must be able to create an environment in which participants feel comfortable in offering comments freely and openly. Because of this, some organizations use external facilitators.

In summary, the focus group is an inexpensive and fast way to determine the strengths and weaknesses of training programs, particularly those that focus on management and supervisory topics. However, for complete evaluation, focus group information should be combined with data from other instruments.

Observations

Another useful evaluation instrument is the observation. This involves observing the participant either before, during, or after an HRD program to record changes in behavior. The observer may be a member of the

HRD staff, the participant's supervisor, a member of a peer group, or an outside party. The most common observer, and probably the most practical, is a member of the HRD staff. An example will help illustrate this method:

A supervisor must effectively conduct disciplinary discussions with employees when their performance is substandard or when work rules are violated. One plant determined that their supervisors were not handling these discussions effectively. An HRD program was developed to teach supervisors how to handle these discussions effectively.

As part of the overall evaluation of the program, the direct observation method was used to gather data about changes in the supervisors' behavior. The superintendents (i.e., the supervisors' immediate superior) were asked to observe their supervisors when they conducted disciplinary discussions before the program began. This observation was not unusual since, in many cases, supervisors involve their superintendents in such discussions as a routine practice.

The superintendents made notes on how supervisors handled the discussions. They noted specific points that should be in the discussions as well as important steps that were omitted.

During the program, supervisors were instructed in effective techniques to conduct a disciplinary discussion following predetermined steps, while observing certain key principles. Supervisors were given an opportunity to practice disciplinary skills in the training sessions.

After the program was completed, the supervisors were observed by their superintendent in each disciplinary discussion they conducted. The superintendents made notes based on whether or not all steps in the discussion were followed and whether or not the key principles were considered. The data gathered from this observation, when compared to the previous method of discussion, gave evidence of a change in behavior on the part of the supervisors.

Additional parts of the evaluation will involve the actual success of those discussions over a period of time, but the direct observation gave immediate evidence of a change in behavior.

Guidelines for Effective Observation

The effectiveness of the observation process can be improved with the following guidelines.

Observers must be fully prepared. All observers must fully understand what information is sought. They must be trained and given a chance to practice observation skills.

The observations should be systematic. The entire process must be planned so that the observation is executed effectively without any surprises. The persons observed should know in advance about the observation and why they are being observed.

The timing of observations should be a part of the plan. There are right times to observe a participant, and there are wrong times. If an observer must observe a participant when times are not normal (i.e., in a crisis), the data collected may be useless.

The observers should know how to interpret and report what they see. Observations involve judgmental decisions. The observer must analyze which behaviors are being displayed and what actions are being taken by the participants. Observers should be trained in how to summarize behavior and report results in a meaningful manner.

The observers' influence should be minimized. It is impossible to isolate the overall effect of an observer. Participants being observed may display the behavior they think is appropriate, and they will usually be at their best. Try to minimize the presence of the observer and downplay the significance of their activity. The observer should dress the same as the person being observed and should stand at a discrete distance. If the observations occur over a long period of time, then the effect will be minimized; however, the effect cannot be eliminated and should be considered in the overall results of the observations.

Planning a Systematic Observation

Planning a systematic observation deserves additional coverage. Several steps are necessary to accomplish a successful observation.

☐ Determine what behavior will be observed.
☐ Prepare the forms for the observers to use.
☐ Select the observers.
☐ Prepare a schedule of observations.
☐ Train observers in what to observe and not to observe.
☐ Inform participants of the planned observations with explanations.
☐ Conduct observations.
☐ Summarize the observation data.

Although these steps are self explanatory, the topic of selecting observers needs additional explanation.

Selecting Observers

This step should be easy to accomplish. The most common observers are independent of the participants, typically a member of the HRD staff. On the other hand, an effective observer may be the participant's immediate supervisor. There are advantages to each.

The independent observer is usually more skilled at recording behavior and making interpretations of that behavior. They are usually unbiased in these interpretations. Using them enables the HRD department to bypass training observers and relieves the line organization of that responsibility. On the other hand, the independent observer has the appearance of an outsider checking the work of others. There may be a tendency for participants to overreact and possibly resent this kind of observer.

The participant's immediate supervisor has the advantage of knowing the work situation. He can usually relate more readily to the behavior expected. His presence should be less noticeable in the work area and relieves the HRD staff from providing someone for this function. A disadvantage may be the supervisor-subordinate relationship. The participant may act unnatural or overreact to the situation. Also, the supervisor may be biased according to how he relates to the participant.

Sometimes it might be more feasible to recruit observers from outside the organization. This approach has an advantage of neutralizing the prejudicial feelings entering the judgmental decisions.

Observation Methods

There are five methods of observation, depending on the circumstances surrounding the type of information needed.

Behavior checklist. A behavior checklist can be useful for recording the presence, absence, frequency, or duration of a participant's behavior as it occurs. A checklist will not usually provide information on the quality, intensity, or possibly the circumstances surrounding the behavior observed. The following box is a sample behavior checklist for observing supervisor behavior on the job. This checklist is useful, since an observer can identify exactly which behaviors should or should not occur. Measuring the duration of a behavior may be more difficult and requires a stopwatch and a place on the form to record the time interval. This factor is usually not as important when compared to whether or not a particular behavior was observed and how often. To make observation more effective, the number of behaviors listed in the checklist should be small and listed in a logical sequence if they normally occur in a sequence. Also, behaviors anticipated to be used more frequently should be placed first so they can be easily checked.

Behavior Checklist

During the discussion the supervisor:

_____ Made the employee feel at ease.

_____ Used empathy.

_____ Explained the problem.

_____ Asked for reasons for the problem.

_____ Asked for help in solving the problem.

_____ Secured a commitment from the employee to correct the problem.

Criticized the employee.

_____ Set a follow-up date.

Coded behavior record. Another method of observation involves a coding of behaviors on a form. This method is more time consuming because the code is entered that identifies a specific behavior. Such a record is useful when it is essential to document (as much as possible) what actually happened. Also, this method is helpful when there are many behaviors that may occur, and it is not appropriate for a checklist system. Another advantage is that coding enhances the use of computers in evaluation. The disadvantage of this system is that the data are very difficult to summarize and interpret. It may be a time-consuming process, because the observer must remember special codes or devise codes as the observation is taking place.

Delayed report method. The third and least useful method of observation is the delayed report. In this observation method the observer does not use any forms or written materials during the observation. The information is either recorded after the observation is completed or at particular time intervals during an observation. The observer tries to reconstruct what has been observed during the observation period. The advantage of this approach is that the observer is not as noticeable, and there are no forms being completed or notes being taken during the observation. The observer can be more a part of the situation and less distracting. An obvious disadvantage is that the information written may not be as accurate and reliable as the information collected at the time it occurred.

Video recording. The fourth method is the use of a video camera to record the behavior of the participant. This technique records exactly what happened in every detail, an obvious advantage. However, there are disadvantages. First, it may be awkward and cumbersome to provide for videotaping of the behavior. Second, when compared to direct observation, the participants may be unnecessarily nervous or self conscious when they are being videotaped. If the camera is concealed, the privacy of the participant may be invaded. Because of this, video recording of on-the-job behavior is not frequently used.

Audio monitoring. The fifth method of observation is monitoring conversations of employees who are using the skills taught in the training program. For example, in a large communication company's telemarketing department, sales representatives are trained to sell equipment by telephone. To determine if employees are using the skills properly, supervisors monitor telephone conversations on a selected and sometimes random basis. An overhead light, visible to all sales representatives, is on when conversations are being monitored, although they do not know which representative is being monitored. While this approach may stir some controversy, it is an effective way to determine if skills are being applied consistently and effectively. For it to work smoothly, it must be fully explained and the rules clearly communicated.

Performance Records

Records are available in every organization to measure performance. Although it may appear awkward to refer to performance records as evaluation instruments, in the context of evaluation, they serve the same purpose as tests or attitude surveys. They enable management to measure performance in terms of output, quality, costs, and time. They are necessary for an accurate evaluation system. Table 5-2 lists common performance records or measurements for an employee or group of employees.

Table 5-2
Examples of Performance Records

• Absenteeism	• Percent of Quota Achieved
• Accident Costs, Accident Rates	• Production Schedules
• Break-in Time for New Hires	• Productivity
• Budget Variances	• Processing Time
• Complaints, Employee & Customer	• Project Schedule Variations
	• Rejects, Scrap
• Cost Reduction	• Reports Completed
• Costs, Overhead	• Sales (Dollars & Number)
• Costs, Unit	• Sick Leave Costs
• Downtime	• Supervisor Bonuses
• Efficiency	• Tardiness
• Employees Promoted	• Terminations, Employee
• Equipment Use	• Time Card Corrections
• Errors, Employee	• Total Output
• Grievances	• Transactions Completed
• Inventory Adjustments	• Turnover
• New Accounts	• Work Backlog
• On-time Shipments	• Work Stoppages
• Overtime	

In determining the use of records in the evaluation of an HRD program, the first consideration should be existing records. In most organizations there will be records suitable for measuring the improvement resulting from an HRD program. If not, additional record-keeping systems will have to be developed for analysis and measurement. At this point, as with many other points in the process, the question of economics enters. Is it economical to develop the record-keeping system necessary to evaluate an HRD program? If the costs are greater than the expected return for the entire program, then it is meaningless to develop them.

Using Current Records

If existing records are available, specific guidelines are recommended to ensure that the measurement system is easily developed.

Identify appropriate records. The performance records of the organization should be thoroughly researched to identify those which are related to the proposed objectives of the program. Frequently, an organization will have several performance measures related to the same item. For example, the efficiency of a production unit can be measured in a variety of ways:

- ☐ The number of pieces produced per hour.
- ☐ The number of on-schedule production units.
- ☐ The percent utilization of the equipment.
- ☐ The percent of equipment downtime.
- ☐ The labor cost per piece of production.
- ☐ The overtime required per piece of production.
- ☐ Total unit cost.

Each of these, in its own way, measures the efficiency of the production unit. All related records should be reviewed to determine those most relevant to the HRD program.

Determine if a sampling plan is necessary. When a large number of participants are involved in a program, a sampling of records is adequate to supply the information needed. Total figures may not be available. If sampling is required, the sampling plan should be structured to provide an adequate sample size and one that is selected on a random basis. An example will illustrate this point:

An orientation program, coupled with new employee training, was planned for new machine operators in one organization. The combination of orientation and entry-level training was expected to reduce scrap and increase the output of new operators. Since the program began with new recruits, their output and scrap rates were collected and monitored. They were compared to the records of a sample of other employees who began work with the company before the program was implemented with approximately the same age and skill. This gave a realistic comparison in the performance of the two groups. Significant differences in performance could most likely be attributed to the new program. This was more appropriate than comparing the new group with the average of the entire work force of machine operators. The performance over a three-month period was monitored through this approach.

Convert current records to usable ones. Occasionally, existing performance records are integrated with other data and it may be difficult to keep them isolated from unrelated data. In this situation all existing related data records to be used in the measurement should be extracted and retabulated to be more appropriate for comparison in the evaluation.

At times conversion factors may be necessary. For instance, the average number of new sales orders per month may be presented regularly in the performance measures for the sales department. In addition, the sales costs per salesman are also presented. However, in the evaluation of an HRD program, the average cost per new sale is needed. The two existing performance records are combined to secure the data necessary for comparison.

Develop a collection plan. A data-collection plan defines when data are collected, who will collect it, and where it will be collected. This plan should contain provisions for the evaluator to secure copies of performance records in a timely manner so that the items can be recorded and are available for analysis.

Developing New Records

In some cases records are not available for the information needed to measure the effectiveness of an HRD program. The HRD staff must work with the participating organization to develop these record-keeping systems if they are economically feasible.

In one organization a new employee orientation system was implemented on a company-wide basis. There were several methods of evaluation planned. One of these involved comparisons in the turnover in the first six months. This early turnover represented the percentage of employees who left the company in the first six months of their employment. An effective employee orientation program could influence turnover. At the time of the program's inception, these records were not available. The organization began collecting early turnover figures for comparison when the program was implemented. This record provided one basis for evaluation of the effectiveness of the program.

In creating new records several questions are relevant:

☐ Which department will develop the record-keeping system?
☐ Who will record and monitor the data?
☐ Where will it be recorded?
☐ Will forms be used?

These questions will usually involve other departments or a management decision that extends beyond the scope of the HRD department. Possibly the administration division, the personnel department, or industrial engineering section will be instrumental in helping determine if new records are needed and, if so, how they will be collected.

Summary

Table 5-3 summarizes the features of instruments presented in this chapter. Each type of instrument is listed with the most appropriate level of evaluation and the advantages and limitations. This figure can serve as a quick aid to compare the various types of instruments used in evaluation. It is adapted in part from an aid developed by the U.S. Office of Personnel Management. With these specific limitations and advantages, it is important to use a variety of instruments in an evaluation effort. For example, Ames Department Stores uses three evaluation instruments for each of their training programs: direct observation, interviews, and performance records.[16]

Chapter 6 will focus on developing the overall evaluation design.

Discussion Questions

1. Before selecting an evaluation instrument, why is it important to analyze the types of data needed and examine how the data will be used in the evaluation?
2. What are the advantages and disadvantages of using standard instruments versus "customized" instruments?
3. Which types of validity would be of most concern for HRD program evaluators? Why?
4. What represents a good validity coefficient? Is the development of a validity coefficient necessary in program evaluation? Explain.
5. How does reliability differ from validity? What represents a good reliability coefficient? Is it necessary to develop a reliability coefficient for an instrument used in evaluation?
6. How could administrative problems cause errors in the use of evaluation instruments?
7. Secure a sample questionnaire and critique its design, following the principles in this chapter.
8. What are the advantages and disadvantages of attitude surveys in evaluation?
9. Is it important to compare survey results with norms from other industries or other organizations in the same industry? Explain.
10. Critique the design and use of a test to measure learning.
11. Why are performance tests important to HRD evaluation?

Table 5-3

Comparison of Common Evaluation Instruments

Instruments	Evaluation Levels				Advantages	Limitations
	Reaction	Learning	Behavior	Results		
Questionnaire	*		*	*	Low cost Honesty increased Anonymity optional Respondent sets pace Variety of options	May not collect accurate information On-job responding conditions uncontrolled Respondent sets pace Return rate rarely controllable
Attitude Survey	*		*	*	Standardization possible Quickly processed Easy to administer	Predetermined alternatives Response choices Reliance on norms may distort individual performance May not reflect true feelings
Written Test		*			Low purchase cost Readily scored Quickly processed Easily administered Wide sampling possible	May be threatening to participant Possible low relations to job performance Reliance on norms may distort individual performance Possible cultural bias
Performance Test		*	*		Reliability Simulation potential Objective based	Time consuming Simulation often difficult High development costs

Method		Advantages		Disadvantages
Interview	*	Flexible Opportunity for clarification Depth possible Personal contact	*	High reactive effects High cost Face-to-face threat potential Labor-intensive Trained interviewers necessary
Focus Groups	*	Flexible Low cost Good qualitative responses Personal contact	*	Effectiveness rests with facilitator Subjective Sometimes difficult to summarize findings
Observation	*	Non-threatening to participants Excellent way to measure behavior change	*	Possibly disruptive Reactive effect Unreliable Trained observers necessary
Performance Records	*	Reliability Objectivity Job-based Ease of review Minimal reactive effects	*	Lack of knowledge of criteria for keeping/discarding records Information system discrepancies Indirect nature of data Need for conversion to usable forms Records prepared for other purposes Sometimes expensive to collect

12. Design and describe a performance test to measure the effectiveness of a training program designed to improve interviewing skills.
13. What are the weaknesses of the interview process?
14. When is it appropriate to use the interview as part of the evaluation process?
15. What are the differences in the interview and the focus group process?
16. What are the problems with the focus group process?
17. When is it appropriate to use observations in the evaluation process?
18. What difficulties are encountered when using evaluation information obtained from observers?
19. What performance records are available in your organization (or one with which you are familiar)?
20. Which is the most effective evaluation instrument? Why?
21. Is it possible to use all seven evaluation instruments in the evaluation of a single program? Explain.

References

1. Gatewood, R. D. and Field, H. S., *Human Resource Selection,* 2nd Edition, Dryden Press: Chicago, Il, 1990.
2. Smith, J. E. and Merchant, S., "Using Competency Exams for Evaluating Training," *Training and Development Journal,* August 1990, pp. 65–71.
3. Morris, L. L., Fitz-Gibbon, C. T., and Lindheim, E., *How to Measure Performance and Use Tests,* Sage Publications: Beverly Hills, CA, 1987.
4. Ghiselli, E. E., Campbell, J. P., and Zedeck, S., *Measurement Theory for the Behavioral Sciences,* W. H. Freeman: San Francisco, CA, 1981.
5. Kaufman, R., "More Than Questionnaires," *Training and Development Journal,* September 1989, pp. 26–28.
6. Sudman, S. and Bradburn, N. M., *Asking Questions: A Practical Guide to Questionnaire Design,* Jossey-Bass: San Francisco, CA, 1982.
7. Rosen, N. "Employee Attitude Surveys: What Managers Should Know," *Training and Development Journal,* November 1987, pp. 50–52.
8. Wilmot, R. E. and McClelland, V., "How to Run a Reality Check," *Training,* May 1990, pp. 66–72.
9. Rotondi, T., "The Assessment Factor in Questionnaire Surveys," *Personnel Journal,* February 1989, p. 92.

10. Henerson, M. E., Morris, L. L., and Fitz-Gibbon, C. T., *How to Measure Attitudes,* 2nd Edition, Sage Publications: Beverly Hills, CA, 1987, pp. 178–181.
11. Lee, C., "Testing Makes a Comeback," *Training,* December 1988, p. 49.
12. Sharon, A. T., "Testing . . . 1,2,3," *Training and Development Journal,* September 1989, pp. 30–33.
13. Fetteroll, E., "Did the Training Work? Evaluation By Interview," *Training News,* pp. 10–11.
14. Erkut, S. and Fields, J. P., "Focus Groups to the Rescue," *Training and Development Journal,* October 1987, pp. 74–76.
15. Ibid, p. 74.
16. Myers, J. and Jones, E., "Training Triumphs at Ames Department Stores," *The Human Resources Professional,* Spring 1990, p. 32.

CHAPTER 6

Evaluation Design

In the model presented in Chapter 4 several steps were devoted to the evaluation process. One step involved selecting the evaluation method and design. This step is perhaps one of the most important among those directly involved with evaluation.

The methods of evaluation are difficult to separate from the evaluation design. However, specific methods are only a part of the process and are discussed in more detail in a later chapter. Evaluation design is a more general view of the process. It requires the development of a complete system to get the desired measurements. Proper design is imperative for effective evaluation. This brief chapter presents the basic elements of design and the various design alternatives.

Elements of Design

In many HRD program evaluations, comparisons are made in the performance of a group of program participants:

☐ To their performance prior to the program.
☐ To another group who did not receive the same program.
☐ To the remainder of the population of potential participants.

There can be various combinations which make up an evaluation design. This section deals with the elements of design with emphasis on the different design approaches. The specific design variations will be presented later.

Control Groups

Control groups and experimental groups frequently appear in designs. A control group is a group of participants who are as similar as possible to those in the experimental group but are not involved in the HRD program: the experimental group does participate. Ideally, the only difference between the two groups is that one participates in the program and the other does not. Therefore, a performance comparison of the two groups should indicate the impact or success of the HRD program. The selection of control groups is presented in Appendix 3 along with guidelines for determining the appropriate sample size.

It is important that the two groups be equivalent in their job settings, skills, abilities, and demographic characteristics. The true control group is formed by random assignment as discussed in Appendix 3. If possible, the identity of the control group should not be revealed. Otherwise, it could affect their performance. With these requirements, control groups may not be practical in real work situations. However, for critical evaluations affecting many participants, control groups are almost essential.

Timing of Measurements

A critical issue in evaluation is the timing of measurements (or tests). Measurements may be taken before the program, during the program, and at subsequent intervals after the program. The post-test part of a design is never omitted because it directly measures the results of a program. Careful attention needs to be given to determining when and how pretests and post-tests are conducted. In each case, participants being tested deserve an explanation about the proposed activity.

When conducting pretests, four general guidelines are recommended:

Do not use the pretest if it alters the participants performance in some way. Pretests are intended to measure the state of the situation before the HRD program begins. The test itself should not have any effect on performance. If there is evidence that the testing procedure will affect performance, then possibly the pretest should be omitted, modified, or given far enough in advance of the program to minimize the effect.

Do not pretest when it is meaningless. In teaching completely new material or providing information that participants do not have at the present time, pretest results may be meaningless. It would just show an absence of the knowledge, skill, or ability. For example, in a foreign language program, it is meaningless to conduct a pretest in the foreign language if the participants are not expected to know it. Instead, a measurement of proficiency in acquiring the foreign language skills after the program is more appropriate (post-test only).

Pretests and post-tests should be identical or approximately equivalent. When scores are compared, they should have a common base for comparison. Identical tests may be used, although they may influence results when they are taken the second time. Similar but equivalent tests may be more appropriate.

The testing should be conducted under the same or similar conditions. The length of time and the conditions under which both tests are taken should be approximately the same.

In addition to pretesting and post-testing, tests may be conducted at different time intervals during and after a program. These tests are called *time series tests* and are recommended, when feasible. Time series tests after a program show the long-term effects of the program and in particular detect whether or not benefits are lasting. Time series tests during the program measure participant progress toward the objectives.

Threats to Validity

When discussing the merits of various evaluation designs, it is appropriate to return to the subject of validity. There are a number of problems (or threats) which can reduce the validity of an evaluation design. Different designs can counteract or offset the effects of these threats.

Time or history. Time has a way of changing things. With time, performance can improve and attitudes can change—even without an HRD program. When observing output measurements of an HRD program, this question should always be asked: "Would the same results have occurred without the program?" This threat to validity can be isolated by modifying the evaluation design.

Effects of testing. It is possible that the actual experience of a test or other instrument can have an effect on performance or attitude even if no HRD program is undertaken. This effect is more likely to happen when pre-tests and post-tests are identical. With enough time between testing, participants reflect on the material and possibly even seek answers to questions that attract their curiosity Also, after the participants know the scope of a program, they may give more favorable responses in the post-test based on their knowledge of what is expected.

Selection. As presented in Appendix 3, the selection of the group to participate in an HRD program can possibly have an effect on the outcome. Naturally, some individuals will perform better than others. If mostly high achievers are selected, then the results will be distorted. The same is true for underachievers. The problem can be resolved by using random selection, if it is feasible.

Mortality. Participants may drop out for various reasons. If pre- and post-tests are used, the number in the group may have changed from one testing to another. This change makes it difficult to compare the results of the two, and it is compounded by the fact that the lower-level performers are the ones who will usually drop out of a program.

These are the most common internal threats to validity.[1] The designs presented next will attempt to overcome these threats in varying degrees.

Selecting the Appropriate Design

Selecting the appropriate evaluation design is a key part of the evaluation strategy. This section presents the common evaluation designs and the relative advantages and disadvantages of each.

One-Shot Program Design

One of the most common, and unfortunately least valid, designs involves the "one-shot" program. This technique involves a single group which is evaluated only once after an HRD program is completed. No data are collected prior to the program. There are many uncontrolled factors that might influence the measurement and invalidate conclusions based on results achieved through this design. However, the information obtained in this one-shot evaluation is better than no evaluation at all.

This design may be useful for measuring the performance of a group when there is no way to measure performance beforehand. Or, possibly, when there is no significant knowledge, skill, or ability existing before the program is conducted.

For example, a group of international sales representatives are trained to speak Spanish before conducting a market survey in Mexico. It makes little sense to evaluate their current ability to speak Spanish before the HRD program is conducted. A measurement at the end of the program to measure their ability to understand and speak Spanish is more appropriate as part of the evaluation process.

This evaluation design is useful when financial, organizational, or time constraints prohibit the use of preprogram data collection. Figure 6-1 illustrates this type of design. Since it is the least effective, it should be a minimum reference point for evaluation and used only when necessary.

Single Group, Pretest and Post-Test Design

To remedy the problem of no data to make comparisons, the next proposed design is the single group, pretest and post-test design as shown in Figure 6-2. This design goes one step beyond the one-shot design by collecting data before and after the HRD program. The knowledge, skills, or abilities possessed by the participants before the program can be compared to the knowledge, skills, or abilities after the program to detect improvements.

The effect of a pretest is one disadvantage of this design. The pretest may "tune the participants in" to the topics and questions they might not ordinarily perceive. Consequently, the changes measured by the post-test may result not only from the HRD program, but also from the fact that the pretest was taken. The effect of external factors is another disadvantage to this design. Changes in the organization, environment, the work setting, or other factors may cause changes in the performance of participants. Without a control-group comparison, it is difficult to isolate the effects of testing and external factors.

Single Group, Time Series Design

A very popular design for evaluating an HRD program involves a series of measurements, both before and after the program. This is

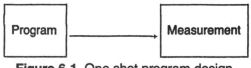

Figure 6-1. One-shot program design.

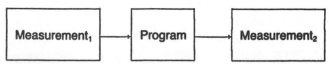

Figure 6-2. Single group, pretest and post-test design.

referred to as a single group, time series design. In this design the experimental group serves as its own control group. The multiple measurements before the program eliminates some of the problems incurred when a separate control group is not used. Repeated measurements after the program not only allows for comparison of the initial results, but enables measurement of the long-term effects of the program. This design, as illustrated in Figure 6-3, may involve any number of measurements practical for the setting. This design eliminates much of the effects of time and selection threats to validity, while the mortality threat is not counteracted.

There can be a number of outcomes in a time series design. These are illustrated in Figure 6-4. In Outcome A, apparently the HRD program had no effect. There was no change in what was measured. Outcome B had a change in output apparently as a result of the program. Outcome C shows a brief change in output as a result of the program; however, the participants returned to the previous level of measurement. There were apparently no lasting effects from the program.

The time series design is extremely useful when measurement data are readily available as part of the organization's performance reporting. With this design, the impact of HRD programs can be compared with previous performance over a significant period of time.

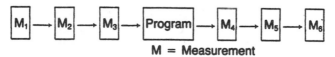

M = Measurement

Figure 6-3. Single group, time series design.

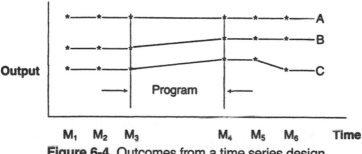

Figure 6-4. Outcomes from a time series design.

Control Group Design

The next design involves the comparison between two groups; one, an experimental group and the other, a control group. This is referred to as a control group design and is illustrated in Figure 6-5.

The experimental group receives the HRD program, while the control group does not. Data are gathered on both groups before and after the program. The results of the experimental group, when compared to the control group, assess the impact of the HRD program.

This design is acceptable only when the two groups are quite similar with respect to the appropriate selection criteria. The participants in each group should be approximately at the same job level, experience, ability, working conditions, and possibly even the location. For example, it is improper to compare first-line production supervisors with middle-level managers in an office environment. With this difference, it is almost impossible to make any sensible analysis of the post-program performance.

The ideal way to select control groups is on a random basis. If the participants for the two groups come from the same population, and can be randomly assigned, then this evaluation design becomes a true control-group design. This random selection not only tends to equalize the groups prior to the program, it also promotes a generalization of the evaluation results to other groups and situations.

However, from a practical standpoint, it may be difficult to assign the participants on a random basis. If this is the case, the shortcomings of the design need to be recognized in the overall results.

The true control-group design is one of the most powerful evaluation designs available, since it combines random selection and the use of a control group. The threats to validity are controlled with this design, except the effects of testing. Since both groups are subjected to the pretest, it can have an effect on performance which cannot be determined. The next design will eliminate all threats to validity mentioned earlier.

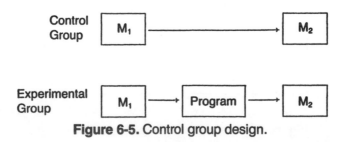

Figure 6-5. Control group design.

Ideal Experimental Design

An evaluation design that represents a more idealistic situation is shown in Figure 6-6. It involves the use of three groups, random selection of participants, and pretest and post-testing on selected groups. As can be seen from Figure 6-6, Group A is pretested, participates in the program, and has a post-test. Group B is pretested, does not participate in the program, but does have a post-test. Group C has no pretest, participates in the program, and does have a post-test.

Group B isolates the time and mortality threats to validity If M-1 and M-2 are equal for Group B, then it follows that neither of these factors influenced the result. The random selection isolates the selection threat.

Group C is used to rule out the interaction of the pretest with the effects of the HRD program. This was the weakness in the true control group design presented previously. If the post-test, M-2, for Group A and C are identical, then we can conclude that the pretest had no effect on performance.

This design approaches the ultimate in experimental designs. From a practical standpoint, obtaining three randomly selected groups may be difficult. The time, expense, and administrative procedures required for this design may prohibit its use. There are other alternate designs which can yield similar reliable results. One alternate design is presented next.

Post-Test Only, Control Group Design

A more practical and less-expensive alternative to the previous design is called the post-test only, control-group design as shown in Figure 6-7.

Only a post-test is used on the randomly selected experimental and control groups. This reduces the effects of a pretest on the participants. Elimination of the pretest reduces the time and expense of the previous evaluation design. In addition, this design isolates almost all of the threats to validity.[2]

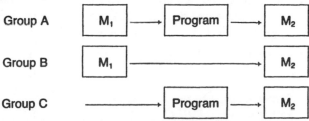

Figure 6-6. Ideal experimental design.

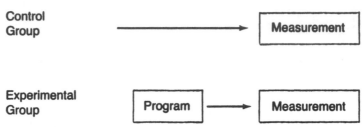

Figure 6-7. Post-test only, control group design.

One problem with this design is the difficulty in determining the amount of change brought about by the HRD program. This design will show that there is a difference between the two groups at the post-test, but the change attributed to the program cannot be determined accurately without the use of a pretest.

Which Design to Choose

The basic types of evaluation designs have been presented. There are many possibilities to construct an evaluation system for an HRD program. These designs can be combined to form a number of other alternate designs. The question of which design to use depends on several factors. More than likely the nature of the HRD program and the practical considerations of the working environment may dictate the appropriate design. The more complex the design, the more costly the evaluation effort. Yet, the results are more valid. The availability of control groups and the ease of randomization are other factors that enter into the decision. And finally, there is no way to isolate completely the effects of factors outside the learning situation.

If a design is less than optimum, then the HRD professional should be prepared to defend the selection in terms of trade-offs. Additional information on evaluation designs can be found in Rutman[3] and Fitz-Gibbon and Morris.[4] Also, a special issue of *Training and Development Journal* contains practical information on designs.[5]

Discussion Questions

1. When is it important to use control groups in the evaluation process? Is this a common practice? Explain.
2. What factors affect the timing of measurements in an evaluation process?
3. Are the threats to validity usually considered in most evaluation schemes? Explain.
4. What type of evaluation designs are used in your organization (or one with which you are familiar)?
5. Which evaluation design is the most commonly used? Why?
6. Suppose you are developing a training program for sales representatives in an effort to boost sales in a medium sized organization. Which evaluation design may be appropriate? Explain.
7. In a single group time series design, how many measurements are necessary? Explain.
8. Why is the ideal experimental design rarely used in evaluation projects?
9. One HRD executive stated, ". . . although we try to show the results of our programs, we are not concerned that much with evaluation designs." What is the basis for this comment?

References

1. Lawler, E. E. III, et al., *Doing Research That Is Useful For Theory and Practice,* Jossey-Bass Inc.: San Francisco, CA, 1985.
2. Spector, P. E., *Research Designs,* Sage Publications: Beverly Hills, CA, 1981.
3. Rutman, L. (ed.) *Evaluation Research Methods,* Sage Publications: Beverly Hills, CA, 1984.
4. Fitz-Gibbon, C. T. and Morris, L. L., *How to Design a Program Evaluation,* Sage Publications: Beverly Hills, CA, 1987.
5. Carnevale, A. P. and Schulz, E. R., "Return on Investment: Accounting For Training," *Training and Development Journal,* July 1990, p. S1–S-32.

CHAPTER 7

Determining HRD Program Costs

Importance of Costs

The cost of providing HRD in an organization is increasing. And, as organizations scramble to fund their budgets, it is imperative that they know where the money is spent and for what purposes. This chapter explores the rationale for determining costs and specific methods and techniques for classifying, allocating, and reporting those costs. Although the methods must be tailored to the organization, a number of fundamental principles and guidelines can be useful for any organization.

Rationale for Developing Cost Data

Probably the most significant reason for undertaking an evaluation is to determine the benefits versus costs of an HRD program. This reason alone makes the development of HRD program costs an important issue, but that is not the entire picture. Even if the cost justification is not planned, there are many other important reasons for monitoring the cost of HRD in an organization. Although these reasons are almost a repeat of the purposes for evaluation, a review should be helpful. They should provide a convincing argument for developing a cost tracking system or taking a fresh look at improving the present HRD costing system. For some organizations, all these reasons may not be appropriate.

To determine the total expenditures for HRD. Every organization should know approximately how much money is being spent on HRD. A few organizations calculate this expenditure now and make comparisons with other organizations, although such comparisons are difficult because of the different bases for cost calculations. Some organizations calculate HRD costs as percent of payroll costs and set targets. For example, Motorola budgets 3.5% of its payroll for HRD. Other organizations calculate HRD costs as a percent of revenues or develop HRD costs on a per employee basis. For example, Arthur Andersen & Co. spends about 9.5% of revenue on training. Total expenditures may go beyond the overall budget for the HRD department and include other costs such as participants' salaries, travel expenses, replacement costs, facilities expense, and other general overhead. An effective system of cost data collection will enable an organization to calculate the magnitude of the total HRD expenditure. Collecting this information will also help top management answer these two important questions:

☐ How much *do* we spend on HRD compared to others?
☐ How much *should* we spend on HRD?

To determine the relative cost of each individual HRD program. The HRD department should know which programs are most cost effective. They need to know if some programs with strong support and management commitment are carrying other programs which are costing more with less results. Monitoring costs by program allows the HRD staff to evaluate the relative contribution of a program and determine how costs in a program are changing. If a program is costing more than it has in the past, it might be time to reevaluate its impact and overall success. It may be useful to compare specific components of costs to other programs or organizations. The cost per participant for one program could be compared to the cost per participant for a similar program. Wide differences may signal a problem, although there may be legitimate reasons for the differences. For example, it may be helpful to know why it costs about $2,000 more to train a journeyman plumber than to train a journeyman electrician.[1] Also, costs associated with items such as program evaluation, program development, or other categories could be compared to other programs within the organization. These comparisons could lead to the development of cost standards.

To predict future program costs. Historical costs provide the best basis for predicting future costs. Cost data from a previous program help develop standardized data to use in estimating the cost of future programs. Sophisticated cost models provide the capability to estimate or predict costs with reasonable accuracy.

To calculate benefits versus costs for a specific program. As presented earlier, probably the most significant reason for collecting costs is to prepare data to use in a benefits versus costs comparison for a program. This makes cost data just as important as the data which determines the economic benefits of the program. This views HRD expenditures as an investment with a potential return.

To improve the efficiency of the HRD department. Controlling costs is a very important management function, and HRD personnel are not exempted from this responsibility. They must be able to monitor and control the costs of developing and delivering programs. Most HRD departments have monthly budgets which project costs by various accounts and, in some cases, by project or program. Cost reports, provided to show how the department is doing, are tools to spot problem areas and take corrective action when necessary. Therefore, from a practical management sense, the accumulation of cost data is a necessity.

Some efficiency measures serve as evaluation tools for HRD departments. For example, at Illinois Bell Telephone Company, seven measures have been calculated to serve as indices for tracking effectiveness and efficiency of the training function.[2] These measures include:

☐ Percentage of class size relative to seats available.
☐ Cost per trainee day.
☐ Instructor teaching time.
☐ Hours of development time per hour of instruction.
☐ Ratio of training department employees to total corporate employees.
☐ Ratio of training budget to total corporate budget.

Two of these measures relate directly to costs (numbers 2 and 7). The others are indirectly related to cost calculations.

To evaluate alternatives to a proposed HRD program. Realistic cost data provides management with the cost of a proposed program. The data can be used to evaluate the cost effectiveness of alternatives to a particular program.

Consider an example involving the decision of whether to use on-the-job training versus classroom training. The servicing division of American Express decided to computerize its data management systems and relocate to a different area of the country. It was faced with the need to train a large number of employees immediately and expected its needs for training to continue into the future. These conditions suggested a mix of computer-based instruction and classic classroom training. The large number to be trained, the radical change in procedure, and the relocation implied an insufficient number of trained supervisors—conditions increasing the costs of pursuing on-the-job training.[3]

To plan and budget for next year's operations. A final reason for tracking HRD costs is in preparation of next year's operating budget. The operating budget usually includes all of the expenditures within the HRD department. It may also include other costs such as participants' salaries and their associated travel expenses, although those expenses may be charged to the participant's department. In recent years the budgeting process has become more scrutinized and more sophisticated. The days of adding a percentage increase to last year's budget is, for the most part, gone. HRD departments are asked to examine their activities and programs carefully when preparing the budget. A few departments are on a zero-based budgeting process where each activity must be justified during the budgeting process. It assumes no carry-over expenses into next year's budget based on the previous year's activity. This process can become the basis for setting priorities for next year's efforts. Proposed projects and their costs are reviewed by top management, and their approval of specific items lets the HRD department focus on the most important efforts for the coming year.

To develop a marginal cost pricing system. HRD expenditure data are important when developing marginal cost pricing strategies. Once management is able to include the cost necessary for employee training when considering a new organizational strategy, it has a better sense of value for pursuing that strategy. Several organizations have developed standard cost data that can easily fit into expansion plans, changes in procedures or policies, and changes in products or services. Standard cost data will allow organizations to quickly factor the investment in human resources.

To integrate data into the human resource information systems. An HRD department should collect training cost data so that these data can be integrated into existing data bases for other human resource functions such as compensation, benefits, and selection information. Some data bases such as PIMS and OASIS presently collect this type of information.[4] These data bases provide information on human resource practices' relative contribution to profitability. Aligning training cost information in these data bases provides information on training's relative contribution to profitability in these organizations. Some of the most sophisticated human resource information systems have training cost components that allow tracking and monitoring of costs. In other cases, cost data are collected separately and fed directly into the system.

In conclusion, these nine reasons provide a convincing rationale for collecting cost data. They clearly show why these data are necessary and why HRD departments should be collecting and monitoring HRD costs. However, in many organizations this type of data is either inaccurate or not available.[5]

General Considerations

Whether developing a cost system or not, there are certain points about costs worth considering. These are presented in the form of helpful advice to the HRD professional.

Collect costs even if they are not used in evaluation. Based on the reasons listed in the previous section, it is important to develop cost data. Too often, an HRD department will neglect to collect and report costs adequately because they are not used in the evaluation process. These costs can be very useful management tools and are necessary for an effective organization.

Costs will not be precise. An accurate reflection of all of the costs associated with a program is almost impossible. There are so many hidden costs that it is difficult to get a completely accurate picture of costs. This lack of precision should not discourage anyone from attempting to monitor and collect costs. A reasonably accurate cost estimate is better than no cost estimate. If used in an evaluation, the costs are probably going to be as accurate as the economic value of the benefit of a program.

Use a practical approach in building a system. The HRD department must define the purposes for developing a cost system before it is designed. There will be trade-offs in accuracy versus the feasibility of maintaining the system. The organization should not be burdened with a vast amount of additional paperwork, calculations, and other analyses that can become unproductive and may not add to the precision of cost data. What is needed is a system that is simple yet as accurate as possible. It should be easy to administer and easy to understand by those who use it. If possible, it should be a part of current systems in use in the organization. Some account titles will be different but the manner of collecting, compiling, storing, and reporting the data should be consistent with established practices within the organization.

Use caution when reporting cost data. As mentioned earlier, cost data may be used for a number of purposes. Taken out of context, without proper explanations, cost data might be frightening to top management.

An excellent example of the misuse of cost data comes from the General Accounting Office (GAO). The GAO examined the training provided to auditors of the Internal Revenue Service and concluded that training had cost the federal government as much as $6.5 billion in lost revenue.[6] The GAO calculated this figure by estimating the revenue that would have been brought in by experienced auditors who were taken off the job to train new employees between July 1, 1986 and September 30, 1988. The GAO investigated the costs of training 1,103 new employees the IRS hired for five offices in the U.S. It figured that the lost revenue was $840 million from those offices. It arrived at the $6.5 billion figure by multiplying its figures to account for the 7,300 people the IRS hired nationwide during that time.

These costs, which were reported in the news, had one major deficiency. The GAO did not bother to calculate the long-term benefits of providing good training to new employees who presumably could go back to the job and bring in even more revenues. They examined only the cost side of the ledger and not the benefits. The GAO report concluded that it is essential the IRS explore alternatives to its present training programs.

The moral of this story: If the costs of a program are reported, the estimated benefits should be reported. Otherwise, a training program can appear prohibitively expensive.

The effort to set up a cost system is considerable. In most organizations there is a formal cost accounting system designed to accumulate cost by department, section, product line, and other categories. This type of system is usually adequate for collecting much of the cost data necessary for developing HRD program costs. However, the effort to set up such a system appears to be time consuming and significant. It may require a modification of the current system and will usually involve input from the finance and accounting sections of the organization. This substantial effort needs to be fully recognized at the beginning of the project.

With those general considerations in mind, a brief look at methods and techniques for establishing costing systems is next.

Cost Classification Systems

There are two basic ways HRD costs can be classified. One is by a description of the expenditure such as labor, materials, supplies, travel, etc. These are expense account classifications. The other is by categories in the HRD process or function such as program development, delivery, and evaluation. An effective system will monitor costs by account categories according to the description of those accounts but also includes a method for accumulating costs by the HRD process/functional category. Many systems stop short of this second step. While the first grouping is sufficient to give the total cost of the program, it does not allow for a useful comparison with other programs or indicate areas where costs might be excessive by relative comparisons. Therefore, two basic classifications are recommended to develop a complete costing system.

Developing a Classification System

When developing an HRD classification system, the following steps can help ensure that the system provides the information needed:

Define which costs will be collected. A system of cost classification may be subject to several interpretations. All relevant costs must be identified. Cost accounts should be clearly defined to reduce possible errors made in misclassifying costs. There should be little doubt where an item should be charged (i.e., office supplies or duplication). Also, the various process/functional categories need to be clearly defined so that items can be properly grouped in those accounts.

Assign the responsibility for developing the system. Because the implementation of a costing system involves the input of others, responsibilities of each individual or department should be detailed to reduce delays in implementation and errors in the final product.

Determine the HRD process/functional categories. Cost categories such as administrative and development costs should be determined early. More on these categories later.

Determine the expense account classification descriptions. Each of the account categories should be defined. These should be developed consistent with the organization's current chart of accounts and in a manner that will ease the application and use of the system. The classifications should be practical and describe the types of costs that make up each account. More on these categories later.

Use standard cost data when appropriate. There are many situations where standard cost data may be useful. Usually developed internally, standard costs can save time and can improve the accuracy of total cost calculations. An example of standard cost data is the percent of payroll for fringe benefits in calculating the compensation of participants. Another example is the average per diem for participants when attending an out-of-town HRD program.

Carefully select data sources. A valid data source is critical to the costing system. The source must be readily available, ideally from an existing system. It should be consistent with any other reports of the same data. Typical data sources are payroll records, budget reports, standard cost reports, travel expense records, purchase orders, and petty cash vouchers.

Computerize the system. In almost every organization the cost accounting system will be computerized. If not, computers should be considered to track the HRD program costs and analyze them efficiently. This procedure can ease the implementation and the acceptance of such a system.

These steps make the development of a costing system easier. Also, they help ensure that the system is implemented smoothly and on a timely basis.

Process/Functional Classifications

Table 7-1 shows the process/functional categories for costs in four different examples. In Column A there are only two categories: (1) support costs, and (2) operating costs. Operating costs include all expenses involved in conducting the HRD program; whereas, support costs include all administrative, overhead, development, analysis, or any other expenditures not directly related to conducting the program. While it is simple to separate the two, it does not provide enough detail to analyze costs on a functional basis. Column B provides a little more detail, because costs are divided into three categories. This is more useful than Column A but does not provide information on program development costs, a useful item to have. Column C provides for development costs as a separate item. It still falls short of what possibly is a more ideal situation. There is no way to track evaluation costs, which are becoming a more significant part of the total HRD process. Column D represents a more appropriate HRD process cost breakdown: analysis, development, delivery, and evaluation. The administrative costs are allocated to one of these areas. This four-phase system has been adopted by the Saratoga Institute in their cost surveys.[7]

Table 7-1
Process/Functional Categories for Cost

A	B
Support Costs	Classroom Costs
Operating Costs	Administrative Costs
	Participant Compensation and Facility Costs

C	D
Program Development Costs	Analysis Costs
Administrative Costs	Development Costs
Classroom Costs	Delivery Costs
Participant Costs	Evaluation Costs

These functional breakdowns are further defined in the following ways.

Analysis cost. These are the costs associated with the initial problem identification, needs analysis, development of objectives, selection of participants, and preparation of the program proposal. Common types of costs are salaries, materials, special equipment, and consulting fees.

Development cost. This category includes costs directly related to the development of the program. Examples are the salaries of program developers, supplies, outside consultant fees, and other costs associated with developing course materials and visual aids. Since these costs are usually substantial, the HRD staff must decide whether to spread these costs over the life of a continuing program or charge them off up front. This matter should probably be discussed with the appropriate accounting personnel.

Delivery cost. This category includes all the costs associated with the delivery of the HRD program, including participant materials, meeting room expenses, salaries and expenses of participants, instructor salaries, equipment rental, and any overhead expenses which can be allocated to the actual program delivery.

Evaluation cost. This last category includes all the costs associated with evaluation. Examples are the evaluation materials and time to administer evaluation instruments, analyze results, and report those results. If a pilot test is appropriate, that cost goes into the evaluation category.

One example of a breakdown for these functional costs is as follows:

Analysis costs	20%
Development costs	35%
Delivery costs	35%
Evaluation costs	10%

These are only rough estimates. The actual divisions will depend on how costs are accumulated in the organization. Also, they will vary considerably with the program with the greatest variance occurring in the development and delivery components. If a program is developed from a similar one now in operation, development costs should be low. However, in a lengthy program involving much participant time, the delivery costs may be much higher.[8]

Expense Account Classifications

The most time consuming step in developing an HRD cost system is defining and classifying the various HRD expenses. Many of the expense accounts, such as office supplies and travel expenses, are already a part of the existing accounting system. However, there will be expenses unique to the HRD department that must be added to the system. The system design will depend on the organization, the type of programs developed and conducted, and the limits imposed on the current cost accounting system, if any. Also, to a certain extent, the expense account classifications will depend on how the HRD process/functional categories have been developed as discussed in the previous section. A description of all of the expenses necessary for a system is inappropriate; however, an example may be useful to illustrate how one classification was established. The following box shows an expense account classification system in one organization with more than 8000 employees. Each account is clearly defined and assigned an account number. Additional accounts might make the system more precise and avoid misallocation of expenses. However, from a practical standpoint, this classification seems to be adequate for most any kind of analysis of HRD costs.

Human Resource Development Costs
Expense Account Classifications

00 — *Salaries and Benefits—HRD Personnel*
This account includes the salaries and employee benefit costs for HRD personnel, both supervisory and non-supervisory.

01 — *Salaries and Benefits—Other Company Personnel*
This account includes the salaries and employee benefit costs for other company personnel, both supervisory and non-supervisory.

02 — *Salaries and Benefits—Participants*
This account includes the salaries and employee benefit costs for participants, both supervisory and non-supervisory.

03 — *Meals, Travel, and Incidental Expenses—HRD Personnel*
This account includes meals, travel, and incidental expenses of Corporate HRD Department employees.

04 — *Meals, Travel, and Accommodations—Participants*
This account includes meals, travel accommodations, and incidental expenses for participants attending HRD programs.

05 — *Office Supplies and Expenses*
This account includes expenses incurred for stationery, office supplies and services, subscriptions, postage, telephone and telegraph service.

06 — *Program Materials and Supplies*
This account includes the cost of materials and supplies purchased for specific programs and includes such items as films, binders, hand-out materials, and purchased programs.

07 — *Printing and Reproduction*
This account includes expenses incurred for printing and reproduction of all material.

08 — *Outside Services*
This account includes the cost incurred for fees and expenses of outside corporations, firms, institutions, or individuals other than company personnel who perform special services such as management consultants and professional instructors.

09 — *Equipment Expense Allocation*
This account includes that portion of original equipment cost allocated to specific HRD programs, including computers.

10 — *Equipment—Rental*
This account includes rental payments for equipment used in administrative work and HRD programs.

11 — *Equipment—Maintenance*
This account includes expenses incurred in repairing and servicing company-owned equipment and furniture.

12 — *Registration Fees*
This account includes employee registration fees and tuitions for seminars and conferences paid for by the company. Membership dues and fees in trade, technical, and professional associations paid by the Company for employees are also included in this account.

13 — *Facilities Expense Allocation*
This account includes an expense allocation for use of a company-owned facility for conducting an HRD program.

14 — *Facilities Rental*
This account includes rental payments for facilities used in connection with an HRD program.

15 — *General Overhead Allocation*
This account includes general overhead expenses prorated to each HRD program.

16 — *Other Miscellaneous Expenses*
This account includes miscellaneous expenses not provided for elsewhere.

Cost Accumulation and Estimation

Cost Classification Matrix

The previous section presented two ways of classifying costs. Costs will be accumulated under both classifications. The two classifications are obviously related and the relationship depends on the organization. For instance, the specific costs that comprise the analysis part of a program may vary substantially with the organization.

A final step in the classification process is to define the kinds of costs in the account classification system which normally apply to the process/functional categories. Table 7-2 represents a matrix which allows represent the categories for accumulating all HRD-related costs in the organization. Those costs, which normally are a part of a process/functional category, are checked in the matrix. Each member of the HRD staff should know how to charge expenses properly. For example, equipment is rented to use in the development and the delivery of a program. Should all or part of the cost be charged to development? Or to delivery? More than likely the cost will be allocated in proportion to the extent the item was used for each category.

Table 7-2
Cost Classification Matrix

Expense Account Classification	Analysis	Development	Delivery	Evaluation
00 Salaries and Benefits—HRD Personnel	X	X	X	X
01 Salaries and Benefits—Other Company Personnel		X	X	
02 Salaries and Benefits—Participants			X	X
03 Meals, Travel, and Incidental Expenses—HRD Personnel	X	X	X	X
04 Meals, Travel, and Accommodations—Participants			X	
05 Office Supplies and Expenses	X	X		X
06 Program Materials and Supplies		X	X	
07 Printing and Reproduction	X	X	X	X
08 Outside Services	X	X	X	X
09 Equipment Expense Allocation	X	X	X	X
10 Equipment—Rental		X	X	
11 Equipment—Maintenance			X	
12 Registration Fees	X			
13 Facilities Expense Allocation			X	
14 Facilities Rental			X	
15 General Overhead Allocation	X	X	X	X
16 Other Miscellaneous Expenses	X	X	X	X

Cost Accumulation

With expense account classifications clearly defined and the process/functional categories determined, it is an easy task to track costs on individual programs. This can be accomplished through the use of special account numbers and project numbers. An example will illustrate the use of these numbers.

A project number is a three-digit number representing a specific HRD program. For example:

New employee orientation	112
New supervisors training program	215
Electrical assembly training	418
Interviewing skills workshop	791

Numbers are assigned to the process/functional breakdowns. Using the example presented earlier, the following numbers are assigned:

Analysis	1
Development	2
Delivery	3
Evaluation	4

Using the two-digit numbers assigned to the expense account classifications (see page 138), an accounting system is complete unless there are other requirements from the existing system. For example, if manuals are reproduced for the interviewing skills workshop, the appropriate charge number for that reproduction is 07-3-791. The first two digits denote the account classification, the next digit the process/functional category, and the last three digits the project number. This system enables rapid accumulation and monitoring of HRD costs. Total costs can be presented:

☐ By HRD program (interviewing skills workshop).
☐ By process/functional categories (delivery).
☐ By expense account classification (printing and reproduction).

Cost Estimation

The previous sections covered procedures to classify and monitor costs related to HRD programs. This is important to monitor ongoing costs to compare with the budget or with projected costs. However, a significant reason for tracking costs is to predict the cost of future programs. This goal is usually accomplished through a formal method of cost estimation unique to the organization.

Some organizations use cost estimating worksheets to arrive at the total cost for a proposed program. The following box shows an example of a cost estimating worksheet to calculate costs for analysis, development, delivery, and evaluation. The worksheets contain a few formulas which make it easier to estimate the cost. In addition to these worksheets, current charge rates for services, supplies, and salaries are available. These data become quickly outdated and are usually prepared periodically as a supplement.

Analysis Costs   *Total*
Salaries & Employee Benefits—HRD Staff   _____
  (No. of People × Average Salary × Employee
  Benefits Factor × No. of Hours on Project)
Meals, Travel, and Incidental Expenses   _____
Office Supplies and Expenses   _____
Printing and Reproduction   _____
Outside Services   _____
Equipment Expenses   _____
Registration Fees   _____
General Overhead Allocation   _____
Other Miscellaneous Expenses   _____
  Total Analysis Cost   ======

Development Costs   *Total*
Salaries & Employee Benefits (No. of
  People × Avg. Salary × Employee Benefits   _____
  Factor × No. of Hours on Project)
Meals, Travel, and Incidental Expenses   _____
Office Supplies and Expenses   _____
Program Materials and Supplies   _____
  Film   _____
  Videotape   _____

Audiotapes   ____
35mm Slides   ____
Overhead Transparencies   ____
Artwork   ____
Manuals and Materials   ____
Other   ____
Printing and Reproduction   ____
Outside Services   ____
Equipment Expense   ____
General Overhead Allocation   ____
Other Miscellaneous Expense   ____

  Total Development Costs   ____

Delivery Costs   *Total*
Participant Costs   ____
Salaries & Employee Benefits   ____
  (No. of Participants×Avg.
  Salary×Employee Benefits Factor×Hrs. or
  Days of Training Time)
Meals, Travel, & Accommodations   ____
  (No. of Participants×Avg. Daily
  Expenses×Days of training)
Program Materials and Supplies   ____
Participant Replacement Costs (if applicable)   ____
Lost Production (Explain Basis)   ____
Instructor Costs   ____
  Salaries & Benefits   ____
  Meals, Travel, & Incidental Expense   ____
  Outside Services   ____
Facility Costs   ____
  Facilities Rental   ____
  Facilities Expense Allocation   ____
Equipment Expense   ____
General Overhead Allocation   ____
Other Miscellaneous Expense   ____

  Total Delivery Costs   ____

Evaluation Costs   *Total*
Salaries & Employee Benefits—HRD Staff   ____
  (No. of People×Avg. Salary×Employee Benefits
  Factor×No. or Hours on Project)

Meals, Travel and Incidental Expense	_____
Participants Costs	_____
Office Supplies and Expense	_____
Printing and Reproduction	_____
Outside Services	_____
Equipment Expense	_____
General Overhead Allocation	_____
Other Miscellaneous Expenses	_____
Total Evaluation Costs	======
TOTAL PROGRAM COSTS	======

The most appropriate basis for predicting costs is to analyze the previous costs by tracking the actual costs incurred in all phases of a program from analysis to evaluation. The organization will begin to see how much is spent on programs and how much is being spent in the different categories. Until adequate cost data are available, it is necessary to use the detailed analysis in the worksheets for cost estimation.

Estimating the time for program development and instructor preparation is sometimes difficult. The time to develop a program depends on the type of program, whether or not a similar one has been developed, the availability of subject-matter experts, and the proposed program format. Of course, the length of the program is another factor. There are shortcut ways to estimate the amount of time involved in developing a program. The Office of Personnel Management estimates the ratio between production and class time this way[9]:

If the Format Is	Development Hours Per Hour of Presentation
Technical, formal courses	5–15
Self-contained for use by other instructors	50–100
Conventional management development	20–30
Programmed instruction	80–120
Technical, on-site training	1–3
Computer-assisted instruction	up to 350

Xerox Corporation estimates the number of hours of development time per one hour of instruction for classroom training to be 15. For computer-based training, it's 130.[10]

Instructor preparation is another area difficult to estimate, particularly if there is very little prior experience at cost accumulation. The preparation hours per classroom hour can vary from 1 to 25 or more depending on the type of program, method of instruction, and competency level of the HRD person.

Formulas, guidelines, or rule-of-thumb methods can be developed by the organization based on past experiences. Although these methods are not as accurate as itemizing the total predicted cost, they can provide a way to get a quick estimate of costs.

One organization developed a rule-of-thumb method for estimating the total cost of training through use of a formula.[11] The formula develops a percentage:

$$\text{Cost factor} \quad = \quad \frac{WS+B+R\&LP+O+Tu+TDC+Tr\&L}{\text{Annual salary}} \quad \times 100$$

where

WS = Weekly salary
B = Benefits
$R\&LB$ = Replacement and lost production costs
O = Overhead costs
Tu = Tuition costs
TDC = Training department costs
$Tr\&L$ = Traveling and living costs

The cost factor (percentage) is multiplied by the total annual salaries of the participants to yield training costs based on a one-week program. A three-day program requires dividing this figure by five (5) and multiplying by three (3). For this organization, the percentage averaged 10%. The percentage can vary considerably with other organizations.

Training Cost Models

In large organizations a training cost model might be appropriate for analyzing and estimating costs. A model is a simplified representation of a real-world situation. It simulates the behavior of HRD costs under various specified conditions. This is accomplished in a step-by-step procedure which enables the user to predict the cost of a proposed HRD program or, in the absence of accurate accounting data, to construct the cost of a program already conducted.

OPM Model. The Office of Personnel Management developed such a model for use in government agencies. The training cost model has been used by various government agencies and is accurate within $\pm 2\%$, based on the actual experience in field validation studies. (Their situation may be unique, since they essentially deal with "canned programs," which they offer much as a school or public seminar.)

In their model there are four simple steps to predict HRD program costs. The first involves making certain basic assumptions about the proposed HRD program. These are:

☐ Length of course
☐ Times repeated each year
☐ Number of participants and salary grade levels
☐ Course methodology
☐ Geographic location

These assumptions were made by a qualified training officer using professional judgment.

The next step involves selecting data from cost data tables. Four major categories for standard cost tables were developed:

☐ Salary
☐ Travel
☐ Development
☐ Production

The actual tables were derived from formulas, thus allowing the user of the model to avoid using the formulas themselves. The third step involved entering the cost data on four individual worksheets:

☐ Course development cost worksheet
☐ Participant cost worksheet
☐ Instructor cost worksheet
☐ Facilities cost worksheet

Each worksheet contained several elements. The fourth and final step involves transferring the cost data to a summary worksheet. This task involves copying data from the previous sheets to a separate sheet and can be done by clerical personnel. When completed, the separate sheet contains the total cost of the proposed HRD program.

This model is tailored for use in government agencies. Similar models can be developed for organizations whose size and frequency of programs justifies the development of such a model. Once developed and validated, the models can be very easy to administer and make the task of cost estimating almost effortless.

Head Model. Another cost model is developed by Head and focuses on five cost variables.[12]

☐ Student cost
☐ Instructor cost
☐ Instructional development cost
☐ Facilities cost
☐ Maintenance cost

To arrive at the cost in each of these areas, it is necessary to identify basic cost factors and calculate the values for each individual program. Some of the variables that influence the five costs include:

☐ Expected course life
☐ Course link
☐ Number of trainees in each class
☐ Number of times the course is held
☐ Geographic location of the course
☐ Average annual salaries
☐ Company's employee benefits percentage
☐ Annual productive days
☐ Average travel and per diem expenses
☐ Number of instructors per class
☐ Lost opportunity cost
☐ Production of materials cost
☐ Development and evaluation time

The model is a result of more than ten years of experimentation and development. It is administered by Instructional Communications Inc., of Denver, Colorado and has been used to develop training cost analyses for a wide variety of organizations, including major utilities, telecommunications, government, retail and banking concerns. According to the model's author, the costs that were identified were truly "eye openers."[13]

Decision-Oriented Cost Model. Although most costs are collected to influence a decision, some models are developed around a comprehensive decision making process. One such model, developed by LaPointe, focuses on the justification to conduct a program.[14] Labeled the Decision Evaluation Cost Model, this model has seven basic steps in its development:

☐ Developing a list of cost elements
☐ Developing and identifying sub-components of each cost element
☐ Developing the model structure
☐ Collecting data to estimate cost for each element
☐ Developing alternative scenarios
☐ Running the model
☐ Developing "what if" analysis

Designed to be used with a spreadsheet on a personal computer, the model is available through Decision Technology & Associates, Chicago.

These and other models enable the HRD manager to calculate the cost of HRD quickly and accurately.

Summary

This chapter presented information necessary to develop a cost system to accumulate, monitor, and report the costs of HRD programs. This information is necessary whether or not it is used directly in a program evaluation. If information is collected for evaluation, it can then be used in the analysis explained in Chapter 10.

Discussion Questions

1. Discuss the importance of monitoring HRD costs in an organization.
2. How do HRD costs in an organization compare to other human resources functions such as recruiting, compensation, benefits, and labor relations?
3. For which reasons does your organization collect costs?
4. How much should an organization spend on HRD? Please explain.
5. Why are HRD practitioners reluctant to monitor costs and report them to management on a program by program basis?
6. Compare the expense account classification system in your organization (or one with which you are familiar) to the one presented in this chapter.
7. Which process-functional cost classification system is appropriate for your organization (or one with which you are familiar)? Explain.
8. Are all costs accounted for in the classification system presented here? Explain.

9. What are the advantages of using the cost classification matrix as presented in this chapter?
10. What are the advantages and disadvantages of using training cost models?
11. An HRD manager stated . . . "There is no way you can ever accurately assess costs of training in an organization." Is this true? Explain.
12. The American Society for Training and Development estimates that employers spend, collectively, $210 billion on training annually. How is this figure calculated and how reliable is it?

References

1. BNA Staff, "Protecting the Training Investment," *Bulletin on Training,* March 1984, p. 4.
2. Coblentz, C., "Macro Evaluation," *Training,* April 1987, p. 12.
3. Mangum, S. L., "On-The-Job vs. Classroom Training: Some Deciding Factors," *Training,* February 1985, p. 76.
4. Carnevale, A. P. and Schulz, E. R., "Return on Investment: Accounting for Training," *Training and Development Journal,* June 1990, p. S1–S32.
5. Bernhard, H. B. and Ingols, C. A., "Six Lessons for the Corporate Classroom," *Harvard Business Review,* September–October 1988, p. 46.
6. Geber, B., "GAO Raps IRS Training," *Training,* June 1990, pp. 16, 21.
7. Fitz-enz, J., "Proving the Value of Training," *Personnel,* March 1988, p. 18.
8. Bennett, B. and Griswold, D. F., "Proving Our Worth: The Training Value Model," *Training and Development Journal,* October 1984, p. 83.
9. Lee, C. and Zemke, R., "How Long Does It Take?" *Training,* June 1987, pp. 75–80.
10. Guilmette, H. and Reinhart, C., "Competitive Benchmarking: A New Concept for Training," *Training and Development Journal,* February 1984, p. 71.
11. Suessmuth, P., "A Rule of Thumb Way to Determine Quickly the Real Cost of Any Training Program," *Training,* October 1976, p. 43–44.
12. Head, G. E., *Training Cost Analysis,* Marlin Press: Washington, D.C., 1985.
13. Ibid, p. 2.
14. LaPointe, J. and Verdin, J. A., "How to Calculate the Cost of Human Resources," *Personnel Journal,* January 1988, pp. 38, 39.

C H A P T E R   8

Data Collection Methods

This chapter covers methods of data collection, sometimes referred to as evaluation methods. The methods directly relate to the material presented in Chapters 5 and 6 which presented instruments and evaluation design. Some explanation is necessary of the differences between instruments, evaluation design, and data-collection methods. Chapter 5 presented the design of instruments used in the evaluation process with little regard to how an instrument was used or whether it was used in conjunction with other instruments. Chapter 6 presented the considerations necessary for the design of a valid and reliable overall evaluation scheme. Data-collection methods are concerned with the practical use of instruments and their applications to collect data. Data-collection methods will usually be part of the evaluation design and use one or more instruments. These methods provide, from a practical standpoint, useful and effective approaches for collecting data necessary to evaluate HRD programs.

In some situations the three terms are almost synonymous. For instance, precourse and post-course testing represents a method of data collection. The instruments are the tests used in the evaluation, and the evaluation design is of the precourse and post-course measurement variety. In another example the distinction is more apparent. Participant follow-up is a method of data collection. From the instrument design standpoint, the concern is only with the design aspects of the questionnaire, interview, or observation to use in the follow-up. In evaluation design, follow-up is one measurement or possibly a series of measurements in the overall design. The data collection method is concerned with the practical applications of the follow-up.

The chapter begins with a presentation on the types of data collected and is followed by an explanation of the most common data-collection methods. To avoid overlap with previous material, this chapter presents only the information that will complement the principles outlined in Chapters 5 and 6.

Types of Data

A fundamental premise of evaluation is to collect data directly related to the objectives of the HRD program. For some reason HRD professionals still have a concern that appropriate data are not available. Fortunately, this is not the case. Most companies already collect the data needed to evaluate training, they just don't recognize the evaluative potential of that data.[1] The confusion sometimes stems from the different types of outcomes planned for training programs. Often, programs have skill and behavioral outcomes that promise trainees will be able to do certain things or behave in certain ways. The outcome of some programs, such as technical training programs, are fairly easy to observe and evaluate. It is easy to measure the speed and quality of an assembly line operator before, during, and after a training program. However, behavioral outcomes associated with effective management are not nearly so obvious or measurable. Demonstrating that a manager is an effective delegator or motivator is much more difficult than demonstrating that an assembly line operator is maintaining quality and quantity standards.[2]

Because of this, a distinction is made in two general categories of data—*hard data* and *soft data*. Hard data are the primary measurement of improvement, presented in rational, undisputed facts that are easily accumulated. They are the most desired type of data to collect. In the long run, the ultimate criteria for measuring the effectiveness of management rest on hard data items, such as turn on investment, productivity, profitability, cost control and quality control. Because changes in these data may lag behind changes in the condition of the human organization by many months, it is highly useful for management planning and control to supplement these measures with interim assessments of measures of attitude, motivation, satisfaction, and skills.[3]

Although a supervisory program designed to build delegation and motivation skills should have an ultimate impact on hard data items, it may be best measured by soft data items. Soft data are more difficult to collect and analyze but are used when hard data are not available. The contrasting characteristics of the two types of data emphasize this point.

Hard data are:

☐ Easy to measure and quantify.
☐ Relatively easy to assign dollar values.
☐ Objectively based.
☐ A common measure of organizational performance.
☐ Very credible in the eyes of management.

Soft data are:

☐ Difficult to measure or quantify directly.
☐ Difficult to assign dollar values.
☐ Subjectively based in many cases.
☐ Less credible as a performance measurement.
☐ Usually behaviorally oriented.

Hard Data

Hard data can usually be grouped in four categories (or subdivisions) as shown in Figure 8-1. These categories of output, quality, cost, and time are typical performance measures in almost every organization. When they are not available, the basic approach is to convert soft data to one of these four basic measurements.

Output. The most significant results which can be achieved are those involving improvements in the output of the work unit. Every organization, regardless of scope, has basic measurements of work output. This may appear in various forms as outlined in Table 8-1. Since these factors are normally monitored by organizations, changes can be easily measured by comparing before- and after-work output.

Quality. Almost as important as work output is the quality of that output. Every organization is concerned with quality, and methods are usually in place to measure it. Many HRD programs are designed to improve quality and the results can easily be documented. The variety of quality improvement measurements is illustrated in Table 8-1.

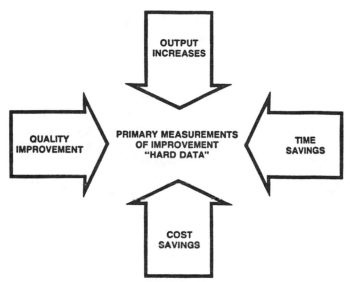

Figure 8-1. The four major categories of hard data.

Cost. Another very significant item for evaluation is improvement in operating costs, administrative costs, and capital expenditures. HRD programs which produce a direct cost savings can easily show a bottomline contribution. A few examples of the types of costs are shown in Table 8-1. There can be as many cost items as there are accounts in a cost accounting system. In addition, costs can be combined to develop any number of combinations needed for evaluation.

Time. The fourth subdivision of hard data is time. This is another factor that is easy to measure in HRD programs and can be just as critical as cost and quality. A time savings may mean a project is completed sooner than was planned, a new product was introduced earlier, or the time to repair equipment was reduced. It quickly translates into additional output or lower operating costs. Examples of time savings monitored in HRD programs are shown in Table 8-1.

The distinction between these four groups of hard data is sometimes unclear, since there are some overlap factors. For example, accident costs may be listed under the cost category, the number of accidents listed under quality, and the lost-time days due to an accident listed under the time category. The rationale? Accidents represent a cost which can

Table 8-1
Examples of Hard Data

OUTPUT	TIME
Units Produced	Equipment Downtime
Tons Manufactured	Overtime
Items Assembled	On Time Shipments
Money Collected	Time to Project Completion
Items Sold	Processing Time
Forms Processed	Supervisory Time
Loans Approved	Break in Time for New Employees
Inventory Turnover	Training Time
Patients Visited	Meeting Schedules
Applications Processed	Repair Time
Students Graduated	Efficiency
Tasks Completed	Work Stoppages
Output Per Hour	Order Response
Productivity	Late Reporting
Work Baccklog	Lost Time Days
Incentive Bonus	
Shipments	**QUALITY**
New Accounts Generated	Scrap
	Waste
COSTS	Rejects
Budget Variances	Error Rates
Unit Costs	Rework
Cost By Account	Shortages
Variable Costs	Product Defects
Fixed Costs	Deviation From Standard
Overhead Cost	Product Failures
Operating Costs	Inventory Adjustments
Number of Cost Reductions	Time Card Corrections
Project Cost Savings	Percent of Tasks Completed Properly
Accident Costs	Number of Accidents
Program Costs	
Sales Expense	

easily be determined. They are usually caused by someone making a mistake and are a reflection of the quality of his efforts. The days lost from the job represents time lost to the organization. In another example an incentive bonus may be listed as output, since the amount of bonus is usually tied directly to the output of an employee or group of employees. However, the bonus is usually presented in cash, which represents a cost to the organization. The distinction between the different subdivisions is not as important as the awareness of the vast number of measurements in these four areas.

Soft Data

There are times when hard, rational numbers just do not exist. When this is the case, soft data may be more meaningful to use in evaluating HRD programs. Table 8-2 shows typical kinds of soft data. Soft data are behaviorally based and difficult to measure accurately or assign dollar values. The soft data have been categorized or subdivided into six areas: work habits, new skills, work climate, development/advancement, feelings/attitudes, and initiative. There may be other ways to divide soft data into categories because there can be many other types of soft data-the possibilities are almost limitless. This grouping of six categories make the presentation easier to follow.

Work habits. Employee work habits are critical to the success of a work group. Poor work habits can lead to an unproductive and ineffective work group, while good work habits can boost the output and morale of the group. The most common and easily documented poor work habits include absenteeism and tardiness, and these can be tied to cost savings much easier than the other types of soft data.

HRD programs for supervisors frequently contain modules to train them to improve the work habits of employees. In some organizations regular systems are in place to record employee work habits such as absenteeism, tardiness, and visits to the first-aid station. In others the poor work habits may have to be documented by the employee's supervisor.

New skills. Skill building is an important area for HRD programs. The successful application of new skills might result in hard-data measurements such as a new employee learning a production procedure. However, they may involve soft-data measurements which are intangible in nature and difficult to relate to a dollar savings. Examples of soft-data skills are making decisions, solving problems, resolving conflicts, settling grievances, and improving listening. Another important point is the frequency with which the new skill is employed. The success of many skill-oriented programs lies in the frequency of use after the program was completed. With the proper amount of preplanning, the

Table 8-2
Examples of Soft Data

WORK HABITS	NEW SKILLS
Absenteeism	Decisions Made
Tardiness	Problems Solved
Visits to the Dispensary	Conflicts Avoided
First Aid Treatments	Grievances Resolved
Violations of Safety Rules	Counseling Problems Solved
Number of Communication Break-downs	Listening Skills
	Interviewing Skills
Excessive Breaks	Reading Speed
Follow-Up	Discrimination Charges Resolved
WORK CLIMATE	Intention to Use New Skills
Number of Grievances	Frequency of Use of New Skills
Number of Discrimination Charges	**DEVELOPMENT/ADVANCE-**
Employee Complaints	**MENT**
Job Satisfaction	Number of Promotions
Unionization Avoidance	Number of Pay Increases
Employee Turnover	Number of Training Programs At-tended
Reduced Litigation	
FEELINGS/ADDITUDES	Requests for Transfer
Favorable Reactions	Performance Appraisal Ratings
Attitude Changes	Increases in Job Effectiveness
Perceptions of Job Responsibilities	**INITIATIVE**
Perceived Changes in Performance	Implementation of New Ideas
Employee Loyalty	Successful Completion of Projects
Increased Confidence	Number of Suggestions Submitted
	Number of Suggestions Implemented
	Work Accomplishment
	Setting Goals and Objectives

frequency and extent of the use of new skills can be monitored and documented, thus providing additional data for a program evaluation.

Work climate. Improving the work climate is another area of importance. Grievances, discrimination charges, complaints, and job dissatisfaction are quite often the result of a poor work climate. The result: less efficiency, less output, unionization drives, or possibly even employee resignations.

Development/advancement. Another important type of soft data is related to employee development and/or advancement. There are two perspectives: (1) the development of participants who attend programs; and (2) in the case of management/supervision, the extent to which they provide developmental opportunities for their employees. Promotions, transfers, pay increases, performance ratings are typical data that indicate improvement in this area.

Feelings/attitudes. Almost every HRD program is designed to get a favorable reaction toward the subject being taught. These reactions provide additional evidence of the success of the program. Some programs are conducted to change attitudes toward employees, the job, or the organization. And finally, a few programs are designed to change the participant's perception of the job or other aspects of the work setting. In all these situations the feelings and attitudes are relatively easy to document with reaction questionnaires and attitude surveys.

Initiative. The final category of soft data involves initiative. In some HRD programs participants are encouraged to try new ideas and techniques. The extent to which employees accomplish what they plan provides additional evidence of the success of the program. Also, the employee's initiative to generate ideas and submit suggestions are further indications that improvement has occurred.

As with the hard data, these subdivisions have some overlap. Some items listed under one category could just as appropriately be listed in another. For instance, consider employee loyalty. Loyalty is related both to the feelings and attitudes of an employee as well as work habits. An employee exhibits loyalty through attitudes and feelings in these situations:

☐ Placing the organization's goals above personal nonwork goals.
☐ Choosing to purchase the company's products rather than those of a competitor.

On the other hand, loyalty may surface in these work habits of an employee:

☐ Returning to work promptly after break.
☐ Studying job information on his own time.
☐ Taking work home when necessary to finish the job.

Soft Data vs. Hard Data

The preference of hard data in program evaluation does not mean that soft data are not valuable. It is usually essential for a complete evaluation of an HRD program. A program's total success may rest on soft-data measurements. For example, in a program to reduce turnover at McDonald's, four key measures of success were identified in the program evaluation. These were:

☐ Trainee turnover
☐ Interview to hire ratios
☐ Participant's evaluation
☐ Reduced litigation

The program was successful in all four measures as reported by the program's developer.[4]

Most programs use a combination of hard- and soft-data items in the evaluation. A comprehensive evaluation would use several hard-data and soft-data measurements. For example, in a maintenance supervisors training program, Travenol laboratories used the following measures of success:

☐ A reduction of costs associated with specific maintenance activities.
☐ Improvement in production equipment and processes.
☐ Changes in maintenance responsibilities and procedures.
☐ Improvement in training of maintenance employees.
☐ Changes in organization and personnel.

These changes included both hard data (production and costs) and soft data (increased training, changes in procedures, and changes in the organization).[5]

Another important point is that soft data are usually the best when evaluating behavior and skill outcomes. For example, in behavior modeling, which has proven to be a very effective approach to building supervisory skills, the evaluation of behavioral and skill outcomes rests almost entirely on soft data. Hultman[6] presents the following generic behavioral modeling skills resulting from a training program for supervisors:

☐ Following procedures
☐ Taking notes
☐ Coaching for content

- ☐ Asking for help in solving a problem
- ☐ Listening
- ☐ Distinguishing effective from ineffective behavior
- ☐ Maintaining self esteem
- ☐ Checking for understanding
- ☐ Coaching for process
- ☐ Giving dialogue feedback
- ☐ Awareness of errors
- ☐ Ability to correct errors
- ☐ Accessing the impact of behavior on others
- ☐ Providing rationale
- ☐ Coaching for special learning needs
- ☐ Responding with empathy

While these are all in the soft-data category, a supervisory training program could have objectives tied to hard-data measurements. The acquisition of skills and changes in behavior could produce hard-data results.

The important point is that there is a place for both hard- and soft-data program evaluation. A comprehensive program will use both types of data. Some programs will rely on soft data as primary measures, while others will rely on hard data as primary measures. Hard data are preferred because of their distinct advantages and level of credibility.

Pre-Program and Post-Program Examinations

A very popular data-collection method involves administering examinations before and after an HRD program. This method measures changes in skills, knowledge, and attitudes.

The guidelines for the design and use of precourse and post-course examinations were covered in Chapters 5 and 6 and will not be amplified further.

Advantages of this type of data-collection method are:

- ☐ They are easy to administer.
- ☐ Improvement can easily be tabulated.

The inherent disadvantages of this type of data-collection method are:

- ☐ Improvement measured during the program does not assure that it will be put into practice on the job.

☐ The effects of testing may have an impact on the post-program scores. The first examination might influence the score on the second.

Nevertheless, the precourse and post-course measurements are used frequently and represent a significant method of data collection for use in evaluation.[7]

Participant Feedback

Feedback from program participants is the most frequently used, and least reliable, method of collecting data for evaluation.[8] The popularity of this form of data collection is astounding. Ratings from reaction questionnaires can be so critical that a person's job may be at stake, as in the case of instructor ratings in school systems.

Feedback forms are used in many places outside the HRD area. Any organization providing a service or product is usually interested in feedback from those utilizing the service or product. Consider this example from the tourism industry:

> At the end of a seven-day Caribbean cruise, the owners of an oceanliner solicited feedback from passengers regarding food, dining room service, bar service, cabin service, entertainment, etc. These questionnaires, referred to as "comment cards," were discussed several times during the cruise. Passengers were assembled on the last day to discuss how the forms should be completed and the importance of leaving them at the proper location. They were so interested in getting a large response that five passengers' names were selected at random to receive gifts on the last day if they turned in their comment cards. Ratings from the comment cards were analyzed by the ship's owners and compared with ratings of other ships in the fleet. These were regarded as significant measures of performance and served as a useful tool to make corrections as necessary. (Although this example is away from the HRD effort, it shows the importance of feedback.)

While participant feedback is popular, it is also subject to misuse. Sometimes referred to as a "happiness rating," it has come under fire from many HRD professionals because it is considered worthless. The primary criticism concerns the subjectivity of the data.[9] Possibly the criticism is unjustified. Some research shows a direct correlation between positive comments at the end of a program and the actual improved performance on the job.[10] This research was based on 90 government supervisors and managers who completed a basic management course. In all the variables examined, trainee reaction was the strongest determinant of on-the-job application of the new management principles. Those participants who enjoyed the program most were the ones who achieved the most on the job. Those who did not like it apparently did not bother to do too much of anything with it. Armed with these data, HRD managers could logically assume that if participants enjoyed the course and said they planned to use the materials, they probably would. A word of caution is in order. This research might be measuring the effect of the self-fulfilling prophecy discussed in an earlier chapter. Other research has produced mixed results on this issue.[11,12]

While there is no good substitute for hard data in evaluating programs, a carefully designed, properly used participant feedback questionnaire at the end of an HRD program might suffice for a more sophisticated evaluation method. There is a definite place for feedback questionnaires in HRD evaluation. A high quality evaluation would be difficult to achieve without feedback questionnaires.[13]

Areas of Feedback

The areas of feedback used on reaction forms depend, to a large extent, on the organization and the purpose of the evaluation. Some forms are very simple while others are very detailed and require a considerable amount of time to complete. The feedback questionnaire should be designed to supply the proper information. The following areas represent a comprehensive listing of the most common types of feedback solicited:

☐ Program content
☐ Instructional materials
☐ Out-of-class assignments
☐ Method of presentation
☐ Instructor/speaker
☐ Program relevance
☐ Facilities
☐ General evaluation
☐ Planned improvements

Objective questions covering each of these areas will provide very thorough feedback from the participants. This feedback can be extremely useful for making adjustments in a program and/or assist in predicting performance after the program. The area of instructor/speaker evaluation deserves additional attention. In some organizations the primary evaluation centers on the speaker, and a separate form may be used for each speaker that covers a variety of areas. This highlights the importance of an effective course leader.

This is illustrated in the instructor evaluation process at Southwestern Bell.[14] The evaluation focuses on five areas for evaluation of the instructor:

☐ General performance criteria referenced to company standards.
☐ Knowledge of the subject matter including familiarity with content and depth of understanding.
☐ Presentation skills which focus on clarity of the presentation, use of audio visual material, pacing of material, maintaining eye contact and accessing learner understanding.
☐ Communications which include the use of understandable language, real-life examples and the promotion of discussion.
☐ Receptivity which includes responsiveness to trainees, responding effectively to questions and maintaining neutrality in responses to student comments.

Appendix 4 provides a detailed participant feedback questionnaire which covers most of the previously listed areas. It was used at the end of a program for new supervisors.

Useful Guidelines

The design information on questionnaires presented in Chapter 5 applies to the design and construction of reaction or feedback questionnaires. In addition to those design principles, there are a number of useful tips that can improve the effectiveness of this data-collection method.

Consider an ongoing evaluation. For lengthy programs, an end-of-the-program evaluation may leave the participants unable to remember what was covered at what time. To help improve the situation, an ongoing evaluation can be implemented. This evaluation form is distributed at the beginning of the program and participants are instructed when and how to supply the information. After each topic is presented, participants are asked to evaluate the topic and speaker. The information is fresh on their minds and can be more useful to the program evaluators.

Try quantifying course ratings. Some organizations attempt to solicit feedback in terms of numerical ratings. Although very subjective, these can be useful to program evaluators. An overall rating is collected by the American Management Association in their public seminars. The AMA monitors these overall ratings to compare them with similar programs and to track increases in ratings over time. With a large number of forms, these ratings can be useful in making comparisons. In some cases, targets or norms are established to compare ratings.[14,15] This can be particularly helpful in courses which are repeated several times. When using a norm scale, a rating that is normally considered good may prove to be quite low when compared to the norm of the factor being rated. Another caution is needed here. Since these ratings are subjective, putting them in numerical terms may create an impression that the data are objective. This point should be clearly communicated when presenting evaluation summaries.

Collect information related to cost savings. It is difficult to get realistic input on a feedback form related to cost reductions or savings, but it is worth a try. The response may be surprising. Just a simple question will sometimes cause participants to concentrate on cost savings. A possible statement might be:

As a result of this program, please estimate the savings in dollars that will be realized (i.e., increased productivity, improved methods, reduced costs, etc.) over a period of one year. $_____ Please explain the basis of your estimate.

_____
_____

Express as a percent the confidence you place on your estimate. (0% = no confidence, 100% = certainty) _____

Allow ample time for completing the form. A time crunch can cause problems when participants are asked to complete a feedback form at the end of a program, particularly if they are in a hurry to leave. Consequently, the information will be cut short in an effort to finish and leave. A possible alternative is to allow ample time for evaluation as a scheduled session before the end of the program. This could possibly be followed by a wrap up of the program and the last speaker. Another alternative is to allow participants to mail the evaluation later. With this approach, a reminder may be necessary to secure all of the forms.

Put the information collected to use. Finally, sometimes participant feedback is solicited, tabulated, summarized, and then disregarded. The information is collected for one or more of the purposes of evaluation.

Otherwise, the exercise is a waste of the participants' time. Too often instructors or program evaluators use the material to feed their egos and let it quietly disappear in the files, forgetting the original purposes for its collection. The last chapter on communicating program results reveals several possibilities for disseminating this evaluation information.

Advantages/Disadvantages

There are some obvious advantages to feedback questionnaires. Two very important ones are:

☐ They obtain a quick reaction from the participants while information is still fresh on their minds. Quite often, at the end of a program, participants have passed judgment on the usefulness of the program material. This reaction can be helpful to make adjustments or to provide evidence of the program's effectiveness.
☐ They are easy to administer, usually taking only a few minutes. And, if constructed properly, they can be easily analyzed, tabulated, and summarized.

The disadvantages to feedback questionnaires are:

☐ The data are subjective, based on the opinions and feelings of the participants at that time. Personal bias may exaggerate the ratings.
☐ Participants often are too polite in their ratings. At the end of a program, they are often pleased and may be happy just to get it out of the way. Therefore, a positive rating may be given when they actually feel differently.

☐ A good rating at the end of a program is no assurance that the participants will practice what has been taught in the program.

In summary, there is a definite place for feedback questionnaires in HRD program evaluation. They can provide a very convenient method of data collection. Ideally, it should be only a part of the total evaluation process.

Feedback from Others

Another useful data-collection method involves soliciting feedback from other individuals closely identified with the participants in the program. Typically, these groups fall into five categories: (1) supervisors of the participants, (2) subordinates of the participants, (3) peers, (4) members of the HRD staff, and (5) specially trained observers.

Supervisors

The most common group for feedback is the supervisors of those attending HRD programs. This feedback provides detailed information on performance improvement which resulted from the HRD program. Possibly the best person to evaluate performance is the participant's supervisor, particularly if he has been instructed to observe the participant. This "feedback from the boss" is usually obtained during a follow-up evaluation using an instrument such as a questionnaire or an interview. The questions on the instrument should be designed to solicit specific information that will reveal as much tangible change as possible. This method can develop very reliable feedback data.

Subordinates

Probably the second most often used feedback group is the subordinates of the participants of an HRD program. This information may not be as reliable as that obtained from the participant's boss but can nevertheless be valuable in the evaluation process. The information will be subjective and may be biased or opinionated, depending on the employee's attitude toward the participant. Generally, with this type of data-collection method, employees are asked about changes or improvements in their supervisor's behavior since he attended an HRD program. Table 8-3 shows an example of results collected from subordinates. Patterned

Table 8-3
Subordinate Evaluation of HRD Program Participants

Effectiveness in Resolving Critical Situations Before and After Supervisory Training* (as Perceived by Employees)	No. of Situations
More effective resolution	7
No change	2
Total	9

*Number of Supervisors=6
(Source: Agway, Inc., Syracuse, New York. Reproduced with permission from Development Dimensions International, Pittsburgh, Pennsylvania.)

interviews were conducted with subordinates of supervisors before the supervisors were trained in a program of Interaction Modeling. Six months after the training, follow-up interviews were conducted to determine how effectively the supervisors handled nine specific employee situations. The results show that there were seven situations where the resolution was more effective after the training program.

Peers

Probably the least used feedback group is the peer group. This involves soliciting feedback from peers to see how participants have performed after an HRD program. This technique is rare, since it is highly subjective and may be unreliable because of the loose ties between the evaluator and the participant. The other two groups have a closer identification. The techniques of data gathering for this type of feedback are through questionnaires or interviews.

A word of caution is in order for collecting information from the previous three groups. Any information collected from another group may tend to put the participant on trial. Members of that group are watching unusually close to see if the participant performs in a particular manner. This close scrutiny, while it may be important to evaluation, may not be appropriate for the acceptance and endorsement of the overall HRD program.

Staff Evaluation

Another group used for feedback purposes is the HRD staff. In these situations, staff members, properly trained in observation techniques, observe participants and provide feedback on their performance. The specific methods of observation used to gather feedback on participant performance were outlined in Chapter 5. Staff evaluation can be very helpful and can represent a very professional and unbiased method of data collection.

Assessment Center Method

The final method of data collection involving feedback from others is a formal procedure called the assessment center method. The feedback is provided by a group of specially trained observers (called assessors), not usually HRD staff members as in the previous section. For years the assessment center approach has been a very effective tool for employee selection. It now shows great promise as a tool for evaluating the effectiveness of an HRD program.[16]

Assessment centers are not actually centers, i.e., a location or building. The term refers to a procedure for evaluating the performance of individuals. In a typical assessment center the individuals being assessed participate in a variety of exercises which enable them to demonstrate a particular skill, knowledge, or ability, usually called job dimensions. These dimensions are important to on-the-job success for individuals for which the program was developed. One organization identified the following job dimensions for first-line supervisors:

☐ Oral communication   ☐ Planning and organizing
☐ Written communication   ☐ Analysis
☐ Reading skills   ☐ Judgment
☐ Initiative   ☐ Sensitivity
☐ Leadership   ☐ Management identification
☐ Delegation   ☐ Technical knowledge

The participants are evaluated or "assessed" by the assessors, and the evaluation is in the form of a rating for each dimension. This process takes anywhere from four hours to three days for the participants to complete all the exercises. The assessors then combine individual ratings and remove subjectivity to reach a final rating for each participant.

In HRD program evaluation the assessment center process gives a rating or "an assessment" of the participants prior to the HRD program. After the program is conducted, the participants are assessed again to see if there are improvements in their performance in the job dimensions. The use of a control group in an evaluation design helps to produce evidence of the impact of training.

When used as an evaluation tool, the participants are placed in a high-risk situation where they are asked to exhibit new and untried behaviors. In selection, this is not the case, since those being assessed will produce lower-risk behavior to second guess the assessors' desired outcomes.

Not all of this type of evaluation requires the use of a preprogram assessment, as was the case with the University of Alabama. For years the University's management institute had been conducting training programs for supervisors and managers. In four weeks of training the participants learned a variety of management skills. In 1980, the institute used the assessment center method to determine if those who had been trained out-performed those without training.

A total of 21 managers were assessed: 10 in an experimental group who had completed the 4 weeks of training, and 11 in an untrained control group. The members for the experimental group were selected at random from more than 50 persons who had completed the program. The untrained control group members were selected to provide a match with the members of the experimental group on demographic variables such as level in the organization, education, background, and experience. The results of the assessment indicated a significantly higher performance in the dimensions assessed in the experimental group. Table 8-4 shows the percentages in each group evaluated as satisfactory or better. The experimental group (E) outperformed the control group (C) in every category.

Table 8-4
Assessment Center Evaluation of an HRD Program

Performance of Experimental and Control Groups at
Alabama's Management Institute*

Dimensions	E................................ 100
Oral communications	C————————————63.7
	E................................ 100
Sensitivity	C————————————63.7
	E................................ 100
Leadership	C————————————72.8
	E........................ 80
Delegation	C————————————63.7
	E............................ 90
Planning & organizing	C————————————72.8
	E........................ 80
Problem analysis	C————————45
	E............................ 90
Judgment	C————————45
	E............................ 90
Decisiveness	C————————————81.9
	E............................ 93.3
Total	C————————————63.6

*Based on a scale of from 0–100%.
(Reproduced with permission from Development Dimensions International, Pittsburgh, Pennsylvania.)

Although the popularity of this method seems to be growing, it still may not be feasible in some organizations. The use of an assessment center is quite involved and time consuming for the participants and the assessors. The assessors have to be carefully trained to be objective and reliable. However, for programs which represent large expenditures aimed at making improvements in the soft-data area, the assessment center approach may be the most promising way to measure the impact of the program. This is particularly true for an organization where the assessment center process is already in use for selection purposes.

Participant Follow-Up

Another common data-collection method is the participant follow-up at a predetermined time after program completion. The follow-up evaluation almost always follows an end-of-the-program evaluation. In fact, in many situations the follow-up relates back to a previous evaluation. This follow-up normally involves the use of a feedback questionnaire, although other variations include interviews and observations. The primary purposes of the follow-up are:

☐ To help measure the lasting results of the program.
☐ To isolate the areas where participants show the most improvement.
☐ To compare the responses at follow-up time with those provided at the end of the program.

The follow-up evaluation usually focuses on learning retention, on-the-job application and organizational impact. In some evaluation models, follow-up evaluation is considered the most important phase of evaluation.[17] It usually occurs three to twelve months after training is completed with the most common time frame being six months. For more comprehensive evaluation, the follow-up could occur at repeated intervals (i.e., at six months or one year intervals). This approach will depend on the organization's emphasis on long-term results from the program.

Useful Guidelines

The design principles used in follow-up evaluation were outlined with the appropriate instrument in Chapter 5. In addition to those principles, here are some useful guidelines that will enhance the effectiveness of this follow-up. Appendix 5 provides a detailed example of a follow-up questionnaire.

Determine progress made since the program. This is an excellent time to determine what the participant has accomplished with the material presented in the HRD program. Ideally, there will be additional data that reflects the success of the program. Each item which required an action at the end of the program should be checked at the follow-up to see what was accomplished.

Ask many of the same or similar questions. To provide the continuity for data comparison, the questions asked on the end-of-program questionnaire should be repeated on the follow-up, if appropriate. For example, a question at the end of a program on the relevancy of the program content to the job could be asked again on the follow-up. By this time, the participant has attempted to use the program material. Different responses to the same question could reveal a problem in program content. If the participant was asked to estimate a dollar savings as a result of the program, then a follow-up question should ask what dollar savings did materialize as a result of the program.

Solicit reasons for lack of results. Not all follow-ups will generate positive results. Some will indicate no improvement or will contain negative comments. A good follow-up will try to determine why the participant did not achieve results. There can be many obstacles to performance improvement such as lack of support from superiors, restricting policies and procedures, or lack of interest on the part of the participant. Identifying these obstacles can be almost as valuable as identifying the reasons for success, since the obstacles can possibly be avoided in future programs.

The follow-up should be carefully planned. A plan should be developed to solicit follow-up information. The plan should answer the questions of who, what, where, when, and how as they relate to the administration of the follow-up. In AT&T, a plan for follow-up is developed in almost the same detail required for program development. The time period for the follow-up is critical. It should be long enough so that the desired improvement can take place, yet short enough so that material is still relatively fresh.

Participants should expect a follow-up. There should be no surprises at follow-up time. The intention to administer a follow-up instrument should be clearly communicated during the program, preferably at the end. Also, participants should know what information is expected from them in the follow-up.

Consider a follow-up assignment. In some cases, follow-up assignments can enhance the evaluation process. In a typical follow-up assignment, the participant is instructed to meet a goal or complete a particular task or project by the follow-up date. The following box shows an example of a follow-up assignment for a new supervisor to conduct discussions presented in the HRD program. A summary of the results

---

Follow-Up Assignment

To reinforce the use of Interaction Management (IM) skills, we are asking you to complete a case study of a successful discussion or series of discussions.

Three months after the end of this program, please document successful discussions that you have held with an employee. This case study should outline:

☐ The problem.
☐ The type of discussion(s) held with the employee.
☐ The significant points of the discussions.
☐ What you agreed to do and when.
☐ The problems you encountered.

Subsequent discussions should be documented. For each discussion, please supply the previous information. When the discussions result in improvement, please note the extent of improvement. If the problem was solved or problems were avoided, please indicate so.

The attached example shows how the discussion should be documented. You might only have one discussion. For instance, handling an employee complaint may require only one discussion. Motivating the average performer may require only one discussion.

The objective of this assignment is to document successful discussions. By successful we mean that you followed the critical steps and accomplished the objective of the discussion. If there was no improvement, explain why you think there was none.

This case study should be typed, reviewed with your department head, and a copy forwarded to the Training and Development Department. Please be precise, accurate, and factual in your reports.

These reports will be used to show improvements as a result of utilizing IM skills. The reports will be reviewed by various members of top management.

If you need assistance, please do not hesitate to call the Training and Development Department.

---

of these completed assignments provides further evidence of the impact of the HRD program. A variation of the assignment is a follow-up case, where participants have the opportunity to test themselves to be sure they have learned the material.[18]

Follow-up information should be shared with the participant's supervisor. Ideally, the participant's immediate supervisor should be involved in the application of what was learned in the HRD program. At a very minimum, the supervisor should know about what results have been achieved and receive the information on the follow-up evaluation.

Completing the follow-up should be required. The follow-up evaluation should not be optional. Participants are expecting it, and the HRD department must see that it is accomplished. This input is essential to determine the impact of the program. Good response from the follow-up evaluations is not difficult to come by. Some organizations, such as Shell Oil, boast of a 100% response on follow-up evaluation after the first reminder.

Advantages/Disadvantages

The follow-up method of data collection has the following advantages:

- ☐ It is easy to administer and easy to tabulate.
- ☐ It provides a more accurate assessment of the impact of the program when compared to the end-of-the-program questionnaire.
- ☐ It helps to measure the lasting results of the program.

The major disadvantages are:

- ☐ The information supplied by the participant may be subjective.
- ☐ It needs the cooperation of the supervisor.
- ☐ There may be intervening factors affecting the results.
- ☐ The participants may not have the opportunity to apply what they have learned.

In summary, participant follow-up is a commonly used technique for collecting evaluation data. Even with its shortcomings it is a very important part of evaluation.

Action Plan Audit

An action plan audit is an extension of the follow-up assignment described in the previous section. In this approach HRD program participants are required to develop action plans as part of the program. These action plans contain detailed steps to accomplish specific objectives related to the program. The plan is typically prepared on a printed form such as the one shown here. The action plan shows what is to be done, by whom, and at what time to accomplish the objectives. The action plan approach is a straightforward, easy-to-use method for determining how participants will change their behavior back on the job. The approach produces data which answers such questions as:

☐ What happened on the job as a result of the HRD program?
☐ Are the improvements the ones expected by the program designers?
☐ What may have prevented participants from accomplishing specific action items?

With this information, HRD professionals can decide if a program should be modified and in what ways, while managers can assess the findings to evaluate the worth of the program.

The Approach

The action plan approach can have a tremendous impact on the organization. In one of Shell Oil Company's sales training programs, participants were required to develop an action plan to secure a new customer. Much of the material in the program was aimed at developing a strategy to convert a potential customer to an existing customer. In the follow-up, the participants indicated whether or not they had success with their potential customer, an easy item to measure. The dollar volume of the new customer is the additional sales resulting from the HRD program. In one example, Shell was trying to sell a major automobile manufacturer. For years they had been trying to get this manufacturer to use Shell's lubricant in its air conditioning system. One salesman picked that manufacturer as a potential customer. Following the strategy developed in the program, the new customer was actually secured, resulting in several million dollars of additional sales. That one example more than paid for the entire cost of the program up to that point.

The action plan approach is used by many organizations with excellent results. Probably the most comprehensive application to this approach

ACTION PLAN WORKSHEET

NAME _____ DEPARTMENT/SECTION _____ DATE _____

INSTRUCTIONS: TO BE COMPLETED AFTER PROBLEM ANALYSIS HAS BEEN CONDUCTED AND KEY AREAS FOR ACTION IDENTIFIED.

OVERALL OBJECTIVE

NO	OBJECTIVE (Goal)	ACTION TO BE TAKEN (What will be done)	PERSON RESPONSIBLE (who)	TARGET DATE (when)	ACTUAL DATE COMPLETED

PAGE _____ OF _____

has occurred in the U.S. Government. The Office of Personnel Management has developed a method called the Participant Action Plan Approach (PAPA).[19] This approach can be used independently as the entire evaluation process, or it can be used in conjunction with other evaluation methods. The approach centers around five basic steps as shown in Figure 8-2. In general, PAPA requires the participant to develop action plans listing behaviors he wants to try when he returns to the job. The plans are based on the content of the HRD program just experienced. After a set time, the participant is contacted to see what changes he has actually been able to implement.

Developing the Action Plan

The development of the action plan requires two tasks: (1) determining the areas for action, and (2) writing the action items. Both tasks should be completed during the HRD program.

The areas for action should come from the material presented in the HRD program and, at the same time, be related to on-the-job activities. A list of potential areas for action can be developed, a list may be generated by the participants in a group discussion, or possibly, a participant may identify an area needing improvement for his particular situation.

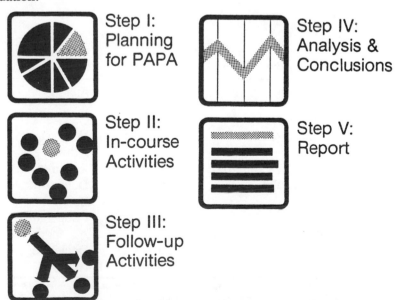

Step I:
Planning
for PAPA

Step IV:
Analysis &
Conclusions

Step II:
In-course
Activities

Step V:
Report

Step III:
Follow-up
Activities

Figure 8-2. The participant action plan approach.

The following questions should be asked when developing the areas for action:

☐ How much time will this action take?
☐ Are the skills for accomplishing this action item available?
☐ Who has the authority to implement the action plan?
☐ Will this action have an effect on other individuals?
☐ Are there any organizational constraints for accomplishing this action item?

The specific action items are usually more difficult to write than the identification of the action areas. The most important characteristic of an action item is that it is written so that everyone involved will know when it occurs. One way to help achieve this goal is to use specific action verbs as shown in Table 8-5. This is only a partial list of the many verbs that can be used to begin an action item. Some examples of action items are:

☐ Learn how to operate the new RC-105 drill press machine in the adjacent department.
☐ Identify and secure a new customer account.
☐ Handle every piece of paper only once to improve my personal time management.

Table 8-5
Active Verbs Used in Writing Action Plans

	Mental Skill	Physical Skill	Attitude
State	Demonstrate	Execute	Choose
Name	Discriminate	Operate	Volunteer
Describe	Classify	Repair	Allow
Relate	Generate (a solution)	Adjust	Recommend
Tell	Apply (a rule)	Manipulate	Defend
Write	Solve	Handle	Endorse
Express	Derive	Manufacture	Cooperate
Recount	Prove	Calibrate	Accept
Learn	Analyze	Remove	Decide to
Identify	Evaluate	Replace	Agree

(Source: Office of Personnel Management, "Assessing Changes in Job Behavior Due to Training: A Guide to the Participant Action Plan Approach," U.S. Government Printing Office (February 1980).

☐ Talk with my employers directly about a problem which arises rather than avoiding a confrontation.

If appropriate, each action item should have a date for completion and indicate other individuals or resources required for completion. Also, planned behavior changes should be observable. It should be obvious to the participant and others when it happens.

Action plans, as used in this context, do not require the prior approval or input from the participant's supervisor, although it may be helpful. Participants may not have prior knowledge of the action-plan requirement for the program. Frequently, an introduction to, and a description of, the process is an integral part of the program.

The action plans should be reviewed before the end of the HRD program to check for accuracy, feasibility, and completeness. At that time, it should be made clear to the participant that the plan will be audited.

The Audit

To tabulate the results achieved from the action plans, an audit (or follow-up) is conducted-usually four-to-six months after the program is completed. This audit will reveal and document what progress has been made toward the planned objectives and reviews the detailed steps that were planned. It can be accomplished through either a questionnaire or interview.

Questionnaires are mailed to participants at the specified follow-up time. The questionnaire has a cover letter followed by a detailed list of questions about the action plan, much like any other audit. The questionnaire has ample space for the participant to describe, for each action item, what was done, how it was done, who was involved, and how often it was tried. The detailed results are documented. If the items were not accomplished, information is gathered to explain why they were not accomplished. Problems encountered or obstacles to success are listed.

Using the previous approach, questionnaires are gathered directly from every participant. Other options that can be just as effective are:

☐ Contacting only a sample of the participants for a follow-up.
☐ Reconvening the class of participants to complete the follow-up questionnaires.
☐ Obtaining input from both the participant and his supervisor.

The interview method of follow-up begins with a letter reminding participants about the follow-up. This letter focuses attention on the action items before the interviews take place. Participants are contacted for an appointment. The participant should be interviewed at his own convenience to minimize distractions on the job. The interview approach should follow the principles outlined in Chapter 5. Basically, the same information is obtained in the interview that is obtained in the question-naire. The difference is that the information is gathered face-to-face or over the telephone.

The impact of the action plan process is impressive. In a medium size manufacturing facility, a training program was developed for first-level supervisors that focused on improving interpersonal skills with employees. Several of the areas tackled were productivity improvement, scrap reduction, absenteeism, turnover, grievances, and safety. These areas were discussed thoroughly and the supervisors improved their skills in how to make improvements in each area and how to handle problems and discussions that may develop. Supervisors were required to develop action plans for improvement in each area and report the results later. In a follow-up six months after the program, the following results were documented for a pilot group:

☐ The department unit hour had increased from 65 to 75. This is a basic measure of productivity, where a unit hour of 60 is considered to be average and acceptable work.
☐ Scrap was reduced from 11% to 7.4%.
☐ Absenteeism was reduced from 7% to 3.25%.
☐ The annual turnover rate was drastically reduced from 30% to 5%.
☐ The number of grievances was reduced 80%.
☐ Lost time accidents were reduced 95%.

These results were achieved by the supervisors practicing what they had learned and reporting results in follow-up evaluation sessions. It's an indication of the impact of a supervisory training program when it is targeted for specific improvements and action plans and follow-ups are used to ensure that those improvements are realized.

Advantages/Disadvantages

The action plan approach is very flexible and has many inherent advantages:

☐ It is simple and easy to administer, and participants can understand the approach.
☐ It can be used with a wide variety of different HRD programs.
☐ It can be used to collect a variety of information and can measure reaction, learning, and results.
☐ It can be used independently as the only method of evaluation or in conjunction with other evaluation methods.

Although there are many advantages, there are at least three disadvantages to this data-collection method:

☐ The method relies on direct input from the participant. As such, the information can be biased and unreliable.
☐ There may be a problem with the type of data collected. It is usually subjective, in the soft-data category. If more concrete information is available through some other method, then it should be used.
☐ It can be time consuming for the participant and, if the participant's supervisor is not involved in the process, there may be a tendency for the participant not to complete the assignment.

Performance Contract

The performance contract is another effective data-collection method. Essentially, it is a slight variation of the action-plan process described in the previous section. It is based on the principle of mutual goal setting which has become a well-established process. It is a written agreement between a participant and the participant's supervisor. The participant agrees to improve performance in an area of mutual concern related to the subject material in the HRD program. The agreement is in the form of a project to be completed or goal to be accomplished soon after the program is over. The agreement spells out what is to be accomplished at what time and with what results. An example of a detailed performance contract is contained in Appendix 6. The example contains the following items:

☐ Subject   ☐ Activities
☐ Objective   ☐ Time
☐ Goals   ☐ Costs
☐ Problems   ☐ Benefits
☐ Solutions   ☐ Commitment
☐ Resources

The commitment section requires both parties to sign the agreement and commit themselves to making the improvements as outlined in the contract.

Steps in the Process

Although the steps can vary according to the specific kind of contract and the organization, a common sequence of events is as follows:

1. The participant and supervisor mutually agree on a subject for improvement.
2. A specific, measurable goal(s) is set.
3. The participant attends the HRD program where the contract is discussed, and plans are developed to accomplish the goals.
4. After the program, the participant works on the contract against a specific deadline.
5. The participant reports the results of the effort to his supervisor.
6. The supervisor and participant document the results and forward a copy to the HRD department along with appropriate comments.

Selecting the Subject

The individuals mutually select the subject or topic for improvement prior to the beginning of the HRD program. The topic can cover one or more of the following areas:

☐ **Routine performance**—includes specific improvements in routine performance measures such as production targets, efficiency, and error rates.
☐ **Problem solving**—focuses on specific problems such as an unexpected increase in accidents, a decrease in efficiency, or a loss of morale.
☐ **Innovative or creative applications**—includes initiating changes or improvements in work practices, methods, procedures, techniques, and processes.
☐ **Personal development**—involves learning new information or acquiring a new skill to increase individual effectiveness.

Requirements for the Contract

The topic selected should be stated in terms of one or more objectives. The objectives should state what is to be accomplished when the contract is complete. These objectives should be:

☐ Written.
☐ Understandable (by all involved).
☐ Challenging (requiring an unusual effort to achieve).
☐ Achievable (something that can be achieved).
☐ Largely under the control of the participant.
☐ Measurable and dated.

The details to accomplish the objectives of the contract are developed following the guidelines under action plans presented earlier.

Reporting Progress

If the contract extends more than one month from the end of the HRD program, participants should possibly submit progress reports outlining what has been accomplished. Upon completion of the contract, a summary report should be submitted to the participant's supervisor. The report outlines the initial objectives and the standards by which the objectives were measured. It reviews the problems encountered and how they were solved, along with specific activities, costs, and benefits. A detailed statement of the results achieved is a significant part of the progress report. In addition, the participant's supervisor, after reviewing the report, makes appropriate comments outlining his satisfaction with the activity. Then the progress report is forwarded to the HRD department and becomes additional data to evaluate the program. Several variations are possible on the follow-up of the performance contract. The methods outlined in the previous section may be helpful to assure that this final report is accomplished and is ultimately received by the HRD department.

The performance contract is another powerful technique to secure impressive results with an HRD program. Tektronix Inc., an electronics company uses this technique in a program for senior managers.[20] Objectives are set for managers prior to the program. During the two-year program, the participants must produce a business impact project that directly relates to Tektronix's business. Past projects have included the design of a new lab and the development of a new distribution method for one of the company's products.

Other Variations of the Contract Approach

There can be many other variations of the goal-oriented approach to applications of material covered in an HRD program. One such variation is the learning contract. This process is promoted by Malcolm Knowles and focuses on a contract to learn a new activity or improve in a particular area.[21] This is a self-contract with the individual. The contract may not even be related to a particular HRD program but instead represent a self-development activity. Also, the results from the contract may or may not be reviewed by other individuals, although Knowles recommends a peer-group review for many types of contracts.

This variation reveals a flexibility in participants developing goals to be accomplished as a result of an HRD program. Basically, four variations of this goal-oriented, post-program behavior have been explored: (1) follow-up assignments, (2) action plan audits, (3) performance contracts, and (4) learning contracts. Table 8-6 shows the basic differences in these data-collection methods.

The six factors make the difference in these four approaches. Other combinations of these four methods enable the HRD professional to develop the custom-designed data-collection method appropriate for the organization while optimizing the transfer of training to assure that results are obtained.

Ex-Post-Facto Evaluation

The underlining theme of the results-oriented model presented in Chapter 4 is that evaluation should be integrated into all elements of the HRD process. Unfortunately, in many real world applications, this is not always possible. Even if evaluation is not part of the program, an ex-post-facto system can incorporate many of the same elements. Obviously participants cannot be pretested or reaction questionnaires cannot be administered at the end of a program. Nor can you normally bring the participants back together for an evaluation. However, it is still possible to develop an evaluation input at all four levels of evaluation using the ex-post-facto approach.[22]

This approach requires follow-up with the participants in the program, gathering input to address each of the four areas of evaluation. As a first

Table 8-6
A Comparison of Goal-Oriented Data-Collection Methods

Features		Follow-Up Assignment	Action Plan Audit	Performance Contract	Learning Contract
Topic selection	Little flexibility	✔			
	Much flexibility		✔	✔	✔
Supervisor participation	Required			✔	
	Optional	✔	✔		
	Unnecessary				✔
Announcement prior to program	Yes			✔	
	No	✔			✔
	Optional		✔		
Techniques discussed in program	Yes		✔	✔	
	No				✔
	Optional	✔			
Specific format required	Yes		✔	✔	
	No				✔
	Optional	✔			
Feedback of results	Required	✔	✔	✔	
	Optional				✔

step, the goals of the program need to be developed based on input from the individuals who designed the program, conducted the program, and those who attended the program. Once the goals are clarified, the evaluation can be addressed at the four levels.

Satisfaction. Regardless of the time that has elapsed since completing the program, participants are capable of providing input on satisfaction. A reaction questionnaire, similar to the one that would have been administered at the end of the program can be provided to the participants. They are asked to evaluate the environment, the presenters, the length, and the content any other items appropriate for feedback questionnaires.

Learning. Based on specific objectives from the program, a test can be developed to assess what the participants learned. The variety of different tests discussed earlier can be used to measure learning.

Behavior. Behavioral change is more dificult to assess but can be evaluated using instruments outlined in Chapter 5. A good methodology for the ex-post-factor approach is a personal interview with the participant and his or her immediate peer group, subordinates and superiors. The interview should be conducted in terms of the behavioral results targeted in the training program.

Results. In this level, an assessment of the ultimate outcomes is developed using a variety of instruments and data collection methods. Performance measures are usually examined as well as specific improvements uncovered.

In summary, the ex-post-facto approach to evaluation is offered for those instances where prior planning for the evaluation process was omitted. It is particularly useful when a program has not been evaluated but suddenly management wants to know about results. The evaluator does not have to wait until the next program is conducted to assess its impact. Using the ex-post-facto approach, the evaluator reconstructs what happened and measures the impact.

Simulation

A final method of data collection is the use of job simulations. This method involves the construction and application of a procedure or task that simulates or models the activity for which the HRD program is being conducted. The simulation is designed to represent, as closely as possible, the actual job situation. Simulation may be used as an integral part of the HRD program as well as for evaluation. In evaluation, participants are provided an opportunity to try out their performance in the simulated activity and have it evaluated based on how well the task was accomplished. The assessment center method covered earlier is actually a simulation. Each exercise is designed to reproduce a work situation where participants exhibit behavior related to one or more job dimension. Simulations may be used during the program, at the end of the program, or as part of the follow-up evaluation.

Advantages of Simulations

Job simulations offer several advantages for the HRD professional.[23] These are highlighted here.

Reproducibility. Simulations permit a job or part of a job to be reproduced in a manner almost identical to the real setting. Through careful planning and design, the simulation can have all of the central characteristics of the real situation. Even complex jobs, such as that of the manager, can be simulated adequately. In addition, simulation can allow the HRD professional to shorten the time required to perform a task in an actual environment.

Cost effectiveness. Although possibly expensive to construct, simulations can be cost effective in the long run. For example, it is cost prohibitive to train airline pilots to fly an airplane utilizing a $50 million aircraft. Therefore, an aircraft simulator is used to simulate all of the flying conditions and enable the pilot to learn to fly before boarding the actual vehicle. In many other situations the cost involved in learning on the job also becomes prohibitive to the point where simulation becomes much more attractive.

Safety considerations. Another advantage of using simulations is safety. In the aircraft simulator example, safety is an important consideration for utilizing a flight simulator. It would be too dangerous for the pilot to learn how to fly an airplane without the use of a simulator. The nature of many other jobs requires participants to be trained in simulated conditions instead of real situations. For example, in training emergency medical technicians, the possible risk of life is too great to have someone learn how to administer emergency medical techniques on a victim as part of the training process. Firemen are trained on simulated conditions prior to being exposed to actual fires. CIA agents are trained in simulated conditions prior to being exposed to their real-world environment. For safety reasons, the applications for simulation are varied.

Simulation Techniques

There are a variety of simulation techniques used to evaluate program results. The most common techniques are presented here.

Electrical/mechanical simulation. This technique uses a combination of electronics and mechanical devices to simulate the real-life situations. They are used in conjunction with programs to develop operational and diagnostic skills. Expensive examples of these types include simulated "patients" or a simulator for a nuclear power plant operator. Other less expensive types of simulators have been developed to simulate equipment operation.

Task simulation. Another approach involves the performance of a simulated task as part of an evaluation. For example, in an aircraft company technicians are trained on the safe removal, handling, and installation of a radioactive source used in a nucleonic oil-quantity indicator gauge. These technicians attend a thorough training program on all of the procedures necessary for this important assignment. To become certified to perform this task, technicians are observed in a simulation where they perform all the necessary steps on a checkoff card. After they have demonstrated that they possess the skills necessary for the safe performance of this assignment, they become certified by the instructor. This task simulation serves as the evaluation of the program.

Business games. Business games have grown in popularity in recent years. They represent simulations of a part or all of a business enterprise. Participants change the variables of the business and observe the effect of those changes. The game not only reflects the real-world situation but represents the synopsis of the HRD program of which it is a part. Given certain objectives, the participants play the game and their output is monitored. Their performance can usually be documented and measured. Typical objectives are to maximize profit, sales, market share, or return on investment. Those participants who maximize the objectives are those who usually have the highest performance in the program.

In-basket. Another simulation technique called an in-basket is particularly useful in supervisory and management training programs. Portions of a supervisor's job are simulated through a series of items that normally appear in the in-basket. These items are typically memos, notes, letters, and reports which create realistic conditions facing the supervisor. The participant must decide what to do with each item while taking into consideration the principles taught in the HRD program. The participant's performance in the in-basket represents an evaluation of the program. In some situations every course of action for each item in the in-basket is rated, and a combination of the chosen alternatives provides an overall rating on the in-basket. This provides a performance score representing the participant's ability to handle the program material in an adequate manner.

Case study. Possibly a less-effective, but still popular, technique of simulation is a case study. A case study represents a detailed description of a problem and usually contains a list of several questions posed to the participant. The participant is asked to analyze the case and determine the best course of action. The problem should reflect the conditions in the real-world setting and the content in an HRD program.

The most common categories of case studies include[24]:

☐ *Exercise* case studies, which provide an opportunity for participants to practice the application of specific procedures.
☐ *Situation* case studies, which provide participants the opportunity to analyze information and make decisions surrounding their particular situation.
☐ *Complex* case studies, which are an extension of the situation case study, where the participant is required to handle a large amount of data and information, some of which may be irrelevant.
☐ *Decision* case studies, which require the participant to go a step further than the previous categories and present plans for solving a particular problem.
☐ *Critical incident* case studies, which provide the participant with a certain amount of the information and withhold other information until it is requested by the participant.
☐ *Action maze* case studies, which present a large case in a series of smaller units. The participant is required to predict at each stage what will happen next.

The difficulty in a case study lies in the objective evaluation of the performance of participants. Frequently, there can be many possible courses of action, some equally as effective as others, making it extremely difficult to obtain an objective measurable performance rating for the analysis and interpretation of the case.

Role playing. In role playing, sometimes referred to as skill practice, participants practice a newly learned skill and are observed by other individuals. Participants are given their assigned role with specific instructions, which sometimes includes an ultimate course of action. The participant then practices the skill with other individuals to accomplish the desired objectives. This is intended to simulate the real-world setting to the greatest extent possible. A difficulty sometimes arises when other participants involved in the skill practices make the practice unrealistic by not reacting the way individuals would in an actual situation. To help overcome this obstacle, trained role players (non-participants trained for the role) may be used in all roles except that of the participant. This can possibly provide a more objective evaluation. The success of this technique also lies in the judgment of those observing the role plays. The skill of effective observation is as critical as the skill of the role player. Also, the success of this method depends on the participants' willingness to participate in and adjust to the planned role. If participant resistance is extremely high, the performance in the skill practice may not reflect the actual performance on the job. Nevertheless, these skill practices can be very useful, particularly in supervisory and sales training, to enable participants to practice discussion skills.[25]

In summary, simulations come in a wide variety They offer an opportunity for participants to practice what is being taught in an HRD program and have their performance observed in a simulated job condition. They can provide extremely accurate evaluations if the performance in the simulation is objective and can be clearly measured.

Summary

Beginning with a discussion of the types of data, this chapter presented the most common methods of data collection. Data can be grouped into two broad categories according to the degree of subjectivity and ease of measurement. Hard data are desired but not always available, in which case soft data are used. The following classifications of methods for collecting both hard and soft data were presented:

☐ Preprogram and post-program examinations
☐ Participant feedback
☐ Feedback from others
☐ Participant follow-up
☐ Action plan audit
☐ Performance contract
☐ Ex-post-facto evaluation
☐ Simulation

A program evaluation may use one or more of these methods to collect data. Each has its own advantages and limitations. The next chapter presents the techniques to analyze data after it has been collected.

Discussion Questions

1. Use examples to illustrate the difference between evaluation instrument design, evaluation design, and data collection methods.
2. Can all data be grouped into either hard data or soft data? Explain.
3. Identify additional hard data and soft data measurements from your organization (or one with which you are familiar).
4. Why is it important to obtain participant feedback in training programs?
5. One HRD manager commented . . . "Smile sheets (participant feedback forms) are not worth the time it takes to complete them. These happiness ratings do nothing but feed the ego of the instructor." Is this true? Explain.
6. Design a participant feedback form for a one-day workshop on improving interviewing skills.
7. What problems occur in collecting feedback from groups other than participants' supervisors?
8. Why are follow-up evaluations important?
9. Design a follow-up assignment for a performance appraisal workshop.
10. To what extent does your organization (or one with which you are familiar) use follow-up evaluation procedures?
11. Do organizations use performance contracts on a routine basis? Explain.
12. What advantages do the action plan audits have over learning contracts?
13. Is the ex-post-facto approach useful? Explain.
14. How have computers influenced the use of simulations in the evaluation process?
15. In your organization (or one with which you are familiar), which types of data collection methods are more commonly used? Why?

References

1. Kelley, A. I., Orgel, R. F., and Baer, D. M., "Evaluation: The Bottom Line is Closer Than You Think," *Training and Development Journal,* August 1984, p. 33.
2. Hennecke, M., "How Do You Know It Works?" *Training,* April 1988, p. 50.

3. Schuster, F. E., *The Schuster Report: The Proven Connection Between People and Profits,* John Wiley: New York, NY, 1986, pp. 69–70.
 4. Desatnick, R. L., "How HRD Took the Bite Out of McDonald's High Turnover," *Training,* September 1982, p. 45.
 5. Rosow, J. M. and Zager, R., "Teaching More for Less: IBM and Travenol Stretch Training Dollars," *The Human Resources Professional,* January–February 1989, p. 18.
 6. Hultman, K. E., "Behavioral Modeling for Results," *Training and Development Journal,* December 1986, p. 61.
 7. Swierczek, F. W. and Carmichael, L., "The Quantity and Quality of Evaluating Training," *Training and Development Journal,* January 1985, p. 96.
 8. Dixon, N. M., "Meet Training's Goals Without Reaction Forms," *Personnel Journal,* August 1987, pp. 108–112.
 9. Erickson, P. R., "Evaluating Training Results," *Training and Development Journal,* January 1990, p. 57.
10. Elkins, A., "Some Views on Management Training," *Personnel Journal,* June 1977, pp. 305–311.
11. Dixon, N. M., "The Relationship Between Trainee Responses on Participant Reaction Forms and Post-test Scores," *Human Resource Development Quarterly,* Vol. I, No. 2, Summer 1990, p. 129.
12. Newstrom, J. W., "Confronting Anomalies in Evaluation," *Training and Development Journal,* July 1987, p. 56–60.
13. Tyson, L. A. and Birnbrauer, H., "High Quality Evaluation," *Training and Development Journal,* September 1985, pp. 33–37.
14. Caldwell, R. M. and Marcel, M., "Evaluating Trainers: In Search of the Perfect Method," *Training,* January 1985, p. 52.
15. Woodard, W., "A Rating Scale for Adult Learning," *Training,* February 1990, pp. 63–64.
16. Byham, W. C., "How Assessment Centers Are Used to Evaluate Training's Effectiveness," *Training,* February 1982, p. 32.
17. Connolly, S. M., "Integrating Evaluation, Design, and Implementation," *Training and Development Journal,* February 1988, pp. 20–21.
18. Smith, M., "Sizing Up Your Training," *Personnel Administrator,* October 1987, p. 64.
19. Office of Personnel Management, "Assessing Changes in Job Behavior Due to Training: A Guide to the Participant Action Plan Approach," *U.S. Government Printing Office,* February 1980.
20. Coblentz, C., "Of Buy-In and Bottom Line," *Training,* December 1987, p. 12.
21. Wehrenberg, S. B., "Learning Contracts," *Personnel Journal,* September 1988, pp. 100–102.

22. Dunn, S. and Thomas, K., "Surpassing the Smile Sheet Approach to Evaluation," *Training,* April 1985, pp. 67–71.
23. Schachter, H. L., "Simulations for Training and Assessment: The Problem of Relevance to the World," *Public Personnel Management,* Vol. 9, 1980, pp. 225–227.
24. Armistead, C., "How Useful Are Case Studies," *Training and Development Journal,* February 1984, p. 75.
25. Robinson, L. J. B., "Role Playing As A Sales Training Tool," *Harvard Business Review,* May–June 1987, p. 35.

CHAPTER 9

Data Analysis

The data-collection methods in the previous chapter yield numerical data which must be analyzed and interpreted to be meaningful. The type of analysis necessary is usually determined when the evaluation is designed. This chapter presents the basic methods of data analysis with emphasis on statistical techniques. It covers procedures appropriate for typical evaluation data developed from HRD programs.

Data analysis is a complex, but important, subject—one that cannot be covered in complete detail in this book. The brief presentation of the techniques and examples in this chapter should give a sufficient overview for most evaluators. Armed with this, the HRD program evaluator should have adequate tools to analyze common evaluation data. To avoid confusion, some evaluators may want to skip this chapter or seek help for its application.

Guidelines for Analyzing Data

Before approaching the use of statistics, a review of a few very basic guidelines for analyzing evaluation data should be helpful.

Review for consistency and accuracy. While this guideline may be obvious, additional checks may be necessary to ensure the accuracy and consistency of the data. Incorrect or insufficient data items should be eliminated. A simple scan of data will usually reveal extreme data points or values that may seem impossible to obtain. Also, accuracy is of utmost importance. The analysis and interpretation will only be as reliable as the data itself. If caution is not exercised to ensure accurate data, then the remaining steps in the process are meaningless.

Use all relevant data. In most evaluations improvement is desired by the person conducting the evaluation. This may provide a built-in bias. Improvement will not always materialize. Some data will be both positive and negative. It may be tempting to eliminate data that does not support the desired outcome. All relevant data should be used for a valid analysis. If not, there should be an explanation of why it was deleted.

Treat individual data confidentially. Frequently, data collected will be the result of individual performances. When analyzing and interpreting data and reporting results, the confidentiality of the sources should be an important concern unless there are conditions which warrant their exposure. The same atmosphere of confidentiality used in collecting data should be used in the analysis and reporting phases. This should be clearly communicated to the participants before the evaluation begins.

Use the simplest statistics possible. There are many ways to analyze data. A variety of statistical techniques are available compare changes in performance. Additional analyses which may serve no further benefit should be avoided. The analysis should be kept as simple as possible and limited to what is necessary to draw the proper conclusions with the data.

As a simple example, suppose the average (mean) number of sales calls is a performance improvement measure for an HRD program on time and territory management for salespersons. Three measures of the average are available: the mean, the median, and the mode. The mean value is needed in the analysis. It does not add anything to the analysis to determine the median and the mode. These two numbers, while they can be easily identified, may serve to confuse the person receiving the evaluation results.

Use of Statistics

The terms "statistics" and "data analysis" are almost synonymous. According to *The Random House Dictionary,* statistics is the "science that deals with the collection, classification, analysis, and interpretation of numerical facts or data, and that, by use of mathematical theories of probability, imposes order and regularity on aggregates of more or less disparate elements." Unfortunately, it seems that statistics frighten those involved in HRD evaluation. Although confusing, the subject can be presented in a simplified manner—yet in enough detail—to be useful in even the most sophisticated evaluations.

This chapter is not intended to make a statistician of the reader. Many other books serve that purpose. The material which follows covers a few very basic concepts and provides enough insight so that simple analyses can be performed on frequently occurring situations. The simple and most useful statistics are presented first, followed by more sophisticated techniques.

Caution: The presentation of one part of the subject of statistics often leads to other possibilities, and it becomes difficult to generalize and simplify the procedures. Many variables can affect the kind of statistics to use and the type of analysis to pursue. Because of this, the HRD program evaluator may need to seek additional resources. Any sophisticated analysis involving all of the concepts in this chapter should be reviewed by someone familiar with statistical methods.

The use of statistics in evaluation has three primary purposes:

1. *Statistics enable large amounts of information to be summarized.* Probably the most practical use of statistics is the summary of information. Under this category there are two basic measures. One is the measure of central tendency, or average, which is the mean, median, and mode. This measure presents, in a single number, a summary of the characteristics of the entire group such as the average absenteeism rate for a group of employees.
   The other category is dispersion, or variance. The most useful measure of dispersion is the standard deviation. This reveals how much the individual items in the group are dispersed. For example, a large standard deviation for an average attendance means that there is a wide variation among the absenteeism records for the group of employees.
2. *Statistics allow for the determination of the relationship between two or more items.* In analyzing data the relationship between one or more items may be important. The term used for this relationship is "correlation," which represents the degree to which the items are related and is expressed in terms of a coefficient. A positive correlation between two items means that as one item increases, the other increases. For example, a high achievement score on a knowledge examination in an HRD program might correlate with a high level of performance on the job. There also can be a negative correlation between items. In this case the correlation coefficient is negative and, as one item increases, the other item decreases.
3. *Statistics show how to compare the differences in performance between two groups.* When performance improves after an HRD program, a likely question can be asked: "Did the improvement occur because of

the program, or could it have occurred by chance?'' In other words, without the HRD program, would the same results have been achieved? And, how accurately can the conclusions be drawn? Statistical analyses enable a confidence level to be placed on conclusions about differences in groups of data. Normally, conclusions are based on a 95% confidence level, which means that 95% of the time, on the average, the conclusions will be correct.

Frequency Distributions

Before reviewing the basic calculations involved in statistics, it is best to cover a useful way to present raw data, called a frequency distribution. For example, the data in Table 9-1 represents preprogram and post-program measurements of performance for a group of 15 employees. A unit hour is a measure of work pace equal to the allowed minutes of work produced in an hour's time. One way to

Table 9-1
Preprogram and Post-Program Measurements

Employee Number	Production Rates (Unit Hours) Before Training	After Training
1	43	47
2	45	59
3	61	79
4	59	69
5	66	63
6	54	55
7	49	51
8	52	58
9	55	72
10	60	63
11	50	61
12	55	60
13	58	65
14	56	63
15	63	67
Total	826	932

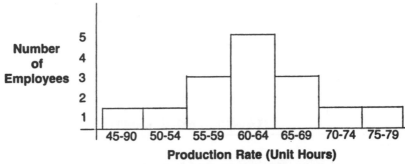

Figure 9-1. A frequency histogram.

present the post-training data is to group it into small ranges, called class intervals, as shown here:

Unit Hours by Class Intervals		Employees in Each Class
45–49		1
50–54		1
55–59		3
60–64		5
65–69		3
70–74		1
75–79		1
	Total	15

These groupings can be plotted on a diagram to yield what is called a frequency histogram as shown in Figure 9-1. This graphical presentation of the data reveals that, after training, more employees had a unit hour rating in the range of 60–64 than any other range. The graphical presentation of data can be useful to show the central tendency (where most of the items are grouped), and also the dispersion (the extent to which the data is scattered).

Statistical Measures

Measures of Central Tendency

As mentioned earlier, the most common measures of central tendency are the mean, median, and mode. The mean is the arithmetic average for a group of numbers. It is calculated by adding all of the values and dividing by the total number. The formula is

$$\bar{x} = \frac{\Sigma x_i}{n}$$

where: i=Subscript used to identify an individual employee.

x_i=The performance level of employee i.

Σ=Summation sign which means that the items following the sign should be added. Therefore, Σx_i is the sum of all the x values.

n=The sample size.

$\bar{x}$=The average value or mean for the sample.

To illustrate a calculation, refer to the data in Table 9-1. The post-training measurements yield a mean value of

$$\bar{x} = \frac{\Sigma x_i}{n} = \frac{932}{15} = 62.13$$

This figure represents the mean level of performance of the 15 employees after the HRD program. The mean is the number which best represents the set of data. It is the most useful statistic to show performance after completing an HRD program.

Another measure of central tendency is the median. The median is the middle value. When the numbers are arranged in order of magnitude, there are an equal number of values above and below the median. In the case of an even number of data items, the median is the average of the two middle values. The post-training data in Table 9-1 can be arranged in order of magnitude to present the following list:

Employee	Unit Hour
1	47
7	51
6	55
8	58
2	59

Table continued

Employee	Unit Hour	
12	60	
11	61	
5	63	Median
10	63	
14	63	
13	65	
15	67	
4	69	
9	72	
3	79	

The median is 63, the eighth number in the list of 15. The median can serve as a useful shortcut to show the estimate of the whole group when the mean is not readily available or is not required.

The final measure of central tendency is the mode. The mode of a set of numbers is the value which occurs with the greatest frequency; i.e., the most common value. In the previous example, 63 is the mode. It occurs three times in the list. The mode has limited application and may not even exist at all in some data. For instance, if all of the employees had different levels of performance, there would not be a mode for the distribution.

In summary, for the post-training data, the three measures of central tendency are:

Mean = 62.13
Median = 63
Mode = 63

This agrees with the conclusion about the frequency distribution in Figure 9-1 (i.e., the majority of employees have a unit hour rating in the range of 60–64). When the three measures are almost equal, the distribution is called normal or bell-shaped.

Measures of Dispersion

The degree to which data varies from the average, or mean, is called dispersion. The most common measures of dispersion are the range, variance, and the standard deviation. The range is the simplest measure of dispersion. It is the difference between the largest and smallest of a set of numbers. In the example of post-training values, the range is 79 minus 47, or 32. This value gives a simple picture of how much the data varies from one extreme point to the other. A larger range usually reflects more dispersion.

The variance is the average value of the squares of the deviations from the mean. It is calculated by the following formula:

$$s^2 = \frac{\Sigma(x_i - \bar{x})^2}{n}$$

Each item, x_i, is subtracted from the mean value, $\bar{x}$, and squared. These squared values are all added and divided by the sample size, n. The variance, denoted by s^2, reflects the degree to which the numbers vary from the mean. By itself, the variance is not very useful, since it represents squared values. A more useful value is the standard deviation, s. It is calculated by taking the square root of the variance

$$s = \sqrt{s^2} = \frac{\sqrt{\Sigma(x_i - \bar{x})^2}}{n}$$

As the name implies, standard deviation represents how much the data deviates from the mean value for the group. If the standard deviation is low, then the data are grouped together very closely to the mean value. If the standard deviation is large, the data are spread throughout the range.

Using the post-training data from Table 9-1, the standard deviation is

$$s = \frac{\sqrt{\Sigma(x_i - \bar{x})^2}}{n} = \frac{\sqrt{899.78}}{15} = 7.75$$

Table 9-2 shows some of the detailed calculations.

In the frequency histogram (Figure 9-1) the data graphically simulates a bell-shaped curve if the center points of each of the rectangles are connected. If there were many items with smaller intervals, the histogram would form a bell-shaped curve as shown in Figure 9-2. Much data in its normal state are distributed in a similar manner. For this kind

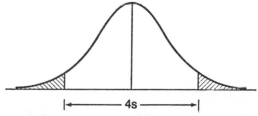

Figure 9-2. The normal distribution or bell-shaped curve.

Table 9-2
Calculating the Standard Deviation

Post-Training Value X_i	$X_i - \bar{x}$	$(X_i - \bar{x})^2$
47	15.13*	228.92
59	3.13	9.80
79	16.87	284.60
69	6.87	47.20
63	0.87	0.76
55	7.13	50.84
51	11.13	123.88
58	4.13	17.06
72	9.87	97.42
63	0.87	0.76
61	1.13	1.28
60	2.13	4.54
65	2.87	8.24
63	0.87	0.76
67	4.87	23.72
		Total 899.78

Sample calculation:
$\bar{x} = 62.13,$ $x_i = 47.$
$x_i - \bar{x} = 47 - 62.13 = -15.13$
(No need to use the minus sign, since the values are squared to get the next column.)

of distribution, which is called a normal distribution, approximately 95% of the values are within two standard deviations of the mean as illustrated in the figure. In other words, two standard deviations on both sides of the mean (for a total of four) account for approximately 95% of the total of the values. Therefore, the range will equal approximately four standard deviations for normal distributions. In our example of post-training measurements, the standard deviation was 7.75. Four times this standard deviation is 31, close to the actual range of 32. This represents a shortcut way to calculate an approximation of the standard deviation.

Measures of Association

In evaluation occasionally there is a need to know if a relationship exists between two or more groups of data. These groups of data may be referred to as variables. This relationship is useful in predicting performance based on program results or prerequisite criteria. The following examples will help illustrate this point.

Example 1. A large manufacturer is evaluating its cooperative education program. Among the aspects of evaluation, the employer wants to know if the grade point average (GPA) of participants in the program is related to their rates of promotion and salary increases after program completion. This answers the question: "Do co-op students with higher grades experience more job success?"

Example 2. An electronics manufacturer employs electronics circuit board testers who test each completed circuit board assembly. Employees selected for this job must complete an initial training program. At the end of the program, a knowledge test is administered. The test covers all the procedures necessary to perform electronic circuit board testing effectively. The test scores at the end of the program are compared to both the production efficiency and quality of their work after training. The efficiency relates to the number of circuit board tests completed. Quality represents the percentage of the circuit boards tested improperly. If there is a direct relationship between the end-of-the-program scores and after-the-program performance, then this not only assists in the validation of the test but also provides a predictor of performance without the expense of a follow-up. Table 9-3 shows the program scores (listed in random order) and production efficiency for this example.

Table 9-3
Performance of Electronic Circuit Board Testers

Test Program Scores (%)	Production Efficiency (%)
75	105
68	95
88	116
92	119
78	111
82	113
74	100
90	120
95	125
100% = Perfect Score	100% = Standard Rate

These two examples illustrate the need to determine if a relationship exists between two variables and also the extent of that relationship. This relationship is called *correlation,* and the degree of that relationship is measured by a *correlation coefficient.*

A basic approach to examining data for a possible relationship is to plot the two variables on a diagram and visually determine the likelihood of the correlation. Figure 9-3 shows a plot, called a scatter diagram, of the two variables from Table 9-3. On the horizontal axis, end-of-program test scores are plotted. On the vertical axis, the circuit board test rate efficiency is plotted. The horizontal axis is referred to as the "X" axis, and the vertical axis is referred to as the "Y" axis. The higher the test score, the higher the efficiency rate of the employee. This reveals a good possibility that there is a relationship between the two.

A relationship between two variables can be expressed in the form of an algebraic equation. The process of determining the relationship or the equation for the relationship between variables is known as *curve fitting.* In the example in Figure 9-3 a straight line approximates the relationship. This is called a linear relationship, and the line through the data is called a *trend line.* This trend line can be drawn as shown in Figure 9-3 and extended to show approximately where data will be located past the data points on the graph.

The method of determining the equation of a relationship is called the *method of least squares.* When the equation of the relationship is known, test scores can be plugged into the equation, and the corresponding values for production efficiency can be calculated. The specific formulas for determining the equations are beyond the scope of this book. There are

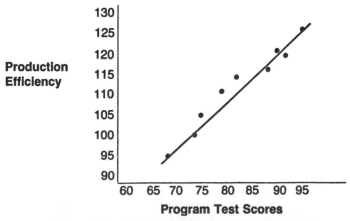

Figure 9-3. Scatter diagram of two variables.

many resources, including several of those listed at the end of this chapter, that are appropriate for providing information on these calculations.

There are several different types of correlation coefficients. The particular coefficient to use depends on the type of data, how the data are arranged, and the relationship between the two variables. Most of the data used in evaluation will be numerical from test scores and performance measurements. For this type of data, the correlation coefficient used is the Pearson's Product-Moment Correlation Coefficient. This coefficient applies only when there is a linear relationship, i.e., a straight-line relationship with no curve in the trend line of the graphical plot of the data. Fortunately, in many cases there is a linear relationship, particularly with performance data. This coefficient will be used in the remainder of this chapter. For additional information on the other correlation coefficients and when they should be used, please consult one of the additional references.

The correlation coefficient varies between -1 and $+1$: the minus denotes negative correlation, and the plus denotes positive correlation. When there is a perfect negative correlation, the coefficient is -1; when there is no correlation between the two variables, the coefficient is 0;

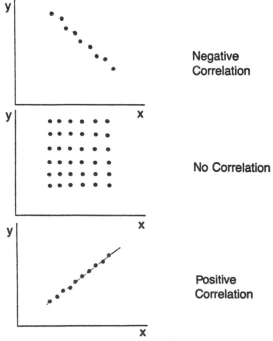

Figure 9-4. Extreme examples of correlation coefficients.

when there is perfect positive correlation, the coefficient is +1. These extreme situations are illustrated graphically in Figure 9-4.

The range between these two extreme values represents the degree of correlation. As a rough guide, Table 9-4 shows ranges of possible correlations and their rough interpretations. These are only approximate, and the actual interpretation of a specific correlation value depends on the confidence placed on that value.

Table 9-4
Ranges of Correlation Coefficients and Their Approximate Interpretations

Correlation Value	General Description
−1.0	Perfect negative correlation
−.8 to −1.0	Very high degree of negative correlation
−.6 to −.8	High degree of negative correlation
−.4 to −.6	Medium degree of negative correlation
−.2 to −.4	Low degree of negative correlation
+.2 to −.2	Probably no correlation
+.2 to +.4	Low degree of positive correlation
+.4 to +.6	Medium degree of positive correlation
+.6 to +.8	High degree of positive correlation
+.8 to +1.0	Very high degree of positive correlation
+1.0	Perfect positive correlation

The formula for calculating the correlation coefficient, r, is

$$r = \frac{n\,\Sigma x_i y_i - (\Sigma x_i)(\Sigma y_i)}{\sqrt{\{n(\Sigma x_i^2) - (\Sigma x_i)^2\}\,\{n\Sigma y_i^2 - (\Sigma y_i)^2\}}}$$

where:

n = The sample size.
x_i = The values on the X axis.
y_i = The values on the Y axis.

Most scientific calculators have this formula pre-programmed on function keys. However, it may be helpful to illustrate the calculation, as shown in Table 9-3, using the two variables of program test scores and efficiency. Table 9-5 shows the calculations in detail. Plugging into the formula, the coefficient is

$$r = \frac{9(83490) - (742)(1004)}{\sqrt{\{9(61866) - (742)^2\}\{9(112782) - (1004)^2\}}}$$

$$= \frac{6442}{\sqrt{(6230)(7022)}} = .97$$

This coefficient represents almost perfect positive correlation.

A word of caution is in order about correlation. The determination of a relationship between two variables does not mean that one necessarily caused the other. There could be other outside factors which influenced the changes. Therefore, as with many areas of statistics, this process provides additional useful information but does not provide the exact answer to the relationship of data.

Table 9-5
Data for Calculating the Correlation Coefficient

Item Number	(x_i) Program Test Score	(y_i) Production Efficiency	$x_i{}^2$	$y_i{}^2$	x_iy_i
1	75	105	5625*	11025†	7875‡
2	68	95	4624	9025	6460
3	88	116	7744	13456	10208
4	92	119	8464	14161	10948
5	78	111	6084	12321	8658
6	82	113	6724	12769	9266
7	74	100	5476	10000	7400
8	90	120	8100	14400	10800
9	95	125	9025	15625	11875
Total	742	1004	61866	112782	83490

Sample calculations:
* $x_i^2 = 75 \times 75 = 5625$
† $y_i^2 = 105 \times 105 = 11025$
‡ $x_iy_i = 75 \times 105 = 7875$

Statistical Inference

In some HRD program evaluations an hypothesis is stated, although it is not necessary. An hypothesis is a proposed explanation of the relationship between two or more variables such as performance and training. An example is: "production employees performance will improve as a result of the training program." The statement is either rejected or not rejected based on the evaluation data, the result of the statistical analysis, and a statistical test. The hypothesis is "tested." (Some individuals prefer to use the terminology "fail to reject" or "not rejected" rather than "accept." The rationale is that in some situations failing to reject the hypothesis on the basis of a single test may not be sufficient to accept the hypothesis.) The development of hypotheses, statistical analyses, statistical testing, and types of errors are presented in Appendix 7. An example is included to illustrate the process.

Statistical Deception

No chapter on data analysis and interpretation can be complete without a few words of caution about statistics that might deceive the reader and result in erroneous conclusions from data gathered in an HRD program. Numerous examples of statistical deception appear regularly. Almost anything can be proved using statistics. Disraeli once said there are three kinds of lies: lies, damned lies, and statistics. The following cautions are presented to show some common ways that statistics can deceive the casual observer, often unintentionally.

Unsupported Results

Presenting conclusions from data without proper statistical analysis is a common deception. Throughout this chapter the necessity for conducting a thorough analysis was presented. If data are properly used in a conclusion, it should be expressed on some level of reliability or confidence. Without support, data are subject to distortion and may be useless.

Biased Sampling

Sampling procedures are presented in Appendix 3. An improperly selected sample used in an experimental versus control-group comparison may yield results which are inconclusive. If the experimental group comprises high achievers and the control group represents the general population, the improvement in the experimental group, from a statistical point of view, may be conclusive. However, because of the bias in the sample selection, the actual results may be completely distorted. Random sampling and proper sample sizes usually can overcome biases in the selection.

Improper Use of Percentages and Averages

Another error involves the use of different bases for comparisons which show an improvement. For example, an HRD program in quality improvement has resulted in the error rate being reduced from 20 units per 1000 down to 15 units per 1000. There are two ways to show that improvement. Normally, it can be expressed as a 25% reduction, a change in 5 divided by 20. However, another way to express the result is that the new error rate is 33% less than the old rate. In this case 5 is divided by 15 to give 33%. There is a big difference in the two numbers.

Another deception comes in the use of averages. It is not unusual for a set of data to have a different value for the three types of averages: mean, median, and mode. An evaluator can select the one that suits the situation, depending on what message is needed. It is disguised under the term "average."

Graphical Distortions

Visual presentation of data in the form of graphs and charts can distort the true comparisons of data. For example, examine the two charts shown in Figure 9-5. The same data are presented in two different charts, only the scale of the vertical axis is changed. The one on the right shows a very small amount of increase; the one on the left shows a large increase in proportion to the horizontal axis. This difference can easily account for a distorted picture of what has happened.

Consider another example. The change in output of the melting department in a steel mill resulting from an HRD program is presented visually. Since the output is in tons of production per employee, a drawing of a blast furnace is used to show the visual differences in the outputs.

	Hypothesis False	Hypothesis True
Reject Hypothesis	Correct Decision	Type I Error
Do Not Reject Hypothesis	Type II Error	Correct Decision

Figure 9-5. Two presentations of the same data.

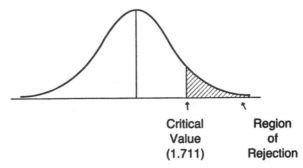

Critical | Region
Value | of
(1.711) | Rejection

Figure 9-6. Distortion in visual presentation.

There was a 50% improvement as shown in Figure 9-6. The blast furnace on the left shows the output before the program; the one on the right is after the program. The one on the right is 50% taller than the one on the left. The basis of comparison is a vertical axis only. However, the taller blast furnace has a wider base. Therefore, a 50% improvement looks like at least a 100% improvement.

Drawing Erroneous Conclusions

Much caution needs to be exercised when data from a single program, particularly on a pilot or experimental basis, are used to make inferences about the entire population. If care is taken to select a random sample and the proper statistical analysis is conducted, then the predictions for the remaining population will usually be accurate. However, without the proper care, distortions can easily come into play. Consider this extreme example. Following a pilot HRD program on work simplification, one participant suggested a way to simplify a procedure which saved the company $10,000 annually. In the report one of the conclusions read this way:

> If every employee could save $10,000, then, with an employment level of 450, the resulting savings would be $4,500,000. And since the program cost is only $50,000, a 9000% return on investment would be realized.

That is an erroneous conclusion. Only one employee had a savings of $10,000. The average savings were closer to $200. Using one statistic to make inferences about the entire population suggested a conclusion far better and vastly distorted.

Another example involves correlation. A correlation does not necessarily show a cause-and-effect relationship. Suppose the production output for a group of employees correlates with age. The older the employee, the greater the output. Using this correlation to draw a conclusion, the best recruiting strategy might be to hire employees in their sixties. Further analysis of the data reveals that the employees in the sample were in their early twenties to mid-thirties. No employees in the forties or fifties were in the sample. More than likely their performance would begin tapering off as they approach middle- and upper-age ranges.

The previous examples illustrate the common methods of statistical deception. They represent traps the HRD program evaluator should avoid when analyzing, interpreting, and presenting data.

Summary

Confused? It is a common reaction. It is easy to get carried away with analysis. Many HRD program evaluators get confused and discard evaluation because of data analysis. Data analysis is important, but it may not be appropriate for every evaluation. When used, it should be kept as simple as possible. If there are problems with data analysis, seek additional resources or help from someone familiar with statistical methods. The next chapter logically follows this one. It presents the methods to measure the return on HRD once the data have been analyzed.

Discussion Questions

1. How important are statistics in the evaluation process?
2. How important is data analysis to the overall evaluation process?
3. It is often said that data analysis is the most confusing, misunderstood, and feared part of evaluation. Why?
4. Why is it important to know about the dispersion of data?
5. What represents a good correlation coefficient? Why?
6. How have computers changed the data analysis process? Please elaborate.
7. How is statistical inference used in the evaluation process?

8. In your organization (or one with which you are familiar), indicate the specific examples of the use of statistics in the evaluation process. Include examples of measures of central tendency, measures of dispersion, measures of association, and statistical inference.
9. Cite examples of statistical distortion in data analysis and presentation. Are they intentional or unintentional?
10. What can be done to take the fear and mystery out of data analysis?

References

1. FitzGibbon, C. T., and Morris, L. L., *How to Analyze Data*, Sage Publications, Beverly Hills, CA, 1987.
2. Witzling, L. P. and Greenstreet, R. C., *Presenting Statistics: A Manager's Guide to the Persuasive Use of Statistics,* John Wiley, New York, NY, 1989.
3. Aczel, A. D., *Complete Business Statistics,* Irwin, New York, NY, 1989.
4. Koosis, D., *Statistics: A Self Teaching Guide* (3rd Edition), John Wiley, New York, NY, 1988.
5. Pfaffenberger, R. C., *Statistical Methods for Business and Economics*, 3rd Edition, New York, NY, 1987.
6. Gotlow, H. S. and Oppenheim, R., *Stat City: Understanding Statistics Through Realistic Applications*, 2nd Edition, Irwin, New York, NY, 1986.

CHAPTER 10

Measuring the Return on HRD

Possibly the ultimate level of evaluation is to compare the financial benefits of a program to the cost of that program. This comparison, which will be referred to as the return on HRD, is the elusive goal of many program evaluators. This chapter explores the various methods of calculating this return.

First, it begins with useful techniques to assign values to program data, particularly in those areas where it is most difficult. Data must be transformed into dollar values before the financial benefit can be calculated.

Second, the methods of comparisons are explored, the most common being return on investment (ROI). A detailed example is presented which shows the calculation of the ROI for a proposed HRD program taken from an actual case.

And finally, an alternate method of measuring the effectiveness of an HRD department is explored. The concept, called a profit center, is gaining increasing attention in the HRD field.

Assigning Values to Data

Chapter 8 described the types of data collected for program evaluation. Before this data can be used to compare benefits versus costs, it must be converted to a dollar value. This section gives additional insight into practical ways to assign values to the data collected. Conversions of hard data (output, quality, cost, time) are discussed first, followed by soft data conversion.

Except for actual cost savings, the easiest program measurement to convert to a dollar value is a change in output. An increase in output can appear in a variety of forms such as increased production, sales, or productivity. Savings in time and improvements in quality are a little more difficult to convert to a dollar value, while the greatest difficulty is encountered when attempting to convert soft data such as changes in attitudes, a reduction in complaints, or the implementation of new ideas.

Value of Increased Output

Changes in output are the goal of many HRD programs. In most situations the value of increased output can be easily calculated, while in a few instances it may be difficult. For example, in a sales training program the change in sales output can easily be measured. The average sales before the program are compared to the average sales after the program. The average profit per sale is usually easy to obtain. Therefore, the increased earnings as a result of increased sales is the increase in sales times the average profit per sale.

In another example consider a packaging machine operator in a pharmaceutical plant. The operator packages drugs in boxes ready for shipment. Operators participate in an HRD program to learn how to increase their output through better use of equipment and work procedures. In this example, the precise value of increased output is more difficult than the sales example. One approach is to calculate the unit labor cost of the packaging operation. Then the additional output of a unit ready for shipment saves the company the unit labor costs. Using this approach, the increase in output times the unit labor cost of packaging equals the cost savings. This figure may not be exact, since increases in output may affect the unit costs. However, this approach is usually accurate enough for measuring the return on an HRD program.

These output factors are normally closely monitored by organizations, and changes can easily be measured. Assigning values then becomes a relatively easy task.

Value of Cost Savings

Assigning a value to cost savings is redundant. An HRD program which produces a cost savings usually has a value equal to the cost savings. However, one item needs consideration when assigning these values: the time value of money. A savings realized at one point in time may be worth more than a savings at another time. A cost savings experienced by an employee or a group of employees over a long period might have a greater value than the actual savings, since costs normally increase during that period. This can best be explained with an example.

A group of government employees operate a distribution center for publications. Supervisors have specific cost control responsibilities for their particular unit. They are held accountable for the direct variable cost and a portion of the fixed costs which are partially under their control. When costs seemed unusually high, the supervisors were trained in cost control techniques for both variable and fixed costs. Supervisors learned how to analyze costs and how to use the various reports to take action to control costs. Both fixed and variable costs were monitored for a six-month period before and after the program to see if there were improvements. Part of these costs included raw materials, wages, and supplies, all of which increased during the one-year period. Therefore, to get a true picture of the value of the cost savings, the first six-month period costs were adjusted upward to what represented a cost target for comparison during the post-program period. Then the actual cost comparison with the target costs gave the value of the cost savings as a result of the HRD program, assuming no other factors influenced the cost savings.

Value of Time Savings

Many programs are aimed at reducing the time for participants to perform a function or task. Time savings are important because employee time is money, in the form of wages, salaries, and benefits paid directly to the employee. There are several economic benefits derived from time savings as described here.

Wages/salaries. The most obvious time savings results in reduced costs of labor involved in performing a task. The dollar savings are the hours saved times the labor cost per hour. The labor cost per hour can be an elusive figure. Generally, the average wage with a percent added for benefits will suffice for most calculations. However, time may be worth more than that. The chart on the following pages presents a method of calculating how much an hour of time is worth considering many other factors. The exercise is designed for management and supervision, but parts of it will be equally applicable to other types of jobs. Although the figure calculated is probably much higher than most people estimate,

(text continued on page 216)

JOHN OR JANE SMITH		YOUR OWN SALARY	
Annual salary	$16,000	Your own annual salary	☐
Fringe benefits at 25%. . . . . (In different companies this ranges between 15% and 35%; we've picked the mid-point).	4,000	Your benefits package . . . . (Use 25% unless you know the figure for your organization.)	☐
Sub-total	20,000 *	Sub-total	☐ *
Overhead: office space, furniture, phone, lights, heat, air conditioning, plus Smith's fair share of the cost of office services (copying machine, cafeteria, building maintenance, supplies, etc).		Overhead: (as defined in left column) This calculated as a percentage of payroll. If your organization's total annual payroll is, say, three million dollars, the total cost of overhead is likely to be close to this amount. Hence, we use 100% or the figure you wrote in the sub-total box above.	
As a percentage of payroll 100%.	20,000 *		☐ *
Secretarial support: Smith shares a secretary, Betty, with Jones. Hence, the "fair share" of Betty's services is 50%. She makes $8000 per year. Thus, 50% of her annual salary is		Secretarial support: Your "fair share" of secretary's annual salary (calculate this percentage on the basis of the proportion of time he/she spends working for you rather than on basis of how many people he/she serves): . .	
	4,000		☐
She, too, has fringe benefits at 25%.		Secretary's fringe benefits (Use 25% unless you know actual figure)	
	1,000		☐
Sub-total	5,000 *	Sub-total	☐ *
She, too, uses her "fair share" of overhead which must be charged to Smith, since her job exists solely to serve Smith (and Jones).			
At 100%	5,000 *	Your own overhead figure	☐ *
Other expenses:		Other expenses:	
Travel, registration, hotel at annual meeting of FEPCA Sub-total	1,200	Any conferences, meetings, or company related travel-hotel you have during the year.	☐
Night school at local college where employer pays tuition		Any educational reimbursement or other "professional development" expenses paid by your employer (e.g. the cost of this course).	
Sub-total	700		☐

JOHN OR JANE SMITH	YOUR OWN SALARY
Other expenses: (cont.)	Other expenses: (cont.)
Entertainment (business lunches or other activity reimbursed by company throughout the year) . . ⬜ $ 100	Any entertainment or other out-of-pocket expenses (e.g., reimbursement for use of personal car on business travel) that your employer has paid for . . . . ⬜
Sub-total . . . . ⬜ 2.000 *	Sub-total . . . . ⬜ *
Total of all boxes followed by an asterisk (*). This is how much you cost your employer annually ⬜ 52,000	Total of all boxes followed by an asterisk (*). This is how much you cost your employer annually ⬜
Note that this figure of $52,000 is the actual cost of Smith to the organization. This assumes a break-even situation. However, if the organization is making a profit, then Smith is expected to contribute his/her "fair share" to that profit (i.e., the organization does not want "break-even" employees, but "profitable" employees). To make 6% profit annually (net, after taxes) a firm must *gross* about 12% profit (assuming a corporate tax in the 50% range). This means that Smith must be worth 12% more than the break-even amount listed above.	If you know what net profit (*after* taxes) your organization made last year (expressed as a percentage), double it to calculate how much you must add to your break-even cost (last box above) to get your total cost plus profit. If you don't know your organization's net profit, use the figures shown in the column at the left. If you work for a non-profit organization, this section does not apply.
Total profit that is Smith's fair share (12% of figure in last box above) . . . . ⬜ 6,240	Total profit that is your fair share ⬜
TOTAL COST PLUS PROFIT . . . ⬜ 58,240	TOTAL COST PLUS PROFIT . . ⬜
Now let's break this figure down into how much Smith is worth per hour. There are 230 working days in the year (after deducting 52 weekends, 10 holidays, 10 vacation days, and 10 sickness or excused absence days). So we divide 230 into $58,240 to get a daily rate of . . . . ⬜ 253	Divide the figure above by 230 (or whatever figure applies in your own case . . . 225, if you have a 3-week vacation, 235 if yours is only a 1-week vacation, etc.). This gives you a daily rate of . . . . ⬜
Now we must divide this by the number of productive ("chargeable") hours in the day. For most managers this is about 4-6 hours. (Deduct time for coffee, "comfort" breaks, socializing, waiting, etc.) For Smith we'll use 5 hours. Dividing 5 into 253 gives Smith an hourly worth of . . . . ⬜ 51	Now divide this by the number of productive hours in your day . . . that is, the number of hours you could legitimately charge for (against a project or profit-producing activity). Dividing the number of productive hours in your day into your daily rate (shown in the box above) gives us your hourly worth of . . . . ⬜

Reproduced with permission of Training House, Box 3090, Princeton, N.J. 08540.

(text continued from page 213)

and may in fact be overstated, the point is very important. The value of employee time is significant and is more than just wages and benefits. Whatever items are used in the calculations must be clearly explained in the HRD evaluation. A conservative figure is probably best, since most managers feel more comfortable in dealing with the average wages plus benefits. However, if more detail is needed or a more accurate reflection of costs is necessary, the other factors should be included.

Better service. Another potential benefit of time savings is better service. This is particularly true when production time, implementation time, construction time, or processing time is reduced so that the product or service is delivered to the client or customer in a shorter period of time. As a result, there is better customer satisfaction, the value of which is difficult to quantify.

Penalty avoidance. In some situations reductions in time can avoid penalties. For example, in processing invoices in accounts payable, a reduction in processing time can avoid late payment penalties and possibly earn a discount for the organization. In another example, a reduction in time to complete a construction project can earn the company a sizable bonus.

Opportunity for profit. A sometimes hidden, but potentially rewarding, benefit of time savings is the opportunity to make additional profit. For example, if a salesperson reduces the average time spent on a sales call, then there is time for additional sales calls. These additional calls can bring in additional sales, which bring in additional profits at no additional sales salary expense.

Training time. Frequently, HRD programs will be improved to reduce the previous training time. With new instructional technology and refinements as a result of program evaluations, a new program can possibly accomplish the same objectives in a shorter period of time. This savings in training time is another important part of a two-fold evaluation: (1) the reduction in the time to conduct the program, and (2) the actual results achieved from the program.

For ongoing HRD programs, there are usually many opportunities for improvement that will result in less training time and which in turn result in a cost savings. An example helps illustrate the simplicity of attaining benefits in time reduction for training programs:

A large metropolitan hospital historically used an outside training program for its nurses. The one-week program was conducted by an association. On the average, the hospital had 65 nurses complete the program each quarter. The hospital administration decided to change the training approach. They designed an internal program utilizing programmed instruction, cassette and workbook exercises, and slide-tape presentations. Two HRD staff specialists developed the program for a total cost of $30,000. This included salaries, fees for outside consultants, artwork, and training course booklets. The new program took only 12 hours when compared to the previous 40 with the same course objectives. The cost of the old method was:

Enrollment per nurse in the one-week public course $400
Salaries paid to each nurse during program $250
Total cost per nurse $650
Multiply 65 trainees times $650 for a cost of $42,250.
The new program has the following costs:
Salaries paid to each nurse during the program (one-third
   of one week's pay) $83
Instructor time per nurse ($2000 per quarter divided by 65) . . . $31
Course materials used by each nurse $10
Development costs ($30,000 divided by 4 years divided
   by 4 quarters per year divided by 65 nurses) $29
Total cost per nurse $153
Multiply 65 trainees times $153 for a cost of $9945.

Therefore, the average savings per quarter for the four-year period is the difference in the two values or $32,305. A significant cost savings can result from a savings in training time. This example uses rough estimates and may omit some of the costs in another setting.

Value of Improved Quality

Quality improvement is an important and frequently used target of HRD programs. Programs are developed to overcome deficiencies in employees which are evident by low-quality output or an excessively high error rate. The cost of poor quality to an organization can be staggering. According to quality expert Philip Crosby, an organization can probably increase its profits by 5 to 10% of sales if it concentrates on improving quality.[1] The measurable impact of a program for quality improvement must be calculated. Then, to calculate the return on a program, the value of the quality improvement must be determined. This value may have several components as illustrated here.

Scrap/waste. The most obvious cost of poor quality is the scrap or waste generated by mistakes. Defective products, spoiled raw materials, and discarded paperwork are all the results of poor quality. This scrap and waste translates into a dollar value which can be used to calculate the impact of an improvement in quality. For example, in a production environment the cost of a defective product can be easily calculated. Basically, it is the total cost incurred at the point the mistake is identified minus the salvage value. In another example, the cost of an error on a purchase order can be enormous if the wrong items are ordered.

Rework. Many mistakes and errors result in costly rework to correct the mistake. The most costly rework occurs when a product is delivered to a customer and must be returned for correction, or when an expensive program has been implemented with serious errors. In determining the cost of rework, labor and direct cost are both significant. Maintaining a staff to perform rework can be an additional overhead cost for the organization. In a manufacturing plant the cost of rework is in the range of 15–70% of a plant's productivity. In banks, an estimated 35% of operating costs could be blamed on correcting wrong work.[2]

Customer/client dissatisfaction. The dissatisfaction of customers and clients represents a tremendous loss for the organization when errors and mistakes are made. In some cases serious mistakes can result in lost business. Customer dissatisfaction is difficult to quantify, and attempts to arrive at a dollar value may be impossible. Usually, the judgment and expertise of sales and marketing management are the best sources to try to measure the impact of dissatisfaction. It may be more realistic to list it as an advantage of improved quality without trying to quantify it.

However, more experts in service quality are insisting that customer and client dissatisfaction can be measured. John Goodman, President of TARP Institute, Inc., a service research company in Washington, D.C., refers to this as measuring the market damage of poor service quality. TARP surveys customers who have had good and bad experiences and asks them whether they are likely to do business with that particular company again. Later, TARP surveys the same people, asking them if they did do business with the company. Then TARP researchers use a formula to measure the monetary damage bad service did to repeat business. TARP also has formulas to measure word of mouth, both good and bad.[3]

Product liability. In recent years premiums for product liability insurance have soared due to an increase in lawsuits brought against businesses. An organization which experiences more than average product defects will usually experience a higher product liability insurance premium. Therefore, better quality can result in less customer complaints; consequently, less lawsuits and lower premiums. It is difficult to make a direct connection between quality and premiums, but through a series of logical deductions and assumptions, a value can be developed. For example, suppose an organization produces pipe fittings by the millions. A defective pipe fitting can cause extensive damage. The number of customer complaints is directly correlated with the scrap rate for the production of the fittings (i.e., the more defects found, the more customer complaints received). In addition, there is a direct correlation between customer complaints and the extent of liability losses. And finally, the liability losses in the previous year determine the liability insurance premium for the coming year. With these assumptions and facts known, an improvement in quality through an improved scrap rate can translate into lower liability losses and a savings in the liability insurance premium.

Inspection and quality control. In some organizations, the response to the demand for improved quality is to hire additional inspectors or beef-up the quality control staff. These inspectors often inspect products after they have been produced or inspect supplier products as they are received. Although some inspection may be necessary to determine the level of quality, it is not the solution to a poorly designed or manufactured product or an ineffective service delivery system. An HRD program, designed to improve quality, should ultimately reduce the level of inspection and quality control required in the process and ultimately result in specific reductions in the number of inspectors, a measure that can be translated into dollar value savings.

Internal losses. There is still another type of loss tied to errors and mistakes that is not covered in the categories mentioned previously They are internal losses caused by employee mistakes. For example, an overpayment to a supplier can possibly represent a loss that cannot be recovered. It does not result in rework or produce any waste, but it costs the company. Similar errors in processing paperwork can create substantial losses.

Employee morale. One final cost of poor quality is employee morale. When mistakes are made, usually other employees have to suffer inconveniences, loss of the use of the product or services, extra time involved in correcting mistakes, or other forms of discomfort or dissatisfaction. Mistakes can lower the morale of the employees affected. However, this subject is difficult to quantify, and it may be best left in a subjective form when presented to management.

Quality improvement example. The previous categories illustrate the extent of the quality problem and how the different components affect the cost of poor quality. These components are sometimes grouped and often referred to, categorically, as preventive costs, appraisal costs, and failure costs. Crosby contends that total expenditures for these items should be no more than 2.5% of sales.[4] Although it may seem challenging to calculate the numbers, some consultants and practitioners are able to make this calculation using surveys. This process requires employees to estimate how much time they spend doing work that falls into each of the three categories above. The figure is then multiplied by the standard labor wage rate, adjusted for benefits costs. Paul Revere Insurance Companies uses a survey process to estimate this cost. Each team is directed to list the amount of time each member devoted to each category in an average week, plus the specific costs incurred by variations from quality standards. The numbers are not precise, but are estimates and resulted in a total figure of 44% of overhead. The result was amazingly consistent among the divisions. This measure provided an indication of the magnitude of the problem and served as a source of ideas for the team throughout the year. Also, it served as a benchmark by which to measure the team in years to come.[5]

An example illustrates the impact of quality improvement resulting from an HRD program:

Twelve health insurance claim processors make up a department charged with the responsibility of processing group claims. Most are relatively new and apparently not very knowledgeable of the procedures for processing claims. The company experienced a 12% error rate (i.e., 12 errors for every 100 claims processed). On the average, the 12 employees process 200 claims per day.

The full extent of the errors are usually uncovered by internal auditors. Frequently, and randomly, internal auditors audit a full day's work of processed claims. The random audits revealed the 12% error rate. Also, they found that 40% of the errors (or 4.8% of the claims processed) result in overpayments to the claimants, while the other 60% represent underpayments. The overpayments are usually regarded as lost funds. If the amounts are substantial, they try to recover the loss. Otherwise, it is usually written off as a loss. The underpayment errors are reprocessed so that claimants get all of the reimbursement due them. Most of the underpayment errors are spotted by the claimants after checking the work of the claims processors. Occasionally, an overpayment is brought to the attention of claims processing; however, the extent of this is negligible. The internal audit also revealed that the overpayments average $21.

When faced with this unusually high error rate and the extent of the overpayments, the company developed and conducted a formal HRD program to improve the skills of claims processors. After the employees were trained, internal audit randomly audited the section to calculate the new error rate of claims processing and average overpayment. After several audits, there was a 5% error rate with an average overpayment of $15. The 60/40 distribution of the errors was the same as before the HRD program.

The average time to reprocess a claim, when discovered, was approximately one-half hour. Almost all of the underpayment claims were brought to the attention of the claims processor before the audit results. The average salary for claims processors including 30% for benefits is $7.80 per hour.

The solution
The net savings because of the error reduction is as follows:

Reprocessing
$12-5=7\% \times 60\% =4.2\%$ less claims to be reprocessed
$4.2\% \times 200$ claims/day $\times 5$ days $=42$ claims per week
$42 \times 1/2$ hour $\times \$7.80$/hour $=\$163.80$ weekly savings

Overpayment
Before training
$12\% \times 200$/day $\times 5$ days $\times 40\% =48$ overpayments per week
$48 \times \$21 = \$1008$ average weekly loss

After the program
$5\% \times 200$/day $\times 5$ days $\times 40\% =20$ overpayments per week
$20 \times \$15 = \$300$ average weekly loss

Net savings
$\$1008 - \$300 = \$708$ weekly savings
Total savings
$\$708 + \$163.80 = \$871.80$ per week
or $\$871.80 \times 50$ weeks $= \$43,590$

Annual savings $= \$43,590$

Value of Soft Data

While soft data are not as desirable as hard data; nevertheless, they are important. The difficulty arises in collecting the data reliably and in assigning values to the data. Almost any assignment of value is subjective and must be used with that in mind. There are a number of approaches to convert the soft data to a dollar value as presented here.

Existing data/historical costs. Frequently, tangible items or historical costs will be intertwined with the soft data. Use as much of that data as possible. For example, the cost for employees being tardy can be calculated by making a number of assumptions about what happens when an employee is absent for a short period of time. Another example is the cost of grievances. Although an extremely variable item, there are historical costs which can form a basis for estimating the cost savings for a reduction in grievances. Tangible hard data, if available, should always be used when estimating the value of soft data items.

Expert opinion. Expert opinions are possibly available to estimate the value of the soft data. The experts may be within the organization, within the industry, or specialists in a particular field. Extensive analyses of similar data may be extrapolated to fit the data at hand. For example, many experts have attempted to calculate the cost of absenteeism. Although these estimates can vary considerably, they may serve as a rough estimate for other calculations with some adjustments for the specific organization. A review of the studies on absenteeism conducted by the experts, reveal some staggering figures. Based on studies conducted in the '70s and '80s, the average cost of absenteeism per incident, when adjusted for inflation, is $80 to $100.[6]

Participant estimation. The participants in an HRD program may be in the best position to estimate the value of an improvement. Either at the end of a program or in a follow-up, participants should be asked to estimate the value of the improvements. They should also be asked to furnish the basis for that estimate and the confidence placed on it. The estimations by participants may be more realistic, since they are usually directly involved in the improvement. With encouragement and some examples, participants can be very creative when estimating these values.

Management estimation. Another technique for assigning a value to soft data is to ask management concerned with the evaluation of the program. This management group may be the superiors of the participants, top management (who are approving the expenditures), or the members of a program review committee whose function is to evaluate the program. This approach solicits an estimate from a group of what it is worth to improve on a particular soft-data item such as the implementation of new ideas, resolving conflicts, or increasing personal effectiveness. When management develops an estimate, it becomes their figure. Even if it is extremely conservative, it can be very helpful in the final analysis of the HRD program.

In summary, the previous methods are very subjective but can help assign a value to soft data for use in calculating a return on an HRD program. One word of caution is in order. Whenever a monetary value is assigned to subjective information, it needs to be fully explained to the audience receiving the information. And, by all means, when there is a range of possible values, use the most conservative one. It will improve the credibility.

Soft data value example. In some cases, it might be appropriate to combine the different techniques previously listed to arrive at an estimation of the benefits from an HRD program. The following is taken from an actual case and focuses on three of the methods cited—historical cost, expert opinion, and management estimation.

Secor Bank, a large, regional federal savings bank was experiencing a higher than desired turnover rate. An HRD program was developed to reduce turnover. To measure the payoff of the program, Secor needed to estimate the cost of turnover, an elusive figure in most organizations. The total cost includes replacement costs (i.e., recruitment, selection, employment testing, and orientation), training costs to bring new employees up to the contribution level of the employees who left the organization, lost production (because new employees are not at full contribution), lost time of individuals involved with the turnover problem (i.e., supervisors, managers and specialists involved in the issues of recruiting and training), and administrative costs tied to all of these processes. Calculating the precise cost of turnover is a difficult chore, and Secor did not want to devote resources to develop it. As a result, a combination of approaches were used to estimate turnover costs.

First, the HRD staff checked the literature to see if turnover had been calculated for financial institutions. In an institution of similar size, the cost of turnover had been developed by the bank's internal audit department and verified by a consultant who was an expert in the field of turnover reduction.[7] The cost of turnover was calculated to be $25,000 per turnover statistic. Thus, this initial figure had the advantage of historical costs developed at a similar institution and had the credibility of expert opinion. However, there is always a question of whether data in one organization should apply to another, even though they are in the same type of business.

Next, the HRD staff met with top executives to agree on a turnover cost value to use in gauging the success of the program. Management agreed on an estimate that was half the amount from the study, $12,500. This was considered very conservative, because other turnover studies typically yield statistics of greater value. However, management felt comfortable with the estimate and it was used on the benefits side of program evaluation. Although not precise, this exercise yielded a figure that was never disputed. For additional information on how to calculate the cost of turnover, see a detailed example in Phillips.[8]

Calculating the Return

The return on investment is an important calculation for the HRD professional. Yet, it is a figure that must be used with caution and care. There are many ways that it can be interpreted, or misinterpreted. This section presents some general guidelines to help calculate a return and interpret its meaning.

Defining Return on Investment

The term "return on investment" (ROI) may appear to be improper terminology for the HRD field. The expression originates from the finance and accounting field and usually refers to the pretax contribution measured against controllable assets. In formula form

$$\text{Average ROI} = \frac{\text{pretax earnings}}{\text{average investment}}$$

It measures the anticipated profitability of an investment and is used as a standard measure of the performance of divisions or profit centers within a business.

The investment portion of the formula represents capital expenditures such as a training facility or equipment plus initial development or production costs. The original investment figure can be used, or the present book value can be expressed as the average investment over a period of time. If an HRD program is a one-time offering, then the figure is all the original investment. However, if the initial costs are spread over a period of time, then the average book value is usually more appropriate. This value is essentially half the initial costs since, through depreciation, a certain fixed part of investment is written off each year over the life of the investment.[9]

In many situations a group of employees are to be trained at one time, so the investment figure is the total cost of analysis, development, delivery, and evaluation lumped together for the bottom part of the equation. The benefits are then calculated assuming that all participants attend the program or have attended the program, depending on whether the return is a prediction or a reflection of what has happened.

To keep calculations simple, it is recommended that the return be based on pretax conditions. This avoids the issue of investment tax credits, depreciation, tax shields, and other related items.

To illustrate this calculation, assume that an HRD program had initial costs of $50,000. The program will have a useful life of three years with negligible residual value at that time. During the three-year period, the program produces a net savings of $30,000, or $10,000 per year ($30,000/3). The average investment is $25,000 ($50,000/2), since the average book value is essentially half the costs. The average return is

$$\text{Average ROI} \ = \ \frac{\text{annual savings}}{\text{average investment}} \ = \ \frac{\$10,000}{\$25,000} \ = \ 40\%$$

Return on investment is sometimes used loosely to represent the return on assets (ROA) or the return on equity (ROE). Equity usually refers to the net worth of a company. The assets represent the total assets employed to generate earnings, including debt. The ROA and ROE are terms that are more meaningful when evaluating the entire company or division in the company. ROI is usually sufficient for evaluating expenditures relating to an HRD program.

Finance and accounting personnel may actually take issue with calculations involving the return on investment for efforts such as an HRD program. Nevertheless, the expression is fairly common and conveys an adequate meaning of financial evaluation. Some professionals suggest a more appropriate name is return on training (ROT), or just return on human resource development. Others avoid the word "return" and just calculate the dollar savings as a result of the program, which is basically the benefits minus costs. These figures may be more meaningful to managers to keep from getting the ROI calculation confused with similar calculations for capital expenditures.

ROI may be calculated prior to an HRD program to estimate the potential cost effectiveness or after a program has been conducted to measure the results achieved. The methods of calculation are the same. However, the estimated return before a program is usually calculated for a proposal to implement the program. The data for its calculation are more subjective and usually less reliable than the data after the program is completed. Because of this factor, management may require a higher ROI for an HRD program in the proposal stage. The detailed example in this chapter will illustrate how the return is calculated for a proposal to implement a program.

When to Use ROI

Early in this book it was stated that the calculation of the return for an HRD program was not feasible or realistic in all cases. Even if the perceived benefits have been converted to dollar savings, the mere calculation of the return communicates to a perceptive manager more preciseness in the evaluation than may be there. Usually, the ROI calculation should be used when the program benefits can be clearly documented and substantiated, even if they are subjective. If management believes in the method of calculating the benefits, then they will have confidence in the value for the return. The nature of the program can also have a bearing on whether or not it makes sense to calculate a return. Management may believe, without question, an ROI calculation for sales training programs. They can easily see how an improvement can be documented and a value tied to it. On the other hand, an ROI for a program which teaches managers the principles of transactional analysis is difficult to swallow—even for the most understanding manager. Therefore, the key considerations are how reliable are the data, and how believable are the conclusions based on subjective data.

Targets for Comparison

When a return is calculated, it must be compared with a predetermined standard to be meaningful. A 30% ROI is unsatisfactory when a 40% ROI is expected. There are two basic approaches to setting targets. First, the normally accepted return on any investment may be appropriate for the HRD program. Second, since the ROI calculation is more subjective than the ROI for capital expenditures, the company may expect a higher target. This figure should be established in review meetings with top management where they are asked to specify the acceptable ROI for the program. It is not uncommon for an organization to expect an ROI for an HRD program twice that of the ROI for capital expenditures.

Additional Methods for Evaluating Investments

There are several methods other than ROI which represent efficiency in the use of invested funds. The most common ones are shown here.

Payback period. A payback period is a very common method of evaluating a capital expenditure. In this approach the annual cash proceeds (savings) produced by investment are equated to the original cash outlay required by the investment to arrive at some multiple of cash proceeds equal to the original investment. Measurement is usually in terms of years and months. For example, if the cost savings generated from an HRD program are constant each year, the payback period is determined by dividing the total original cash investment (development costs, outside program purchase, etc.) by the amount of the expected annual savings. The savings represent the net savings after the program expenses are subtracted. The payback period is simple to use but has the limitation of ignoring the time value of money.

To illustrate this calculation, assume that the initial program costs are $100,000 with a three-year useful life. The annual net savings from the program is expected to be $40,000. Then

$$\text{Payback period} \quad = \quad \frac{\text{total investment}}{\text{annual savings}} \quad = \quad \frac{100,000}{40,000} \quad = 2.5 \text{ years}$$

The program will "pay back" the original investment in 2.5 years.

Discounted cash flow. Discounted cash flow is a method of evaluating investment opportunities that assigns certain values to the timing of the proceeds from the investment. The assumption, based on interest rates, is that a dollar earned today is more valuable than a dollar earned a year from now.

There are several ways of using the discounted cash flow concept to evaluate capital expenditures, such as a large investment in an HRD program. The most popular one is probably the net present value of an investment. This approach compares the savings, year by year, with the outflow of cash required by the investment. The expected savings received each year is discounted by selected interest rates. The outflow of cash is also discounted by the same interest rate. Should the present value of the savings exceed the present value of the outlays after discounting at a common interest rate, the investment is usually acceptable in the eyes of management. The discounted cash flow method has the advantage of ranking investments, but it becomes difficult to calculate and may be too complex for the average user.

Internal rate of return. The internal rate of return (IRR) method determines the interest rate required to make the present value of the cash flow equal to zero. It represents the maximum rate of interest that could be paid if all project funds were borrowed and the organization had to break even on the projects. The IRR considers the time value of money and is not affected by the scale of the project. It can be used to rank alternatives, and specifying a minimum rate, can be used to make accept/reject decisions when a minimum rate of return is specified. A major weakness of the IRR method is that it assumes that all returns are reinvested at the same internal rate of return. This can make an investment alternative with a high rate of return look even better than it really is and a project with a low rate of return look even worse. For additional information on the IRR and a comparison of IRR, Discounted Cash Flow, Payback and ROI, see Mosier.[10]

Cost-benefit ratio. Another method of evaluating the investment in HRD is the cost-benefit ratio. Similar to the ROI, this ratio consists of the total of the benefits derived from the program expressed in dollars, divided by the total cost of the program also expressed in dollars. A cost-benefit ratio greater than 1 indicates a positive return. A ratio of less than 1 indicates a loss. The benefits portion of the ratio is a tabulation of all the benefits derived from the program converted to dollar values as described earlier in this chapter. The cost portion includes the total cost in all the cost categories as outlined in Chapter 7. The ratio has been used to evaluate projects, particularly in the public sector, beginning in the 1900s with the passage of the River and Harbor Act of 1902.[11] This Act mandated that individual projects be justified by comparing benefits with costs. Since then, it has been used for project evaluation in a variety of different settings.

Many HRD practitioners prefer to use the cost-benefit ratio because it is not usually connected with standard accounting procedures. Although the benefits are converted to dollar values, steering away from the standard accounting measures is a more comfortable approach.

Sometimes there is a feeling that the accounting measures communicate a preciseness that is not always available when calculating the benefits or the cost portion of the equation. For more information on the cost-benefit ratio, see Hawthorne.[12]

Utility analysis. Another important and interesting approach for developing the return on investment in HRD is the use of utility analysis. Utility is a function of the duration of a training program's effect on employees, the number of people trained, the validity of the training program, the value of the job for which training was provided, and the total cost of the program.[13]

Utility analysis measures the economic contribution of a program according to how effective the program was in identifying and modifying behavior, hence the future service contribution of employees. Schmidt, Hunter, and Pearlman derived the following formula for assessing the dollar value of a training program:[14]

$$\Delta U = T \ N \ dt \ SDy - N \ C$$

where:
- ΔU = Dollar value of the training program.
- T = Duration and number of years of a training program's effect on performance.
- N = Number of employees trained.
- dt = True difference in job performance between the average trained and the average untrained employees in units of standard deviation.
- SDy = Standard deviation of job performance of the untrained group in dollars.
- C = Cost of training per employee.

Of all the factors in this formula, the validity of the program and the value of the target job are the most difficult to calculate. The validity is determined by noting the performance differences between trained and untrained employees. The simplest method for obtaining this information is to have supervisors rate the performance of each group. The value of the target job, SDy, is estimated by supervisors and experts in the organization.

This approach seems to have promise and has been reported significantly in literature. An excellent example of the application of utility analysis concept involving the effects of a training program in supervisory skills on a performance rating of 65 bank supervisors was recorded by Mathieu and Leonard.[15] In this example, the time effect of utility was factored into the formula and produced estimates of the total at $34,000 for the first year and increasing to almost $200,000 for year 20.

Consequences of not training. For some HRD program efforts, the consequences of not training can be very serious. A company's inability to perform adequately might mean that it is unable to take on additional business or that it may be losing existing business because of an untrained work force. This method of calculating the return on training has received recent attention. Jackson has described a four-step method to calculate the consequences of not training.[16] This method involves:

☐ Establishing that there is an actual or potential loss.
☐ Obtaining an estimate of what the business is worth in actual or potential value and if possible, its value to the organization in terms of profit.
☐ Isolating the factors involved in lack of performance, which may create the loss of business or the inability to take on additional business. This includes lack of staff, lack of training, inability to staff quickly, inadequate facilities in which to expand, inadequate equipment, excessive turnover, etc. If there is more than one factor involved, determine the impact of each factor on the loss of income.
☐ Estimating the total cost of training using the techniques outlined in Chapter 5 and comparing costs with benefits.

This approach has some disadvantages. The potential loss of income can be highly subjective and difficult to measure. Also it may be difficult to isolate the factors involved and to determine their weight relative to lost income. This approach is only helpful in business organizations and usually where there is an expanding market.

ROI Calculation: A Case Study

The following case study is taken from an actual situation. It involves an ROI calculation prior to program approval. To avoid complication, some of the detailed information has been omitted.

The Setting

The company employs a large number of machine operators who operate a variety of machines including lathes, drill presses, and milling machines. The company was experiencing a shortage of machine operators. New recruits were largely untrained, inexperienced operators from outside the company.

New operators were trained on the job by their supervisors, using regular production equipment. This created some problems because the new trainee was not productive during the early days of employment, and the production machine was virtually out of service. The traditional on-the-job training methods were perceived as not being effective, and the training time for new operators appeared to be excessive. In addition, the problems of high scrap and excessive machine downtime were often by-products of poor initial training. Too often, a new operator in the midst of frustration left the company and became a turnover statistic.

A structured training program taught by an experienced instructor, away from the pressures of production, was tried on a pilot basis. The results were outstanding, and management was interested in implementing the program for all new operators.

A major issue in restructuring the program was the question of where the training should take place. Management concluded that the training should take place out of the production environment where the trainee could learn under close supervision of an instructor. As a result, the company explored the possibility of building a separate training facility to house the machine operator training program. The HRD department was charged with the responsibility for developing a proposal for the project. This involved designing the complete program, developing the preliminary design of the facility, and calculating the expected ROI.

There were other obvious benefits of a separate facility. Low-tolerance production could be performed in the training center. Limited, small-scale research and development could be conducted there. However, these benefits were not to be used to justify the new program. The HRD department was asked to confine its evaluation to the improved performance of machine operators.

Program Benefits

There were several areas identified for potential cost savings. Most of these were developed after an analysis of the performance of the employees in the pilot training program when compared to employees without training. The following performance measurements were isolated:

☐ Reduction in time to reach a standard proficiency level.
☐ Improvement in the scrap rate for the new employees.
☐ Reduction in turnover of new employees.
☐ Improvement in the safety record.
☐ Reduction in equipment maintenance expense after training.

These were the tangible items used in the analysis. Additional, more subjective benefits included:

☐ Improved attitude and morale.
☐ Reduced absenteeism.
☐ Reduction in training responsibilities for supervisors.

Because of the difficulty in measuring the additional benefits, they were not used in calculating the proposed cost savings.

The improvements in the five measurement factors were estimated in the following manner. First, the pilot program results were analyzed for each of the five areas. Next, experienced production management personnel were heavily involved in the program design. They estimated the extent of improvements in each of the areas as a result of the structured training in a separate facility. The two approaches provided a combined basis for estimating the potential improvements in each area.

Training time. Company records indicated that more than $65,000 was charged to trainee losses in the machining areas during the year. These losses were essentially lost production as a result of trainees taking more time than allowed to learn to operate a machine at a standard rate. Based on the pilot program and management estimations, the trainee losses could be reduced by 50% with a structured training program in a separate facility. This results in a savings of $33,000.

Machining scrap. There are many factors which contribute to machining scrap. With new and inexperienced operators, one of the biggest factors is lack of training. It was estimated that there could be a 10% reduction in total scrap costs with the new training program. In machining areas the annual cost of scrap was $1,450,000 for all product lines. A 10% reduction results in a $145,000 savings. This figure was significant, since the potential for scrap reduction was high. Management felt that the estimate was conservative.

Turnover. At the time of this analysis, the turnover rate in the machining area was 22 employees per month. Management felt that a large percentage of this turnover was directly related to ineffective and/or insufficient training. It was estimated that an effective training program could reduce this turnover rate by at least 20%. The turnover of 22 per month translates into 264 per year. The approximate cost to hire a new employee was estimated to be $500 representing a total annual cost of $132,000. A 20% savings is $26,000.

This estimate was conservative. The $500 cost to hire a new employee was an estimate of the initial processing cost, including a physical examination and unproductive time in the first week of employment. On the average, new employees who left the company during the training program worked longer than one week. Therefore, the cost to the company was probably greater than $500, since some lost production occurred after the first week.

Accidents. The number of first-aid injuries in the machining area was averaging 552 per year with the majority of them involving relatively new employees. The total cost in a year for these accidents (including outside medical costs, worker's compensation, and first aid) was $34,000. It was estimated that accidents could be reduced by 25% with an effective training program which emphasized safety practices. This would result in an annual cost savings of $8500.

Maintenance expense. Effective training of new employees should result in less maintenance required on production machines. Much of the current, unscheduled machine downtime is caused by new employees improperly operating equipment during their training period. It was estimated that the unscheduled maintenance expense could be reduced by 10% each year with the implementation of the training program. The annual unscheduled maintenance costs for the machining areas were $975,000. The annual savings would be $97,500. This estimate was considered very conservative.

Savings summary. The total projected annual savings are as follows:

Training time		33,000
Machining scrap		145,000
Turnover		26,000
Accidents		8,500
Maintenance expense		97,500
	Total	$310,000

Program Costs

The cost for the proposed program involved the construction of a building, the acquisition of the necessary equipment, the salaries and expenses of two instructors, and the additional administrative overhead expenses connected with the training program. The most efficient approach was to construct a new facility on existing idle property. This design was a 30 ft × 50 ft metal fabricated building at a proposed cost of $90,000. The initial program development cost was estimated to be $10,000.

The equipment cost was less than expected. Most of the equipment planned for the new facility consisted of surplus equipment from the production line to be modified and reconditioned for use in training. The total equipment cost was estimated to be $95,000. This figure included $7000 initial installation expenses. The equipment cost included the equipment for staffing two offices for the instructors and providing them with various training aids, including overhead projectors.

The salaries of two instructors plus expenses were estimated to be $40,000 per year. The overhead costs, which include normal maintenance, were estimated to be $15,000 each year.

The total investment is $195,000 (95+90+10).

Calculating the Return

A comparison of the costs with the savings yields the following calculations. The first-year net savings are

Annual gross savings	310,000
Less annual expenses	65,000
Net savings	$245,000

The ROI, assuming a first-year total write-off on the building, equipment, and the program development is

$$\text{ROI} = \frac{245,000}{195,000} = 126\%$$

Realistically, the investment in the buildings, equipment, and development should be spread over several years. Assume a useful life of five years for the building, equipment, and program development. The average book value for these items is 195,000/2=97,500. The new average return is

$$\text{ROI} = \frac{245,000}{97,500} = 251\%$$

These estimates of return may seem unusually high in this example. This can be attributed to the following reasons:

☐ The equipment costs were unusually low, using the salvage value plus costs for reconditioning. New equipment would cost much more, but have a longer useful life.
☐ There was no additional investment in land, since idle property was used. A land purchase would have added significantly to the investment.
☐ The cost savings were very high. Indeed, they may be overstated, since they include estimations based, in part, on subjective judgments.

A Few Words of Caution

The HRD professional should use caution when developing, calculating, and communicating the return on investment for HRD programs. The ROI calculation is a very important item which should be a goal for many HRD programs. However, there are a few cautions which need consideration.

Do not confuse the return on HRD with other financial returns. There are many ways to calculate the return on funds invested or assets employed to produce earnings. The calculation for a return on an HRD program needs to be based on as much tangible data as possible. Its method of calculation and its meaning should be clearly communicated. Most important, it should be an item accepted by management as an appropriate measure for HRD evaluation.

Involve management in calculating the return. Management ultimately makes the decision on whether or not a return is acceptable. They should be involved in defining how a return is calculated and setting targets by which programs are considered acceptable within the organization. After all, a good return in their eyes is what is most important.

Approach emotional and sensitive issues with caution. Occasionally, sensitive and controversial issues will be generated when discussing a return on HRD. It is best to avoid debates over what is measurable and what is not measurable unless there is clear evidence of the issue in the specific program under discussion. Also, there is sometimes a tendency to consider some items so fundamental to the survival of the organization that any attempt to measure it is unnecessary. For example, if a program is designed to improve customer service, there may be a tendency to avoid the measurement and subsequently not calculate the return on the assumption that if the program is well designed, it will improve customer service. This may not be enough for some cost conscious managers. Finally, avoid debates on the return on investment for programs that are considered to be "pet projects" of the CEO or other high-level officials. It may be best to avoid calculating the return on these projects even when their economic value is questionable.

Teach others the methods for calculating the return. Each time a return is calculated for a program, the HRD manager should use this opportunity to educate other staff members and other colleagues in the organization. Even if it is not in their area of responsibility, they will be able to see the value of this approach to HRD evaluation. When possible, each project should serve as a case study to educate the HRD staff on specific techniques and methods.[17]

Do not boast about a high return for HRD. It is not unusual to generate what appears to be a very high return on investment for an HRD program. Several examples in this chapter have illustrated the possibilities. A person boasting about a high rate of return will be open for possible criticism from finance and accounting personnel, unless there are undisputable facts on which the calculation is based.

Do not try to use ROI on every program. The HRD professional should recognize that there are some programs that are difficult to quantify. An ROI calculation may not be feasible. Other methods of presenting the benefits may be more appropriate.

Converting to a Profit Center

Another approach to measuring the return on HRD is to convert the department to a profit-center concept. The concept involves a conversion of the HRD department from a budget-based center to one that either breaks even or generates a profit. The revenue comes from the sale of products, programs, or services delivered to the user departments. This can take the place of individual ROI calculations or can be used in conjunction with them. Although the concept is in the embryonic stage, many organizations have at least planned for the conversion.

Since the first edition of this book, there has been considerable progress on the implementation of profit centers. For example, Control Data made the transition from an expense-based to a profit center concept and included the entire corporate personnel staff.[18] Based on Control Data's successful experience, the process needs to be carefully planned and integrated into the organization on a gradual basis. It is particularly difficult for the staff members to adjust to it. These issues are covered in more detail in this section.

One company with a tremendous track record with this concept is the chemical giant, DuPont. Created almost twenty years ago, the DuPont profit center has 150 employees delivering expertise on safety, quality assurance, environmental management, regulatory compliance, and other topics through consulting, seminars, training aids, films and interactive video. Basically, DuPont offers three types of services:

- ☐ Courses designed to be administered at client sites
- ☐ Seminars conducted by DuPont consultants
- ☐ Management consulting services

According to DuPont, their profit center concept has been very successful and they believe that it can be done by other HRD departments.[19]

Rationale for Conversion

No department wants to be a burden on others. Yet many HRD departments are considered as staff overhead. Line organizations must work a little harder to pay for the department's services and products. The HRD staff is referred to as excess, overhead, burden, or an administrative expense. Those references create frustrating conditions for many professional HRD personnel. One way to move from that posture to one of a self-sufficient nature is to convert the HRD department to a profit center.

Some organizations, by the nature of their structure, are forced into the profit-center concept. One such organization is Belk Stores, a soft-goods retail chain of almost 400 stores in 17 southeastern states with 35,000 employees. Each store is basically a wholly owned corporation, with its own Board of Directors. A member of the Belk family serves as a majority stockholder of the Board to provide coordination and continuity within the chain of stores. Within the limits set by the Board of Directors, the store manager operates autonomously. He is responsible only for the bottomline results.

The HRD department is one of the several corporate services available to the stores. This department provides HRD programs as requested by each store. If a store manager does not want to participate in a program, he does not have to. There is little or no pressure to force their participation or involvement. The HRD department must offer a service which yields an ROI for the store. Otherwise, it will not be used. This structure forces the department to become a profit center.

Another reason for conversion is that the concept lessens the need to calculate the ROI for individual programs. The profit generated from revenues is used to calculate an overall return for the department. Unprofitable programs will disappear or be subsidized by profitable ones. However, there is still a need for evaluation because of all the other purposes other than cost/benefit comparisons.

Some professionals perceive the HRD profit-center concept as being the same as an existing HRD/consulting firm. There are hundreds of firms providing consulting services and HRD programs as their sole source of revenue. They develop and customize in-house programs to meet their clients' needs. They have survived and made a profit, with many of them being very successful. The internal HRD department should be able to provide the same programs or services—at a profit.

If the profit-center concept is effective, the HRD department must negotiate or establish fees and prices for parts or all of their efforts. There are several types of profit-center concepts, and many considerations are necessary before making this conversion. The remainder of this chapter will be devoted to these issues and an initial discussion of the true profit center.

Sources of Revenue

A "typical" HRD department has several sources of revenue. These are usually divided into the following categories.

Professional services. These services include professional staff time devoted to assisting an organization in conflict resolution, problem solving, needs analysis, or other activities aimed at developing the personnel in the organization. They may also include all the development work necessary to produce an HRD program.

Program fees. These fees include all fees for seminars, workshops, or HRD programs. They may cover the costs for delivering an HRD program as well as factors for overhead, analysis, development, and evaluation.

Products. This covers the self-contained packaged programs sold to the various departments or divisions within the organization. For example, a self-sufficient computer-based instruction course does not necessarily need any assistance from the HRD staff. This program is sold as a product with a fixed price.

Administrative services. These services include charges for routine and standard services provided by the HRD staff. Examples are processing tuition refund requests, coordinating outside seminar participation, or maintaining a human resources planning system.

A few organizations have another source of revenue, or outside income, that results from the sale of services and programs to other organizations. In addition to Control Data and DuPont, General Motors, Xerox, and Westinghouse are only a few of many organizations now selling their programs to the public.

Fee/Price Determination

The determination of the fees, charges, or prices for revenue items is very critical to the success of a conversion. The prices must be high enough for the department to generate the revenue to yield the desired profit, yet low enough to be competitively priced. There are three basic approaches to setting fees.

Fee negotiation. The HRD staff and the client organization, whether a department, division, or section, can negotiate a fair and equitable fee for the services offered. This is a particularly useful approach when determining the fee to charge for professional assistance. Some consideration might be given to using a rate similar to those set by external HRD consulting firms providing the same or similar service.

Competitive pricing. Another possibility is to price the program or service equal to or less than the market price for the same or similar items. This is probably the best approach when pricing a product such as a packaged HRD program or a workshop similar to one offered publicly. The HRD staff must show how their prices compete with those that are commercially available. Ideally, it should be less than what the organization can buy outside. Of course, the quality should be better, and the specific tailoring to the organization should be a definite plus. This procedure is difficult when a program is needed, and there are no programs commercially available for comparison. In this case similar programs in terms of length, content, and difficulty might be used for comparison purposes.

Administrative service charges. The third approach is to establish a service charge for providing a service to the organization. This charge is determined internally with input from accounting personnel. It represents a fair and equitable charge for providing the service. An example is a 10% service charge for processing all tuition refund applications.

Variations of the Profit-Center Concept

The concept just described is the true profit center. With fixed or negotiated fees or prices, the revenue offsets the expenses, and the additional funds represent profit generated by the HRD department. The ROI is the earnings divided by the investment in resources to deliver those products and services. When in practice, this concept is utopia. Realistically, it may be a long way off for many organizations. There are other variations, short of the true profit center, which may be appropriate for some organizations, at least on an interim basis.

Protected profit center. A profit center that is subsidized to ensure the availability of resources is called a protected profit center. Basically, this approach involves pricing those services and products when they can easily be priced and subsidizing other programs and essential services. This approach assumes that it is difficult to establish prices for a number of services. Other departments and sections may not utilize the HRD department to supply those services, and the result may cause inefficiencies. For example, in the tuition refund program mentioned earlier, if a department was not willing to pay a 10% service charge, the results could be unacceptable. The department might want to resort to processing their own tuition refunds, possibly jeopardizing the standards of the program. An easy way out is to subsidize the department to provide funds necessary to administer those programs.

Cost center. This approach involves estimating the cost of the various services and products delivered and charging the client for those costs. All department costs are allocated in some way to user departments. This approach requires detailed and accurate cost forecasts and cost accumulation. Also, when parts of the organization refuse to use a program or service, the cost for providing that service to other parts of the organization may increase. For example, suppose 10 departments share the cost for an HRD program and 2 departments decide not to participate. All costs, including prorated development costs, as well as delivery, have to be spread over 8 departments instead of 10, thereby raising the overall cost of those departments. This approach provides little incentive for HRD departments to try to keep costs at a minimum, and there is no opportunity for a profit.

Break-even center. This variation is similar to the cost center concept, except that fees and prices are established to enable the department to reach a break-even point at year end. Higher prices are established for popular or frequently offered programs to offset losses on programs or services difficult to price or which represent a loss to the department. With this approach, users of the programs, services, or products may not get what they pay for. They may pay more for some programs and less for others when they should cost approximately the same. Another problem is the lack of the opportunity to profit in the HRD department.

Considerations for Conversion

There are several critical factors to consider when converting from the present-status operation to one of the versions of a profit-center concept. The strength or weakness of these factors may determine if such a move is feasible.

Gradual change. A conversion from an expense-based department to a profit center requires a gradual change. Management may have difficulty with the concept of paying for these services. One organization approached the conversion with the following 10 steps:

1. Establish HRD accounts in each department.
2. Allocate all costs of outside programs/seminars to user departments.
3. Allocate the costs of special, non-routine HRD programs.
4. Charge each user department for tuition refunds of their employees.
5. Charge a fee for participation in major programs.
6. Set prices for all formal HRD programs.
7. Charge all management trainee salaries to the sponsoring department.
8. Negotiate fees for new program development.
9. Negotiate fees for consulting work.
10. Charge an administration fee for all regular support services.

It took approximately five years to move from a centralized budget-based department to a self-sufficient profit center.

Effective products and services. The products and services provided by the organization must be effective and be perceived as a worthwhile investment. The HRD department must have an excellent reputation, with good results from past programs; otherwise, such a conversion could be disastrous.

Management commitment and support. A successful conversion requires good management support and commitment at all levels. Management must not only see the need for effective HRD, but be willing to pay for it. They must be willing to invest today for a return tomorrow. They must be willing to let employees participate in programs and be involved in the development and implementation of new programs.

HRD staff commitment. Another obvious consideration is the total commitment of the HRD staff. This is mentioned because, too often, a major change is implemented at the initiation of one key individual in a department or section. A successful conversion will require the commitment and involvement of the entire staff. Otherwise, the department could drop out of existence. This was a key to Control Data's successful conversion.

Competitive fees/prices. All revenue items must be competitively priced. Charging more than the competition on the basis of providing a better product will not carry very much weight with a profit-minded executive. While it may be true, the departments are seeking bottomline results, and they must be convinced that they will be getting a superior product.

Method of charges. Straightforward, equitable methods of charging departments must be devised. One problem that may surface is the concept of double charges. In many organizations the HRD department is funded through direct charges or allocations to all the producing departments, regardless of their participation in these programs. If a department is charged an additional fee when their employees participate in an HRD program, then in effect they are being double-charged. This approach has caused some conversion efforts to fail.

A more realistic approach is to credit those departments for the amount of the fees or prices of the products and services used. This reduces the allocation to HRD and saves the department money. This also encourages use of the products and services of the HRD department. If the participation is sufficient, the credits can offset the charges. Thus, in effect, each department is receiving a benefit from the HRD department equal to their original budget allocations.

This approach can be illustrated with an example. Suppose a department has a $15,000 cost allocation incurred in their overhead expenses for the HRD department. When the department sends a participant to an HRD program or otherwise uses a service of the HRD department, the predetermined fee or price is credited to the department. If the department uses more than $15,000, the excess amount is charged against the department. A manager interested in HRD will certainly use the total allocation for the department, assuring that $15,000 worth of HRD products and services are used.

Profit-center impact. One final factor should be considered before pursuing the conversion. The impact of the profit-center concept should be assessed thoroughly in the organization. This impact analysis includes the types of courses delivered, services provided, the reaction of the management group, and the reaction of the HRD staff.

Some courses will die a natural death because no one will pay for them, particularly those perceived as unnecessary. This may cause concern. For instance, suppose all supervisors have been required to participate in an Equal Employment Opportunity (EEO) workshop. The company feels that it is imperative that all supervisors understand the various laws and company commitment toward EEO. Departments paying for this program may be reluctant to send participants if the program is not perceived as essential. These issues must be addressed up front before conversion.

Some insight into the potential impact may be gained from a survey of the management group to determine to what extent management will utilize the department's services if they must pay directly for them. The results of this survey could very well determine whether or not it can work. Negative attitudes could signal problems ahead or at least pinpoint areas where attention is needed before implementing a conversion plan.

Caution. Of all concepts introduced in the first edition of this book, the profit center approach has been slow to develop. Perhaps this is because of the issues raised in this chapter. It is a bold step and though not yet widely adopted, it holds great promise for the future.

An important concern when implementing this process is to examine the philosophy and structure of the organization. The profit center concept is not as effective when training is decentralized to the lowest level in the organization. With decentralization, it is difficult to pinpoint precise costs that can be charged to the user organization. In essence, a highly decentralized approach moves the cost of training nearest to the user organization and itself is a step toward the concept of paying for services provided.

Overall, the profit center approach is a legitimate, viable alternative for many organizations. It should only be tackled where human resource development is respected and is already considered to be a contributing force in the organization. A conversion that succeeds can be very rewarding to the HRD department. A failure can be disastrous. For additional information on converting an existing department to the profit center concept see Mercer.[20]

Discussion Questions

---

1. Identify a common output measurement and convert it to a dollar value. How difficult is this process?
2. Identify a measure taken from the quality control field and convert it to a dollar cost savings. Comment on the difficulty of this conversion.
3. Identify a times savings measure and convert it to a dollar value. Why is time savings so difficult to calculate?
4. Select at least two soft-data measurements and convert them to a dollar value of savings.
5. Which of the approaches to converting soft-data measurements is most appropriate? Why?
6. An HRD executive was quoted as follows, "The conversion of soft data to a dollar value creates an illusion of a precision that does not exist. As a result, we do not use soft data savings in any of our evaluation projects." Explain the concern that generated this comment.
7. In what type of projects would the calculation of a return on investment be most appropriate? What type would be least appropriate?
8. What are some advantages of return on investment over other types of quantitative evaluations?
9. What are the advantages of using the cost/benefit ratio over the other financial measures?
10. Search the literature for an example where a return on investment has been calculated. Critique the approach and the results.
11. What are the advantages of utility analysis?

12. Why has the profit center concept been slow to develop?
13. Develop a plan to convert the HRD department in your organization (or one with which you familiar) from an expense-based to a profit center concept.
14. What are some natural barriers to the use of the profit center concept?
15. Under what conditions should a profit center approach be considered?
16. What important precautions should be taken when dollar values are tied to program evaluations?

References

1. Crosby, P. B., *Quality Is Free,* Mentor Books, New American Library, New York, NY, 1979.
2. Zemke, R., "Cost of Quality: You Can Measure It,"*Training,* August, 1990, pp. 62–63.
3. Zemke, ibid p. 62.
4. Zemke, ibid p. 63.
5. Townsend, P. L., *Commit To Quality,* John Wiley, New York, NY, 1986.
6. Goodman, P. S., Atkin, R. S., et al., *Absenteeism,* Jossey-Bass, San Francisco, CA, 1984, p. 308.
7. Creery, P. T. and Creery, K. W., *Reducing Labor Turnover in Financial Institutions,* Quorum Books, New York, NY, 1988.
8. Phillips, J. J., *Recruiting, Training and Retaining New Employees,* Jossey-Bass, San Francisco, CA, 1987, pp. 19–24.
9. Brealey, R. and Myer, S., *Principles of Corporate Finance,* McGraw-Hill, New York, NY, 1984.
10. Mosier, N. R., "Financial Analysis: The Methods and Their Application to Employee Training," *Human Resources Development Quarterly,* Spring, 1990, p. 48.
11. Thompson, M. S., *Benefit-Cost Analysis for Program Evaluation,* Sage Publications, Beverly Hills, CA, 1980. p. 1.
12. Hawthorne, E. M., *Evaluating Employee Training Programs,* Quorum Books, New York, NY, 1987.
13. Sheppeck, M. A. and Cohen, S. L., "Put a Dollar Value on Your Training Programs," *Training and Development Journal,* November, 1985, p. 61.
14. Schmidt, F. L., Hunter, J. E. and Pearlman, K., "Assessing the Economic Impact of Personnel Programs on Workforce Productivity," *Personnel Psychology,* Vol. 35, p. 333–347, 1982.
15. Mathieu, J. E. and Leonard, R. L., Jr., "Applying Utility Concepts to a Training Program in Supervisory Skills: A Time-based Ap-

proach," *Academy of Management Journal,* Vol. 30, No. 2, June, 1987.

16. Jackson, T., *Evaluation: Relating Training to Business Performance,* University Associates, San Diego, CA, 1989.
17. Spencer, L. M., Jr., *Calculating the Human Resource Costs and Benefits,* John Wiley, 1986.
18. Noer, D. W., "Ready, Set, Turn a Profit!" *Training and Development Journal,* May, 1985, p. 38–39.
19. Rutigliano, A. J., "Training Inc.: DuPont Makes the Most of A Corporate Resource," *The Human Resources Professional,* November–December, 1988.
20. Mercer, M. W., *Turning Your Human Resources Department Into A Profit Center,* AMACOM, 1989.

CHAPTER 11

Computers and HRD Evaluation

A major development in the HRD field in the 1980s was the use of computers in training, education, and development, and from all indications, the 1990s will see a continuation of this. This change is more pronounced in large organizations. At IBM, for instance, computer technology was used to deliver more than 5% of the company's education in the early 1980s. Today that figure stands at 30%, and by the end of the 1990s, IBM estimates that 60% of the company's training will be delivered by the use of computer technology. Although IBM may be one of the leaders in this effort, others are not changing as rapidly. For example, Northern Telecom, Inc., which has a reputation for effective, technology-based training, still conducts 90% of its training in the classroom.[1]

After several decades of research and development with computer-based training, two points have become increasingly clear: (1) Computer-based training will not replace all other methods of training and development as some had predicted, and (2) computer-based training is not going away as some others had hoped.[2] It is obvious that computer-based training will be integrated into the mainstream of the delivery and administration of the HRD function.

If computer-based training was used only as a method of training delivery, then its coverage would be presented in another chapter or perhaps covered very little at all. However, computers have gone far beyond the process of delivering training through a self-paced format. They have become an integral part of HRD and an important aspect of evaluation. For example, in addition to providing a method of training delivery, computers are used in a variety of applications such as

☐ Tracking, collecting, and analyzing costs for HRD
☐ Collecting data for evaluation
☐ Test scoring and analysis
☐ Comprehensive analysis of all evaluation data
☐ Training administration and recordkeeping

Because of these applications, computers have become an integral part of evaluation. Consequently, this chapter focuses on the use of computers in training with an emphasis on the evaluation process. It presents the types of computer-based training, the advantages of computers over other traditional methods of training, applications of computers in training, computers and training evaluation, and finally, a comprehensive case example on the use of computers.

Types of Computer-Based Training and Basic Concepts

As with most topics tied to computers, there is a proliferation of terms and acronyms that tend to complicate the basic understanding of the issues. This section presents basic definitions in computer-based training that are consistent with those reported by the American Society for Training and Development.[3] Figure 11-1 shows the relationship of the principal components of computer-based training that are explained in this section.

Computer-Based Training

The term computer-based training (CBT) is the umbrella that includes all forms and uses of computers to support training or learning. The components of computer-based training are computer-assisted instruction (CAI), computer-managed instruction (CMI) and computer-supported learning resources (CSLR). Other terminology has been used interchangeably with computer-based training. When there is a focus on the learner instead of the instructor, computer-based learning (CBL) is sometimes used. When there is a focus on education, the term computer-based education (CBE) is used. Because computer-based training was originally developed in a university setting, the term naturally applied to it was education. Hence, CBE is the oldest of the several synonymous

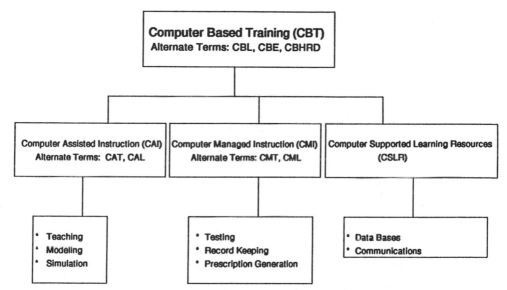

Figure 11-1. Basic terminology and relationships in computer-based training.

terms of use. With the increasing use of the term human resource development, some prefer to use computer-based human resource development (CBHRD) as the preferred term. Because of its widespread use, the term computer-based training will be used throughout this chapter.

Computer-Assisted Instruction

CAI is defined as the use of a computer to deliver instruction. The modes of CAI are drill and practice, modeling, tutorial, and simulation. Generally, drills take less time and cost less to develop than tutorial CAI. Under drill and practice, the computer presents a problem to the trainee, waits for an answer, and tells the trainee if the answer is right or wrong. In a tutorial, concepts may be introduced, examples may be presented, and practice may be part of the process. If a trainee finds information too simple or too difficult, a program may branch to another lesson or segment in line with the trainee's abilities. Modeling and simulations make it possible for trainees to experience events or explore environments that would otherwise be too expensive, dangerous, or time consuming to encounter.

Computer-assisted instruction is an outgrowth of programmed instruction developed in the 1960s. In programmed instruction, trainees could control their own progress lesson by lesson by providing responses to questions and problems contained in the program. Trainees could branch out to different parts of the program based on their responses. In CAI, storing lessons in a computer rather than pages of a book has major advantages. First, the sheer volume of the material is better controlled and managed through the use of a computer. In a comprehensive program that involves a tremendous amount of branching, a computer can handle the material much better than a programmed text. To provide a modest amount of remedial text in a programmed instruction format would require a work of tremendous complexity.

A second advantage is the speed in using a computer. Trainees can interact quickly with the computer through the terminal and move efficiently through the material. In a programmed instruction text, the movement is sometimes cumbersome and slow to generate. With the trainee engaged in the program, there is almost continuous dialogue with the computer. The trainee makes frequent inputs to the system and so the responses flow quickly.

Computers are usually programmed to vary the instruction to the ability level of the trainees and provide remedial instruction for those who have less capability. Some systems provide initial testing on all training objectives and the trainees receive instruction only in accordance with those objectives in which he or she does not perform satisfactorily. When trainees with varying degrees of experience are participating, this feature can save considerable time.[4]

Computer-Managed Instruction

The second major part of CBT is computer-managed instruction. CMI realizes its advantage from the full capabilities of a computer to track and monitor student progress. CMI includes a computer-assisted testing, which involves the use of computers to deliver and score tests. This has proven to be an inexpensive process in which test items are quickly scored and analyzed on a computer.

In addition to testing, CMI involves prescription generation and recordkeeping. Whereas CAI in the truest sense is used mainly to deliver specific lessons, the computer system can serve a wide range of purposes in course management. Through the use of CMI, students will be routed to different resources, appropriate to their needs. At the start of the course, the computer can assist in diagnosing a trainee's specific knowledge and skill deficiencies, his or her performance on the entry test and determine whether he or she needs further instructions on a particular subject and if so, to what depth.[5] Recordkeeping involves the full range of administrative support activities to manage trainee records and ensure that the HRD department functions efficiently.

Computer-Supported Learning Resources

By definition, a computer-supported learning resource is any form of computer support or function that supports learning other than those that teach (CAI), test, prescribe, or keep records (CMI). The modes of CSLR are data base and communications. CSLR data bases are similar in purpose to traditional non-computer learning resources such as the library. The CSLR, along with CAI and CMI are the components of computer-based training. For the remainder of the chapter, the term "computer-based training" will be used to cover computers in training including CAI, CMI, and CSLR.

Interactive Video Discs

The interactive video disc (IVD) represents a combination of a video disc and CAI media. The computer controls the lessons interfaced with the program. It also presents a lesson that may involve the completely automatic play of a video disc sequence. A question is asked and depending on the answer, the learner may be shown any one of several video sequences. Based on the response, a particular still or motion video sequence will be displayed. In many ways, this technology offers the power of both media.

The interactive video disc grew during the 1980s and promises to be an important training tool for the 1990s. The interactive video disc has been enhanced in the following ways:[6]

☐ Post video discussions are added where trainers follow a video training session with a question/answer discussion period.
☐ Discussions are allowed during the video using the pause function of the VCR.
☐ Case studies are presented where a dramatic, illustrative scene is presented.
☐ The use of searching/skipping where trainers find that generic video tape contain segments of little or no value to trainees.

One reason interactive video discs seem more promising is that it appears that standards are now being developed. In the early models of IVD, hardware was incompatible and specifications were different. It now appears that the Interactive Video Industry Association will be developing standards.[7]

Advantages of Computer-Based Training

The use of computers in training has grown dramatically in the last ten years. This is fueled in part by the continuing improvement in the technological and computer industry along with the cost reductions of computer technology and associated equipments. In addition, some inherited advantages of computer training have assisted this growth. Today's technology and applications of the use of computers in training focus around six important advantages, presented in this section.

Cost Effectiveness

Because of the need to sink large sums of money into hardware for the delivery of training, a decision to use computer-based training was difficult to justify in the past. However, with lower cost computer equipment, greater capabilities of equipment, and the demand for large-scale delivery mechanisms, the costs are now overshadowed by the tremendous benefits. Computers, in many applications, are the most cost effective way to deliver training. There is overwhelming evidence that, under the right circumstances, computer-based training is considerably more cost effective than classroom training and has produced learning that is equal to or superior to what classrooms can provide.[8] Table 11-1 shows typical costs and benefits of providing computer-based training.

Self-Paced Learning

Probably the most publicized advantage for using computer-based training is the self-paced learning process. As described earlier, computers enable individuals to learn at their own pace and adjust to their own abilities. This feature differentiates computer-based training from classroom training, training films, and other methods of delivery.[9] The advantages of self-paced learning hinge around three important concepts: interaction, continuous testing and reinforcement, and trainee self-sufficiency.

Table 11-1
CBT Costs vs. Benefits*

Costs	Benefits
Start-up	To trainees
* people	* more effective use of time
* equipment	* available when needed
* facilities	* consistent presentation
On-going	* reduced travel time and cost
course production including	* special short-term requirements
* design	can be met
* authoring	* not away from place of work or
* entry into computer	home
* correction	* practical training made more
* review	effective
* validation	* may be available any time
* other media	* home study may be possible
course presentation including	To HRD department
* equipment costs	* reduced instructor time
* instructor time	* easier trainee monitoring
* time of computer personnel	* accurate trainee monitoring
course updating	* less classroom space needed
	* incentive to improve courses

* *Taken in part from Christopher, D. and Whitlock, Q.*, A Handbook of Computer Based Training *(2nd Edition), Kogan Page, London, 1988 p. 172.*

From the time a trainee switches on a computer to the time the program is complete, each screen is presented as a result of a trainee's response. In a well designed program, responses determine what happens, as well as when and how long the program will last. The program's progress and a trainee's success are geared by what a trainee does or fails to do. Training cannot proceed unless the trainee takes the initiative.

Built-in testing and even remedial training is incorporated into many CBT programs. Depending on the nature of the material and the type of knowledge being taught, these tests follow some of the types of tests presented earlier in this book. The trainee must show a mastery of the test items to proceed with the remainder of the material.

An important distinguishing feature of most CBT is that it is self-sufficient. Training self-sufficiency is important in cost justifications since the trainee needs little or no outside help beyond the computer and the program. In this way, self-paced learning is also self-taught.

There are a variety of circumstances and requirements in which self-paced characteristics of CBT are particularly advantageous. According to Ganger, CBT has a definite advantage when:

☐ The instruction is complex and multilevel computer systems must be delivered to heterogeneous, variously qualified trainee communities.

☐ The training seeks to involve trainees in their own career development, thereby adding empowerment to the educational process.[10]

Efficiency

While the self-paced learning concept itself is sufficient, there are other factors that add to the efficiency of computer-based training. Studies have shown that individualized instruction takes less trainee time on average than group instruction.

Individualized instruction decreases the total training time from 30% to 50% depending on which study is examined.[11] Computer simulations created in a computer-based training network can collapse time. In situations where trainees are learning to operate equipment in which waiting times are typically involved, computer simulation can compress waiting time significantly.

An additional aspect of efficiency is in the use of subject matter experts. In effect, with CBT, these experts can be replicated without losing their productive capacity. Highly specialized technical courses are usually instructed by experts. Using computers allows organizations to replicate the process without taking the time of the individual expert. And finally, there is the situation when computers enable trainees to schedule and use their time more efficiently. For example, sales representatives who have meetings cancelled can use this time with a computer-based training program.

Situational Advantages

There are some situations in which the computer has an obvious advantage. One such situation is where computer systems or software is being taught in a training program. Because trainees will be at the computer terminal, it makes much more sense for computers to be used in the process. The most practical way to teach a software language is to use a computer. Another situation is when nothing else works. In teaching autistic children or other children with severe handicaps, traditional methods just don't work. A computer has a better chance at making progress with these special audiences.[12] Then there are situations when accuracy is of absolute importance, times when training *must* work. For example, training technicians at a nuclear power plant, mechanics for an airline, or surgeons in a medical school are situations where training effectiveness must be as near perfect as possible. Computer-based training seems to enhance this accuracy requirement.

Information Distribution

In situations where an organization must deliver a substantial amount of information to employees in widely separated or dispersed locations, computer-based training has been particularly useful. This is particularly true when training material contains periodic or unscheduled updating and changes. A computer-based program can be downloaded from a centralized location, sent to the mainframe at the division or headquarters location, and on to hundred of locations throughout the world. Trainees at each site receive exactly the same program. This brings uniformity to procedures and expertise. Furthermore, employees receive training simultaneously. Perhaps most importantly, CBT programs can be updated or changed more effectively than written material or classroom instruction.[13]

Availability of Computers

In most organizations, a computer terminal is readily available. In financial institutions, for example, almost every employee has access to a computer terminal that is used in the normal activities at work. In other businesses, more and more employees have computer terminals, either PC based, networked with a group of computers, or tied to a mainframe computer. With this availability, training programs can be developed to be presented on existing equipment avoiding additional purchases of terminals or additional facilities for training.

Also, when compared to other forms of training, CBT requires little or no support logistics. Instructors, classroom space, travel arrangements, and field preparations are eliminated because the training comes to the trainee at the work site. This advantage is particularly appropriate when training occurs over time or when turnover creates a flow of new trainees.[14]

Applications of Computers in Training

Virtually any type of training program can be converted to a computer-based format. However, some programs have inherent advantages because of the nature of the program, the audience, location of the trainees and the magnitude of the training task. To illustrate the variety of computer-based training, four actual case studies are presented to show the applications of computers in training.

Clerical Training at a Bankcard Center

The first example is taken from the financial industry and was reported by Dean and Whitlock.[15] Barclaycard is one of the two main credit card companies in the United Kingdom operated by major banks. As with any credit card company, the operations are highly computerized. At Barclaycard, approximately 80 tasks were identified that require human input, and included such actions as issuing cards, debiting or crediting customer accounts, or replacing lost or stolen cards. Detailed procedures are developed to assist the clerical employees in using the computer to access information and to process these tasks as needed. There were 1,500 people who were trained on these procedures.

New employees entering the company must be trained in the use of these procedures as well as in the selection and interpretation of computer-based information programs that provide information to carry out their particular tasks. Before 1977, lectures, demonstrations, and exercises in a classroom were used for this type of training. A decision was made to use the IBM mainframe computer to provide this training.

Because the volume of the training materials was high and the demand for terminals used in the production area was constant and heavy, management decided that computer-based training would be accomplished on special terminals located near workstations. New employees at Barclaycard learned many of the day-to-day tasks performed in work groups through CBT courses. Training was efficient and effective and Barclaycard reports a tremendous success in the twelve years since the program's implementation.

Sales Training

A second example is taken from the computer services industry and was reported by Reinhart.[16] In 1987, Xerox Corporation was experiencing a decrease in its printer sales. The software package called "Xerox Integrated Composition Software" (XICS) was identified as an important starting point for selling large centralized printers. Researchers have found that for each XICS software package sold, 2.4 centralized printers were sold. Data showed that sales representatives had not been selling XICS well. Sales were less than half of what Xerox had predicted. A Xerox problem solving team had determined that previous XICS training had been ineffective and new sales representatives had not even had the training. Obviously, there was a need to improve XICS training.

After forming a team to develop a program, management decided that computer-based training would be used instead of classroom training by experts, on-the-job training, or self study. Computer-based training not only served the needs on a cost-benefit basis, but it posed several other advantages. It was self-paced and could address a variety of trainee backgrounds. It was modular and could easily be integrated with other training. It was able to reach a target population quickly, and it offered an innovative approach to the subject.

Xerox implemented the program on a pilot basis and then evaluated the program on both content and strategy, using a variety of measurements and measurement instruments, including telephone surveys, observations, and one-on-one and group interviews. Pre- and post-testing was also a part of the process. The computer-based program had a significant impact on primary customers as well as the sales force. Sales representatives who took the course learned about application selling. Many customers are now developing new applications for XICS software. At the close of 1988, XICS was at 150% of the plan. In a follow-up survey, the training program attributed more than $4.6 million to revenues.

Basic Skills Training in the Army

The third example is taken from government and was reported by Wilson.[17] Because of discouraging trends about the shortage of skilled workers to staff jobs both in and out of the military, more than eight years ago, the education division of the U.S. Army recognized the problem and began to work on it. A sharp decline in the available recruiting population began in 1988 and is to continue through the late 1990s. To maintain the same level of recruitment it had been achieving, the Army would have to sign up one out of three high school graduates in 1992, a task that was considered to be impossible. Instead, the Army decided that upgrading the basic skills of the available population would be a more reasonable approach to the employment problem. In addition, the Army faced a congressional mandate and close scrutiny by the General Accounting Office (GAO). The GAO stated that the Army should:

☐ Identify basic skills required for job performance.
☐ Enroll those people who need basic skills and teach only the skills they need to learn to perform their jobs.
☐ Centralize management so that the Army's basic skills program would be administered uniformly at all locations.

The solution was a new program that became known as a job-skills education program (JSEP), developed jointly by Florida State University and Ford Aerospace Corporation.

JSEP is the largest computer-based skills program every developed for adults. It was designed to teach basic skills that students need to be trained for jobs. It contains more than 300 lessons that cover more than 200 basic skills. Each version of JSEP takes more than 100 megabytes of disk space and includes more than 10,000 graphics.

JSEP is made up of three major kinds of lessons:

☐ Verbal lessons, which teach reading and writing skills.
☐ Quantitative lessons, which teach computational skills.
☐ Learning strategy modules, which teach students how to learn.

About 90% of the lessons are on computer, the rest are on paper. Each lesson is job related. All lessons are self-paced and individualized and are controlled by a student management system. There are many possible paths that students may take through JSEP depending on performance at particular places in the program. Because the individual prescriptions are based on occupations and because of the multiple paths of each program, no two JSEP students will follow the same course of study. Army JSEP students average from 80 to 100 hours to complete their prescriptions. Students with lower reading abilities will take longer.

Overall, the program enjoys the normal benefits available through computer-based training. More than 20 Army posts around the country now use JSEP. Thousands of soldiers have completed their JSEP prescriptions and plans are underway to expand the program's use. In addition to its use in the Army, it is now available commercially for use in a classroom environment or a smaller field location. It offers industry and government a solution to the basic skills deficiency of current and future employees.

Medical Education at a University

In this fourth example, the CBT system involves a large time-shared computer used exclusively for CBT at a university and is reported by Kearsley.[18] The terminals are high-resolution graphic displays that accept touch input. Twenty terminals are located in the CBT learning center and four additional terminals are available elsewhere for instructors to offer courses or examine student records. Most of the courses were developed at the university. Instructors can either learn the authoring language and write courseware themselves, or work with programmers on the staff. The medical facility provides one semester of time to three instructors per year for the specific purpose of creating or revising CBT courseware.

To take advantage of the CBT system, the medical faculty had to acquire its own terminals and communication controllers. In this scenario, CBT provides mainline instruction and therefore replaces the previous classroom approach. The center is open 76 hours per week. The utilization rate is about 50% for a total of 760 actual students hours per week. This translates into a cost per student hour of $5.80. For medical education at the university level, this is an attractive per student hour cost.

These four brief examples show the wide variety of applications of computer-based training and highlights some of the advantages of this technology in replacing other methods of delivery. It also highlights the integration of evaluation with training because many of the systems require testing and evaluation as part of the program.

Evaluation and Computers

While the previous material in this chapter emphasized the use of computers in HRD, it is important to focus on how computers have enhanced the evaluation process. Five reasons why computers have strengthened evaluation of the HRD process are outlined here.

Accuracy

An inherent advantage of computers in any field is the accuracy enjoyed by computers. Rarely, if ever, do computers make a mistake. They seldom fail to add, subtract, multiply, or divide correctly. They do not forget or omit data. They also have tremendous storage capabilities.

However, computers are not fool-proof and they will only process information that is supplied by humans. Therefore, if errors are entered into the system, there will be errors on the output side of the system.

Speed

Computers are fast and are getting faster. They can quickly analyze data that previously took hours to do by hand. In a sophisticated data collection and analysis, the task can be completed in a matter of seconds or minutes with computers. Data analysis software is readily available to analyze evaluation data to provide faster responses and quicker results. Computers now allow accurate, on-the-spot assessments of trainees' responses. For example, a customized spreadsheet makes it possible to obtain immediate and ongoing monitoring of trainees' responses. The computer only takes a few minutes to assess trainee responses to a session. The results are more participation, improved communication between trainer and trainees, and better training programs.[19]

Cost Monitoring

Another important advantage of computers in evaluation is tracking and monitoring costs. Costs must be tracked and monitored for a efficient training program administration as well as to provide data for a cost-benefit analysis. Computers enhance the analysis of cost data, enabling trainers to quickly tabulate costs by various cost categories. Expense account classifications and process/functional categories for costs can be routinely monitored on an ongoing basis and tabulated by program or time periods. It would be difficult, if not impossible, to monitor costs without the use of computers. In addition, computers enhance the use of training cost models described in Chapter 7. Cost models use complicated formulas that facilitate computer tabulation and analysis.

Build-In Evaluation

For computer-based training programs, testing and evaluation is usually built into the system. Some use pre- and post-course testing while others test student progress throughout the program. Effective CBT programs evaluate not only student progress but also how the student reacted to and used the program and the difficulties encountered. An effective program would monitor the following:

☐ Pre- and post-test results.
☐ The time each trainee has spent on the computer and the overall program.
☐ The responses of all trainees in the use of a portion of the program.
☐ Extended remedial learning.
☐ Path selections.
☐ Trainees' evaluation of the program.
☐ Difficulties trainees have encountered with the program.

This information is collected automatically as part of program design. It is this feature of CBT programs that help enhance overall evaluations and represent an important step toward accountability of the training effort.

Training Administration

Although not exclusively related to evaluation, training administration is an important element in the effective and efficient delivery of training programs. It is important to keep track of training attendance records, course completion records, and follow-up data, as well as coordinate correspondence in an efficient manner. Organizations need a simple way to process routine information on courses, schedules, and instructors, and develop reports for course and program statistics, charge back information to accounting, etc. Many organizations have found a solution by computerizing training administration. This process involves the use of a database program to store employee information, course information, schedules, costs, and other training information. Lists and reports can be generated that would normally take hours to assimilate manually. In a recent review of major software packages, it was shown that the training administration involved the following types of data:

☐ Course title, time, date, location
☐ Participants (name, title, address, employee number)
☐ Registration and placement (status, course roster, attendance, waiting list)
☐ Instructors
☐ Costs
☐ Calendars

Computerized training administration is essential for effective and efficient use of trainee staff and trainee time and to ensure that records are kept properly to reflect the progress of trainees. The following is a listing of what one commercially available software package* can accomplish for the HRD department:

- ☐ Print enrollment confirmation memos.
- ☐ Keep complete employee training histories.
- ☐ Show all training activity in a time period.
- ☐ Show training activity by department or division.
- ☐ Schedule courses.
- ☐ Sort training activity by job title, EEO classification, sex, department or any other criteria you require.
- ☐ Print course catalogs.
- ☐ Export data to mainframe computers.
- ☐ Import data electronically from mainframe computers and slash manual data entry time.
- ☐ Waitlist trainees automatically.
- ☐ Enroll trainees automatically from waitlist.
- ☐ Print course rosters.
- ☐ Produce training plans for individuals or departments.
- ☐ Relate specific job qualifications to course curriculum.
- ☐ Provide evaluation data on course content, instructors, and training materials.
- ☐ Handle billing and chargeback information.
- ☐ Share data with other personal computer programs, including Lotus 1-2-3 and dBase III.
- ☐ Track job performance indicators.
- ☐ Produce individual transcripts.
- ☐ Produce key information for training needs analysis.
- ☐ Track and document training program development costs.
- ☐ Keep departmental budget.

Case Study: Implementation of a Career Development Plan

To illustrate the use of computers in HRD, the following case on career development is presented. It shows the dramatic impact of computers in an actual setting, and emphasizes built-in evaluation, even

---

* *TR Plus Software, produced by HRD Software, 22 Amherst Road, Amherst, MA 01002. Used with permission.*

in a subject difficult to evaluate. The system is developed by Conceptual Systems, Inc. and has a trade name of CareerPoint.[20] While it has been implemented in a variety of organizations, its implementation in Corning Glass Works won the ASTD Career Development Organizational Award. The following description will explain the program with excerpts of how the program is used at Corning, Unisys, and Secor Bank. This material is furnished by Conceptual Systems and is reproduced with permission.

System Overview

CareerPoint is a micro-computer-based career development system that provides employees at all levels with a complete program of career development information and planning, fully within the context of the specific organization and workplace. After only a few hours on Career-Point, employees produced their own career development plans. This ultimate output, in the form of a step-by-step action guide, is fully individualized and fully tested against both sound career development theory and objective organizational realities.

Every aspect of the system has been structured to focus responsibility for career development on employees, encouraging them to manage their own careers while providing the organization with a fully integrated structure for supporting employee development. Each user gains the knowledge and skills essential to effective, long-term career management with clear links to the organization's actual human resource needs and the related career opportunities.

Designed to be efficient and highly user friendly, CareerPoint uses the best available instructional and computer technology to aid career development efforts and to expand each user's sense of his or her career possibilities. Among these advanced features are on-line assessments; immediate on-line scoring and storage of all responses; the ability to search public and organizational databases for information on training, positions, and educational options; and the capability for full customization of content, text, screen displays, graphics, and user-accessible databases.

CareerPoint's proven effectiveness is quite literally by design; it draws in the most well-researched and sophisticated career planning theories. These proven concepts and instruments have been used in thousands of organizational and other career programs over many years, and their validity has been demonstrated with abundant empirical evidence.

Theoretical Foundations

CareerPoint integrates many proven career concepts and assessment systems that combine to measure, validate, and inform each user's progress toward a career plan. Chief among these foundations are those that address the concept of "Career Fit," the all-important alignment between person, place, and position.

Holland's Self-Directed Search. The most comprehensive of CareerPoint's conceptual bases is Holland's concept of vocational congruence, the fit between individual interests and the organization's needs. Holland's Self-Directed Search (SDS) is the instrument used in CareerPoint to assess career interests, and is a key mechanism through which employees can search the system's position database. The SDS thus measures the "position" fit for a potential employee-job combination.

The SDS employs Holland's "ideal" types of people and work environments, against which real people and work settings are measured. According to the Holland typology, there are six such person/position types: realistic (R), investigative (I), artistic (A), social (S), enterprising (E), and conventional (C).

The SDS assesses the three types that a given person most closely resembles, and assigns a three-letter summary code (e.g., RIE) to the individual. Positions and job families also have a unique three-letter code, reflecting the dominance to particular personality types and other traits within a given occupation or job category.

In CareerPoint, the SDS links the personal and position codes and then gives each user a list of "matching" positions and job families. This result provides crucial information about a person's "type" and their degree of fit with available job options.

The power of Holland's SDS typology lies in the fact that it respects the complexity of people and positions, while providing an effective means of locating good matches and clarifying poor ones. Further, this highly practical information helps both employees and employers identify and resolve person-position congruence problems.

The Work Environment Scale. A well-known and well-tested inventory, the Work Environment Scale helps individuals articulate their perceptions of existing work environments, specify their ideal workplaces, and assess their expectations of the work setting. This information can then be used to compare actual and ideal settings, or employer and manager perceptions of those environments, to bring about positive change in the workplace. The subscales of this useful inventory assess three dimensions of a given workplace environment: relationship, personal growth, and system maintenance and change.

The Myers-Briggs Type Indicator. The Myers-Briggs Type Indicator (MBTI) is well known as a means of assessing "personality" issues. The Myers-Briggs system assesses four areas of personal style and preference in perception and judgment—how individuals take in data and how they make decisions based on that data. The MBTI theories form the basis for CareerPoint's "person" concepts, and the optional on-line version compares an individual's four-letter MBTI code to the code for a given job or type of work, to help in determining the desirability of various career options for that individual.

Together, these three theoretical bases and parallel assessment tools are the key in the CareerPoint system. They provide a clear picture of each user's possible "Career Fit" with a potential position or career choice, and along with creative computer technology, they help to make the CareerPoint system so effective and rewarding for the individuals and organizations it serves.

Modules/Menus

As a whole, CareerPoint consists of 12 modules, accessed by a series of simple-to-use menus. The modules are structured in accordance with a proven career development model that embodies these key career development concerns:

- [ ] What is career development?
- [ ] Am I satisfied with my job?
- [ ] What are my skills and interests?
- [ ] What are my top career options?
- [ ] What are my goals?

Before covering those issues, CareerPoint users enter basic demographic information and receive a "how-to" tutorial on the use of the computer and the CareerPoint program. The system's instructional flow then moves through the four key steps in career development: self-assessment, reality checking, goal setting, and development planning.

The 12 modules are as follows:

1. How do I use the system?
2. What should I know about the organization?
3. What are my values, interests, and preferences?
4. What are my skills?
5. How do I identify job opportunities?
6. What are my goals for attaining a position?
7. What is my development plan for reaching my goals?
8. What skills should I have for job searching?
9. How do I create a resume?
10. What is my career planning summary?
11. Final hints.
12. System evaluation.

Users can select any of these practical questions and modules from the system's main menu; if specific menu choices are not made, CareerPoint automatically advances users along the most logical sequence. To illustrate the system's capability, two modules are explained in more detail. Module G focuses on individual development plans and Module L focuses on system evaluation.

Module G: What Is My Development Plan for Reaching My Goals?

In Module G, users synthesize information from the preceding modules to identify forces that will help or hinder achievement of their career goals and to develop detailed "next-step" plans. In the first section, the user begins developing an action plan for the goal by completing a force field analysis, which identifies positive and negative forces affecting that goal. In section two, the user identifies three goal obstacles and specific plans for overcoming them. This exercise can be done repeatedly. The information is then summarized at the end of the section.

The last section alerts users to the importance of education and training opportunities. Various options are presented, including general information on technical schools, higher education, organizational training, and documentation of prior learning. Users can also access the CareerPoint Training Calendar, a database of training opportunities that can be customized to fit a wide range of specific organizational offerings.

Peterson's College Database is also available on-line, giving users instant access to this well-known source of information on two-year and four-year colleges. These data are the same as found in the print versions of the famous Peterson's Guides.

Module L: System Evaluation

The last module focuses on evaluation of career development. In this module, CareerPoint owners can get feedback on the system's effectiveness and the usefulness of information it provides. Users respond on a scale of one to five to a set of eight specific questions on the system's ease and efficacy. The last section concludes with questions about the user's next step and actual planning of his or her development plan.

Also, as part of the evaluation, the system generates reports for managers who are tracking, assessing, and tabulating employee career development activities. The first of these is the general usage report for a given time period, which is accompanied by an interpretation of such data as the total number of sessions, average time per session, number of users, etc. The second is a demographics report giving the distribution of CareerPoint users by age, sex, years with the organization and job classification. For example, all demographic categories can be customized to meet manager's needs. A third report focuses on content analysis. It provides distributions of job satisfaction levels, Holland codes, Work Environment Scale Averages, Myers/Briggs types, Career Leverage Inventory scores for career-move options, skills and values, evaluation responses, and next items. As with other reports, different content analysis can be generated for different user groups ranging from all system users to those in selected categories to individuals.

In the Unisys system, evaluation not only focuses on the use of the CareerPoint system just described, but in the frequency of enrollment in training and development activities, the amount of attrition (voluntary reduction in force) and evidence of new skill sets. At Secor Bank, these evaluations are used, but in addition, system use is correlated with attitude survey results, focusing on career development needs and activities.

At Corning, an analysis of pre- and post-questionnaire results indicated that an increase of 47% of employees had completed career plans. Further, there was a 33% increase of supervisors' helpfulness in assisting employees with career planning. Also, in a re-administration of a climate survey, the most significantly improved item was related to career planning. Employees felt more positive about making career plans because they better understand and participate in their own career planning and their given information about opportunities.

System Flexibility

CareerPoint system has many special features that make it a very flexible, organization specific system. In addition to its many embedded features, CareerPoint offers several important components that enhance the ease of use, the impact and value of the user's efforts and results, and the ways in which the system supports the organization's efforts to implement and adapt career development as a key to broader HRD. There are express menus, skills analysis, customizing options and interactive compatibility making CareerPoint a flexible system. Figure 11-2 shows the overall structure of CareerPoint. CompScan, as shown in the figure, is a highly capable, but extremely flexible system that organizes, assesses, and reports on competencies by position or job family. CompScan's raw assessment data and resulting position profiles

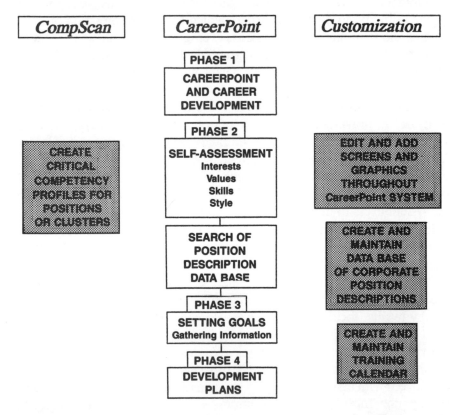

Figure 11-2. CareerPoint career development system reproduced with permission from Conceptual Systems Inc.

can easily be accessed by CareerPoint for use in job description reviews, skills gap analyses and many other position and skills-related applications. Summit, CareerPoint's authoring system, can be used to generate any kind of independent instructional and informational programs. All Summit content can be accessed and referenced by CareerPoint users for direct training or other purposes.

In summary, CareerPoint is a highly interactive system designed to enhance career development in an organization. Built in evaluation features enhance its accountability as an important tool for HRD managers.

Discussion Questions

1. In what ways have computers had an effect on the evaluation process?
2. Contrast the IBM and Northern Telecom examples. Why is one so far ahead of the other in the use of computer technology when they both have progressive HRD departments?
3. Contract CBT, CAI, CMI. What are the major differences?
4. To what extent is computer-based training used in your organization (or one with which you are familiar)?
5. Review a specific application of computer-based training. What advantages led to the decision to use CBT?
6. Computers have some advantages over traditional methods of training. Which are most important? Why?
7. The four applications of CBT presented in this chapter represent large scale implementations. Do all CBT projects need to be large scale systems? Explain.
8. Discuss the importance of computers in the evaluation process.
9. Is it possible to have a thorough evaluation without the use of computers? Explain.
10. Most CBT programs have some type of built-in evaluation. Explain how this works and why it is important.
11. What are the advantages of having computerized administration of training records?
12. What are the strengths and weaknesses of the system used in the case on career development? What type of organization is best suited for this system?
13. Critique the evaluation of the case study on career development. What additional data might be helpful in evaluating this system? Is it possible to calculate a return on investment for this example? Explain.
14. There has been a dramatic increase in the use of computers in HRD in the 1980s. How will the use of computers in the 1990s be different?

References

1. Geber, B., "Goodbye Classrooms (Redux)," *Training*, January 1990, pp. 27–28.
2. Mayo, G. D. and DuBois, P. H., *The Complete Book of Training: Theory, Principles and Techniques*, University Associates, San Diego, CA, 1987.
3. American Society for Training and Development, *Computer-Based Training Today: A Guide to Research, Specialized Terms and Publications in the Field*, ASTD Press, Washington, D.C., 1987.
4. Mayo and DuBois, p. 80.
5. Dean, C. and Whitlock, Q., *A Handbook of Computer Based Training*, (2nd Edition), Kogan Page, London, 1988.
6. Lookatch, R. P., "How to Talk to a Talking Head," *Training and Development Journal*, September, 1990, pp. 63–65.
7. Geber, B., "Coming Soon: Interactive Videodisc Standards," *Training*, January 1990, p. 92.
8. Geber, B., "Goodbye Classrooms (Redux)," *Training*, January 1990, pp. 27–28.
9. Ganger, R. E., "Computer Based Training Works," *Personnel Journal*, September 1990, pp. 85–87.
10. Ibid, p. 86.
11. Zemke, R., "Evaluating Computer Based Instruction: The Good, The Bad and the Why," *Training*, May 1984, pp. 23–24.
12. Ibid, p. 23.
13. Ganger, p. 87.
14. Ibid, pp. 85–86.
15. Dean and Whitlock, p. 163.
16. Reinhart, C., "Developing CBT—The Quality Way," *Training and Development Journal*, November 1989, pp. 85–89.
17. Wilson, L. S., "An On-Line Prescription for Basic Skills," *Training and Development Journal*, April 1990, pp. 36–41.
18. Kearsley, G., *Costs, Benefits and Productivity in Training Systems*, Addison-Wesley, Reading, MA, 1982.
19. Weatherly, N. L. and Gorosh, M. E., "Rapid Response with Spreadsheets," *Training and Development Journal*, September 1989, p. 75.
20. Much of this material is taken from documents supplied by Conceptual Systems, Inc., 1010 Wayne Avenue, Suite 1420, Silver Spring, MD 20910.

CHAPTER 1 2

Evaluating Outside
Resources

Of the $30 billion that U.S. employers spend annually on training and development, 31%, or $9 billion, goes to outside providers in a supplier network of consultants, colleges, vocational schools, government agencies, professional associations, trade unions, conference providers, packaged training suppliers and other organizations.[1] Collectively, they represent an important tool for cost effective training and development. According to a two-year study conducted by the ASTD, the linkage between the training suppliers and training departments is very strong and the relationship is productive. The report states that most training linkages come about simply because few in-house HRD departments can meet all of the organization's training needs. Employers usually contract with outside providers when internal training functions lack the expertise, time, facilities or staffing to create necessary training services. Outside services range from needs analysis and instructional design guidance to off-the-shelf or customized packaged programs. This chapter explores four common types of outside resources that HRD departments use:

☐ Seminars
☐ Packaged training programs
☐ HRD consultants
☐ External facilities

Each of these services bring on unique evaluation challenges. With outside seminars, the organization is interested in maximizing the benefits derived from employee participation. Steps must be taken to ensure that the right seminar is selected, and the seminar material is put to proper use.

When purchasing a packaged training program, the evaluation of the results of those programs is no different than evaluating an internally produced program. However, it must be evaluated prior to purchasing to ensure that it is appropriate for the organization before funds are allocated for procurement.

The same logic applies to using external consultants. The programs they develop or conduct internally follow regular evaluation procedures. The most critical activity, however, is evaluating their capabilities prior to contracting for their services.

As part of an organization's philosophy toward training delivery, a decision must be made concerning the use of external facilities. Several factors influence this decision in addition to the decision of which facility to use.

Each of these unique evaluation opportunities will be explored in this chapter.

Evaluating Outside Seminars

The Problem

The seminar business is a big business. Each year nearly one million managers and executives attend some kind of seminar, workshop, or conference. The seminar fees alone approach $3 billion per year. Every employer is flooded with flyers promising programs that will instill or revive professional or managerial skills. With all this activity, many still question the benefits either to themselves or to the people they send. People who go to seminars these days sometimes learn more than anything else the importance of picking the seminars carefully.

An HRD manager in one organization received this memo from the employment manager:

> The course in New Orleans was the worst that I have ever attended. The instructor did not follow the outline as presented to us and was totally unprepared to discuss the subject matter. He would start talking

about a subject and forget where he was and then ask the class to tell him what he was talking about.

The next instructor was a substitute. The day was a complete waste of time. He read from a book most of the time, and the class got up and left before it was over.

Approximately a week after the course was over, I received a letter from the first instructor boasting about the high ratings he received from the class. He mentioned that his book was sold out of its last printing and said he was available as a consultant if we needed him.

A situation like that has to frustrate even the most understanding HRD professional. Yet, it is not uncommon. Too many organizations develop and present poorly designed and ineffective seminars.

A common objection to seminars is the content. Many participants complain about the information being too general and offering few solutions to problems. Speakers represent another area of complaint. Occasionally, speakers are ill-prepared, lack the necessary expertise, and sometimes have less experience than those in the audience. Others complain that knowledgeable speakers hold back during seminars because they do not want to give away their secrets; they want to hold out for consulting fees after the program is conducted.

There appears to be too little attention paid to the quality of seminars. In the past, companies relied on the participants to provide the necessary quality control. The participants' ratings at the end of the program provided input to program designers and speakers. Too often these ratings were ignored as long as new participants enrolled. A few companies even registered formal complaints with the seminar sponsors with little or no success.

To provide good quality control, two actions are needed. First, each organization must do a careful job of pre-screening the seminar and obtaining the necessary information to avoid a disaster. Second, each organization must evaluate the program and assure that the information is put to effective use in the organization.

Concern for Evaluation

Employees attend seminars for a variety of reasons. Because some of these are the wrong reasons, there may be general apathy toward evaluation of outside seminars.

One reason participants attend seminars is to get out of the office. The seminar is a reward for performance or represents a change in pace in their regular work routine. These participants are more concerned with the location and the dates of the seminar rather than the content or quality of the program. Fortunately, this reason for attending seminars is diminishing. Tight budgets and emphasis on accountability has forced some organizations to spend less money on unnecessary and unneeded seminars. There must be an identifiable need to attend. If the participants attend a seminar for other than its original purpose, it is difficult to evaluate the seminar objectively. It is also more difficult to implement the information collected in the program.

There is another reason for lack of concern about evaluation. Some argue that, regardless of the effectiveness of the seminar, an energetic and enthusiastic employee will be able to get some new ideas out of the program and put them into practice. This is questionable thinking. Consider the cost involved in a typical one-week program. The seminar fee will be between $700 and $1,200. The salary, including benefits of the participant during the one week, will average more than $800. Travel expenses could easily add another $1,000. These three together represent an investment of $2,500–3,000 for an employee to attend a one-week training program. Also, depending on the type of work, a replacement may be necessary at an additional cost.

Now for the important question: Would an organization spend $3,000 on equipment without some prior evaluation or comparison of the different brands, models, and specifications? Most likely the answer would be no. What can a company do to get the best seminar for its money?

Getting Additional Information on Seminars

The answer to the previous question lies in getting proper information early so that the seminar can be evaluated prior to attendance. The following six guidelines are recommended to get a complete profile of the seminar. All the information may not be necessary for a given seminar or for a specific situation in the organization.

Beware of the brochure. Never judge a seminar on its brochure. Professional organizations conducting seminars are careful to design a very attractive brochure. They may have flashy headlines and be printed in a myriad of colors. It is difficult to distinguish between a sales pitch and real information. A good brochure will list all of the information needed to make a decision:

- [ ] Ample information about seminar leaders.
- [ ] A complete and detailed agenda.
- [ ] A detailed explanation of the costs.
- [ ] The method(s) of instruction and other items to enhance the learning environment.
- [ ] Evaluation data, if any is available.
- [ ] The target audience.

Of course, necessary information about the location, registration cutoff, refund policy, and other administrative details are standard items to be included in any brochure.

Ideally, the brochure should contain enough information to answer initial questions, stimulate interest, and provide input to help decide whether to attend or seek additional information.

Gather additional details. When additional information is needed, the seminar sponsor should be contacted for a more detailed outline and other facts pertaining to how the program will be conducted and its target audience. Additional information might be needed about the sponsoring organization. Some are well known and have very good reputations. Others may be new to the business and not as careful to present a quality program. Typical questions to ask are:

- [ ] How will the program be conducted?
- [ ] How many participants have attended?
- [ ] Who designed the program?
- [ ] How long has the current instructor conducted the program?

Answers to these questions give additional insight into the overall program content, its purpose, and its method of instruction.

Check out the speakers. Most outside seminars will usually be as good as the speaker. If different speakers handle the same program, there may not be any similarity between them. Ask about specific speakers for the program in question. Check them out. See what experience they have had not only in conducting seminars but in practicing the topic at hand. Questions to ask are:

- [ ] Do they have a track record in accomplishing what they will be discussing?
- [ ] Do they have any experience in the field?
- [ ] What have been their ratings in the past?
- [ ] Why are they conducting this program?

That last question deserves an additional comment. Most seminar leaders are either consultants or college professors, since their work schedules are usually flexible enough to allow them to conduct seminars. Unfortunately, those in other fields who are successfully applying many of the techniques discussed in seminars are too busy practicing their trade to conduct seminars for others. This is unfortunate, not because of poor quality of instruction from professors or consultants, but because many seminar participants do not have the opportunity to interface with individuals who have a track record in the field.

One organization recently challenged a university in its selection of a speaker. The seminar title was "How to Manage the Training and Development Department." It was conducted by one of the professors at the university, who had never been a manager of a training department nor had he ever worked as a member of a training staff. Regardless of the ability of the professor, it is difficult to build the credibility needed for the subject of the seminar without some relevant experience.

Check with previous participants. A list of previous participants can provide an excellent source of unbiased information. If this can be secured, contact as many previous participants as feasible who are located in the same area, in the same field of work, and with job titles similar to the prospective participants. Typical questions to ask are:

- □ Why did you attend the program?
- □ What was your overall reaction to the program?
- □ Did it meet the program objectives?
- □ What results have you achieved because of this program?
- □ Was the speaker effective?
- □ Was the program material up to date?

If an organization refuses to give you a list of participants, ask them why. If they do not have a good reason, possibly they could have many dissatisfied past participants. Obviously, there are no past participants for first-time presentations of a seminar. It might be wise to wait until it is offered again.

Investigate the learning environment. The program and the environment in which a seminar is conducted should be designed for maximum learning. The method of instruction is usually one area that reveals much information about the learning environment. If the method is a lecture only-type program, it may result in very little learning. On the other hand, discussion with active participation and involvement from the participants increases the chances that they will learn more.

The facility also can enhance the learning environment. Programs conducted at a conference center, as opposed to a local hotel, will usually have a better learning environment, especially if the center is designed for conferences only.

A final note about the learning environment involves the use of hand-out materials. This material can support the information presented in the program and provide for additional analysis and follow-up when the participant is back on the job. Ideally, hand-out material should be used in class as the subject is presented and have space provided for notes.

Secure additional evaluation data. Occasionally, the sponsors of successful repeating seminars have collected additional information on their effectiveness. This information may be in the form of dollar savings as the result of a program, testimonial letters from participants, or analysis of changes which have taken place on the job as a result of the program. Most likely such evaluation data are contained in the program announcement. However, it may be too detailed to present, or it could have been collected after the brochure was printed. In any case, it should be secured if available. If the organization does not collect such information, or does not think it is important, then maybe the effectiveness of the seminar should be questioned. Also, an organization reluctant to give additional information about their programs may have a reason for their actions. It's analagous to developing a product but not being willing to indicate how it is to be used. When faced with this situation, the best approach is to ignore the sponsoring organization completely, not just the seminar in question.

Preprogram Planning

The success of a seminar back on the job involves the combination of company policy, management support, and careful planning by the HRD department. The HRD department should be the central agency for coordinating, processing, and approving participants' attendance in outside seminars. This is the case with many organizations now. For others, it is a trend. There should be only one department charged with this responsibility, and certainly the HRD department is the most likely place. Otherwise, it is difficult to know what activity is taking place with outside attendance, and it is difficult to gather the necessary base of information to give advice and help select the right seminars. The term "advice" needs some amplification. The HRD department should know which frequently offered programs are effective. The department can be a very helpful resource to the organization in identifying appropriate seminars and providing evaluation data when asked.

Management support is necessary for obtaining maximum effectiveness from an outside seminar. Support must come from the top down and represent a general philosophy and attitude of the organization toward expenditures for an outside HRD program. Participants must be allowed time to attend programs. Helping them select the appropriate program is another area where support is needed. Finally, requiring improvement or the implementation of the material presented after attendance is the most significant area of support.

Preprogram planning can help ensure the success of the offsite venture. This is where the HRD department can have a significant impact. After the program is selected and the decision is made to send a participant, the HRD department should get in touch with the participant and his supervisor. This communication has three general purposes:

☐ To give the necessary administrative details about the seminar (i.e., location, travel arrangements, payment of fees).
☐ To send a copy of the evaluation form which is required to be completed after attendance.
☐ To require the participant and his supervisor to discuss the program prior to attending.

An evaluation form should be sent to participants prior to their attending the program. There should be clear instructions on what is required in the evaluation process. Evaluation forms for outside programs can come in many varieties. The following form provides a section to evaluate the program as well as space for indicating what action will take place as a result of attending the program. It also has space for an estimate of the dollar savings over a period of one year. The dollar-savings information, if appropriate, can be useful in summarizing the effectiveness of outside programs.

The communication between the participants and their supervisors prior to attendance is important. Unfortunately, many seminar attendees depart for the seminar with no discussion about what is expected when they return. Ideally, they should discuss the following areas:

☐ Program content.
☐ Important areas of the seminar.

OUTSIDE DEVELOPMENT PROGRAM EVALUATION

INSTRUCTIONS: Please complete this form immediately after attending your seminar, training program, or conference and return to the Training & Development Department within one week of program completion. Your information will be valuable to others in evaluating this program for future participation. Important: After completing this form your supervisor and Department Manager should then review it and forward it to the Training & Development Department.

Name _____

Department _____

Course _____

Date attended _____ Cost $ _____

Location of Program ____ _____ Length ____ ____

Sponsoring Organization _____

_____

Instructor _____

Briefly describe the content of the program ____

_____

What specific knowledge, techniques, or ideas were learned and how do you plan to apply them on your job? (use example)

Planning of work   _I will plan and organize my time to_
Example   _increase my productivity a minimum of_
                            ten percent (10%) within the next month

1 _____   _____

2 _____   _____

As the result of this course, the change in your thinking or new ideas, please estimate (in dollars) the amount of money that will be saved (i.e. increased productivity, improved methods, reduced costs) over a period of one year. $ _____ Explain— _____

Please put a (✔) check in the column which best answers the following questions:

	RATINGS				
	1. Inadequate	2. Marginal	3. Adequate	4. More than Adequate	5. Outstanding
GENERAL					
How would you rate this course overall					
How well did this course meet its announced goals and contents					
General interest of course material to you personally					
How applicable was this course material to your job					
CONTENT					
How would you rate the difficulty or technical level of the material					
How up-to-date, factual, and reliable was the information .					
How practical was the material presented					
INSTRUCTION					
Effort and preparation made by instructor					
Competence of instructor in material presented					
Instructors ability to effectively communicate material covered					
Instructors ability to handle questions					
Your satisfaction with amount and type of discussion allowed in class					
OUT-OF-CLASS STUDY					
The amount and difficulty of homework or self-study expected of you					
Relationship of homework assignments to material covered in course					
Degree to which homework is helpful					
Value of textbooks, notes or handouts provided by the instructor					

Signed _____

Supervisor _____ Manager _____
             Initial   Initial

Date
Received _____
T&D

☐ Areas where additional information is needed.
☐ Potential on-the-job applications of the material.

Prior discussion of the previous areas can stimulate the participant's involvement in the program, increase eagerness to attend, and help ensure that the material is put to use on the job. In addition, these discussions can enhance follow-up evaluation efforts that may be planned by the HRD department. As a side benefit, the discussion improves the boss-subordinate relationship.

Participants will frequently have many questions about attending a seminar and will usually want to know why they were selected and what is expected when they return. A typical reaction, if not perceived as a reward, is that it may be punishment; that something is wrong with their performance. A thorough discussion can alleviate these concerns.

Post-Program Activities

After the program is conducted and the participant returns to the job, the crucial part of the process begins. The evaluation form should be returned within the specified period of time. The participant's supervisor should sign the form to ensure that there has been a post-program discussion. A memo from the HRD department, with a copy to the participant's supervisor, should serve as a reminder if the form is not returned when required. If the discussion is not held in a timely manner, the participant may feel that the program was unnecessary or that management is not interested in what happens after attending a seminar. If a follow-up evaluation is planned, it should be communicated at this time.

Once the evaluation form is returned, it should be reviewed by the HRD department for completeness and accuracy. Two areas need particular attention: (1) the actions planned by the participant, and (2) the dollar savings with appropriate explanations. If these are left blank, then it should be returned to the participant with an explanation of the importance of the information. It is not unusual to get an adverse reaction when asked about dollar savings for attending the outside program. Savings are difficult to quantify, and even the best estimate can be unrealistic. The HRD department should insist on this information if it is feasible for the program. One such approach is to answer formally any adverse comment about the information (see memo). The memo, to a frustrated marketing manager, explains why dollar savings are required on the evaluation form. This approach, if handled diplomatically, can

MEMO

To: Marketing Manager

From: Jack Phillips   Date: May 8, 1991

Subject: Outside Program Evaluation

Thank you for your evaluation of the course you attended on industrial product management. On the evaluation form you indicated that to estimate the dollar savings is an exercise in nonsense. I'd like to challenge that statement. It is true with some seminars and courses, applications of ideas and techniques gained in the seminar are difficult to measure in terms of the overall benefit to the company. While this appears to be the case with your course, we should not forget the purpose of attending outside programs.

Whenever a supervisor or manager attends a course, the value of that course to the company depends on what the participant does with the information gained in the program, however difficult it is to estimate. The mere presence of the question relating to dollar savings tends to make some people think more precisely in terms of saving money, reducing waste or increasing profits. Such exercises are very sensible and necessary.

For too long, training and development personnel have taken the attitude that there is no way to tie training programs to dollar savings. While it is extremely difficult, we will continue to pursue this at every opportunity. We will ask each person to go through the exercise. Some day maybe the exercise will generate an additional idea that will help us save money.

Thanks for your comments and for completing the evaluation.

DR:ds

increase support, not only in the evaluation of outside seminars but also in the evaluation of internal HRD programs.

Building a Data Base

The HRD department should function as a central agency for all employees attending outside seminars. This enables the department to build a data base that represents the accumulation of current information on the effectiveness of programs, and the collection of information on programs suitable for specific HRD needs. Seminar participants should be encouraged, or possibly even required, to keep the HRD department informed about the effectiveness of these programs. This can keep future participants from attending ineffective programs. Some independent firms are attempting to perform this function as a service to other organizations.[2] Although this service can provide information on various programs, it can be unreliable because it is collected on a voluntary basis.

Another reason for establishing a data base is to keep track of costs of outside program attendance. This activity can represent a significant expenditure. Cost summaries of registration fees and travel expenses can be developed and reported frequently.

A final reason for establishing a data base is to evaluate the overall impact of outside program attendance. In addition to evaluating the impact of an individual program, the organization may want to know if the ROI for this total expenditure is acceptable. This can be accomplished only through proper completion of evaluation forms coupled with the follow-up discussed in the next section. Armed with this information, the HRD department can calculate an approximate ROI for this expenditure, at least on an annual basis, if required.

Follow-Up

The last and final effort from the HRD department to ensure the successful application of an outside seminar is through a follow-up procedure. This follow-up involves a formal contact with the seminar participant in a predetermined period of time after attending the program, usually three months or six months. The purpose is to determine what changes have taken place as a result of attending the program. Follow-ups are usually limited to programs with at least a week's duration. Specific activities planned at the end of the program are audited to see if they were accomplished. Additional relevant data on improvement directly attributed to the program are collected.

The follow-up is usually in the form of a questionnaire sent to the participant from the HRD department with a copy to the participant's supervisor. To make this process effective, the participants must:

☐ Know in advance that the follow-up will be conducted.

☐ Have the full support, cooperation, and commitment of their superior to put into practice the items agreed to at the end of the program.
☐ See the need for supplying this information to the HRD department.

This follow-up should not be very time consuming yet contain enough detail to provide a complete evaluation. Most of the techniques of follow-up for internally conducted HRD programs (discussed in Chapter 8) apply to the follow-up of an outside program.

A few organizations conducting seminars provide their own follow-up to see what impact the seminar has had on the participant. Others follow-up on a random basis. This represents an encouraging trend and provides invaluable marketing information that can lead to program improvements.

Evaluating Packaged Programs

Today there are more commercially available packaged training programs than ever before. Organizations developing and marketing such programs have mushroomed in recent years. Faced with this deluge of programs and information, the HRD specialist may be confused about the decision to build or buy a program, and further confused in the choice of which one to buy if a purchase is planned.

A survey of Fortune 500 firms reveals the extent to which organizations use external suppliers for training programs.[3] The survey revealed that 85% of the Fortune 500 use external suppliers representing 27% of their total human resource development. The survey also revealed that HRD executives expect the use of external suppliers to increase in the future. This trend of increased use of purchased programs makes the decision to select a supplier a difficult one. This section outlines a recommended approach to address this question.

Evaluation Questions

The decision to make or buy a program is extremely difficult for HRD specialists, particularly in larger organizations. There are usually three major objections to outside purchases:

☐ The belief that a program must be developed in-house to be effective and be accepted.
☐ No other organization has the same training needs.

☐ Parts of the program may conflict with practices or philosophies within the organization.

These objections may not be valid. Employees are willing to accept programs developed by external suppliers. The "not-invented-here" syndrome does not seem to bother many program participants. The training needs may be unique but chances are, at least for commonly required skills, the training needs in one organization are similar to others. Finally, in response to the last objection, commercially available programs can be tailored to the organization's needs or questionable portions can be eliminated.

Before making the decision, it is necessary to first determine the training needs. The steps in the results-oriented HRD model presented in Chapter 4 are appropriate for outside programs as well as those internally developed. Outside programs should be evaluated to see if they meet the proposed internal requirements.

A list of questions can be developed to assist in the evaluation. The following yes/no form shows an example of evaluation questions. The list is very thorough and compares the organizational requirements to the specifications of commercially available programs. This list can be used to eliminate available programs which will not fulfill the needs. It does not, however, select the best one. That subject is explored in the next section.

Ranking of Proposed Programs

After suitable commercially available programs have been identified, the next consideration involves cost effectiveness. Is it more cost effective to develop or purchase the program? It is a relatively simple process to estimate the development costs versus the costs of the purchase. Usually, if a program is available that will meet the organization's needs, it is more cost effective to purchase the program, since the development costs have been spread over a number of organizations. To duplicate the effort may be cost prohibitive. In very large organizations where internal program development costs can be allocated over many participants, an internal program may have an economic edge over a program purchased from a commercial supplier.

After the decision is made to purchase an existing program, the last and final decision is to select the best one from those available. There may be a number of reasons for selecting one program over another. The relationship with the supplier, the reputation of the supplier, or the

---

Evaluation Questions

YES	NO	
____	____	1. Are the program learning objectives consistent with internal objectives?
____	____	2. Is the recommended length of the program consistent with internal plans?
____	____	3. Are evaluation procedures designed into the program?
____	____	4. Does the content match the requirements from the needs analysis?
____	____	5. Is the method of presentation compatible with existing practices?
____	____	6. Does the program design require participants to be actively involved in the learning process?
____	____	7. Are the program materials suitable for the target audience?
____	____	8. Are there procedures/methods to ensure the transfer of training to the job?
____	____	9. Can the program be used without modification?
____	____	10. Does the program allow for skill practices?
____	____	11. Are supporting materials available for the participant's supervisor?
____	____	12. Is the program attractively packaged?
____	____	13. Are the audio-visual requirements compatible with existing hardware?
____	____	14. Is instructor training for internal personnel available?
____	____	15. Is the program available on a trial basis?
____	____	16. Are examples of program success available?
____	____	17. Are the costs for the program competitive?

---

unique advantages of a particular program may all be factors in selecting the one best program. However, if there has been no experience with the supplier and the reputation of the program is not a strong factor, then the internal decision makers must objectively compare the programs. A comparison ranking is a simple yet effective procedure to select the best program. This procedure involves listing the most important criteria used to select the program. Next, assign a weight to each criterion. Then, compare each program, and rate how it best fits the criteria. A three represents the best fit, two the second best, and a one the third best fit for each criterion. These rankings are then multiplied by the weight to give an overall value for each program by criteria. These are added to give a total weighted ranking for each program. The program with the highest number represents the best program. This procedure is illustrated in Table 12-1 for the selection of an HRD program for supervisors. Three programs are among the finalists that met the basic requirements as outlined in the previous section. The criteria for selection are shown in the left column of the figure. The relative importance (or weight) of each criterion is listed next. The rankings (one, two, or three) are forced rankings in that each of the three programs are compared and a choice of a three, two, or one is required. The rankings for each program are multiplied by the importance factor to give a value by each criterion. When the totals are calculated, Program B has the highest number and should be selected assuming there are no other factors available for making that determination.

Table 12-1
Selection Chart for an HRD Program for Supervisors

Selection Criteria	Relative Importance	Program A Rank	Value	Program B Rank	Value	Program C Rank	Value
Course content	30	2	60	3	90	1	30
Cost	25	3	75	2	50	1	25
Instructional method	10	2	20	1	10	3	30
Supplier reputation	10	1	10	3	30	2	20
Ability to customize	15	3	45	2	30	1	15
Media compatibility	10	2	20	1	10	3	30
Ease of implementation	20	2	40	3	60	1	20
Results orientation	20	1	20	3	60	2	40
			290		340		210

Selecting the individuals to do this ranking is very important. Key individuals in the HRD department, as well as key managers from the line organizations, make an unbeatable team. For a supervisory HRD program, the head of the HRD department, as well as the person responsible for management development, are two individuals recommended for this task. Two line managers who will have participants in the program could make up the two other individuals ranking the program. Together they should reach a consensus on relative rankings of each of the programs.

Test Before Purchase

Another approach to evaluate a packaged program is to test it before the program is actually purchased. There may be a tendency to react too fast to an attractive training program with a successful track record. To save time and implement a program quickly, an HRD professional may prematurely purchase a program before it is thoroughly evaluated. A pilot test following one of the evaluation designs outlined in Chapter 6 can provide two very important pieces of information:

☐ The program can be evaluated to see what results are obtained within the organization.
☐ The reaction of the participants and the adaptability of the program to the organization's personnel can be judged before purchase.

These factors are necessary before the program is purchased and implemented. Otherwise, it is embarrassing to have the program flop after the purchase. In addition, a pilot test period can give the HRD professional more time to familiarize himself with the supplier and to reflect over the initial decision. If the results are there and the program wears well with the participants, then the decision is obviously a good one.

Guaranteed Results

One final area concerning evaluation of packaged programs is securing guaranteed results from the supplier. Until recently, few if any HRD program suppliers offered a written guarantee. Now these guarantees are beginning to appear in brochures and advertisements. One organization makes this promise: "If you and we agree up front on the desired results; and if you agree to install the courses via our ten-step model, then if you aren't satisfied with the results, we will refund the entire cost of the course materials."[4] The concept may appear to be a sales gimmick. However, the concept may be appropriate when selecting programs representing large expenditures. A supplier with an effective and proven program should be willing to guarantee results. HRD professionals should use caution when dealing with guarantees, since the results of any program will depend to a large measure on how it is implemented in the organization. Before suppliers will offer guarantees, they will certainly ask for some assurances that the program is implemented properly, possibly even by their own personnel. Nevertheless, the question of guaranteeing results and the response from the supplier might give additional insight into the effectiveness of the program.

Evaluating External Consultants

The third area of outside resources involves the use of consultants or instructors. The term "consultant" will be used to refer to any individual who assists in internal HRD efforts but is not a regular employee of the organization. The work of the consultant may not be confined to conducting a program but may include determining training needs, developing programs, or otherwise solving performance deficiencies.

Concern for Evaluation

The use of external consultants is increasing. Their work can interface with any HRD department's plan of activities. Before contracting for their services, consultants should be thoroughly evaluated for at least three major reasons.

Program results. One of the key reasons for prior evaluation is to try to determine if the results that may be achieved by the consultant. The HRD department will be held accountable for those results whether the program is conducted internally or by an outside consultant. An HRD department should expect no less from an outsider than they expect from the regular internal professionals.

Cost effectiveness. Consultants are expensive and their costs must be justified. The organization, and in particular the HRD department, must be convinced that the use of their time is cost effective when compared to other alternatives. An effective prior evaluation can help ensure that the project will be cost effective.

Problem avoidance. An ineffective consultant will reflect unfavorably on the HRD department. Since the consultant will be identified as being part of the HRD department's efforts, a failure can be potentially embarrassing and hinder future programs. An up-front evaluation can possibly prevent this situation from happening.

Areas of Initial Evaluation

There are many approaches to evaluating consultants prior to engaging their services. The following eight areas represent a comprehensive evaluation process which can lead to a more effective consultant/client relationship and help ensure that the desired results are obtained.

Related work experiences. The consultant should have related work experience. Usually, the organization is seeking expertise for a project, and the consultant should be a specialist in that area. Similar consulting projects, programs conducted in the same field, and other past experiences may be necessary. Publishing articles or books and conducting public seminars can be evidence of successful previous experiences. They can easily be reviewed for applicability to the organization's needs. Beware of those consultants who specialize in everything and can tackle a project regardless of the problem.

References. Consultants should be asked for references, or possibly a complete client list. Several of these clients should be contacted. Too often the client list is an exaggerated document. It contains only the best clients and does not show the extent of the previous assignments. Specific questions about clients can reveal factual information. If the consultant is a frequent seminar leader, possibly attending one of the seminars can give some additional insight into his capabilities.

Beware of the package containing letters of recommendations. They are usually developed at the request of the consultant and may represent only a minority opinion of the consultant's effectiveness. Check the clients who have not written letters.

Successful projects. Effective consultants will usually have a long list of successful projects which produced measurable improvements. The consultant should be asked to supply information about those successes along with client contacts to verify them. A few consultants develop and update a summary of major projects. The summary shows the results achieved in measurable terms on each major project undertaken.

Even the most effective consultant may not have a success in every project. Some efforts will not produce results, and other organizations may not require any type of measurement system to see if results were achieved. The responses to these situations should be carefully analyzed. It may reveal more insight into the consultant's effectiveness.

Consultant demand. Effective consultants are busy. They will have several clients with many projects in various stages of completion. Ideally, there should be a good balance between the consultant who is not busy and one who is too busy. If they are not busy, this may be an indication that no one wants to use them. They may not be able to produce the desired results. If they are too busy, then they may not be able to spend the required time on a proposed project and will sometimes send a substitute. This is usually true with top-rated consultants, those who have developed an excellent reputation. They may be involved in the initial meeting to land a client account and quickly disappear when the work begins. There may be no problems with this approach-as long as it is clearly communicated in the beginning.

Costs. Costs are definitely a factor in evaluating a consultant, although it may not be the primary item for consideration. In employing a consultant clients usually get what they pay for. Fees can vary considerably, and obviously the more effective results-oriented consultants will demand higher fees. Compare the consultant's costs with what is expected and with the projected benefits from his work. Then compare his costs to the costs of other consultants, either for the same project or similar projects. Itemizing costs is another issue. Beware of a consultant who is vague and gives a wide range of possible costs for a consulting project. Rest assured the value on the upper end will be the final figure.

Personality. The meshing of personalities in selecting consultants is far more important than people realize. The consultant must fit into the organization. He must be able to gain the respect and confidence of the management group and be able to influence key individuals. The personality, work habits, and other subjective traits demand consideration. The consultant's sensitivity to people is a key indicator of his ability. The consultant who listens attentively to people will not only get the information needed, but also the cooperation necessary to complete the project.

Questions asked. An effective consultant will know which questions to ask to gather additional insight into performance deficiencies. The consultant should be able to probe a problem and look for causes. A consultant who asks few questions about the potential assignment may reveal inexperience with the problem at hand.

Professionalism. A final area of evaluation involves professionalism. This should not be an area for evaluation. However, there are still many individuals who operate as consultants who are not professionals. Usually, individuals become consultants because they are specialists in their fields and want to help others, or they become so skillful that their services are in great demand. These consultants are usually professional in their approach. There are other individuals who are consultants because they cannot do anything else and consequently are very ineffective.

The professional consultant will exhibit excellent communication in all phases of the contact. He will exhibit good business conduct, have excellent follow-up, and present a detailed plan of what will happen at what time and with various responsibilities assigned.[5] A professional consultant will give favorable responses to the questions in the following list.

Selecting the Right Consultant

Using the previous eight areas of evaluation, it is possible to develop a simple ranking form that will enable the organization to select the best consultant, assuming that more than one is available in the area of

Table 12-2
Evaluation Chart for External Consultants

Area of Evaluation	Weight	Consultant #1 Rating	Value	Consultant #2 Rating	Value	Consultant #3 Rating	Value
Related work experience	10	2	20	2	20	4	40
References	8	3	24	4	32	1	8
Successful projects	10	4	40	4	40	1	10
Consultant demand	5	1	5	2	10	1	5
Costs	7	4	28	3	21	2	14
Personality	4	4	16	3	12	3	12
Questions asked	4	2	8	2	8	4	16
Professionalism	8	3	24	4	32	1	8
Total			165		175		113

Does the Consultant . . .

1. Listen to determine the client's needs, or is there an attempt to fit textbook solutions or predetermined techniques or products to the client's problems?
2. Use the "first team" or the "top brass" to sell the service and then hand the job over to less experienced people who are often inadequately supervised?
3. Overcommit and make promises beyond their ability to deliver within the agreed-upon time frame?
4. Misrepresent areas of strength and expertise, or is there openness in stating what they are and are not good at?
5. Write out in clear, measurable terms what work will be done and with what results?
6. Refer to other client organizations and divulge names or confidential information obtained while working for another organization?
7. Share with upper management information that was given in confidence during employee interviews or survey research?
8. Criticize management (collectively or by name) when talking with employees, or vice versa?
9. Use the client's name without permission in inferring a testimonial or endorsement?
10. Bill the client for services that could have been done as well and less expensively by the client?
11. Use materials or technology from other organizations without acknowledging the source or the commission (retainer, finder's fee, etc.) they may be receiving?
12. Violate copyrights by reproducing protected material or modifying it slightly and claiming it as original?

Questions for the Professional Consultant (Reproduced with permission of Training House, Box 3090, Princeton, N.J. 08540.)

expertise desired. This process is illustrated in Table 12-2 and is very similar to the ranking of the packaged program presented earlier.

Each of the eight areas are listed on the form. Others are added if appropriate for the evaluation. A relative weight is assigned to each area. For example, a weight of 10 is given for the item considered most important, and a 1 for the item considered least important. There could be several 10's or 1's, depending on the relative importance of each area. Next, each consultant is rated against each of the areas of evaluation. A simple rating system can be developed such as:

4	Excellent, perfect fit.
3	Above average, good fit.
2	Average, ok.
1	Fair, barely acceptable

Each consultant is then rated. These ratings are multiplied by the relative importance to generate an overall value for each area of evaluation. The numbers are added, and the consultant with the highest number represents the best fit for the assignment. A word of caution: assigning numerical values to subjective ratings might show a more precise evaluation than is actually the case. For additional information on selecting consultants see Shenson.[6]

Evaluating External Facilities

In the last two decades, specially designed training facilities have been developed for use by major organizations heavily involved in the HRD process. These conference centers provide a distraction-free environment ideal for training, customer presentations, board meetings, and sales and marketing reviews. These centers are a response to a corporate trend toward smaller, regional meetings. Twenty years ago there were only a handful of such centers. Today there are more than 300 facilities generating $3.5 billion in annual revenues.[7]

Internal vs. External

To a certain degree, the use of external facilties is influenced by the philosophy of the organization. Some organizations want to have all education and training conducted in its own facilities. Others do not want the investment in buildings and equipment and rely extensively on external facilities. Several factors influence the extent of external facility use.

Costs. For many organizations, it is more economical to use external facilities unless there is a heavy and consistent demand for the facility's use within the organization. State-of-the-art conference centers are expensive to build and represent a drain on financial resources. Unless there is a utilization rate of 70% to 80%, an organization may be unwisely allocating its resources when it invests in the construction of separate training facilities. In addition to the initial investment, facilities are expensive to maintain and operate. Not only is there routine maintenance but there is a constant need for support staff. Coordinators, specialists, and technicians must be available to keep the center running efficiently. Because of this significant commitment, some organizations see external facilities as a more cost effective approach. External facilities represent a way for organizations to pool resources to deliver training and development in a specially designed conference facility. Although the per week cost for external facilities may be high, there is no cost when they are not in use.

Convenience. Sometimes the convenience factor forces organizations to use external facilities. Training needs may vary and it may be more appropriate to conduct training programs in different geographical areas of the country. It may be impossible for the organization to have adequate training facilities in all areas. Therefore, contracting for the use of a facility in a particular geographic region provides a convenience to the HRD staff and program participants. Specially designed conference centers are located in virtually every major metropolitan area.

Recreational interface. For HRD programs lasting a week or more, there is a need to integrate recreational activities with training programs. Although the specially designed conference centers were created to give HRD professionals and meeting planners an alternative to crowded resort areas, they are often located in areas where recreation can be integrated into the program. It is not always possible for an organization to have recreational facilities at or near its own training facilities. When they do, it is usually restricted to one geographic region at division or corporate headquarters. In the winter it may be desirable to meet in warm climate areas, near the coast. In the summer, it might be more appropriate to be in mountain resorts. Many of the commercially available training facilities are located near recreational centers or resort areas. They are readily available and offered as a part of the conference center service.

State-of-the-art technology. It has become increasingly important for organizations to have the latest in technological development available in their training programs. While it may become increasingly expensive for an organization to continually upgrade all of its training facilities, most of the commercial facilities will have the latest state-of-the-art equipment and are committed to make changes as technology improves. Meeting rooms typically offer ample electronic hook ups for computers and access to data, video and audio distribution lines. In addition, larger meeting spaces are usually equipped with audio/visual control rooms and have provisions for front and/or rear screen projections. They also come equipped with personal computers, interactive video equipment, and other state-of-the-art technology for an effective HRD delivery. An organization not interested in this initial and continuing investment may prefer to use conference centers.

Training demand. The final area for consideration is the actual demand for training. Although closely related to costs, it brings into focus other factors. For example, during periods of high growth, which relate to heavy training and development needs, existing facilities may not be able to meet requirements on a readily available basis. External facilities may be required just to meet the volume of short-term activity. In this case, the organization has little choice but to go to an external facility. Specially designed conference centers are usually available on a shorter notice than high demand resort facilities.

The above factors need to be carefully weighed in deciding the extent to which organizations should use external facilities. In many organizations it will be a blend of both. Routine programs are conducted in existing facilities and other programs, such as executive conferences are conducted in external facilities.

Selecting the Appropriate Facility

After the decision is made to use external facilities, the question of which facility to use becomes an issue. Several important questions must be addressed in this selection.

Location and convenience. Just as the location is important in the decision to use external facilities, it also becomes a consideration in deciding which facility to use. It is usually important for the facility to be easily accessible to most of the participants. The convenience to transportation facilities is another important area of consideration. In some cases, it may be best to be near a metropolitan area. In other HRD programs, it may be better to be in a secluded, quiet location. The selection depends on the type of training needed as well as the time available for the participants to travel to and from the facility.

Facility design. The design of the facility is an extremely important consideration. Conference centers have been designed with the learner in mind. Specific design criteria focus on issues such as heating and ventilation, color, acoustical considerations, wall covering, windows, lighting and furniture, as well as overall architectural design.[8] Every detail is planned with the objective of maximizing comfort and learning. The first conference centers were developed by large corporations seeking isolated, off-premise facilities for corporate retreats. These early centers emphasized seclusion and minimal distraction for corporate and adult education programs. The focus on learning as well as the ease in presentation make the participation in these facilities an enjoyable and meaningful experience.

Support services. The support staff can be a critical issue in deciding which conference center to use. The support staff's availability, capability, and quality are extremely important to program success. Facility owners go to extremes when providing excellent customer service to their guests. They have specially trained personnel such as:

☐ Conference planner or coordinator who assists meeting planners in all phases of the conference planning and operation, from designing the program to conducting the postconference evaluation.
☐ Conference concierge who provides support services such as typing, transcribing, photocopying, mailing, etc.
☐ Security personnel who protect valuable audio/visual inventory and also secure the confidentiality of meetings and attendees' safety.
☐ Technical support personnel who provide assistance to ensure that equipment works properly.

Availability. The facility must be available when needed by an organization. Some facilities, because of their reputation, may not be available unless reserved for more than a year in advance. This is sometimes beyond the scope of many organizations where training may be planned only two or three months in advance. Marketplace changes may dictate a swift reaction with a corresponding heavy training schedule. Availability becomes a critical issue. The meetings at conference centers are usually planned on a shorter notice than the resort centers or hotels.

Costs. Cost must be a factor in selecting a facility. Specially designed conference centers are not inexpensive and the user pays for the services provided. The cost can be significant and will vary from one facility to another. Cost comparisons must consider the support staff arrangements, conveniences, locations, and other items that tend to affect cost. Sometimes the cost can be negotiated or even reduced through contractual arrangements for a fixed amount of use per year.

Reputation. References from current and former clients can be helpful when selecting the facility. A complete list of clients for a particular period of time should be obtained, not just a list of individuals who are satisfied. Some organizations such as the International Association of Conference Centers have attempted to provide information on the quality of conference centers. To qualify for membership, facilities must be dedicated to meetings and meeting related activities and meet a variety of criteria. For example, a facility must provide comfortable, high-quality meeting rooms as well as a range of audio/visual equipment and knowledgeable people who can operate it. Furthermore, the facility must derive 60% of its business from meeting related activities.[9]

Collectively, these factors can help an organization select an external facility for meeting HRD needs. The result will be a facility that is conveniently located, within the budgetary constraints of the organization, and is one in which the learning process in enhanced.

Summary

This chapter presented ways to evaluate the use of outside resources: outside seminars, packaged programs, external consultants and external facilities. The typical HRD department will use all four external resources. The evaluation of these resources is critical to the success of the overall effort. In each case evaluation can help the organization receive the expected benefits. The impact of packaged programs and external consultants is evaluated using the methods presented for internal evaluation. The concepts presented in this chapter focused on techniques to evaluate the packaged program before purchase or the consultant before contracting for services. This is a very necessary and important part of evaluation.

Discussion Questions

1. Most of the books and articles on evaluation omit reference to evaluating outside resources; yet 31 % of HRD expenditures are placed with outside resources. Explain this situation.
2. Why do so few organizations attempt to evaluate the results achieved by employees participating in outside seminars?
3. Critique an outside seminar you recently attended. Would the procedures outlined in this chapter be helpful to evaluate the seminar? Explain.
4. The American Management Association (AMA) is the largest provider of outside seminars. Consequently, AMA has been the subject of criticism in the content and quality of their programs; yet AMA's seminar business continues to increase. Explain the rationale for this situation.
5. What techniques are helpful to get seminar participants to estimate a dollar savings as a result of attending the external program?
6. What are the advantages and disadvantages of using external off-the-shelf programs?
7. Apply the list of evaluation questions to an off-the-shelf program. How many no's result from this brief analysis?
8. How useful is the selection procedure outlined in Table 12-1? Explain.
9. Review the supplier brochures for of-the-shelf packaged programs. To what extent do they guarantee that results can be achieved with the program?
10. When should an organization buy a training program?
11. Why is it important to carefully evaluate consultants before engaging their services?
12. What approaches are typically used to evaluate consultants in an organization? Explain.
13. Consider one or more consultants in your organization (or one with which you are familiar). Apply the proposed ranking system to evaluate those consultants. Is the process helpful? Explain.
14. How can an organization hold a consultant accountable for the results achieved?
15. What is the appropriate blend of the use of internal versus external consultants?
16. Why has the use of external facilities increased in recent years?
17. What factors has your organization (or one with which you are familiar) used in selecting outside facilities? Explain.
18. Apply the evaluation criteria outlined in this chapter to compare several conference facilities. Comment on the outcome.

19. What is the appropriate blend of the use of external versus internal facilities? Explain.

References

1. ASTD, *Training Partnerships: Linking Employers and Providers*, ASTD Press, Washington, D.C., 1990.
2. Bellizzi, C. and Piontkowski, M., "Semi-trends: Changing Times in the Seminar Game," *Training,* June 1990, pp. 35–40.
3. Ralphs, L. T. and Stephan, E., "HRD in the Fortune 500," *Training and Development Journal,* October 1986, p. 74.
4. Taken from an ad, "Can Trainers Guarantee Results," Training House, Princeton, N.J.
5. Gebelein, S. H., "Profile of an Internal Consultant: Roles and Skills for Building Client Confidence," *Training and Development Journal,* March 1989, pp. 52–58.
6. Shenson, H., *How to Select and Manage Consultants,* Lexington Books, Lexington, MA, 1990.
7. *"Personnel Journal* 1990 Guide to Conference Centers," *Personnel Journal,* September 1990, pp. 109–111.
8. Swor, J., "Site Design: Meeting of the Minds," *Training,* December 1987, pp. 88–92.
9. Ibid, p. 111.

CHAPTER 13

Management Influence on HRD Program Results

There are many factors outside the scope and direct control of the HRD department and program participants which have a significant impact on the overall success of programs. These factors primarily relate to the actions and attitudes of the management group in the organization. These managers make decisions to allocate resources for HRD programs, participate in program development, allow participants to attend programs, and reinforce what has been taught in a program. This chapter explores the influence of the total management group and the environment outside the HRD program development and delivery. Although the HRD department has no direct control over these factors, it can exert a tremendous amount of influence on them.

Several terms used in this chapter need additional explanation: *management commitment, management support, management involvement, reinforcement, maintenance of behavior,* and *transfer of training.* First, management commitment is used primarily in reference to the top management group. Its meaning goes deeper than a pledge or promise. It includes the actions of top management to allocate resources and lend support to the HRD effort in the organization. Management support for HRD programs refers to the supportive actions of the entire management group, with emphasis on middle and first-line management. The actions include a wide range of activities which can have a tremendous impact on the success of HRD programs. Management involvement refers to the extent to which management and other professionals outside the HRD department are actively engaged in the HRD process in addition to participating in programs. Since management commitment, support, and involvement have similar meanings, they are used interchangeably in current HRD literature. Although these definitions will help to keep them separated, there will be some overlap in their use in this chapter.

Reinforcement, maintenance of behavior, and transfer of training have similar meanings. Reinforcement refers to actions designed to reward or encourage a desired behavior. The goal in this case is to increase the probability of the behavior occurring after a participant attends an HRD program. Maintenance of behavior refers to the actions of the organization to maintain a change in behavior on the job after the program is completed. Transfer of training refers to the extent to which the learned behavior from the HRD program is used on the job. These three terms will be presented together in one section on reinforcement.

This chapter emphasizes the fact that the HRD department is not primarily responsible for HRD in the organization. The department only serves as the coordinating agency or facilitator for HRD. The management of the organization is ultimately responsible for development through their commitment, support, reinforcement, and involvement; the extent of their influence will ultimately determine the success of any HRD effort.

Top Management Commitment

A Commitment Check

Each chief executive officer (CEO) has some degree of commitment to HRD. The extent of commitment usually varies with the style, attitude, and philosophy of the chief executive. A heavy commitment to HRD usually correlates with a successful organization. As a first step in approaching the subject of top management commitment, it is sometimes helpful to review the extent of commitment currently prevailing in the organization. The following commitment checklist presents a self-test for the chief executive. In just a few minutes a CEO can examine the extent to which his organization is committed to HRD. The interpretation of the number of "yes" responses to the test may vary with the organization.

CEO: Check Your Commitment to HRD

Yes   No

_____   _____   1. Do you have a corporate policy or statement on HRD?

_____   _____   2. Do you hold managers accountable for the training, education, and development of their subordinates?

_____   _____   3. Does your organization set goals for the extent of employee participation in formal HRD programs?

_____   _____   4. Is your involvement in HRD more than written statements, opening comments, or wrap-up sessions?

_____   _____   5. Did you attend an outside development program in the past year?

_____   _____   6. Do you require your immediate staff to attend outside development programs each year?

_____   _____   7. Do you occasionally audit an internal HRD program conducted for other managers?

_____   _____   8. Do you require your managers to be involved in the HRD process?

_____   _____   9. Do you require your managers to develop a successor?

_____   _____   10. Do you encourage line managers to help conduct HRD programs?

_____   _____   11. Do you require your management to support and reinforce HRD programs?

_____   _____   12. Do you require your top managers to have self-development plans?

_____   _____   13. Is your HRD manager's job an attractive and respected executive position?

_____   _____   14. Does the top HRD manager report directly to you?

_____   _____   15. Does the HRD manager have access to you regularly?

_____   _____   16. Do you frequently meet with the HRD manager to review HRD problems and progress?

____	____	17. Do you require a formal top management review of all HRD programs at least annually?
____	____	18. Do you require a proposal for a major new HRD program?
____	____	19. When business declines, do you resist cutting the HRD budget?
____	____	20. Do you frequently speak out in support of HRD?
____	____	21. Do you often suggest that HRD personnel help solve performance problems?
____	____	22. Do you require the HRD department to have a budget and cost control systems?
____	____	23. Is the HRD department required to evaluate each HRD program?
____	____	24. Do you ask to see the results of at least the major HRD programs?
____	____	25. Do you encourage a costs-benefits evaluation for major HRD programs?

One approach is to view the results in this way:

Number of Yes Responses	Explanation
More than 20	Excellent top management commitment, usually tied to a very successful organization.
More than 15	Top management commitment is good, but still some room for additional emphasis.
More than 10	Poor top management commitment, much improvement is necessary for the HRD department to be effective.
Less than 10	Almost no top management commitment; HRD barely exists in the organization, if at all.

It is recommended that this test be taken by the chief executive in the organization. It can be an eye-opening exercise and can have a favorable impact on the thinking of a chief executive, particularly if there has been little effort to secure additional commitment for the function.

Areas of Commitment

The self-test for the CEO reveals many places where commitment is needed. These can be grouped into 10 general areas of emphasis which show strong top management commitment as outlined here. These 10 commitment areas need little additional explanation. Some are obvious requirements for a successful HRD effort. Many of these items have been discussed previously as requirements for a results-oriented HRD philosophy in the organization. The details of the other items have been or will be covered in other sections.

The Ten Commitments

For strong top management HRD commitment, the chief executive officer should:

1. Develop a mission for the HRD function.
2. Allocate the necessary funds for successful HRD programs.
3. Allow employees time to participate in HRD programs.
4. Get actively involved in HRD programs and require others to do the same.
5. Support the HRD effort and ask other managers to do the same.
6. Place the HRD function in a visible and high-level position close to the chief executive.
7. Demand that each HRD program be evaluated in some way.
8. Insist that HRD programs be cost effective and require supporting data.
9. Set an example in self-development.
10. Create an atmosphere of open communication between the chief executive and HRD personnel.

Increasing Commitment

Now for the big question. How can top management commitment be increased? That represents a puzzling question for many HRD professionals. Quite often the extent of commitment is fixed in the organization before the HRD person becomes involved in the development process. It has evolved slowly over time and varies widely in practice. The amount of commitment does not vary with the size or nature of the organization. It usually depends on how the function evolved, the attitude and philosophy of the top management group toward HRD, and how the HRD function is administered. That last item contains the answer to the question of increasing commitment. The HRD department can have a significant impact on future top management commitment for the department and the function. The following six areas represent items which can help to increase commitment to HRD in an organization.

Results. Top management commitment will usually be increased when HRD programs are obtaining the desired results. This is almost like a vicious cycle. Commitment is necessary to build an effective program where results can be obtained. And when results are obtained, commitment is increased. But nothing is more convincing to a group of top executives than for the HRD programs to produce measurable results that they understand and see as valuable to the organization.[1] When a program is proposed, additional funding is usually based solely on the results the program is expected to produce.

Management involvement. Commitment is increased when there is extensive involvement on the part of all levels of management in the HRD process. This involvement, which can be in almost every phase of the HRD process, shows a strong cooperative effort toward people development in the organization. Chief executives want their managers involved. It represents team spirit. Specific techniques for increasing involvement are covered later in the chapter.

Professionalism. A highly professional HRD unit can help improve the commitment from the top management group. The achievement of excellence is the goal of many professional groups. The HRD department should be no different. The department must be perceived as a professional unit in all steps in the HRD process. A professional department will welcome criticism, adjust to the changing needs of the organization, have excellent relationships with other managers, and will practice what is being taught in the programs.[2] Professionalism will show up in the attention to detail in every HRD program—detail that is often overlooked by nonprofessionals.

Communicating needs. The HRD department must be able to communicate development needs to top management and make them realize that HRD is a necessary, integral part of the organization. This communication may be in the form of proposals or review sessions with the top management group. When chief executives see a need, they will respond through additional commitment.

Resourcefulness. The HRD department should not be a narrowly focused function. Too often the department is regarded as capable in certain areas such as technical training, audio-visual support, or management development. They are not often regarded as problem solvers. The department should be seen as being versatile, flexible, and resourceful. When this happens, they will be used to help solve performance problems in the organization and not confined just to a formal development activity. The result: additional commitment will be forthcoming.

Practical approach. The HRD department must be oriented toward the practical. A department dwelling too much on theories and ideological and philosophical efforts may be regarded as a non-contributor in the organization. While there is a place for theoretical processes, much of the efforts of HRD within the organization should be oriented toward practical application. Programs should normally be how-to in nature. They must be taught by experienced people who understand the program content as well as the business. This practical approach will help ensure additional commitment.[3]

Management Support

Ideal Support

Support from the management group (middle and first-line management) is important to overall program success. Before discussing the techniques involved in improving the support for, and reinforcement of, HRD programs, it is appropriate to present what is considered to be the ideal support. Ideal support occurs when a participant's supervisor reacts in the following way concerning the participant's involvement in an HRD program:

☐ Gives enthusiastic endorsement and approval for participants to be involved in HRD programs.
☐ Volunteers personal services or resources to assist in the HRD effort.

□ Makes a commitment with the participant prior to attending the program that outlines what changes should take place or what tasks should be accomplished after the program has been completed.

□ Reinforces the behavior change resulting from the program; this reinforcement may be demonstrated in a variety of ways.

□ Conducts a follow-up of the results achieved from the program.

□ Gives positive rewards for participants who have outstanding accomplishments as a result of attending the HRD program.

This kind of support for an HRD program represents utopia for the HRD profession. The remainder of this section will explore ways to approach this idealistic supportive environment.

Preprogram Support

Support is necessary before the program is conducted as well as afterward. Several effective actions are available prior to an HRD program that can have a significant impact on what takes place in the program and what happens back on the job. These are summarized here.

Agreements and commitment. An important technique is to execute preprogram agreements or commitments. One type of agreement is between the HRD department and the participant's supervisor. This agreement spells out what the supervisor agrees to do and in turn what the HRD department will do. An example of this type of agreement is shown in the following box.

AGREEMENT

Between the Training Department and _____ of the _____.

I would like to enroll _____, who reports to me, to attend the Challenge of Management course being held on the following dates: _____.

We have discussed the course objectives and content, and agree to make the following commitments so that the training will have maximum impact:

1. The participant named above will attend _____ meetings, one per week, lasting seven hours each. We will work together to arrange work flow and deal with "crash projects" and crises in such a way as to keep them from interrupting the course.

2. The participant will spend 2–3 hours in preparation for each class meeting, going through the pre- workshop assignments and self-assessments. I agree that these exercises require analysis and discussion by both of us, and will make the time available to work together. (Average time: 20–30 minutes per week.)

3. During the week following each class meeting, I will meet with the participant to review the Action Plan that spells out how the concepts and skills covered in the workshop might best be applied back on the job. We will agree on how and when the Plan might best be implemented. (Average time: 30 minutes per week.)

(Continued on page 308)

(Continued from page 307)

4. I will meet with the participant subsequently, as needed, to provide help in carrying out the Action Plan. And I will plan to attend the "Executive Briefing" to be held 6–8 weeks after the course is over, at which time my participant and the other participants will each report on the composite results of their Action Plans as carried out to date.

5. If the participant misses a class meeting or weekly review meeting with me for reasons beyond our control, we will reschedule and make up the loss (e.g., in another cycle of the course or a special meeting with the instructor). If we miss two such meetings in a row, we understand that the participant will be disenrolled and rescheduled, if we so desire, in a subsequent cycle.

The Training Department agrees to meet the following responsibilities:

• to deliver a high-impact program that emphasizes skills development and hands-on learning.

• to provide a forum where participants can learn from one another as well as from the instructor.

• to avoid embarrassing any individual or department in class.

• to maintain confidentiality of any sensitive information that might be brought up in class.

• to serve as liaison between the group and top management on organizational issues.

• to make the learning experience enjoyable as well as beneficial.

Participant's supervisor: _____ Date:_____

Participant: _____ Date:_____

For Training Dept: _____ Date:_____

Reproduced with permission of Training House, Box 3090, Princeton, N.J. 08540.

This contract describes briefly the HRD program, the various requirements of each party, and is usually secured in a meeting with the supervisors of the participants prior to the beginning of the HRD program.

Other types of agreements involve commitments between the participant and the participant's supervisor. These may be in the form of action plans or performance contracts which were thoroughly discussed in Chapter 8. They provide a very effective preprogram commitment to a desired outcome.

Defining responsibilities. Another area of preprogram activity involves defining and distributing the responsibilities of both the participants and the supervisors of the participants. Some organizations develop policy statements, brochures, or other documents that give the specific duties of each party. Figure 13-1 shows an example of a brochure in use at Dana Corporation. The brochure clearly defines the responsibilities of supervisors and managers when their employees are involved in HRD programs. It gives specific instructions regarding education programs

WHEN THEY'RE
GOING TO A
PROGRAM . . .

THEY'VE BEEN
TO A PROGRAM
AND ARE NOW
BACK ON THE JOB . .

Figure 13-1. A brochure defining responsibilities for supporting HRD programs. (Copyright © Dana Corporation, Toledo, Ohio. Reproduced with permission.)

and what they should do to facilitate the development of their subordinates. Other organizations define these responsibilities in policy statements and procedure manuals. The responsibilities of participants are sometimes defined prior to, or at the beginning of, an HRD program. This way, they are fully aware of expectations, particularly those related to getting the desired results.

Instructions to participants. Communication with participants prior to an HRD program is very important. Participants are usually concerned about the reasons for their involvement in a program. They may wonder if they are being rewarded for good performance or punished for doing something wrong. They may have much curiosity about the program, its purpose, and who is attending. Much of this preprogram anxiety can be eliminated if the participants have straightforward information in the following areas:

- ☐ The basis for their selection.
- ☐ The purpose of the program, including a brief review of the program content.
- ☐ The administrative details of the program (time, place, dates, etc.).
- ☐ Typical results achieved by others attending the same or similar programs.
- ☐ Instructions about preprogram assignments, if any.
- ☐ The specific topics or areas discussed which are most important to the participant's job.

This prior information can put the participant at ease and enhance the learning that will take place in the program. It will help assure that results are achieved and strengthen the relationship between the participant and the participant's supervisor. In addition, participants will have a clearer picture of why they need to attend the HRD program.

Management attendance. For many HRD programs, it is important that the supervisors of the participants attend the program first. This will help defuse the typical comment too often heard in programs: "My boss should be here for this!" This management attendance, if feasible, will enable the boss to review the course material and experience the program in the same way as the participants. They usually attend separate sessions but cover essentially the same material. For some situations, a scaled-down version will be more appropriate.

There seems to be great resistance to managers attending HRD programs designed for their subordinates. Sometimes there is a feeling, based on the nature of the position, that the manager does not need full exposure to the program. Some suggest that the program description or a brief outline, along with an explanation of their responsibilities, is enough to ensure that proper results are achieved. This approach usually falls short of an optimum situation. It is difficult for a manager to have a clear understanding of the program unless he experiences it. And, as an additional benefit, quite often the managers are more effective after attending the program. Without this preprogram participation, many programs will be doomed to failure because of the lack of interest and support on the part of management.

Timing. The timing of an HRD program is very critical. Participants should attend the program at a time when they need the skills or knowledge. This point may seem trivial, but too often participants attend programs and acquire knowledge or develop skills before they are allowed to use them. A significant gap between the time the knowledge or skills are acquired and when they are put into use can diminish the transfer of training.

For example, consider the timing of a presupervisory training program. The purpose of the program is to develop the necessary skills for the participant to be an effective new supervisor. Some argue that the skills should be acquired and developed prior to assuming the supervisory responsibilities. Others argue that the optimum time is immediately after the responsibilities are assumed. Still others argue that the supervisor should function on the job for a brief period before attending the program so that the supervisor can relate the material to situations on the job. The timing of some programs may not be as critical as this example; but nevertheless, it deserves serious attention.

Post-Program Support

In many HRD programs participants are expected to do something different after the program is completed. This may be in the form of follow-up assignments, action plans developed in the program, or fulfillment of the preprogram contract or agreement between the participant and the participant's supervisor. These planned actions of the participants must be monitored to assess what change has taken place. Otherwise, the entire follow-up is negated. The key is that the follow-up activity must be of real use and highly integral to the actual job, not just an exercise or make-work task.[4] Specific follow-up techniques were presented in Chapter 8.

For most of these follow-up activities, the participant's supervisor is the key person to be involved, whether or not the design of the follow-up assignment necessarily includes the supervisor. The supervisor needs to see the results achieved and understand the importance of the improvement. Some follow-up assignments require the participant to funnel the accomplishments through the supervisor. The supervisor is required to add comments about the significance of the improvement and the assistance provided to help produce these results.

Close monitoring of these follow-up actions can often reveal a success story. An effective HRD program will usually generate a few very significant successes. These success stories can help build support for the HRD department if they are communicated effectively to the management group. Specific methods for this type of communication are discussed in the next chapter. The next section presents reinforcement, the most important part of post-program support. For additional information on management support, see Spector.[5]

Reinforcement

The Need for Reinforcement

In results-oriented HRD there must be a strong partnership between the participants and the participant's supervisor. This partnership can be viewed as part of a three-legged stool representing the major components of results-oriented HRD. One leg of the stool is the discussion leader who conducts the program. The next leg is the participant who experiences the program. The third leg is the participant's supervisor who reinforces what is being taught. Without any leg of the stool, results-oriented HRD collapses.

The necessity of getting the participant's supervisor involved as an integral part of the HRD process cannot be understated. Too often participants return from an HRD program to find many obstacles to successful application of a program. Faced with these obstacles, even some of the best participants revert back to old habits and forget most of what was learned in the program. In fact, regardless of how well the skills training is conducted in the classroom, unless it is reinforced on the job, most of the effectiveness is lost. Several research studies have supported this assumption.[6,7]

The reason for this painful finding lies in the nature of its field. By definition, a new skill feels awkward and uncomfortable. Instant results are not always forthcoming. In learning a skill participants go through an awkward or frustrating period illustrated in Figure 13-2, where the skill does not feel natural and is not producing the desired results. This period sometimes is called the *results dip* and is a difficult time for most participants. However, those who persist gain the expected reward that is obtained from the new behavior. If the participant continues the new behavior or skill, it eventually feels more natural and begins to result in better performance.

The previous figure illustrates what should happen after a skills HRD program. Unfortunately, such results are not always the case. Without proper reinforcement, particularly during the results dip, participants may not maintain the acquired skills. They may drop back to the familiar

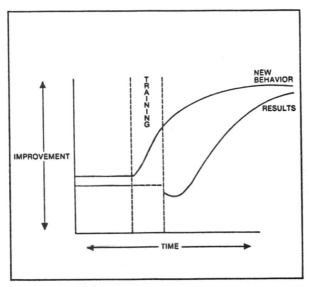

Figure 13-2. On-the-job improvement in performance resulting from new behavior. (From *Training and Development Journal,* American Society for Training and Development. Reprinted with permission. All rights reserved.)

old way of behavior with no change as illustrated in Figure 13-3. This reinforcement on the job is a necessity to make the skill part of the participant's make-up.[8]

Sources of Reinforcement

Management reinforcement. The primary focus for reinforcement is on the group identified as the supervisors of the participants in the HRD program. This group can exert a significant influence on the participant's behavior after attending an HRD program by providing reinforcement in the following ways:

☐ Help participants diagnose problems to determine if new skills are needed.
☐ Discuss possible alternatives for handling specific situations.
☐ Act as a coach to help the participants apply the skills.
☐ Encourage participants to use the skills frequently.
☐ Serve as a role model for the proper use of the skills.
☐ Give positive rewards to participants when the skills are successfully used.

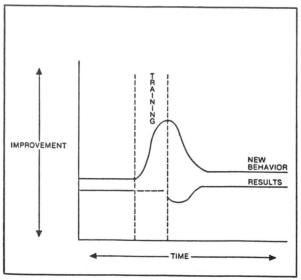

Figure 13-3. No on-the-job improvement in performance. (From *Training and Development Journal,* American Society for Training and Development. Reprinted with permission. All rights reserved.)

Each of these activities will serve to reinforce what has been taught and can have a tremendous impact on the participants.

Management reinforcement workshops. A management reinforcement workshop is an effective technique to ensure management reinforcement for an HRD program. This program is conducted for supervisors of the participants in an HRD program. The primary focus of the workshop is to teach these supervisors how to reinforce the behavior taught in an HRD program. The supervisors typically are exposed to the same material the participants will experience, but emphasis is placed on applications of management reinforcement techniques.

Self-reinforcement. Reinforcement can come from sources other than the supervisor. When participants practice skills and achieve success with those skills, then this result provides reinforcement to use them again. This self-reinforcement causes some participants to do well in HRD programs in spite of the obstacles on the job that may hinder success. Participants may try new skills if they feel an obligation to give it a try or they may be curious to see if they will actually work in a realistic setting. Regardless of the reason for trying new skills, if they are successful, even without reinforcement from others, the impact of that success reinforces them to give it a try again.

Peer reinforcement. An often overlooked group that can provide reinforcement is the peer group. This group includes coworkers at the same level of the participant engaged in the same or similar kinds of activities. When some participants are successful with the application of new skills, this success can encourage others to try those skills. Also, it can spawn intergroup coaching among the peer group. In a cooperative environment participants who are most successful will sometimes show others how to utilize the skills to get the desired results. Some HRD departments establish support groups to provide this reinforcement.[9]

Improving Supportive Relationships with Managers

Degrees of Support

Probably the key area of support involves the post-program activities. In this context the terms "support" and "reinforcement" are almost synonymous. When support is exhibited, it helps reinforce what the participants have learned. Before pursuing the specific techniques for improving the post-program support and reinforcement, it is useful to classify managers into four different types according to their degree of support. The term "manager" is primarily used to represent the supervisor of a participant in an HRD program. The same analysis can apply to other managers above that level. A label has been attached to each type of manager that best describes their attitude and actions toward HRD programs and the HRD department.

Supportive. This manager is a strong, active supporter of all HRD efforts. This manager wants to be involved in programs and wants his subordinates to take advantage of every appropriate opportunity He vigorously reinforces the material presented in programs and will require participants to put it to use successfully He will publicly voice approval for the HRD efforts, give positive feedback to the HRD department, and frequently call on the department for assistance, advice, and counsel. This manager is definitely a friend of the department and a very valuable asset.

Responsive. This manager supports HRD programs, but not as strongly as the supportive manager. Hc will allow subordinates to participate in HRD programs and will encourage them to get the most out of the activity This manager will usually voice support for programs, realizing that it is part of his responsibility but will not usually go out of his way to show unusual interest in the HRD department or activities. This manager will reinforce the material presented in the program, probably at the prodding of the HRD staff.

Non-supportive. This manager will privately voice displeasure at HRD on a formal basis. He will reluctantly send participants to programs and do so only because everyone else does or because it is required. This manager thinks the organization is spending too much time in HRD efforts and will not hesitate to mention how he made it without all of this formal training. In private conversations this manager will usually criticize the HRD staff and their efforts. When participants return from a program, there is very little (if any) reinforcement from this manager— even if instructed to provide reinforcement. In fact, this manager's actions may destroy the value of the program. A typical comment after a program will be, "Now that the program is out of the way, let's get back to work."

Unresponsive. This manager will work actively to keep participants from attending HRD programs with a variety of excuses. He will try to destroy the HRD effort and will openly criticize programs and the HRD department. This manager believes that all training and development should be accomplished on the job. When participants return from a program under this kind of leadership, there is usually negative reinforcement, with typical comments such as, "Forget what was discussed in that program and get back to work." Fortunately, this type of manager is rare in today's setting; however, there may be enough of these individuals to cause some concern for the HRD staff.

Improving the Relationship

The degree to which management supports HRD programs is based on how they perceive the worth of HRD, the function and role of the HRD department and, in some cases, the actions of members of the HRD staff. To improve management support, the HRD department should carefully analyze each situation and work on improving the relationship with an individual manager or with the management group. This improvement requires a series of critical steps outlined here:

1. *Identify the key managers where support is necessary.* This step involves selecting key managers or management groups where support

is necessary or critical to the success of an HRD program. They may be the decision makers, the entire middle-management group, or all of senior management. Individuals selected should be strong leaders, either formally or informally.

2. *Analyze and classify the degree of support.* Following the descriptions in the previous section, managers should be classified according to their degree of support for the HRD function. Input from the entire HRD staff may be helpful to classify all key managers.

3. *Analyze reasons for support or non-support.* Managers will usually show support (or non-support) of HRD programs based on a series of facts, beliefs, and values related to HRD. Each of these elements needs further explanation. A *fact* is something that is indisputable and can be proven without doubt. A *belief* is an interpretation of the meaning of past or present experiences and is used to predict what will happen in the future. A *value* is the worth assigned to a particular belief. An example of a fact is a statement such as, "Each of my employees has spent at least two weeks in training this year already." An example of a belief is "Supervisory training has not improved any of my supervisors." An example of a value is, "All training should occur on the job." The various degrees of support outlined previously are usually based on the facts, beliefs, or values assigned to the HRD effort by individual managers. The key emphasis of this step is to try to analyze the basis for the manager's support. Which facts, beliefs, or value systems caused an individual's behavior? Once these are established, an approach can be developed that may work with the individual manager to improve the supportive relationship.

4. *Select the best approach.* The strategy for dealing with a particular manager depends on his degree of support. Supportive managers are a welcome sight to the HRD department. There is little need for any concentrated effort other than to show appreciation for the support they give. Possibly they should be involved in HRD programs in the capacities described in the next section. This involvement will usually keep them as supporters of the department.

Responsive managers need to be sold on the results of HRD programs so they will remain supporters. They see this as a responsibility and are looking for a return on their investment, whether their investment is in dollars allocated to HRD or the time of participants involved in programs.

The next two types of managers represent challenges to the HRD department. The primary attention should be focused on non-supportive managers. In reality, they can represent a large number in the organization. The analysis in the previous step should reveal the basis for the non-support—either facts, beliefs, or values. Depending on the basis, the problem can be tackled by providing additional information, getting them involved in the HRD effort, showing them the results of HRD programs, or showing the extent of top management commitment to HRD.

Unresponsive managers are a threat to the HRD department. They cannot be ignored unless they are only a very small minority. If these managers are regarded as leaders in the organization, then the HRD department is in for definite trouble. There is no place in a professional organization for that kind of thinking or behavior. Dealing with these managers may require confrontations and possibly a few sessions with the manager's immediate superior. They must be reminded of the top management commitment to the HRD effort. This approach can possibly stop the manager from working against the HRD department; otherwise, efforts to show results or get those managers involved in the program will usually be fruitless.

5. *Adjust the approach if necessary.* Managers are individuals, and what works for one may not work for another. If an attempt to change a manager's behavior does not work, possibly another approach can be successful. If a manager's action is perceived to be based on a belief but instead is based on a value, then an adjustment in approach is necessary. The key point is that each manager responds differently. The HRD staff should analyze the effect of their efforts to increase support, and make adjustments in the strategy to improve it. The primary concern is to move more managers from the non-supportive to the responsive or supportive categories.

The specific actions to increase support and ensure the transfer of training vary widely. Zemke and Gunkler identified 28 techniques for transforming training into performance on the job.[10] Broad and Newstrom have isolated 89 actions to ensure transfer of training.[11] The actions involve the efforts of the organization, manager, supervisor, trainer, and trainee.

Management Involvement

Management involvement in the HRD process is nothing new. Organizations have practiced it successfully for many years, although it does not show up as often as it should. There are almost as many opportunities for management's involvement in the HRD process as there are steps in the results-oriented HRD model presented in Chapter 4, although realistically management input and active participation will only occur in the most significant ones. Line management should be involved in most of the key decisions of the HRD department. The primary vehicles for obtaining or soliciting management involvement are presented here.

Program Leaders

Probably the key area of involvement is the use of management and professional personnel as course leaders or instructors. Their use presents some unique challenges to the HRD department. Not everyone has the flair for leading a discussion in a development program. Discussion leaders should be carefully chosen based on the following criteria:

☐ Knowledge and expertise in the subject area
☐ Presentation skills
☐ Reputation in the organization
☐ Availability

The requirement of knowledge and expertise is usually the largest single reason for soliciting outside assistance. HRD personnel cannot be experts in the majority of the programs conducted. Although the subject-matter expertise is developed into the program, it may be more meaningful to the participants to have a leader knowledgeable in the subject matter.

Good presentation skills are very important. Even the most well-respected and knowledgeable manager will fall flat if he cannot make an effective presentation. Although it may be possible to assist a manager in developing presentation skills, it may not be feasible because of time constraints.

A good reputation in the organization is another important factor. Managers who are respected because of their ability or position will add credibility to the program. Similarly, managers who are considered to be substandard performers or an improper role model will have a negative impact on the program.

Finally, availability is important. While it may not be the norm in every organization, effective managers are usually extremely busy individuals. They may not have the time to assist in conducting programs.

However, equally effective managers, because of unusual factors, may not be using all of their skills. They are likely candidates for an assignment as a course leader. Sometimes top management will insist that even the busiest line managers are involved in the HRD effort. This attitude makes HRD a high priority and can have a favorable impact on the program.

After outside course leaders are selected, the next major task is to prepare them for their assignment. This is a time-consuming process if it is done correctly. In some cases the actual time involved in preparing others to conduct a program will be greater than the time required for the HRD staff to prepare for the program. Detailed lesson plans, course objectives, a prepared script, visual aids, handouts, and other items should be developed for each course leader. If feasible, course leaders should have a chance to practice a session before presenting it to a group of participants. The HRD staff should critique the session and offer constructive suggestions. At a minimum an HRD staff member should monitor the first presentation and provide feedback to the leader. This is important to keeping the quality of the program high.

The extent to which outsiders are involved in HRD programs can vary considerably. In some efforts the entire program is conducted by the HRD staff. At the other extreme, some programs are conducted entirely by line management. The right combination depends on these factors:

☐ The professional ability of the HRD staff.
☐ The capability of line management and other professional personnel.
☐ The value placed on having line management and other professional personnel identified with the program.
☐ The size and budget of the HRD staff.
☐ The physical location of the program as compared to the location of line management personnel.

There may be other factors for the specific organization. In one company the right combination for a two-week supervisory program is shown in Figure 13-4. Outside involvement was high in this example, with the HRD staff conducting only slightly more than 21% of the program.[12]

The example for management involvement in the HRD process needs to be set at the top of an organization. For example, at Aetna Life and Casualty, Ronald Compton, president, is actively involved.[13] He conducts the first hour and a half of the Aetna management process course.

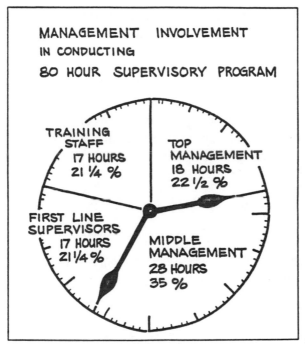

Figure 13-4. The extent of management involvement in a two-week training program.

Also, he or the chairman will speak at every session of the advanced management course. Compton also takes part in the strategic management seminars. This sets the tone within Aetna for active participation.

The use of non-HRD staff personnel in HRD programs creates a strong atmosphere of teamwork. In an organization where management involvement in a program was high, there were periodic "faculty" meetings and an occasional faculty appreciation luncheon. In these meetings the results of the program were presented along with proposed changes and general information about the program's future. This approach created high team spirit and, at the same time, reminded managers that their contribution was appreciated and necessary to make the program effective.

Advisory Committees

Many organizations have developed committees to enhance line management involvement in the HRD process. These committees act in an advisory capacity to the HRD department. They may have other names such as councils or, as in the case of Fluor Corporation, people development boards. As shown in Table 13-1, committees can be developed for individual programs, specific functions, or for multiple functions. They can be one-time committees or standing committees, depending on the duration of the program. Committees can be used in many stages of the HRD process, from needs analysis to communicating program results. The HRD staff benefits from management input and from its commitment as well, once the committee buys into a particular program. It is difficult for managers to criticize something of which they are a part.

Typical duties of a committee are to:

☐ Review the results of a needs analysis.
☐ Approve the proposed design of the program.
☐ Review the methods of presentation.
☐ Recommend potential discussion leaders for the program.
☐ Review the program results.

Table 13-1
Types of HRD Committees

Responsible for:	Examples:
*Individual Program	New Supervisor's Development Program Committee
	Account Executive's Training Program Committee
	Product Knowledge Course Committee
	Apprenticeship Training Committee
*Specific Function	Sales Training Committee
	Nurses Development Committee
	Quality Control Training Committee
	Underwriting Training Committee
*Multi-functions	Management Development Committee
	Faculty Development
	Skills Training Committee
	Government Compliance Training Committee

Committees can meet periodically or on an as-needed basis. Usually, the purpose of a meeting is to review specific activities in the program to secure input, support, and endorsement for that activity. The business of the committee should be conducted in a professional manner, including precise agendas and brief meetings which consume very little time of the members. Otherwise, members may lose interest and not attend.

The selection of the individual members for the committee is very important. Committee members should be key managers and influential executives who can make things happen, are knowledgeable and respected within the organization. A committee comprised of ineffective managers commanding little respect in the organization will be less effective. The committee could get bogged down in irrelevant matters and lose the clout and credibility that it could otherwise have.

Before deciding whether or not the committee is appropriate, the HRD department should determine if the potential benefits outweigh the time that must be taken to work with the committee. Some organizations have a committee for every HRD program, while others manage to survive without them.

HRD Task Forces

Another potential area for management involvement is through the use of an HRD task force. The task force consists of a group of employees, usually management, who are charged with the responsibility for developing an HRD program. Task forces are more useful for programs beyond the scope of HRD staff capability. Also, the time required to develop a program can be reduced considerably with the help of a task force.

A major difference in the function of a task force and committee is that the task force is required to produce something. They must devote a considerable amount of time to developing the program. The time required may vary from a two-week assignment to a six-month, full-time project. This time span, of course, depends on the nature of the program being developed and the availability of assistance for the task force.

The selection of members for the task force is more critical than it is for committees. A typical task force may include members of management or non-management with the expertise needed for the project. Including management on the task force can add credibility and influence that might be needed to make the program a success. The disadvantage in using management is that they may not be available to contribute the time necessary for completion of the project. The backgrounds of the individuals are extremely important. They should represent a variety of experiences necessary for the program development and implementation.

For example, in a training program with the Allstate Insurance Companies, a task force was assembled to develop a program for a complex word processing system. Four participants were selected who represented each of Allstate's four main segments: Eastern, Midwestern, Southern, and Western. Each was experienced and had a thorough technical knowledge of the subject matter. In addition, each brought a specialist's insight into a different aspect of the course content. In another example from Goodyear Tire and Rubber Company, a maintenance training program was developed using the task force approach. The task force was made up of an engineer who designed the equipment to be maintained, a local plant engineer, a maintenance manager who had participated in the original start-up of the equipment, and a training manager familiar with performance-based training.

The task force approach is very economical. It relieves the HRD staff from the time-consuming activity of program development which may be an impossibility in a subject unfamiliar to the staff. It not only is the proper way to go, in some cases it is necessary to achieve the desired results.[14] And, the additional involvement on the part of management and professional personnel can help improve the credibility of the HRD program and enhance the results.

Managers as Participants

It may sometimes be appropriate for managers to attend programs designed for their subordinates. Participation can range from attending the full program to auditing a portion to examine its content. This approach may not be feasible for all types of HRD programs. For specialized courses designed for only a few individuals, managerial participation may not be practical or desirable. It works best when one or more of these conditions exist:

☐ *A high percentage of the manager's subordinates will attend the program.* In this case it is important for the manager to know program content and observe the dynamics of the learning process. This will help the manager understand why most of his or her subordinates must attend.

☐ *Support and reinforcement from the manager are essential to the program's success.* In this case the manager must know what role he or she must take to support the program and reinforce skills that are taught. The success or failure of many training programs often depends on the reinforcement received by the participants when they return to their jobs. The manager's role is critical in this instance.

□ *It is essential for the manager to have the same knowledge or skills that the subordinates will get from program attendance.* Although the program may not be intended for the management group, it may be important that they receive all or part of the information that their subordinates receive. For example, in a new products-application course designed for sales representatives, it may be important for sales managers to attend the program so that they will have a thorough understanding of the new information. Although it may not be essential to them in performing their jobs, it is helpful in keeping them up-to-date on product developments.

Involving Managers in Training Evaluation

A final major area in which managers can be involved in the HRD process is in the evaluation of HRD programs. Although management is involved to a certain extent in assessing the ultimate outcome of training programs, this process focuses directly on evaluation through a team or committee approach. One such approach was developed by Coffman in what he describes as the Training Impact Assessment Process (TIA).[15] This process requires managers to examine collectively what happens to their employees as a result of training. TIA has six steps:

1. Invite key clients to participate in assessment sessions
2. Asks clients to gather data on the effectiveness of training
3. Ask sub-groups to share positive results of training
4. Ask sub-groups to share negative or unachieved results
5. Have the entire group reconvene to share overall results
6. Consolidate lists, agree on actions and set a follow-up date.

This process has been used for over ten years and produces excellent results. In addition, by involving managers and executives and showing them how evaluation can work, increased commitment and support for HRD programs should follow.

New Roles for Managers

The approaches described are primary ways to involve managers in the HRD process when the focus is on achieving results. As stated earlier, there are many other ways in which managers can be involved. In essence, these six types of management involvement define new training roles for managers in an organization. Carswell and Straub have pinpointed five roles that managers can fulfill in developing this results-oriented approach.[16] These are

1. Training as a developmental assignment.
2. Managers training line employees.
3. Managers as subject-matter experts.
4. Managers reinforcing training.
5. Managers included in needs assessment.

It is imperative that managers assume these key roles. And the HRD staff must communicate frequently about the results achieved from programs. Collectively, this process will increase support and commitment as well as enhance input from each training role.

Benefits of Management Involvement

In summary, there are six major benefits from using management and professional personnel in the HRD process:

☐ It adds more credibility to the program than it might otherwise have.
☐ The program belongs to the management group, since they have been involved in the process of developing, conducting, or evaluating it.
☐ The program participants and HRD staff have more interaction with other management which makes for a stronger working relationship.
☐ It sharpens the skills of those managers involved in the process.
☐ It is more economical to use other managers and professional personnel than to add staff to the HRD department.
☐ It rewards good managers for their contributions to the HRD effort.

All of these advantages should encourage more organizations to use the skills and expertise of management personnel in the HRD process. The HRD department cannot afford to ignore the influence of the management group—in particular, key line and staff managers. Otherwise the HRD programs may not achieve desired results.

Summary

This chapter explored the influence of the management group on HRD program results. The HRD department cannot afford to ignore the influence of this group. Their actions and attitudes can have a significant impact on the success of the entire HRD effort. Management commitment, support, reinforcement, and involvement were each discussed along with specific approaches to obtain improvement. Although the HRD department has no direct control over these factors, it can exert a tremendous amount of influence on them.

The next, and final, chapter presents useful techniques for communicating program results.

Discussion Questions

---

1. Administer the CEO commitment survey to the CEO in your organization (or one with which you are familiar). Interpret the results.
2. What represents an adequate score on the Commitment Survey? Explain.
3. An HRD consultant was quoted as saying, ". . . Training is too serious a business to be left in the hands of trainers. It requires a full and active participation of top management." Explain.
4. Explain with practical examples the difference in management commitment, management support, management involvement, management reinforcement, maintenance of behavior, and transfer of training.
5. To what extent can management commitment be increased in an organization? Why?
6. Assess the degree of management support in your organization (or one with which you are familiar). How does it compare with the ideal management support outlined in this chapter?
7. An HRD consultant was quoted as saying, ". . . If we believe the boss plays a role in most everything a subordinate does, why is the boss suddenly exempted when it comes to the training process?" Explain.
8. Classify the key managers in your organization (or one with which you are familiar) according to the four types of managers as outlined in this chapter. Develop a strategy to improve the support from each manager.
9. If reinforcement is so important to training success, then why do so few programs emphasize specific techniques of reinforcement?
10. One HRD executive was quoted as saying, ". . . Without reinforcement, soft-skills training will never take." Please comment.
11. Detail specific actions that are critical to the reinforcement of training.
12. Identify the specific ways in which managers can be involved in the training programs. Which are most effective? Which are least effective?
13. What is the optimum balance of the degree of involvement of managers versus HRD staff members?

14. What can be done to ensure that managers are effective discussion leaders?
15. How are managers involved in HRD in your organization (or one with which you are familiar)?
16. Describe how peer support groups can enhance the transfer of training.
17. What are the advantages of advisory committees in HRD? What type of committees would be appropriate in your organization (or one with which you are familiar)?
18. What are the differences between advisory committees and task forces? Cite examples of each.
19. Why are managers reluctant to attend programs designed for subordinates? What are the advantages of their attendance in these programs?
20. Identify additional benefits of management involvement in addition to those listed in this chapter.

References

1. Paquet, B., Kasl, E., Weinstein, L., and Waite, W., "The Bottom Line," *Training and Development Journal,* May 1987, pp. 27–33.
2. Bell, C., "Building a Reputation for Training Effectiveness,"*Training and Development Journal,* May 1984, p. 50.
3. Quick, T. L., "Five Top Human Resource Professionals Speak Out: The Importance of HRD in Business," *Training News,* May 1987, pp. 10–19.
4. Goulde, R. A., "Management Training? Get Serious,"*New Management,* Vol. 4, No. 3, Winter 1987, p. 30–33.
5. Spector, A. K., "Strategic Steps to Management Support," *Training and Development Journal,* February 1988, pp. 42–43.
6. Wexley, K. N. and Baldwin, T. T., "Post Training Strategies for Facilitating Positive Transfer: An Empirical Exploration," *Academy of Management Journal,* Vol. 29, No. 3, 1986, pp. 503–520.
7. Gist, M. E., Bavetta, A. G., and Stevens, C. K., "Transfer Training Method: Its Influence on Skill Generation, Skill Repetition and Performance Level," *Personnel Psychology,* Vol. 43, 1990, pp. 501–523.
8. For more information see Rackham, N., "The Coaching Controversy," *Training and Development Journal,* November 1979, pp. 13–14; and Paquel, Kasl, Weinstein, and Waite, 1987, pp. 27–33.
9. Kruger, M. J. and May, G. D., "Two Techniques to Ensure That Training Programs Remain Effective," *Personnel Journal,* October 1989, pp. 70–75.

10. Zemke, R. and Gunkler, J., "28 Techniques for Transforming Training into Performance," *Training,* April 1985, pp. 48–63.
11. Taken from a presentation by Dr. Mary Broad and Dr. John Newstrom at the 1989 annual meeting of the American Society for Training and Development.
12. Phillips, J. J., "Getting Managers Involved in HRD,"*Personnel,* July 1985, p. 10.
13. Galagan, P. A., "Ronald E. Compton: Underwriting Business with Training," *Training and Development Journal,* October 1989, p. 35.
14. Coffman, L., "How to Keep Good Programs Alive," *Training,* October 1987, pp. 77–80.
15. Coffman, L., "Involving Managers in Training Evaluation,"*Training and Development Journal,* June 1990, pp. 77–80.
16. Carswell, P. and Straub, C., "On the Road to Management Support," *Training,* July 1990, p. 58.

CHAPTER 14

Communicating
Program Results

With results in hand, what next? Should they be used to justify new programs, gain additional support, or build good will? How should they be presented? This chapter will answer these and other questions concerning the communication of HRD program results.

The worst course of action is to do nothing. Communicating results is almost as important as achieving results. The old saying, "Results will speak for themselves" is not always accurate. If they are "spoken" in the wrong places, the key individuals may not receive the proper information. Getting results without communicating them is like planting seeds and failing to fertilize and cultivate the seedlings. The yield will just not be as great.

This chapter provides useful information to help present evaluation data to the various audiences. It covers both oral and written reporting methods.

The Process of Communicating Results

General Principles

The skills required for communicating results effectively are almost as delicate and sophisticated as those involved in getting the results. Yet, the communication process may be no different than other types of communications in business and professional settings. Regardless of the message, the audience, or the media, a few general principles are important when communicating HRD program results.

The communication must be timely. Usually, program results should be communicated as soon as they are known. From a practical standpoint, it may be best to delay a communication to a convenient time such as the next edition of the newsletter or the next general management meeting. Several questions about the timing must be answered. Is the audience ready for it in view of other things that may have happened? Are they expecting it? When is the best time to have the maximum effect on the audience?

The communication should be targeted to specific audiences. The communication will be more efficient when it is designed for a particular group. The message can be specifically tailored to the interests, needs, and expectations of the group.

The media should be carefully selected. For particular groups, some media may be more effective than others. Face-to-face meetings may be better than special bulletins. A memo to top management may be more effective than the company newspaper. The proper selection of a communication method can help improve the effectiveness of the process.

The communication should be unbiased and modest. It is important to separate facts from fiction and accurate statements from opinions. The various audiences may accept communication from the HRD department with skepticism, carefully searching for biased opinions. Boastful statements sometimes turn off the recipient, and most of the content of the communication is lost. Observable, believable facts carry more weight than extreme or sensational claims, although such claims may get audience attention.

The communication must be consistent. The timing and the content of the communication should be consistent with past practices. A special communication at an unusual time may provoke suspicion. Also, if a particular group, such as top management, regularly receives communications regarding major program outcomes, then they should always receive communication even if the results are not good. If some results are omitted, it might leave the impression that only good results are reported.

Testimonials are more effective if they are from individuals the audience respects. Attitudes and opinions are strongly influenced by others, particularly by those who are admired or respected. Testimonials about HRD program results, when solicited from individuals who are generally respected by others in the organization, can have a strong impact on the effectiveness of the message. This respect may be earned from leadership ability, position, special skills, or knowledge. The converse of this is true. A testimonial from an individual who commands little respect and who is regarded as a sub-standard performer can have a negative impact on the communications.

The audience's attitude toward the HRD department will affect communication strategy. Attitudes are difficult to change. A negative or hostile attitude toward the HRD department may not be changed by the mere presentation of facts. However, the presentation of facts alone may strengthen the opinion of those who already agree with the department. It helps reassure them and provides a defense in a discussion with others. An HRD department with high credibility and respect in the organization may have a relatively easy task in communicating results. Low credibility, on the other hand, may create a problem when trying to be persuasive in communications. The assessment of the credibility of the department should be an important consideration in developing the overall strategy toward communication. Communicating program results, assuming the results are significant, should have a positive effect on increasing the credibility of the department.

These general principles are important to the overall success of the communication effort. They should serve as a checklist to the HRD professional when disseminating program results.

A Communications Model

The process of communicating program results must be systematic, timely, and well planned as illustrated in the model in Figure 14-1. The model represents six components of the communication process which normally should occur in the sequence shown.

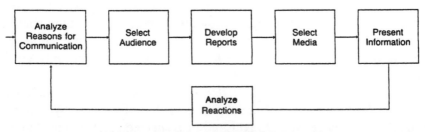

Figure 14-1. A communications model.

The first step is one of the most important. It consists of an analysis of the need to communicate HRD program results. Possibly there is a lack of support for the HRD effort, or there is a need to justify a new program or continue funding for a project. Maybe there is a need to restore confidence or build credibility for the HRD department. Regardless of the need, a very key part of the process is to outline the specific reasons for communicating the results of the program.

The second step involves selecting the target audiences for the communication. The audiences range from top management to past participants, each with their own special communication needs. All groups should be considered in the communications strategy. Maybe a specific group needs winning over through a special targeted communication.

The third step is concerned with developing written material to explain program results. This can come in a wide variety of possibilities, varying from a brief summary of the results to a detailed research report on the evaluation effort. Usually, a complete report is developed; then selected parts or summaries from the report can be used for the different media.

Selecting the media is the fourth step. Some groups respond more favorably to certain methods of communication when compared to others. A variety of approaches, using both oral and written presentations, are available to the HRD professional.

In the fifth step the information is presented. The product is delivered. This must be done with utmost care, confidence, and with every bit of professionalism possible.

The last step, but not of least significance, is the process of analyzing the reactions to communications. This can be very informal and unscientific and still be very helpful. Possibly tuning in to the reaction of a specific group will suffice. Positive reactions, negative reactions, and lack of comments are all indicators of how the information was received. For an extensive and more involved communications effort, a formal and structured feedback process may be necessary. These reactions could trigger an adjustment to the communications on the same program results or give input to make adjustments for future communications.

This communications model is not intended to make the process complicated. There is usually more than one audience who receives the results of an HRD program, and each audience has its unique needs. All the components of the model should be given consideration (even if on an informal basis) before the communication strategy is developed. Otherwise, the full impact of the effort may be diminished.

Reasons for Communications

The reasons for communicating program results depend on the organization and specific needs. The most common reasons are:

☐ To secure *approval* for HRD programs; to allocate resources of time and money.
☐ To gain *support* for the HRD department.
☐ To build *credibility* for the HRD department's actions.
☐ To obtain a *commitment* for a subordinate to attend an HRD program.
☐ To create a *desire* to attend a particular program.
☐ To enhance *reinforcement* of the HRD process.
☐ To show the *importance* of measuring the results of HRD programs.
☐ To stimulate *interest* in what the HRD department is doing.

There may be other reasons for communicating results. A list should be developed tailored to the organization.

Target Audiences

General Principles

When approaching a particular audience, the following questions should be asked about each potential group:

☐ Are they interested in the subject?
☐ Do they really want to receive the information?
☐ Is the timing right for this audience?
☐ Are they familiar with the views of the HRD department?
☐ How do they prefer to have results communicated?
☐ Are they likely to find the results threatening?
☐ Which medium will be most convincing to this group?

There are three general principles in communicating with a specific audience:

Get to know the audience. To the greatest extent possible, the HRD department should get to know each audience. Some of this will certainly come easy (i.e., communicating with program participants). However, top management or various segments of the management group may not be known to the HRD staff as well as they should be.

Find out what information is needed and why. Each group will have its own needs relative to the information desired. Some want detailed information while others want brief information. Do not try to outguess the audience.

Try to understand each audience's viewpoint. This relates back to principle number one—knowing the audience. Each will have a particular viewpoint about the results. Some may be in favor of it, some against it, and others neutral. The staff should use empathy and try to understand the differing views. With this understanding, communications can be tailored to each group. This is especially critical when the audience is anticipated to react negatively to the comments.

Selecting the Audience

There are many people who should receive information on HRD program results. Determining which group needs what information deserves careful thought. Problems can arise when a particular group receives inappropriate information or when another is omitted altogether. A sound basis for a proper audience selection is in the reason for communication, discussed in the previous section. Table 14-1 shows the common target audiences and the basis for selecting the audience. Each group deserves a few comments.

Table 14-1
Common Target Audiences

Audience	Reason for Communication
Top Management	Secure approval
All management	Gain support/build credibility
Participants' superiors	Obtain commitment/build credibility
Potential participants	Create desire
Current participants	Enhance reinforcement
HRD Staff	Show importance
All employees	Stimulate interest
Stockholders	Secure endorsement

Probably the most important target audience of all those listed is the top management group. These individuals are responsible for the allocation of resources for the HRD department. They need information to help justify the expenditures and to gauge the effectiveness of the function.

All management should be informed about HRD program results in a more general way. Management's support for, and involvement in, the HRD process is important to the success of the effort. Also, the department's credibility is another key item of concern. Communicating program results to management can help in each of these areas.

The importance of communicating with the participants' superiors is probably obvious. In many cases they must allow participants to attend the programs. A good return on the investment improves their commitment to HRD, not to mention the department's credibility.

Occasionally, results are communicated to create a desire to participate in a program. This is especially true for programs offered on a volunteer basis or those offered to the general public. These potential participants are an important target for communicating results.

Participants need feedback on the overall success of the effort. Some individuals may not have been as successful as others in achieving the desired results. Communicating the results adds additional peer pressure to practice what was taught and improve results for the future. For those achieving good results, the communication will serve as a reinforcement of the HRD process. This target audience is often overlooked in communicating results under the assumption that since the program is over, the participants do not need to know about the overall success.

The HRD staff must receive the information about program results. For small staffs, the person doing the evaluation may be the same person who conducted the program. For larger departments, evaluation may be a separate function. In either case, the program designer and developer must have the information on the program's effectiveness. This is necessary so that adjustments can be made if the program is to be repeated.

All employees and stockholders may be less likely targets. General interest news or stories may build respect for the function in the eyes of employees. Good will and positive attitudes toward the organization may also be a by-product of program-results communications. Stockholders, on the other hand, are more interested in the return on their investment.

While Table 14-1 shows the eight most common target audiences, there can be others in a particular organization. For instance, all management or all employees could be subdivided into different departments, divisions, or even subsidiaries of the organization. The number of audiences can be large in a complex organization.

Communicating with Top Management

No group is more important, than the top management group when it comes to communicating program results. Improving communications with this group requires developing an overall strategy which may include all or a part of the following actions:

Strengthen the relationship with the CEO. There should be an informal and productive relationship established between the individual responsible for HRD and the chief executive officer of the organization. Each should feel comfortable with open communications regarding HRD needs and program results. One approach is to establish frequent, informal meetings with the chief executive to discuss problems with the current programs, training needs, and performance deficiencies in the organization. Frank and open conversations can give the CEO an insight not possible from any other source. Also, it can be very helpful to the HRD manager in determining direction for the HRD effort.[1]

Show how HRD programs have helped solve major problems. While hard results of specific programs are comforting for an executive, solutions to immediate problems may be more convincing.

Distribute memos on program results. When an HRD program has achieved significant results, let appropriate top executives know about the results. This can easily be done with a brief memo outlining what the program was supposed to accomplish, when it was conducted, who attended, and the results achieved. As shown in the following memo, this should be presented in a for-your-information format with careful attention to state only facts and very little opinion.

Include top executives on all important communications regarding HRD programs. Communications on HRD programs, plans, activities, and results should include the top executive group, unless of course, it is too insignificant. Frequent information from the HRD department, as long as it is not boastful, can have a positive impact on the top group. They are reminded that the department exists and it is doing something worthwhile.

Appoint top executives to HRD committees. An effective way to enhance commitment from the top group is to ask them to serve on an HRD committee. These committees give input and advice to the HRD staff on a variety of issues, including training needs, problems with the present programs, and program evaluation. Committees come in a wide variety as illustrated in the previous chapter. Whatever the scope, these

---

MEMO

To: Top Executive Group

From: Jack Phillips   Date: 3/27/91

Subject: Explorations in Managing

On February 25–27, twenty-eight middle managers attended "Explorations in Managing." The purpose of the program was to develop managerial skills and improve the manager's relationships with his or her subordinates.

The managers were asked to complete a detailed evaluation questionnaire at the end of this program. Part of this questionnaire asked about improvements in personal effectiveness and estimated savings as a result of attending the program. A summary is presented below.

Twenty-six managers indicated an increase in personal effectiveness averaging 22.7% (the range was from 5% to 50%). Twenty managers provided estimates of annual dollar savings to the company as a result of this program. The estimates ranged from $1,200 to $360,000 with a total of $862,000. Nineteen managers provided a confidence level on their dollar estimates. The average confidence level was 48%, ranging from 20% to 100%. The formulas used to arrive at the dollar estimates varied considerably. The most common were based on improvements in personal effectiveness, improvement·in efficiency of subordinates, reduction in operating costs, reduction in scrap and increases in output.

If the total dollar estimates are reduced by the average confidence level, the total savings are reduced to $454,500. As you can see, these estimates are quite high. Even if the total is divided by a factor of ten, the savings are still significant compared with the cost of the program which was approximately $5,000.

Since these questionnaires were administered on the last day of the program, they no doubt reflect the general feeling toward the whole social experience. We would expect a less optimistic report six months after the program and plan to follow up at that time to see to what extent these estimates held true. If you have any specific questions about this program, please give me a call.

JJP:ds

committees can be helpful in letting each executive know what the programs are accomplishing.

One effective example involved the appointment of several executives to a committee for a management trainee program. This program was designed for entry-level college graduates who were being developed for management positions. They met frequently to review the program, monitor the results, and make changes to correct problem areas. The results of this program were in the form of successes on the job and the reduction of turnover of new college graduates. The executives knew the results of the program on a continuous basis. This top executive involvement was crucial to the success of the program.

Conduct an HRD review. A very effective way to communicate HRD program results to top executives is through the use of an HRD review meeting.[2] While this review can be conducted more frequently, an annual basis is common. The primary purpose is to show top management what has been accomplished and what is planned for the future. It can last from two hours to two days, depending on the scope of the meeting and the amount of HRD program activity. A typical agenda for this review meeting is shown in Table 14-2.

Table 14-2
Annual HRD Review Agenda

Annual Human Resource Development Review Meeting	
Time	Topic
8:00	Review of HRD programs for the past year.
10:30	Methods of evaluation for each program and the results achieved.
11:30	Significant deviations from the expected results (both good and bad).
12:00	Lunch.
1:00	Basis for determining training and development needs for next year.
1:45	Planned programs for the coming year (secure support and approval).
3:15	Proposed methods of evaluation and potential payoffs.
4:00	Problem areas in the HRD process (lack of support, where management involvement is needed, or other

	potential problems which can be corrected by top management).
4:30	Concerns from top management.
5:00	Adjourn.

Obviously, this meeting cannot be taken lightly. It may be the single most important event on the HRD department calendar during the year. It must be planned carefully, timely executed, and controlled in a manner to accomplish its intended purpose. This approach has been used in many companies, and the reaction has been extremely favorable. Top management wants to know what the department is doing, what results have been achieved and, most of all, they want to have input into the decisions for new programs.

Developing an Evaluation Report

The type of formal evaluation report depends on the extent of detailed information presented to the various target audiences. Brief summaries of program results with appropriate charts may be sufficient for most communication efforts. For other situations, particularly with significant programs requiring extensive funding, the amount of detail in the evaluation report is more crucial. A full evaluation report may be necessary. This report then can be used as the basis for the information for the specific audiences and various media.

The report may contain the following sections:

☐ Management summary
☐ Background information
☐ Evaluation strategy
☐ Data collection and analysis
☐ Program costs
☐ Program results
☐ Conclusions and recommendations

These seven components produce a very thorough evaluation report. Each is explained here in more detail.

Management Summary

The management summary is a brief overview of the entire report explaining the basis for the evaluation and the significant conclusions and recommendations. It is designed for those individuals who are too busy to read a detailed report. It is usually written last but appears first in the report for easy access.

Background Information

The background information describes why the program was conducted and gives a general description of the program. If applicable, the needs analysis which led to the implementation of the program is usually summarized. The program objectives are presented as well as information on the program content, length, course materials, instructors, facilities, and other specific items which provide a full description of how the program was presented. The extent of the detailed information depends on the amount of information the audience needs.

Evaluation Strategy

The evaluation strategy outlines all of the components that make up the total evaluation process. Several of the components of the results-oriented HRD model presented in Chapter 4 are discussed in this section. It begins with the specific purposes of evaluation for this particular program. Next, the evaluation design is explained with the appropriate rationale. The instruments used in the design are also described and presented as exhibits. Any unusual characteristics of the instrument design are discussed, and the procedures for participant selection are outlined. Finally, other useful information related to the design, timing, and execution of the evaluation is included.

Data Collection and Analysis

This section explains the methods used to collect data as outlined in Chapter 8. The data collected are usually presented in the report in both raw and finished formats. Next, the methods of analysis of the data are presented with interpretations. If appropriate, the hypothesis is stated along with the information on the confidence level.

Program Costs

Program costs are presented in this section. A summary of the costs, by cost components (functional/process category) or by particular accounts, may be appropriate. For example, analysis, development, delivery, and evaluation costs are four recommended categories for cost presentation. The assumptions made in classifying costs are discussed in this section.

Program Results

The program results section presents a summary of the results with charts, diagrams, tables, and other visual aids. If applicable, conclusions from the cost/benefit comparison are discussed along with the ROI. Various program benefits are outlined so that the section gives a complete picture of the evaluation.

Conclusions and Recommendations

This section presents the overall conclusions based on all the material presented up to this point. If appropriate, brief explanations are presented on how each conclusion was derived. A list of recommendations or changes in the program, if appropriate, should be provided with brief explanations for each recommendation. It is important that the conclusions and recommendations be consistent with one another and with the findings described in the previous section.

These components make up the major parts of a complete evaluation report. It can be scaled down as necessary. The evaluation report is a proven technique to communicate results.[3]

Communication Media

There are many approaches available to communicate program results. The most frequently used media are management meetings, HRD newsletters, the organization publication, other written materials, and success stories. These are explained next with useful tips and examples.

Management Meetings

Management meetings represent a fertile ground for communicating program results, if used properly All organizations have a variety of meetings and in each kind, in the proper context, HRD results can be an important part of the meeting. A few examples will illustrate the variety of meetings.

Staff meetings. All the way through the chain of command, staff meetings are held to review progress, discuss current problems, and pass along information. These meetings can be an excellent forum to discuss the results achieved in an HRD program if the program is related to the activities of the group. Information on program results can be sent directly to executives to use in staff meetings, or a member of the HRD staff can attend the meeting to make the presentation.

Supervisory meetings. Regular meetings with the first-line supervisory group are quite common. Typically, items are discussed which will possibly help supervisors be more effective in their work. A discussion of an HRD program and the subsequent results can be integrated into the regular meeting format. In one example a new safety training program was announced in a routine supervisory meeting. After the training, the results were discussed at subsequent supervisory meetings until the end of the year.

Panel discussions. Although not common in all organizations, panel discussions can be very helpful to show how a problem was solved. A typical panel might include two or more supervisors discussing their approach to a solution of a problem common to other supervisors. A successful discussion, based on the results of a recent HRD program, can provide convincing data to other supervisors and to top management.

Management clubs. Management clubs, leadership associations, and local company chapters of the National Management Association are becoming increasingly popular. These organizations usually open their membership to all professional, technical, and managerial employees. Regular meetings are a major part of their activities, with the majority of them on management-related topics. HRD program results can be an appropriate topic in these meetings. In one company a monthly meeting featured a member of the HRD staff discussing the results of an assessment center. In a spotlight presentation the staff member outlined the program statistics since its inception and the specific results achieved. This presentation was very helpful in getting additional support, while showing management that the program has worked.

Annual "State of the Company" meetings. A few organizations have initiated an annual dinner meeting for all the members of management where the CEO reviews progress and discusses plans for the coming year. A few highlights of major HRD program results integrated into the CEO's speech can have a positive effect on the HRD department. It shows top executive interest, commitment, and support. The program results are mentioned along with operating profit, new facilities and equipment, new company acquisitions, and next year's sales forecast.

In summary, whenever a management group is convened in significant numbers, evaluate the appropriateness of communicating an HRD program announcement or program result.

HRD Newsletter

Although usually limited to large HRD departments, a highly visible way to communicate program results is through the use of an HRD newsletter. Published on a periodic basis, monthly or quarterly, a newsletter usually has a two-fold purpose:

☐ To inform management about the activities of the HRD department.
☐ To communicate the results achieved by the HRD programs.

Possibly a more subtle reason for a newsletter is to gain additional support and commitment from the management group. This newsletter is published by the HRD staff and is usually distributed to management personnel, or at least to key managers in the organization. The format and scope of the newsletter can vary considerably A simple photocopied two-page newsletter, front and back, may work well for a small organization, while an offset, four-color, 10-page newsletter may be appropriate for a large organization whose budget can afford it. Regardless of format, there are a number of topics appropriate for this newsletter. A sampling of common topics is presented here.

Schedule of courses. A running schedule of planned courses should be an integral part of this newsletter. In addition to registration information, a brief description should be presented which includes:

☐ Method of presentation
☐ Who should attend
☐ Prerequisites (if any)
☐ Expected outcomes

Plans for new programs. An ongoing training needs analysis or an update on a program in the development stage might be appropriate for the newsletter. This could generate interest in a program before it is developed and stimulate comments about proposed program content, scheduling, and possible instructors.

Reactions from participants. A brief summary of the reactions from end-of-program evaluations may be appropriate to report initial success. Also, brief interviews with participants after a program might be of interest.

Program results. The key ingredients of this newsletter are reports about the results achieved from HRD programs. A headline, "Productivity Improvement Course Nets Cost Savings of $150,000," will draw the attention of a profit-minded manager. Any significant results which can be documented should be presented in an easily understood format. The method(s) of evaluation should be outlined, along with the measurement of the impact or return on the program. This might be a regular feature, possibly with a catchy title such as Focus on Results.

HRD philosophy and policy statements. Another possibility for a newsletter includes comments from a top executive about the organization's philosophies or policies regarding the development of employees. Sometimes this can be used to refine a formal philosophy. In one company the HRD manager developed what he thought would be the ideal philosophy of a chief executive and discussed it with the CEO. After a few modifications, it became the published philosophy of the company in regard to developing human resources.

Manager's spotlight. A section of the newsletter featuring a key supportive manager can be very useful. Emphasis is placed on the manager's efforts and involvement in HRD activity. Statements or interview comments on the following topics may be useful:

☐ Management's support for HRD.
☐ Management involvement in various phases of HRD.

☐ Expectations of participants.
☐ The need for program results.
☐ The need for self-improvement.

Instructor's spotlight. A section spotlighting a member of the HRD staff can focus additional attention on results. This is an opportunity to recognize outstanding individuals who are getting excellent results with their HRD programs, and it can highlight unusual achievements or accomplishments.

While the previous list may not be suited for every newsletter, it represents topics which should be presented to the management group. When presented in a professional manner, the newsletter can improve the management's support and commitment to the HRD effort. A word of caution is in order. The newsletter should not be too boastful; otherwise, it might turn off even the best of managers. Facts should be presented, leaving out most of the opinions of the HRD staff. Facts are hard to dispute, and opinions and comments from executives outside the training department will be respected.

The Organization Publication

To reach a wide audience in their communication efforts, HRD professionals can use in-house publications. Whether in a newsletter, magazine, or newspaper format, this publication usually reaches all employees. The material for this publication should be limited to general interest articles, announcements, and interviews. The communication can be effective if the information is carefully selected. A few types of articles are presented here.

Program results. Results communicated through this media must be significant to arouse general interest. For example, a story with a headline, Safety Training Program Results in One Million Hours without a Lost Time Accident, will catch the attention of many people because they are involved in the effort and know that the results are significant. A report on the accomplishments of a group of participants may not create any interest unless the audience can relate to those accomplishments.

For many HRD programs, results are achieved weeks or even months after the program is completed. It is not something that occurs overnight. Participants need reinforcement from many sources for them to use what has been taught. This is particularly true for skills-oriented training. If a program is communicated to a general audience, including the participant's subordinates or peers, there is additional pressure on that participant to put into practice what was taught in the program.

In one program supervisors were taught to use specific discussion skills with their employees to improve performance and work habits, administer disciplinary action, etc. When an article in the company newspaper appeared describing the skills, the supervisors who had attended the program increased their use of those skills. The participant's subordinates (i.e., the employees) were expecting the supervisors to do something different as a result of the program after reading about it in the company newspaper.

Building interest. Stories about participants involved in an HRD activity and the results they achieve create a favorable image. Employees see the company investing time and money to improve their performance in current assignments as well as preparing them for future assignments.

This communication provides information about programs that employees otherwise may not have known about and sometimes creates a desire for them to be involved. This desire to participate may be necessary to obtain quality applicants. It might even stimulate self-development among employees, particularly if programs are offered after hours to enhance career possibilities.

One organization had a program for potential supervisors. Although it was not communicated as a presupervisory program, it was understood that the participants were being groomed for supervision. It was a highly visible program involving department visitations as well as classroom training. Information about the participants was published in the company's monthly newspaper. It resulted in a long list of employees expressing a keen desire to be selected for future programs.

Participant recognition. General audience communication can bring recognition to participants in a training program, particularly those who excel in some aspect of the program. When participants are selected for a prestigious and sought-after slot in a training program, public recognition can enhance their self-esteem.

Human interest stories. There can be many human interest stories developed as a result of HRD activities. A rigorous program with difficult requirements for selection can provide the basis for an interesting story on participants who have completed it.

In one organization the editor of the company newspaper attended a very demanding HRD program and wrote a stimulating article about what it is like to be a participant. The article gave the reader a tour of the whole course, what was covered, how it was presented, and its effectiveness in terms of the results achieved. It made an interesting story about a difficult development activity.

The benefits are many and the opportunities are endless for HRD departments to utilize the in-house publication to let others know what is happening in HRD.

Other Written Materials

In addition to memos, reports, and newsletters, other forms of written communications can be effective in getting the message out about HRD program results. Brochures, booklets, and pamphlets have proven to be effective in a variety of applications. Four examples are presented here.

Program brochures. A program brochure might be appropriate for programs conducted on a continuing basis where participants are selected from many potential applicants. A typical brochure is printed on standard-size paper and folded twice. It should catch the eye, be attractive, and present a complete description of the program, with a major section devoted to results obtained with previous participants, if available. Measurable results and reactions from participants, or even direct quotes from individuals, could add spice to an otherwise dull brochure. Figure 14-2 is a portion of a brochure that highlights the bottomline results.

Program catalogs. A catalog of programs can be distributed to the management group, particularly in large organizations. This catalog describes the programs for the coming month, quarter, or year. Some necessary items to include are descriptions of the programs, the schedule and duration, the instructor, and most important, the results expected. If the program has been offered in the past, presenting evaluation data can have an impact on those making a decision whether or not to attend. The catalog should be attractively packaged and reflect the concept of getting results. Figure 14-3 shows the cover of a program catalog for Ford Motor Company. The upward trend in the spelling of "Improving Managerial Performance" implies increased performance.

DOCUMENTED BOTTOM-LINE RESULTS

In a wide range of applications the average initial project completed in eight weeks by each Resources Management participant has generated between $5,000 and $30,000 for the organization, based on the *annualized* return to be obtained from that project.

Thus the first-project results, impressive in themselves, represent only the tip of the iceberg. As successful projects are continued on an ongoing basis, and new RM projects developed from year to year, the return on investment multiplies many times over.

Case Study #1
Major Commercial Bank

Twenty-six Resources Managment projects were completed in the trust and trust services departments, including rescheduling work hours to reduce clerical overtime, maximizing interest "float," reducing the cost of security transfers and implementing data processing efficiencies.
Bottom-line savings: $1,147,000 annually from initial projects.

Case Study #2
Technical Instrument Manufacturer

Projects included a method of updating federal contract proposals to reflect latest price changes, elimination

of five operations in the assembly and testing of gyros, plus personnel allocation and compensation policy efficiencies.
Bottom-line savings: $287,000 annually from initial projects.

Case Study #3
Heavy Industry

Projects included design alterations of certain manufactured parts to cut assembly time and expense, elimination of unnecessary computer reports, resale of scrap paper and a procedure to penalize vendors for defective merchandise.
Bottom-line savings: $155,000 annually from initial projects.

Case examples related to your organization are readily available from DDI.

Figure 14-2. A portion of a program brochure. (Reproduced with permission from Development Dimensions Intl., Pittsburgh, PA.)

Recruiting brochures. For some programs, candidates are recruited from outside the organization. Brochures are developed to help bring individuals into programs for management trainees, nurses, account executives, salespersons, and other entry-level professional jobs. These brochures, while they are attractive, usually devote little attention to the results obtained from the program. Most brochures aim to describe the program and the entrance requirements. Information should be included on the success of those completing the program, and possibly a few quotes from past participants about the importance of the program.

Special achievement. Occasionally, the HRD department may have an opportunity to publicize a success story—an achievement linked to an HRD program. A pamphlet on this story, developed and distributed to the management group in general management meetings or staff meetings, can be beneficial if there is a direct tie with an

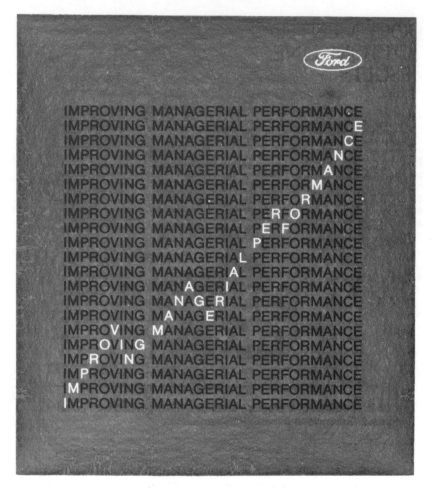

Figure 14-3. A program catalog.

HRD program. The brochure should be aimed at reducing costs, improving productivity, or other tangible areas, and should show what an employee, a group of employees, or a department has achieved in these areas. It should detail what was done, how it was done, and what was achieved with subtle tie-ins to HRD programs. Figure 14-4 shows the cover of a special achievement pamphlet. Note the emphasis on results. An explanation of the contents of the pamphlet is presented in a later section.

If developed and presented in a professional manner, these brochures, booklets, and pamphlets are effective and inexpensive vehicles to let others know about HRD programs and the results they have achieved.

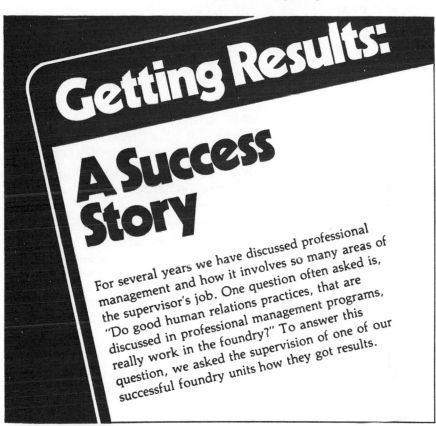

Figure 14-4. Example of a success story pamphlet.

Success Stories

A final approach to communicating program results involves the use of the subtle success story (SSS), which was mentioned earlier. In this approach success stories are publicized when a success can be linked to an HRD program. Publicity is usually low key, and initially it may not be obvious who began the communication or even why it was communicated. The subtle idea is to let the management group see a successful performance story which was a result of an HRD program. For examples of success stories, see DuJardin.[4]

Publicizing success stories can have several advantages.

Program results. Most important, it shows the entire group a success that is related to HRD. The most effective managers, who are looking for results out of the HRD department, will certainly tie the two together.

Encouragement. It can provide encouragement for those who have completed the program but did not get similar results. If they try the skills, techniques, and methods taught in the HRD program, then they should be able to get similar results.

Rewards and reinforcement. To the employees who are being featured, it reinforces the importance of what they have done. To the entire group, it reinforces what is being taught in the HRD program. Also, it is a very positive reward for those who are being recognized for their success. It shows them if they practice what was taught, the organization will give them due recognition.

The subtle approach is taken so that unnecessary attention is not directed to the HRD department. No one wants to listen to a department tooting its own horn about its programs. With this approach, the critics will not treat valuable information as propaganda.

A Case Example

These various methods for communicating HRD program results can be creatively combined to fit any situation. Here is an effective example utilizing three approaches: a success story, management meetings, and a pamphlet.

A production unit had achieved outstanding results through the efforts of a team of two supervisors. These results were in the form of key bottomline measures, such as absenteeism, turnover, lost-time accidents, grievances, scrap rate, and unit hour. The unit hour was a basic measure of individual productivity.

These results were achieved through the efforts of the supervisors applying the basic skills taught in a supervisory training program. This fact was mentioned in the beginning of a presentation made by the supervisors. In a panel discussion format with a moderator the two supervisors outlined what they do to get their results. It was presented in a question-and-answer session at a monthly meeting for all supervisors. They mentioned that many of the techniques were learned in the training program.

The comments were published in pamphlet form for distribution to all supervision through their department head. The title of the publication is *Getting Results: A Success Story.* The cover of the 8 1/2 x 11 four-page pamphlet is shown in Figure 14-4. The contents are more important. On the inside cover the specific results are detailed, along with additional information on the supervisors. A close-up photograph of each supervisor taken during the panel discussion is included on this page. The next two pages present a summary of the techniques used to secure the results. Figure 14-5 shows a copy of these two pages. The pamphlet was used in staff meetings as a discussion guide to cover the points from the panel discussion. Top executives were also sent copies.

In addition, the discussion was video-taped and used in subsequent training programs as a model of applying what is taught. The pamphlet served as a handout.

From all indications, the communications effort worked. Favorable responses were received from all levels of management. Top executives asked the HRD department to prepare and conduct similar meetings. Other supervisors began to use more of the approaches presented by the two supervisors.

Analyzing the Reaction to Communication

The best overall measurement of the effectiveness of communicating program results is the commitment and support from the management group. The allocation of resources when requested and strong top management commitment are clear tangible evidence of how well management perceives HRD program results. In addition to this overall measurement, there are a few techniques the HRD department can use to measure the effectiveness of its communication efforts.

Whenever results are communicated, those involved in the communication effort, or even the entire HRD staff, should try to gauge the reaction of the target audiences. These reactions may include non-verbal gestures, oral remarks, written comments, or indirect actions which reveal how the communication was received. Usually, when results are presented in a meeting, the presenter will have some indication of how the results were received by the group. The interest and attitudes of the audience can usually be quickly evaluated.[5]

During the presentation, questions may be asked or in some cases the information challenged. Of course, these items should be explained at the time they are presented. In addition, a tabulation of these challenges and questions can be useful in evaluating the type of information to include in future communication. Positive comments about the results are certainly desired and, when they are made, either formally or informally, they should also be noted and tabulated.

Sixteen ways to get results with your employees.

1. Help employees with problems.
Whenever an employee develops a problem, either discuss it with him and try to reach a solution or send him to someone who can help. Make the appointment yourself, to insure that he is getting proper counsel. Follow-up to insure that the problem was solved.

2. Be friendly to your employees.
This seems extremely fundamental, but is important. Just the simple gesture of speaking to each employee in the morning or responding to them in a friendly manner can help create a friendly working atmosphere that most employees want. This should be genuine and sincere, not false friendliness just when you want something.

3. Recognize and reward employees.
Employees want to be recognized. Give them recognition on birthdays, employment anniversaries, outstanding performance, or other special occasions. Use a blackboard or other means to communicate particular achievement and recognition of the work group.
Keep a calendar of the special events; such as, birthdays and anniversaries, so you won't forget. These records are easily available from Industrial Relations.

4. Know your employees.
This seems basic, but it is also very important, You must know what your people will respond to and try to satisfy those needs individually. Some can take more kidding than others. Some need more attention than others. Learn how to handle each one.

5. Get employees involved.
Employees will usually want to do more when they are involved in the operation. Whenever there is a problem in the work group, discuss it with key members of the group and let them help handle the problem.
Get employees involved in special activities such as housekeeping contests, safety meetings and exchanging gifts at Christmas.

6. Show employees that you care.
Employees appreciate your concern. A simple act of showing that you are concerned about their welfare can go a long way to get employees to work with you. Take steps to insure that each man is properly paid. Check material to see if it is properly reported in a

timely manner. When there is a discrepancy, let the employee know before they see the posting sheets. Whenever an employee is hospitalized, visit him. Send a fruit basket. It certainly pays for itself in return performance.
Show concern by assuming that each employee's job is in the right classification. If not, work with the proper departments, and through your boss, to get a reclassification.

7. Communicate openly and honestly.
Employees need to be communicated with. A blackboard or bulletin board in the department can be a useful communication tool. It can be used to communicate important announcements such as changes in the break time caused by breakdowns.
Hold regular meetings with the employees and let the employees take part in these meetings.
Level with these employees and let them know where they stand.

8. Criticize employees in private.
When employees need correcting do it privately, with a cool head. Don't use strong language. Tackle the problem, not the person. If employees are treated fairly . . . and as human beings . . . they will usually respond to requests for improvements.

9. Set an example for your employees.
Employees don't mind doing something if they know that the supervisors would do it that way. Set an example, show enthusiasm and practice what you preach.

10. Develop teamwork.
Teamwork can only result when employees are working together toward a common goal. A good working relationship must be maintained with everyone on the team; not just the employees, but with the unit millwright, timekeeper and dispatcher.
Work closely with Production Planning and Control to produce what is on the line-up, as scheduled.

11. Look for new ideas and new ways.
Don't be afraid to try new ideas or look for improvements in the operation of the unit. Make changes whenever necessary. The spare parts cabinet was an innovation to help minimize down time. Switching to shell cores on as many jobs as possible has been a new process that helped reduce scrap.

12. Give and get cooperation from service departments.
Approach service departments in a friendly manner and they will usually respond the same way. Treat other departments the way you want to be treated. When a department responds, tell them you appreciate it. Occasionally, write a note to their boss to show your appreciation.
Follow-up with service departments when they forget or delay on a request. Again, do this in a friendly manner.

13. Establish controls and follow-up.
To be an effective supervisor you must control your unit and follow-up on requests to insure an effective operation. Don't procrastinate, keep copies of written requests. For instance, when you request something from another department, write them a note and send a copy to your boss and keep a copy for follow-up.
Keep your finger on the budget. Know what causes fluctuations, so you can try to control them.

14. Stay organized.
The only way to be effective is to be organized at what you are doing. Keep a daily "To Do" list. Keep a calendar to show the follow-up dates on the particular items that have been requested from your boss or from service departments.

15. Plan for interruptions.
In any production unit interruptions will occur. The more planning you can do to prepare for those interruptions the better off you are. One example was the construction of a spare parts cabinet to keep small, frequently needed, parts. Work with the millwright to keep it stocked and this can reduce downtime by enabling fast repairs.
Cross training employees on different machines will help to insure uninterrupted operations when there is an absence.

16. Meet all responsibilities
Meet all responsibilities including safety, housekeeping, administering policies, etc. For example, unit #2 won the Housekeeping Contest and continued to maintain good housekeeping after the contest. They try to correct all OSHA violations as soon as an inspection is completed. And later follow-up to insure these violations stay corrected.

Figure 14-5. Partial contents of a success story pamphlet.

HRD department staff meetings are an excellent arena for discussing the reaction to communicating program results. Comments can come from many sources, depending on the particular target audiences. Input from different members of the staff can be summarized to help judge the overall effectiveness.

When major program results are communicated, a feedback questionnaire may be used on an entire audience or a sample of the audience. The purpose of this questionnaire is to determine the extent the audience understood, and believed, the information presented. This is practical only when the effectiveness of the communication has a significant impact on the future actions of the HRD department.

Another approach is to survey the management group to determine the perception of the results obtained by the HRD department. In such a survey specific questions should be asked about program results: What does the management group know about the results? How believable are the results? What additional information is desired about the HRD program? This type of survey can help give the HRD department guidance, not only in communicating the results but in altering the mission of the department.

The overall purpose of soliciting reactions is to make adjustments in the communication process—if adjustments are necessary. Although the reactions may involve intuitive assessments, a more sophisticated analysis will provide better information to make these adjustments. The net result should be a more effective communication process.

Summary

This chapter presented the final step in the results-oriented HRD model introduced in Chapter 4. Communicating program results is a crucial step in the overall evaluation process. If this step is not taken seriously, the full impact of the program results will not be realized.

The chapter began with the general principles of communicating program results. A communications model was presented which should serve as a guide for any significant communications effort. The various target audiences were discussed and, because of its importance, emphasis was placed on the top management group. A suggested format for a detailed evaluation report was presented. Much of the remainder of the chapter included a detailed presentation of the most commonly used media for communicating program results, including meetings, periodic publications, and other written materials. Numerous examples were included to illustrate the concepts.

Discussion Questions

1. Why is communication the often neglected final phase of the results-oriented process?
2. An HRD executive was quoted as saying, ". . . We don't see a need to communicate program results to a wide variety of audiences. The individuals who achieve the results know what they have done and that is what is important to us." What is wrong with this philosophy?
3. Consider a recent evaluation project in your organization (or one with which you are familiar). What communication of results were planned and executed? What specific reasons for communication were addressed?
4. In the evaluation project identified in #3, what were the target audiences for communication? Why?
5. Why is it important to communicate to program participants the results that were achieved by all participants?
6. Which of the target audiences are most important? Why?
7. Should an evaluation report be prepared for each training program? Explain.
8. In your organization (or one with which you are familiar), develop an HRD review meeting agenda indicating the topics and emphasis of the meeting.
9. In your organization (or one with which you are familiar), which types of management meetings would be appropriate for communicating program results?
10. Under what conditions would an HRD newsletter be appropriate?
11. What are the disadvantages of using the organizational publication to promote program results?
12. Why are organizations reluctant to include program results in training catalogs and brochures?
13. Identify a success story in your organization (or one with which you are familiar) which relates to the results achieved from training. Write the success story in a format to present to top management.
14. What are the strengths and weaknesses of the success story approach to communicating program results?
15. What precautions are important when communicating results from HRD programs?

References

1. Lawrie, J., "Selling Management Development to Managers,"*Training and Development Journal*, February 1989, pp. 54–57.
2. Ellig, B. R., "Improving Effectiveness Through An HR Review," *Personnel,* June 1989, pp. 56–62.
3. Carew, J., "Four Steps to Selling Your Programs," *Training and Development Journal,* June 1989, pp. 68–70.
4. Du Jardin, P. E., "The Effects of Advanced Management Programs: Three Case Studies," *Management Review,* August & September 1985.
5. Cook, J. R. and Panza, C. M., "ROI: What Should Training Take Credit For?" *Training,* January 1987, pp. 59–68.

APPENDIX 1

Fear and Loathing on the Evaluation Trail

by Bernadine Eve Bednarz
University of Wisconsin—Extension

Last spring, after leading a successful training program, I asked participants for an evaluation of the presenters. Thirty out of 65 participants submitted written evaluations.

I passed the results on to the presenters. Jack, one of the trainers involved in the program, called to tell me he was surprised that I had included this comment about one of the presenters: "She is intelligent, yet has not found her own style—having become a poor carbon copy of the famous person who led the workshop." Jack thought it was a cruel, insensitive remark and felt I could have translated it into kinder terms. Jack said he too had struggled in being compared to famous people.

Last week I passed out evaluations for another program. A comment about one of the presenters was: "Due to Justin's zero personality, I find it hard to concentrate on the information she has to offer in her apparently very effective program."

The next day I had three phone calls and one letter from members of the planning committee who felt that the remark was "impolite" and "deadly." They suggested that I should have changed "zero personality" to "retiring personality."

In light of these responses I devised the following list of suggestions for participants evaluating training programs:

1. Make your language acceptable and gentle. If not, I will change it for you.
2. Never call anyone a sexist, racist, ageist, male chauvinist pig, fascist, moderate, conservative, Communist, Socialist, Democrat, Republican, or Whig.
3. Do not tell presenters to improve anything. They do not need it.
4. If you say something hurtful, I will make it palatable.
5. Never mention your disappointment if objectives have not been met. Conceal vigorously.
6. Do not use phrases like "Could you," "Have you thought about," "Is there any chance you would change . . ."
7. Do not take this evaluation too seriously because we won't.
8. Please wear a hood over your face so you will not be recognized when handing in your comments.
9. Sign the name of another participant so we can unjustly blame them.
10. Write out two evaluations with contradictory statements to create confusion: "the room was too hot/the room was too cold"; "he was the best trainer in this area/this man was vastly incompetent."
11. Focus on the insignificant and unimportant parts of the workshop: the dust on the floor, naked light bulbs, no chairs to sit on.
12. Never be specific. Just say, "I never liked John and like his presentation less."
13. Do not challenge sacred cows. They are the leaders in this field, and you are not.
14. Write illegibly, use arcane language.
14. Trainers are fragile; tread carefully.

Reports on how this worked will follow.

APPENDIX 2

Procedure for Program Evaluation

(Large Utility)

Subject. Program Evaluation

Purpose. To define the Corporate Training Department's evaluation standards and establish the procedures for implementing these standards, consistent with the following:

The philosophy of Corporate Training is to evaluate training programs at the highest level possible without allowing the evaluation process cost to exceed potential benefits. Practical application of this philosophy ensures efficient evaluation manpower utilization.

Procedure. The evaluation process is designed to: (1) determine the impact of training programs on business objectives, and (2) improve Corporate Training programs and their impact on employee development. Within this process, four levels of evaluation have been established:

Levels of Evaluation	
I. Participant Reaction	Evaluation of how the participants feel about the course. Participants are asked to share their perceptions of how applicable the completed training will be to them in thier work environment. Learning is not measured.
II. Participant Knowledge and Skills	Evaluation of the knowledge and skills learned as specified in course objectives. Achievement of course objectives is evaluated.
III. Job Performance Outcomes	Evaluation of course-related performance on the job after training has been completed. Behavioral change on the job after training is documented.
IV. Business Contribution	Evaluation of productivity directly attributable to training. Includes evidence showing the training's impact on the accomplishment of business objectives.

(Reproduced with permission from Alabama Power Company, Birmingham, Alabama. Ron Stone, Manager—Corporate Training Department.)

Table A2-1 illustrates the process used by Corporate Training. Although it is desirable to evaluate all training at the highest level possible, cost/benefit considerations require judicious selection of evaluations conducted beyond Level II.

Measuring Job Performance Outcomes (III) and Business Contribution (IV) is extremely time consuming for both the evaluator and the client, and the validity of the evaluation hinges on isolating productivity attributable to training from productivity gained from other variables.

Evaluation Process

Evaluation Decision

All programs conducted by Corporate Training will receive, at a minimum, evaluation at Level II by the appropriate T&D section or by Training Research and Evaluation (TR&E). Those courses to be evaluated by the TR&E section at Level II will be selected by the Supervisor of Training Research and Evaluation after consulting with appropriate Corporate Training management. Decisions on conducting Level III and IV evaluations will be made by the Manager of Corporate Training in consultation with his staff. All decisions concerning selection of course evaluations will be based on the following criteria:

1. Cost of the evaluation vs. benefits.
2. Potential validity and value of evaluation data.
3. Resources available to conduct the evaluation.
4. Impact on the accomplishment of Company goals.
5. Evaluation requirements of T&D sections.
6. External requirements or mandates.
7. Time (Corporate Training, clients, others) required to accomplish the evaluation.
8. Pilot programs (will have high priority).
9. Program visibility and the accomplishment of business objectives.

Evaluation Reports

Level I—Participant Reaction. Training and Development sections will design, implement, and analyze reaction instruments to meet their specific needs. Guidelines to assist in the development of reaction instruments are detailed in Foundations for Training (FFT), "Developing Course Objectives and Evaluation Instruments." A file of sample reaction instruments is located in the TR&E section. Individual Training and Development sections will maintain a file of reaction instrument summaries for trend identification purposes.

Level II—Participant Knowledge and Skills. In all cases course offerings will be evaluated for achievement of objectives by either the T&D section or by TR&E. Records should be maintained to help in identifying trends or unsatisfactory learning outcomes. A "Course Evaluation Report" will be provided to the T&D section supervisor and Corporate Training management at the conclusion of Level II evaluations conducted by the TR&E section. Use of the "Course Evaluation Report" format for evaluations conducted by the T&D sections is optional.

Level III—(Job Performance Outcomes) and Level IV—(Business Contribution). Evaluations at the two highest levels will be treated as special evaluations requiring customized formats for reporting data to management. Once the decision has been made to evaluate at these levels, the Supervisor of TR&E will confer with the Manager of the appropraite T&D section to determine the required reporting documents. These reports will be prepared for the Manager of Corporate Training, with copies disseminated to company management at his discretion.

Responsibilities

Training and Development Sections

1. With the assistance of the client, establish business and general course objectives.
2. Develop general objective(s) for each module of instruction.
3. Develop specific objective(s) for each module of instruction.
4. Evaluate all courses at Evaluation Level II, "Knowledge and Skills" (see Table A2-1).
5. Assist Training Research and Evaluation during joint course evaluations at the agreed level of evaluation.
6. Evaluate instructor performance.
7. Maintain a file on course evaluations. The file should include, but not be limited to tests, test analyses, reaction summaries, follow-up action taken as a result of formal course evaluations, and analyses of course objective achievement.
8. Provide Training Research and Evaluation a copy of all Training Service Proposals.

Training Research and Evaluation Section

1. Assist Training and Development sections in their development of course objectives.
2. Assist Training and Development sections in the development of evaluation instruments that measure achievement of course objectives.
3. Assist Training and Development sections in the analysis of evaluation results.
4. Schedule Training Research and Evaluation course evaluations in such a manner to ensure both comprehensive coverage and maximum utilization of evaluation resources.
5. Provide section supervisors with Course Evaluation Reports for all Level II evaluations conducted by the Training Research and Evaluation section. Conduct a thorough review of each Course Evaluation Report with the section supervisor.
6. Provide the T&D Managers and the Manager of Corporate Training copies of all Level II course Evaluation Reports. Evaluation reports for Level III and IV evaluations will be provided to the Manager of Corporate Training and other company management, as appropriate.
7. Respond to Training and Development section requests for assistance in any area of research or evaluation to the maximum extent consistent with available resources.

Table A2-1
The Evaluation Process

Level of Evaluation	Responsibilities	
	Training and Development Sections	Training Research and Evaluation
I. Participant Reaction	YES A. All courses should be measured for participant reaction. B. Analyze results, summarize findings, and maintain a file for documentation.	YES A. Upon request, provide T&D sections with support in the design of reaction instruments. B. Provide the T&D sections support in analyzing the instrument's data.

II. Participant Knowledge and Skills	YES
	A. All courses will be evaluated for accomplishment of course objectives.
	1. Subjective assessment of learning (minimum evaluation).
	2. Objective assessment of learning (desired evaluation).
	  a. When practical, measure achievement of specific objectives through the use of post-tests, oral recitations, and/or demonstrations.
	  b. When practical, measure the amount of learning that has taken place by comparing pretest results to post-test results.
	B. Summarize and analyze evaluations for course/modular objective achievement. Use of the "Course Evaluation Report" format is optional.
		YES
		A. On a selective basis, analyze achievement of course/modular objectives.
		B. Provide a "Course Evaluation Report" to the T&D section supervior, T&D Managers, and the Manager of Corporate Training whenever TR&E conducts a Level II evaluation.
		C. As required, provide support in the development of Needs Analysis instruments, course/modular objectives, and pretests and post-tests.
		D. Upon request, assist T&D sections in evaluating design, development, and implementation methods and techniques that impact on desiredx learning outcomes.

III. Job Performance Outcomes

YES
Although the TR&E section will have primary responsibilities for performance evaluations, T&D sections will:
A. prepare and conduct pretests and post-tests.
B. assist the TR&E section in conducting pre-course and post-course interviews as appropriate.

YES
Evaluations will be made on a highly selective basis. TR&E will have primary responsibility for the evaluation of changes in participant performance related to specific training.
A. With the concurrence of Corporate Training management, select courses for performance (Level III) evaluations.
B. Coordinate the scheduling of pre-course and post-course interviews conducted by TR&E and the appropriate T&D sections.
C. Once the evaluation is complete, provide a formal report to the Manager of Corporate Training and additional company management, as appropriate.

IV. Business Contribution

NO
Training Research and Evaluation will be responsible for all evaluations that measure the impact training has on the accomplishment of business objectives.

YES
On a highly selective basis:
A. Measure results of changes in performance by course participants after a course has been completed.
B. Analyze the cost/benefit of the course. Specify contributions toward the achievement of business objectives.
C. Provide a formal report to the Manager of Corporate Training and additional Company management, as appropriate.

APPENDIX 3

Sample Selection

When the evaluation involves the use of a sample group of participants, the selection of the sample becomes an important issue. There are two major concerns: (1) the make up of the sample (sample selection), and (2) the size of the sample. Sample selection can be accomplished in relatively easy steps.

Simple Random Sampling

With simple random sampling participants are selected on a random basis. This eliminates prejudice or unevenness in the selection of those who will participate in an HRD program. Without a random sample selection, the validity of the evaluation can be questioned. The sample might not be an accurate representation of the overall group it is supposed to represent.

The most common process for random selection from a relatively small population is through the use of random number tables. A random number table is a computer-generated table of random numbers. Table A-3 shows a table of random numbers. An example illustrates the use of this table:

Ten production supervisors are to be trained on an experimental basis from a group of 100 production supervisors. The selection is made on a random basis. The supervisors are numbered beginning with 00 up through 99. The numbers in the table are grouped in pairs, since only two digits are needed. From the table, the first 10 two-digit random numbers are 51, 77, 27, 46, 40, 42, 33, 12, 90,

Table A-3
Random Number Table

51772	74640	42331	29044	46621	62898	93582	04186	19640	87056
24033	23491	83587	06568	21960	21387	76105	10863	97453	90581
45939	60173	52078	25424	11645	55870	56974	37428	93507	94271
30586	02133	75797	45406	31041	86707	12973	17169	88116	42187
03585	79353	81938	82322	96799	85659	36081	50884	14070	74950
64937	03355	95863	20790	65304	55189	00745	65253	11822	15804
15630	64759	51135	98527	62586	41889	25439	88036	24034	67283
09448	56301	57683	30277	94623	85418	68829	06652	41982	49159
21631	91157	77331	60710	52290	16835	48653	71590	16159	14676
91097	17480	29414	06829	87843	28195	27279	47152	35683	47280
50532	25496	95652	42457	73547	76552	50020	24819	52984	76168
07136	40876	79971	54195	25708	51817	36732	72484	94923	75936
27989	64728	10744	08396	56242	90985	28868	99431	50995	20507
85184	73949	36601	46253	00477	25234	09908	36574	72139	70185
54398	21154	97810	36764	32869	11785	55261	59009	38714	38723
65544	34371	09591	07839	58892	92843	72828	91341	84821	63886
08263	65952	85762	64236	39238	18776	84303	99247	46149	03229
39817	67906	48236	16057	81812	15815	63700	85915	19219	45943
62257	04077	79443	95203	02479	30763	92486	54083	23631	05825
53298	90276	62545	21944	16530	03878	07516	95715	02526	33537

(Source: Spiegel, M.R., Theory and Problems of Statistics, Schaum's Outline Series, McGraw-Hill Book Co., New York, 1961, p. 349.)

and 44. The supervisors corresponding to those numbers are selected for the program.

This process is simple and easy to follow. It removes selection bias and adds more credibility to the sample.

Stratified Random Sampling

Sometimes a simple random sampling method will not give the kind of representative sampling desired. In the previous example suppose that the 100 supervisors were in three departments with one department containing 40 supervisors and the other two containing 30. There is a requirement to have the sample distributed in proportion to the number of supervisors in each department. Four supervisors must be selected from the large department, and three each from the other two to yield a sample size of ten. Through the simple random sampling procedure, this random selection may not occur. Stratified random sampling will assure the desired make up. The population of 100 supervisors can be stratified into the three groups, and then simple random sampling can be applied to each of the three groups. In this example the supervisors in the large department are numbered 00 through 40. In the other two departments the supervisors are numbered 00 through 30. The same tables are used to select four from the first department and three each from the other two departments. The digits are selected in pairs, as before. When a number is selected that exceeds the numbers attached to a supervisor, it is tossed out. For instance, 27 would be the first number used since 51 and 77 are larger than 40. The same procedure is repeated for the next two departments until a total of 10 supervisors are chosen.

In this example the population was stratified according to the departmental units. There are other useful ways for the population to be stratified. Examples are age, sex, work location, output, sales volume, or geographic location. Overall, stratification provides a basis for a sample to be more representative of the true population.

Systematic Random Sampling

The two previous methods for selecting random samples are useful for simple selection when the population is relatively small, which is the case in most HRD evaluation efforts. However, occasionally the population may be large. For instance, suppose a telephone company has 1000 telephone repairers to be trained. In an experimental training effort a group is selected to participate in the program. Using the two previous methods to select the sample group, all telephone repairers are listed, assigned numbers, and selected using the table of random numbers. With a group this large, this process can become cumbersome and lengthy.

A more useful procedure is to use what is called systematic sampling. This procedure involves selecting employees on some systematic basis such as every tenth person. In the previous example assume a sample size of 25 repairers is needed for the experimental group. The list of all repairers is divided into groups of 40 (1000 ÷ 25). Using simple random sampling, a selection is made from the first group of 40. Suppose this selection yields the twenty-first name. From each of the remaining 24 groups, the twenty-first name is selected. This process will give a precision that is approximately equivalent to that obtained by the simple random sampling when the population is randomly ordered.

Systematic sampling has several advantages. One, of course, is the ease in drawing the sample. Much time and effort are saved. Another advantage is that the process is efficient. The sample is usually spread out more evenly over the population and is thus more representative of the population. As a result, the information per unit cost is greater. However, this spread could depend on a particular characteristic of the population and may not apply in every case. Because of these advantages, systematic sampling is widely used when the population is large.

Simple Cluster Sampling

The final sampling method presented is cluster sampling. This method is another time-saving procedure used when a sample is selected from a fairly large population—one that is grouped into clusters. In the previous example of 1000 telephone repairers suppose the telephone repairers are in 10 operating units scattered among 3 states with 100 repairers in each unit. The time involved in using random sampling, coupled with the administrative cost involved in selecting participants from all 10 operating units, may prohibit the use of one of the earlier techniques. These two problems can be overcome if it is recognized that the telephone repairers are actually grouped into clusters of 10 operating units. If we desire a sample size of 50, we can select 5 operating units at random and then select 10 repairers at random in each of the 5 units. The samples are confined to 5 operating units, eliminating the need to involve the other 5 operating units. This assumes, of course, that the characteristics in those other 5 units were approximately the same as the 5 selected. This technique can be useful anytime the population under consideration can be divided into a number of similar clusters. The ultimate savings is in preparation, cost, and administration of the sampling process.

The previous four methods are fairly straightforward and simple. They are purposely presented this way in order not to confuse the reader. The subject of statistics, particularly in the sampling theory, is no simple process. Those who desire more precision, especially when the parameters and characteristics of the sampling process are more complex, should seek additional information.[1]

Sample Size Determination

The question of sample size is now addressed. An example will illustrate the importance of sample size:

A large insurance firm has 200 employees who process claims. The average time to process a claim is a closely monitored factor. An HRD program is proposed that will improve the time to process claims. Initially, the program will be conducted with a small pilot group, and their performance will be compared with that of the entire population of claims processors in that organization. How large a group should be undertaken? A more general question is, "How many people must participate in the program, on a pilot basis, before we can make general statements about all the people who will complete the program?" If the size is too small, the conclusion from the pilot group may be invalid. An unnecessarily large sample can add additional expense.

While the question of sample size seems to be simple, the answer is very complex. From a statistical basis, there are four significant factors which affect the sample size.

The size of the population from which the sample is drawn has an influence. If the population is small, then certainly the sample size should be larger in proportion to the total. If the population consists of 10 claims processors, to make an accurate judgment about that population, a sample size of 10 is probably needed (i.e., the entire population). As the population increases, the required sample size in proportion to the population is smaller.

The sample size also depends on the variation of the data being observed. In the previous example it is the time to process a claim. The greater the variance, the larger the sample size needed. The measure for this variance is called *standard deviation,* and it is described in more detail in Chapter 9.

Through the sample, an estimate of a new average time to process claims is determined, if all of the claims processors complete the HRD program. Therefore, the sample is used to predict a value. The precision of the estimate is another factor that determines the sample size. The term "precision" refers to the accuracy desired for the prediction. Should the estimate be within two hours of the actual new average time if everyone completes the program? The less precision, the larger the sample size.

In statistical estimation there is a possibility of an error. When a value is predicted, based on a sample, there will be a possibility that the sample does not accurately predict the real value. This refers to the reliability of the estimate and is sometimes expressed in a confidence value. If an evaluator wants to be 95% confident that the estimate is indeed a true predictor, then the reliability of the sample should be

95%. The higher the reliability, the larger the sample size required. Confidence values are discussed in more detail in Chapter 9.

To summarize briefly, the actual sample size selected to make an estimate depends on four factors:

☐ The actual size of the population of prospective participants.
☐ The variation in the quantity to be predicted.
☐ The precision of the sample estimator.
☐ The reliability of the precision.

These factors can be related to formulas to select the sample size. For large and small populations, the formulas will be slightly different. One fairly simple formula for sample size when the population is more than 30 is:

$$n = \frac{(z\sigma)^2}{d^2}$$

where n is the sample size, z is the reliability coefficient which denotes the reliability, σ represents standard deviation, and d represents the precision. An example will illustrate sample size calculation:

A sequence of operations on an assembly line takes a predetermined amount of time to complete, on the average. A large number of employees perform this assembly sequence. A proposed HRD program will possibly reduce this assembly time. A pilot group will be trained, and their new times for completing the assembly sequence will be calculated. It is anticipated that the average times will be reduced significantly with this training. It is assumed that the variation (standard deviation) in time for participants who complete the program will be approximately equal to the variation in times for all the assemblers. The present average time has been 30 minutes and the standard deviation has been 2. It is desired that the estimate of the new average time to complete the assembly be correct to within one minute and that the reliability of this precision be 95% (i.e., being 95% confident that the estimate will be correct within one minute). How many employees should be involved in the pilot program?

Solution: The 95% reliability translates into a reliability coefficient of 1.96 or approximately 2. For our purposes, this translation should be accepted on faith. A detailed analysis can be found in almost any standard text on statistics. The standard deviation is 2. The precision is 1. Plugging into the formula, we have the following:

$$n = \frac{(z\sigma)^2}{d^2} = \frac{(2 \times 2)^2}{1^2} = 16$$

The sample size needed is 16. If 16 employees are used in the experiment, the new average time to complete the assembly can be estimated with the desired reliability and precision.

An analysis of the formula reinforces the previous conclusions about the relationship between the various factors and the sample size. A larger sample size is needed when:

• The bound on precision is smaller.
• The standard deviation is larger.
• A greater reliability is desired.

From a logical point of view, tighter precision and reliability necessitates a larger sample size. A more precise and reliable estimation requires a sample size closer to the actual size of the population.

There is a non-statistical factor that influences the sample size: comfort level. Decision makers for a proposed program should consider (based on their perceptions) what sample size is desired for an experiment. What size makes them "comfortable?" This factor may be just as important as the statistical basis for determining the sample size.

There have been many attempts at creating tables to select a sample size based on predetermined characteristics. While these may be helpful when the conditions change very little, they might not be helpful for a variety of applications in the HRD development area.

In summary, the information about sample size selection can be a complex question. It is recommended that a sample as large as possible be used—one that is convincing to the decision makers for the program. If a detailed statistical verification is needed to support your sample size selection, more detailed references on statistics may be necessary.[2]

References

1. Yamane, T., *Elementary Sampling Theory,* Prentice Hall, Englewood Cliffs, N.J., 1967, pp. 48–236.
2. Ibid., pp. 56–59.

New Supervisors' Development Program Evaluation Questionnaire

Take a few minutes to think about the entire program and give us your answers to the following questions. This information will be very helpful to us in planning future sessions.

General Evaluation

1. The following objectives were stated for the program. To what extent did the program achieve its objectives?

	Completely Successful	Generally Successful	Limited Success	Failed
A. To improve your understanding about the nature, requirements and responsibilities of the supervisor's job	☐	☐	☐	☐
B. To increase your knowledge of basic supervisory principles	☐	☐	☐	☐

(continued on next page)

(continued)

	Completely Successful	Generally Successful	Limited Success	Failed
C. To develop skills to successfully conduct the most common supervisor/subordinate discussions	☐	☐	☐	☐
D. To increase your effectiveness as a leader through a better understanding of human behavior	☐	☐	☐	☐
E. To improve your knowledge of policies within which you must work	☐	☐	☐	☐
F. To enhance your knowledge of how the company functions and the services available to the supervisor	☐	☐	☐	☐

2. If you wish to explain any of the above ratings, please do so.

_____

_____

_____

3. What was your overall reaction to this program?

Excellent ☐

Better than expected ☐

Satisfactory ☐

Below Average ☐

4. Did you feel that the program met your needs as a supervisor?

Yes ☐

Uncertain ☐

No (Please explain) ☐

_____

_____

_____

5. Do you feel that you appreciate more the importance of your job as a supervisor having completed this course?

Yes ☐

Uncertain ☐

No ☐

6. Do you feel that you will be better able to do your job after attending this program?

Yes ☐

Uncertain ☐

No ☐

7. Do you have a better attitude about your job now that you have completed this program?

Yes ☐

Uncertain ☐

No ☐

8. Would you recommend that other new supervisors attend this program?

Yes ☐

Uncertain ☐

No ☐

9. Did you think the number of students in the class was:

Just right ☐

Too few ☐

Too many ☐

(continued on next page)

(continued)

10. When and how did you first learn that you had been select-
    ed to attend this program?

    _____

    _____

    _____

Instructor Evaluation

11. Although you rated each instructor at the end of his or
    her presentation, please provide the following overall
    evaluation on the effectiveness of all the instructors
    as a whole:

	Very Effective	Better Than Expected	Somewhat Effective	Not Effective
A. Knowledge of subject	☐	☐	☐	☐
B. Organization and preparation	☐	☐	☐	☐
C. Style and delivery	☐	☐	☐	☐
D. Responsiveness to participants	☐	☐	☐	☐
E. Creating appropriate learning climate	☐	☐	☐	☐

12. Comments about the instructors_____

    _____

    _____

Method of Presentation

13. Do you think too many instructors were involved in this
    program?

    Just right   ☐

    Too few   ☐

    Too many   ☐

14. How do you rate the balance of lectures, group discussions, and group exercises?

    Too much lecture   ☐

    Too much discussion   ☐

    Too many exercises   ☐

    Good balance   ☐

15. How helpful were the group exercises?

    Very helpful   ☐

    Helpful   ☐

    Not helpful   ☐

16. How did you feel about the pacing of the program?

    Too fast   ☐

    Just right   ☐

    Too slow   ☐

17. Did you have enough skill practice time?

    Yes   ☐

    Uncertain   ☐

    No   ☐

Program Content

Please refer to the list of modules for the entire program while answering these questions.

18. What did you like best about the program?

    _____

    _____

    _____

19. What did you like least about the program?

    _____

    _____

    _____

(continued)

20. If any of your attitudes about supervising have changed, please indicate what has changed and what part of the program had the most significant impact on bringing about that change.

    _____

    _____

    No change ☐

21. Which module will be most useful to you on your job?

    _____

    _____

22. What do you think should be added to the program?

    _____

    _____

23. What do you think should be dropped from the program?

    _____

    _____

24. Do you rate the program length

    Just right   ☐

    Too short   ☐

    Too long   ☐

25. How well was the program content logically sequenced?

    Very well sequenced ☐

    Suitable   ☐

    Poorly sequenced   ☐

26. How valuable was the program content to your current job?

    Very valuable   ☐

    Some value   ☐

    No real value   ☐

27. How much did the program duplicate what you had learned somewhere else?

    Very much duplication ☐

    Some duplication ☐

    Very little duplication ☐

28. How do you rate the balance of theoretical and practical material in the program?

    Too theoretical ☐

    Good balance ☐

    Too practical ☐

29. Which term below do you feel best describes the teaching level of this program?

    Very difficult ☐

    Difficult ☐

    Suitable ☐

    Easy ☐

    Too easy ☐

30. Comments about program content _____

    _____

    _____

Instructional Materials

31. Did you think enough audio-visual aids were used?

    Just right ☐

    Too few ☐

    Too many ☐

(continued on next page)

(continued)

32. How do you rate the quality of the audio-visual aids?

    High quality ☐

    OK ☐

    Below expectations ☐

33. In your opinion, were the number of handouts you received during the program sufficient?

    Just right ☐

    Too few ☐

    Too many ☐

34. How do you rate the quality of the handout material?

    High quality ☐

    OK ☐

    Below expectations ☐

35. Was the handout material relevant to the course content?

    Yes ☐

    Uncertain ☐

    No ☐

Out-of-Class Assignments

36. What did you think of the pre-program assignment?

    Very valuable ☐

    Some value ☐

    No real value ☐

37. What did you think of the evening assignments?

    Very valuable ☐

    Some value ☐

    No real value ☐

38. How do you rate the difficulty of the assignments?

   Very difficult   ☐

   Suitable   ☐

   Easy   ☐

39. How do you rate the relevancy of the assignments to the course material?

   Very relevant   ☐

   Suitable   ☐

   Not relevant   ☐

Facilities

40. Did you like the seating arrangement of the classroom?

   Yes   ☐

   Uncertain   ☐

   No   ☐

41. Did you think your chair was comfortable?

   Yes   ☐

   Uncertain   ☐

   No   ☐

42. How do you rate the service (breaks, lunch, etc.)?

   Excellent   ☐

   Better than expected   ☐

   Satisfactory   ☐

   Below average   ☐

43. How do you rate the physical classroom environment (temperature, lighting, noise, etc.)?

   Excellent   ☐

   Better than expected   ☐

   Satisfactory   ☐

   Below average   ☐

(continued on next page)

(continued)

44. How do you rate the housing accomodations (if applicable)?

    Excellent ☐

    Better than expected ☐

    Satisfactory ☐

    Below average ☐

Planned Improvements

45. As a result of this program, what do you estimate to be the increase in your personal effectiveness, expressed as a percent?

    _____%

46. Please indicate what you will do differently on the job as a result of this program (please be specific):

    1. _____

    2. _____

    3. _____

    4. _____

47. As a result of any change in your thinking or new ideas about supervising which you have learned, please estimate (in dollars) the amount of money which you will save the company (i.e., reduced absenteeism and turnover, reduced employee complaints, better teamwork, increase in personal effectiveness, etc.) over a period of one year:

    $_____

48. What is the basis of this estimate?

    _____

    _____

49. What confidence, expressed as a percentage, can you put in your estimate? (0% = No Confidence; 100% = Certainty)

    _____%

50. To what degree will your on-the-job environment encourage
    you to use the skills and concepts presented in this program?

    To a great degree   ☐

    To some degree   ☐

    No encouragement   ☐

    It will discourage their use   ☐

APPENDIX 5

New Supervisors' Development Program Follow-Up Evaluation Questionnaire

As a former participant in the New Supervisors' Development Program, you can best evaluate the immediate, long-range, and lasting effects of the program. It has been several months since you completed the program, and we are interested in your opinions about the program's success. Since you have had time to reflect on the material and attempt to put it into practice, we need your frank comments regarding several aspects of the program.

General Evaluation

1. The following objectives were stated for the program. To what extent did the program achieve its objectives?

	Completely Successful	Generally Successful	Limited Success	Failed
A. To improve your understanding about the nature, requirements and responsibilities of the supervisor's job	☐	☐	☐	☐
B. To increase your knowledge of basic supervisory principles	☐	☐	☐	☐
C. To develop skills to successfully conduct the most common supervisor/subordinate discussions	☐	☐	☐	☐
D. To increase your effectiveness as a leader through a better understanding of human behavior	☐	☐	☐	☐
E. To improve your knowledge of policies within which you must work	☐	☐	☐	☐
F. To enhance your knowledge of how the company functions and the services available to the supervisors	☐	☐	☐	☐

2. If you wish to explain any of the above ratings, please do so.

_____

_____

_____

3. Did you feel that the program met your needs as a supervisor?

Yes ☐   *(continued on next page)*

(continued)

Uncertain ☐

No (Please explain) ☐

_____

_____

_____

4. Do you have a better attitude about your job now that you have completed this program?

Yes ☐

Uncertain ☐

No ☐

5. The features of the New Supervisor's Development Program which were most significant to you were:

_____

_____

_____

6. Too much time was spent on _____

_____

Too little time was spent on _____

_____

7. Which module has been most helpful to you on your job?

_____

_____

_____

8. Please make any comments about the program (i.e., the instructors, the material used, the subject areas, etc.) which would help us to make future programs more valuable.

_____

_____

_____

9. At what point do you feel this training should be held?
    (i.e., before becoming a supervisor, when first assigned,
    after several months, after several years) Please give
    your reasoning.

    _____

    _____

10. What follow-up training (if any) would you suggest?

    _____

    _____

On-The-Job Support

Formal development programs can fail or succeed because of conditions that may or may not be controllable. Please indicate which
of the conditions below reflect your opinion regarding your on-
the-job opportunities to use what you learned during the program.

11. Indicate the extent to which you are allowed to practice
    what you learned:
    I have not been able to practice anything I learned.   ☐
    I have not been able to practice much of what I learned. ☐
    I have been able to practice most of what I learned.   ☐
    I have been able to practice all of what I learned.   ☐

12. When you returned to the job, your boss:
    Ignored the effects of the training I received.   ☐
    Was neutral regarding the training I received.   ☐
    Was moderately interested in the training I received. ☐
    Assisted me in trying to practice what I learned
        during the program.   ☐

13. As a supervisor I feel that:
    My department has not allowed me to practice the
        skills I learned.   ☐

(continued on next page)

(continued)

My department is neutral regarding new supervisory
practices. ☐

My department has allowed me to practice some of
what I learned. ☐

I have support from the Company president down to
my boss to allow me to use what I learned. ☐

14.   Since completing the program I feel that:

Informal department practices and precedents have kept
me from using what I learned. ☐

Informal department practices and precedents are
neutral in allowing me to use what I learned. ☐

There has been a strong interest in allowing me to
demonstrate what I have learned. ☐

15.   If you want to explain any of the above ratings, please do so.

_____

_____

_____

Improvements Since the Program

16.   What are you now doing as a supervisor that you were not
doing prior to the program?

_____

_____

_____

17.   What have you stopped doing as a supervisor since attending the program?

_____

_____

_____

18. Can you describe any changes in you, your work, or your upward-downward relationships that were caused in some substantial part by your attending this program?

    _____

    _____

    _____

19. Have you used the reference and reading material provided during the program?

    ☐ Yes   ☐ No

20. As a result of this program, what do you estimate to be the increase in your personal effectiveness, expressed as a percent?

    _____%

21. As a result of any change in your thinking or new ideas about supervising which you have learned, please estimate (in dollars) the amount of money which you have saved the company (i.e., reduced absenteeism and turnover, reduced employee complaints, better teamwork, increase in personal effectiveness, etc.) since the program:

    $_____

22. What is the basis of this estimate?

    _____

    _____

23. What confidence, expressed as a percentage, can you put in your estimate? (0% = No Confidence; 100% = Certainty)

    _____%

24. In my opinion, the overall program was _____

    _____

    _____

    _____

Performance Contract

SUBJECT	State the specific area(s) or topics you have picked for improvement.

OBJECTIVE	What do you want to accomplish? What is your purpose, or broad objective?

GOALS	How will you know what you've accomplished? Your specific targets or yard-sticks by which you will measure improvement.

Reproduced with permission of Training House, Box 3090, Princeton, N.J. 08540.

PROBLEMS

What barriers, resistance, interruptions, obstacles, etc. (anticipated and unforeseen) might you encounter as you implement your Action Plan? Number them.

SOLUTIONS

How do you plan to avoid or to deal with the problems that you've just enumerated? Number to correspond with your list at the left.

RESOURCES

What people will you need to implement this plan? Time required? (Did you include your own time?) What other resources — equipment, materials, outside assistance?

ACTIVITIES	TIME
List in sequence the steps required to bring about the desired change. Indicate the time period for each in the column to the right, using actual calendar dates and estimates of the number of hours required for each activity listed.	

COSTS

List the costs of implementing your action plan, including both initial capital investments (if any) and any changes in operating costs.

BENEFITS

Itemize the dollar benefits and estimate the value of any intangible benefits.

COMMITMENT

In signing below, we agree to make the commitment of time and money needed to carry out this Action Plan as outlined. We further agree to meet at the time(s) noted below to review progress and modify the schedule of Activities described on Page 3 as may be needed to achieve our Goals and thereby meet our Objectives.

Signatures: Date/Time for Progress
                                               Review(s)

_____   _____

_____   _____

Today's date:_____   _____

APPENDIX 7

Statistical Inference

The Hypothesis

A hypothesis is a proposed explanation of the relationship between two or more variables such as performance and training. An example is: "production employees performance will improve as a result of the training program." The statement is either rejected or not rejected based on the evaluation data, the result of the statistical analysis, and a statistical test. The hypothesis is "tested." (Some individuals prefer to use the terminology "fail to reject" or "not rejected" rather than "accept." The rationale is that in some situations failing to reject the hypothesis on the basis of a single test may not be sufficient to accept the hypothesis.)

The hypothesis differs from a problem statement or objective in that it provides a tentative answer to the problem, i.e., the training leads to improved performance. A key point to remember is that when an hypothesis is used, a statistical analysis is necessary. This appendix on statistical inference presents the common types of statistical analyses used in hypothesis testing.

Occasionally a null hypothesis is stated. The null hypothesis states that there is no improvement as a result of an HRD program. If the evaluation data and analysis proves otherwise, then the null hypothesis is rejected. The conclusion: there is improvement caused by something other than chance, probably the HRD program. This conclusion is reached based on a specified confidence level, which is discussed later. This null hypothesis may not be formally stated in an evaluation, but it is assumed and is the basis for performing the statistical analysis.

Errors in Hypothesis Testing

As mentioned previously, in hypothesis testing the HRD program evaluator has two choices: (1) reject the hypothesis, or (2) fail to reject the hypothesis. Depending on the decision, there will be a possible error involved in making either one of those decisions. Figure A7-1 shows the possible combinations. If the hypothesis is false and it is rejected, then it is the correct decision. If, on the other hand, the hypothesis is true and it is rejected, then there is an error, usually called a Type I error. If the hypothesis is not rejected and it is true, then it is a correct decision. However, if the hypothesis is not rejected and it is false, there is another error, usually referred to as a Type II error.

Which error is more serious? It depends on the situation. For example, an organization has a large sales force. Management is considering a proposal to purchase a packaged HRD program which is designed to increase the sales output of the participants. A pilot program is planned. If the results of the pilot program are good, the packaged program will be purchased and implemented for the entire sales force. The null hypothesis which forms the basis of the evaluation is: "there will be no increase in sales as a result of the program." Preprogram and post-program measurements are taken, and an analysis is conducted to see if that hypothesis is either rejected or not rejected. The Type I error occurs when the hypothesis is true (there is no increase in sales), yet it is rejected. This means that the program is purchased and all salespersons are trained, although there will be no effect on sales

	Hypothesis False	Hypothesis True
Reject Hypothesis	Correct Decision	Type I Error
Do Not Reject Hypothesis	Type II Error	Correct Decision

Figure A7-1. Possible errors in hypothesis testing.

output. This error could be very costly. The Type II error, on the other hand, means that there is an improvement in sales, yet the hypothesis is not rejected and the program is not purchased. The consequences may not be nearly as great. The substantial expenditure is avoided, yet increases in sales will not be realized. A program is discarded that will increase sales. However, another program will probably be examined or developed if the goal is to try to improve the sales output.

As this example illustrates, there is usually more at risk in the Type I error. The probability of making a Type I error is called the *level of significance* and has the symbol α. The most common value for the level of significance is .05. This figure means that there is a 5% chance that a Type I error can be made. If everything else is held constant, raising the level of significance will decrease the probability of making a Type II error. Consequently, lowering the level of significance increases the probability of a Type II error.

Statistical Tests

The process of testing an hypothesis involves calculating a statistical test value and comparing it with a value from an appropriate statistical table, based on a predetermined level of significance. The comparison of these two values determines whether or not the hypothesis is rejected or not rejected.

The type of test statistic depends on the type of data being compared. To keep the presentation simple, the analysis will be confined to comparisons of mean values, since these are probably the most common types of program evaluation data. Typical comparisons are average values of experimental groups versus control groups or average values before and after a training program for the same group. The formula for the test statistic, t, is as follows:

$$t = \frac{\bar{x} - \mu}{\sigma/\sqrt{n}}$$

where:
  $\bar{x}$ = Sample mean (post-program measurement or experimental group measurement).
  μ = Population mean (preprogram measurement or control group measurement).

σ = Population standard deviation. If this value is unknown, the sample standard deviation, s, is used.

n = Sample size (number of participants).

The use of this statistic can be illustrated by an example. In the previous example of the packaged program to train salespersons, the null hypothesis, H_o, was that there is no difference in the average sales of participants before and after the program. The alternative hypothesis, H_a, is that the average sales after the program are greater. These are represented in the following way:

H_o: $\bar{x} = \mu$

H_a: $\bar{x}$ is greater than μ ($\bar{x} > \mu$)

This is a one-sided analysis, since the interest is only in greater sales. Another alternative hypothesis would be that the average sales after the program are either less than or greater than the average sales before the program. This analysis observes changes on both sides of the preprogram average sales and is shown this way

H_a: $\bar{x}$ is not equal to μ ($\bar{x} \neq \mu$)

This is called a two-sided analysis. For most evaluation uses, the one-sided analysis is appropriate. The reasoning is simple. If postprogram average sales were actually less than the preprogram average sales, then without any statistical analysis, the conclusion is that there was no improvement in sales. The interest is only in improvement. Therefore, the alternative hypothesis for most program evaluations involves this one-sided analysis.

As might be expected, the one-sided analysis involves what is referred to as a one-tailed test. The test statistic is compared to a critical value from Table A7-1 which contains values for both the one-tailed and two-tailed test. The critical value selected for the one-tailed test depends on two factors: (1) the degrees of freedom, and (2) the level of significance. The degrees of freedom are one less than the sample size

df = n − 1

Table A7-1
Critical Values for the t Distribution

df	Level of significance for one-tailed test					
	.10	.05	.025	.01	.005	.0005
	Level of significance for two-tailed test					
	.20	.10	.05	.02	.01	.001
1	3.078	6.314	12.706	31.821	63.657	636.619
2	1.886	2.920	4.303	6.965	9.925	31.598
3	1.638	2.353	3.182	4.541	5.841	12.941
4	1.533	2.132	2.776	3.747	4.604	8.610
5	1.476	2.015	2.571	3.365	4.032	6.859
6	1.440	1.943	2.447	3.143	3.707	5.959
7	1.415	1.895	2.365	2.998	3.499	5.405
8	1.397	1.860	2.306	2.896	3.355	5.041
9	1.383	1.833	2.262	2.821	3.250	4.781
10	1.372	1.812	2.228	2.764	3.169	4.587
11	1.363	1.796	2.201	2.718	3.106	4.437
12	1.356	1.782	2.179	2.681	3.055	4.318
13	1.350	1.771	2.160	2.650	3.012	4.221
14	1.345	1.761	2.145	2.624	2.977	4.140
15	1.341	1.753	2.131	2.602	2.947	4.073
16	1.337	1.746	2.120	2.583	2.921	4.015
17	1.333	1.740	2.110	2.567	2.898	3.965
18	1.330	1.734	2.101	2.552	2.878	3.922
19	1.328	1.729	2.093	2.539	2.861	3.883
20	1.325	1.725	2.086	2.528	2.845	3.850
21	1.323	1.721	2.080	2.518	2.831	3.819
22	1.321	1.717	2.074	2.508	2.819	3.792
23	1.319	1.714	2.069	2.500	2.807	3.767
24	1.318	1.711	2.064	2.492	2.797	3.745
25	1.316	1.708	2.060	2.485	2.787	3.725
26	1.315	1.706	2.056	2.479	2.779	3.707
27	1.314	1.703	2.052	2.473	2.771	3.690
28	1.313	1.701	2.048	2.467	2.763	3.674
29	1.311	1.699	2.045	2.462	2.756	3.659
30	1.310	1.697	2.042	2.457	2.750	3.646
40	1.303	1.684	2.021	2.423	2.704	3.551
60	1.296	1.671	2.000	2.390	2.660	3.460
120	1.289	1.658	1.980	2.358	2.617	3.373
∞	1.282	1.645	1.960	2.326	2.576	3.291

Source: Taken from Table III, p. 46 of Fisher and Yates: Statistical Tables for Biological. Agricultural and Medical Research, published by Longman Group Ltd., London, (previously published by Oliver and Boyd, Edinburgh), and by permission of the authors and publishers.

The level of significance, α, is the probability of a Type I error and is selected based on the confidence desired in the outcome of the analyis. The most common value for α is .05. For example, a sample size of 25 participants and $\alpha = .05$ yields a critical value of 1.711 for a one-tailed test in Table A7-1. If the test statistic, t, calculated from the previous formula is larger than this critical value, then the null hypothesis is rejected. There is an increase in sales caused by something other than chance, usually the HRD program.

This result is shown graphically in Figure A7-2. The values of the test statistic greater than the critical value are in what is called the *region of rejection*. The remaining values are in the *non-rejection region*.

Detailed Example

This process of statistical tests can be further explained and summarized by presenting a detailed example of a calculation. Refer to the data presented in Table 9-1. This example compares the production output of a group of employees before and after an HRD program. Using that data, determine if the change in average output is the result of the training program or chance. Use a level of significance of .05.

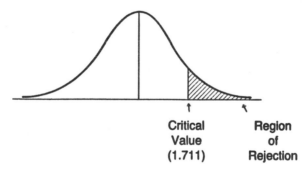

Critical   Region
Value   of
(1.711)   Rejection

Figure A7-2. A one-tailed test.

Setting up the hypothesis

H_o: $\mu_a = \mu_b$
H_a: $\mu_a = \mu_a > \mu_b$

where:
μ_a = Mean unit hour after training.
μ_b = Mean unit hour before training.

This is a one-tailed test, since the interest is only in improvement after training.

Determining the critical value

There are 15 items in the sample. Therefore, the degrees of freedom are

$$df = n - 1 = 14$$

The critical value from Table 9-6, based on $\alpha = .05$ is

$$t_{cv} = 1.761$$

Calculating the test statistic

The standard deviation of the post-training data is 7.75, from a previous calculation. This figure can be substituted for the population standard deviation (all production workers), which is unknown. In reality, this may be a known factor. The preprogram mean value is

$$\mu_b = \frac{\sum xi}{n} = \frac{826}{15} = 55.07$$

The post-program mean is from a previous example

$$\mu_a = \bar{x} = 62.13$$

The test statistic is

$$t = \frac{\bar{x} - \mu_b}{\sigma/\sqrt{n}} = \frac{62.13 - 55.07}{7.75/\sqrt{15}} = \frac{7.06}{2.001}$$
$$= 3.528$$

The test statistic is larger than the critical value. Therefore, the null hypothesis, H_o, is rejected. The results can be attributed to the HRD program, assuming no other variables entered the picture.

Index

A

Absenteeism, 222
Accidents, 233
Achievement, special, 349–350
Action plan
  active verbs for, 176
  advantages of, 178–179
  audit of, 177–178
  definition of, 173
  developing the, 175–177
  disadvantages of, 179
  form for, 174
  participant, 174–175
Active verbs, 176
Ad, behavior modeling, 36
Adjustments, program, 76
Administration of instruments, 87
Advancement, data for, 157
Advisory committees, 321–323
Aetna Life and Casualty, 30, 320
Agreement
  preprogram, 307 (*Also see*
    Contract.)
Agway, Inc., 165
Alabama, University of, 167–168

Allstate Insurance Companies, 324
Alternate form method, 86
American Association of
  Collegiate Schools of
  Business, 33
American College Testing
  Program, 34
American Express, 130
American Management
  Associations, 24, 163
American Society for Healthcare
  Education and Training
  (ASHET), 24
American Society for Training
  and Development (ASTD), 8,
  24, 26, 33, 51, 248, 263,
  271, 313–314
American Telephone and
  Telegraph Company, 170
  (*Also see* Bell System.)
Analysis, utility, 229
Analysis cost, 136
Analysis of data, (*See* Data
  analysis.)
Application outcomes, 46

401